# 子連れ狼

# LONE WOLF AND CUB

子連れ狼

story
**KAZUO KOIKE**

art
**GOSEKI KOJIMA**

**DARK HORSE MANGA™**

translation
**DANA LEWIS**

lettering & retouch
**DIGITAL CHAMELEON**

cover illustration
**FRANK MILLER** with **LYNN VARLEY**

publisher
**MIKE RICHARDSON**

editor
**MIKE HANSEN**

assistant editor
**TIM ERVIN-GORE**

consulting editor
**TOREN SMITH** for **STUDIO PROTEUS**

book design
**DARIN FABRICK**

art director
**MARK COX**

Published by Dark Horse Manga, a division of Dark Horse Comics, Inc.,
in association with Soeisha Inc.

Dark Horse Comics, Inc.
10956 SE Main Street, Milwaukie, OR 97222
www.darkhorse.com

First edition: December 2000
ISBN: 1-56971-505-X

5 7 9 10 8 6

Printed in Canada

To find a comics shop in your area, call the
Comic Shop Locator Service toll-free at 1-888-266-4226

# THE BELL WARDEN

子連れ狼

*By* **KAZUO KOIKE**
**& GOSEKI KOJIMA**

# V O L U M E

# 4

# A NOTE TO READERS

*Lone Wolf and Cub* is famous for its carefully researched re-creation of Edo-Period Japan. To preserve the flavor of the work, we have chosen to retain many Edo-Period terms that have no direct equivalents in English. Japanese is written in a mix of Chinese ideograms and a syllabic writing system, resulting in numerous synonyms. In the glossary, you may encounter words with multiple meanings. These are words written with Chinese ideograms that are pronounced the same but carry different meanings. A Japanese reader seeing the different ideograms would know instantly which meaning it is, but these synonyms can cause confusion when Japanese is spelled out in our alphabet. *O-yurushi o* (please forgive us)!

# LONE WOLF AND CUB

# TABLE OF CONTENTS

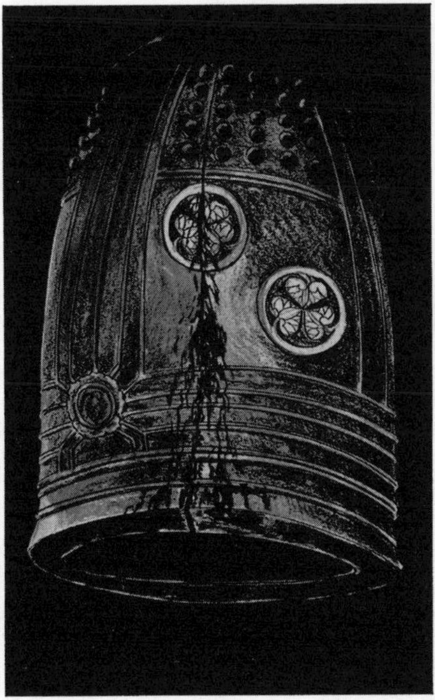

the twentieth

# Tsuji Genshichi the Bell Warden

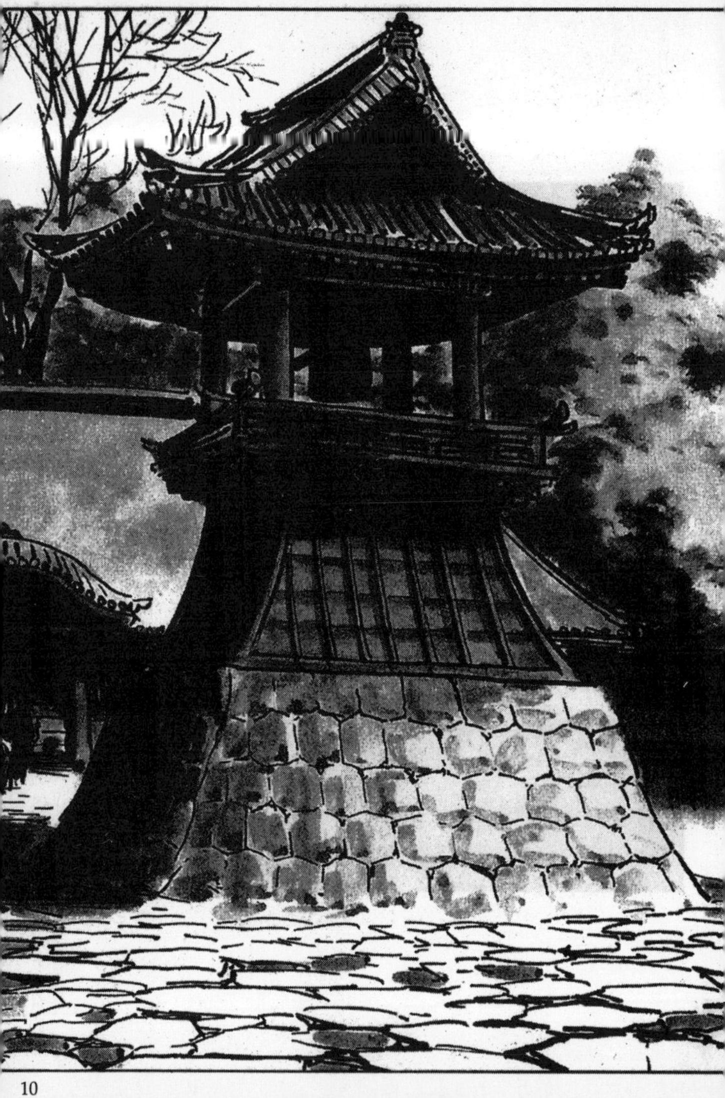

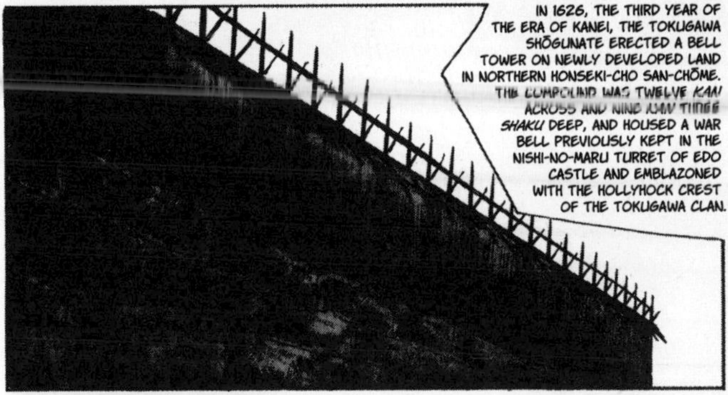
IN 1626, THE THIRD YEAR OF THE ERA OF KANEI, THE TOKUGAWA SHŌGUNATE ERECTED A BELL TOWER ON NEWLY DEVELOPED LAND IN NORTHERN HONSEKI-CHO SAN-CHŌME. THE COMPOUND WAS TWELVE *KAN* ACROSS AND NINE *KAN* THREE *SHAKU* DEEP, AND HOUSED A WAR BELL PREVIOUSLY KEPT IN THE NISHI-NO-MARU TURRET OF EDO CASTLE AND EMBLAZONED WITH THE HOLLYHOCK CREST OF THE TOKUGAWA CLAN.

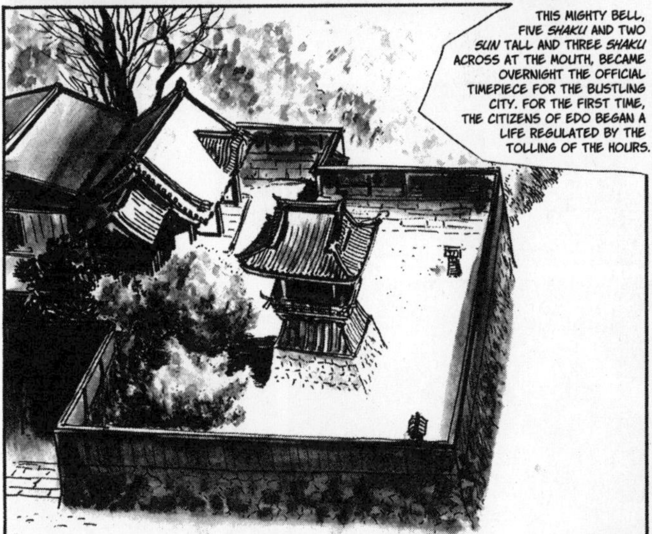
THIS MIGHTY BELL, FIVE *SHAKU* AND TWO *SUN* TALL AND THREE *SHAKU* ACROSS AT THE MOUTH, BECAME OVERNIGHT THE OFFICIAL TIMEPIECE FOR THE BUSTLING CITY. FOR THE FIRST TIME, THE CITIZENS OF EDO BEGAN A LIFE REGULATED BY THE TOLLING OF THE HOURS.

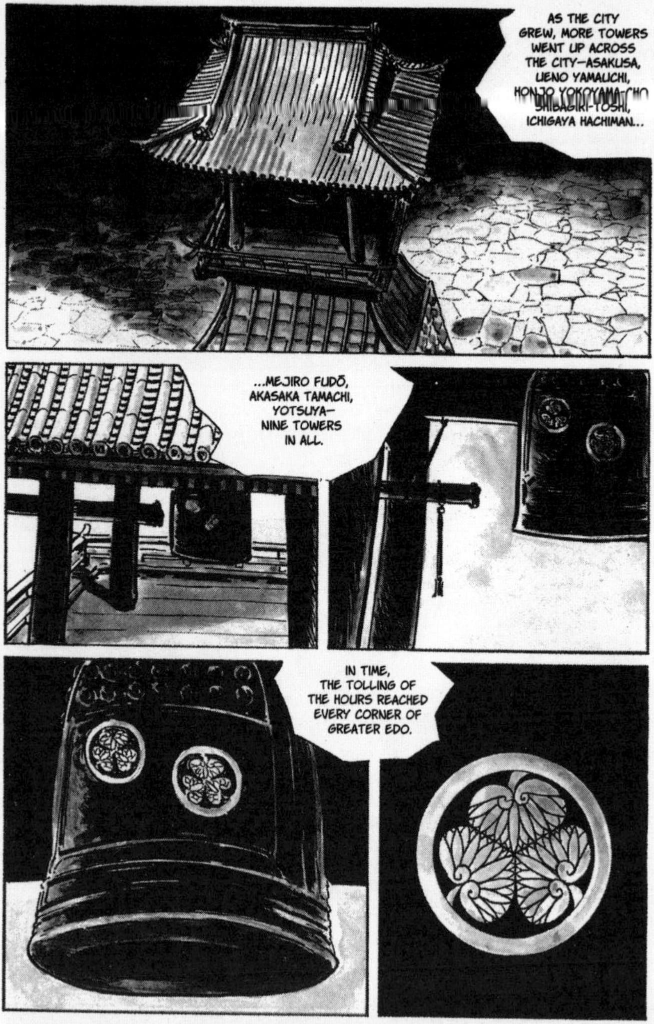
AS THE CITY GREW, MORE TOWERS WENT UP ACROSS THE CITY—ASAKUSA, UENO YAMAUCHI, HONJO YOKOYAMA-CHO SHIBAGIKI-TOSHI, ICHIGAYA HACHIMAN...
...MEJIRO FUDŌ, AKASAKA TAMACHI, YOTSUYA—NINE TOWERS IN ALL.
IN TIME, THE TOLLING OF THE HOURS REACHED EVERY CORNER OF GREATER EDO.

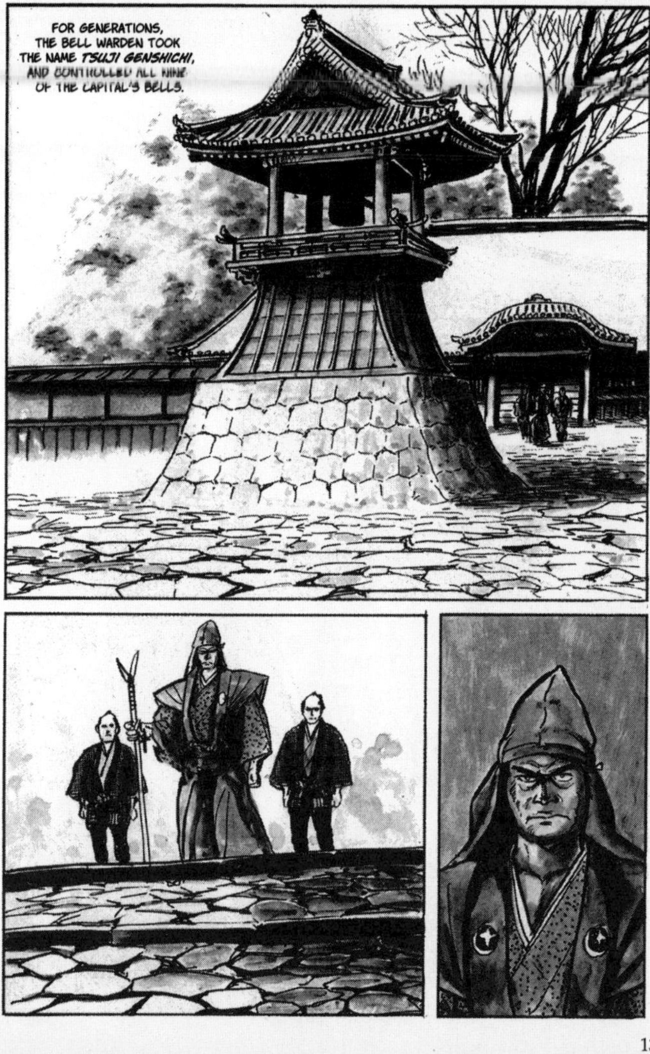
FOR GENERATIONS, THE BELL WARDEN TOOK THE NAME *TSUJI GENSHICHI*, AND CONTROLLED ALL NINE OF THE CAPITAL'S BELLS.

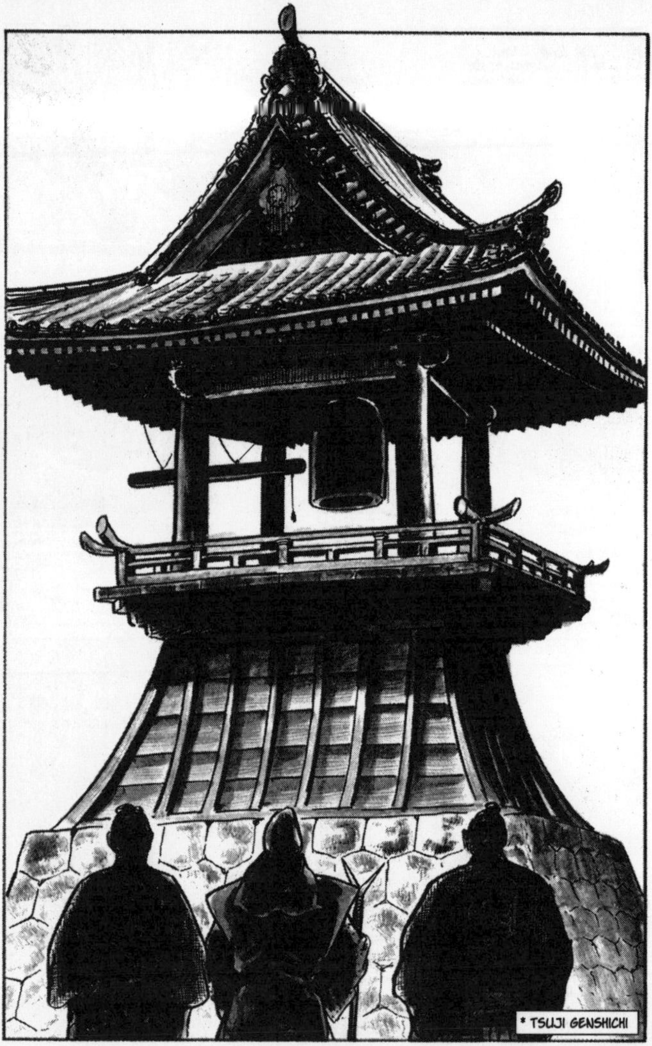
* TSUJI GENSHICHI

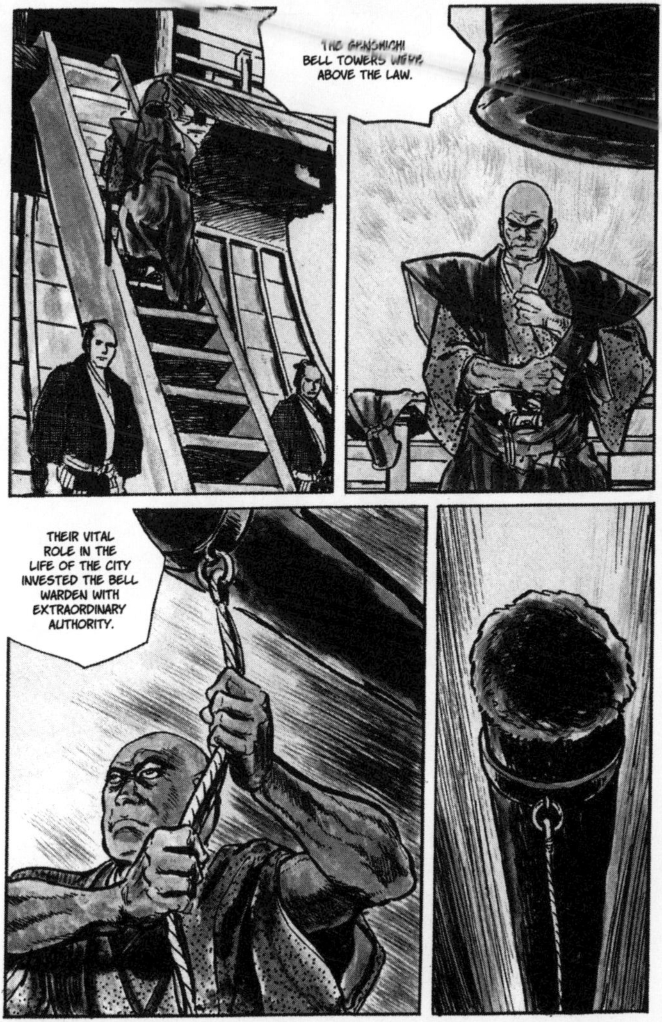
THE GENSHICHI BELL TOWERS WERE ABOVE THE LAW.
THEIR VITAL ROLE IN THE LIFE OF THE CITY INVESTED THE BELL WARDEN WITH EXTRAORDINARY AUTHORITY.

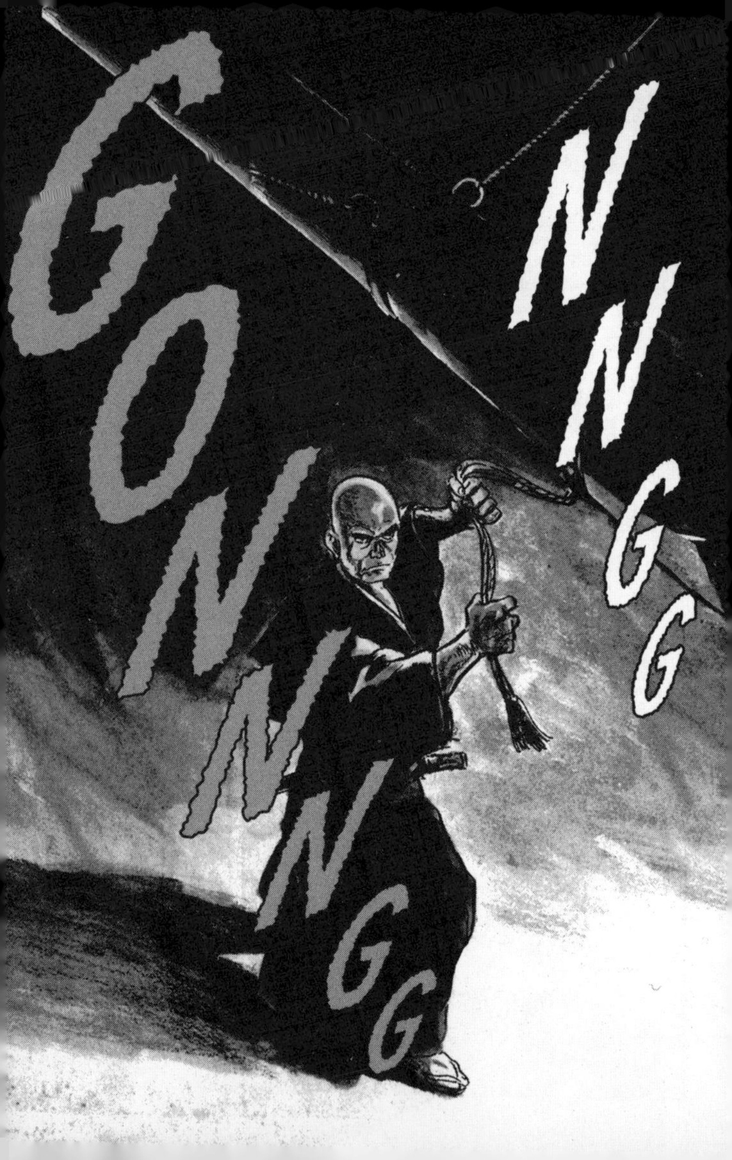
GONNNGG
NNGG

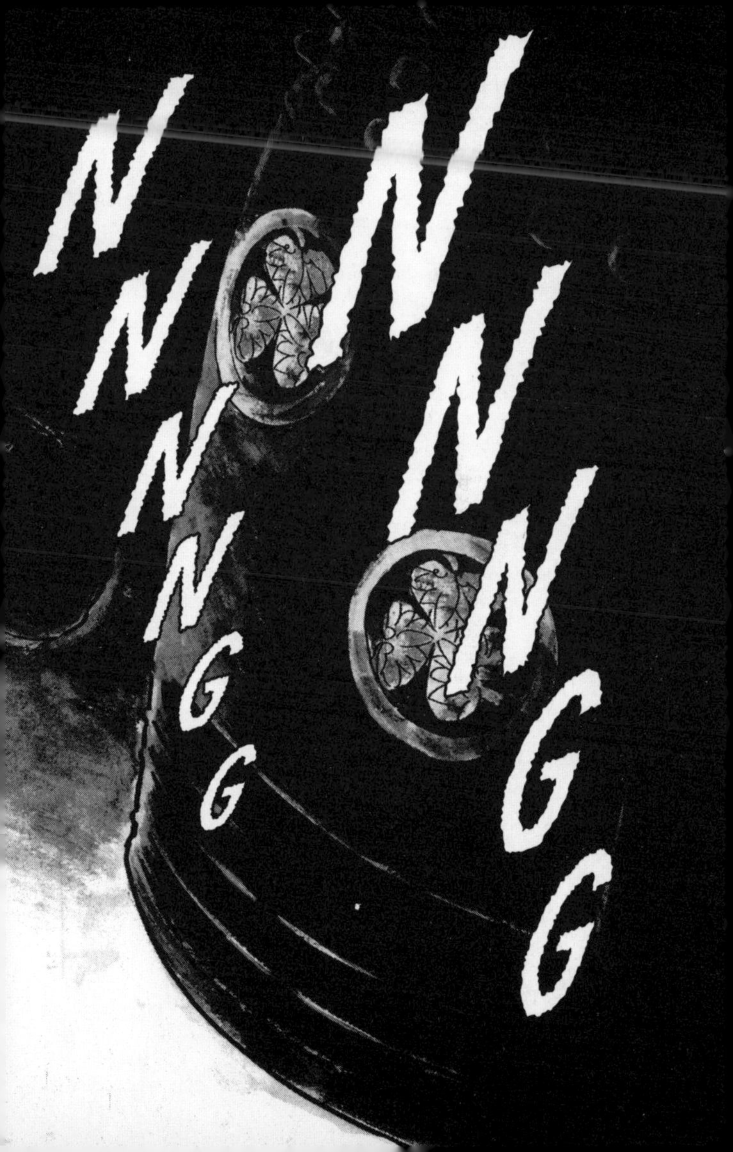
NNNNGG
NNNNGG

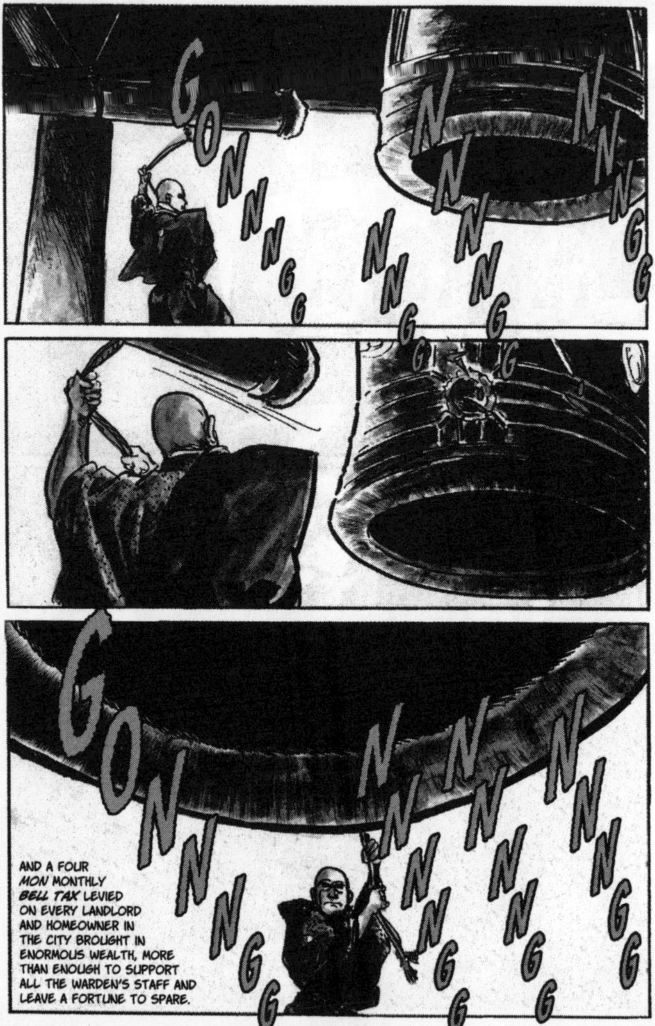
GONNNGG
NNNNGG
GONNNGG
NNNNGG
AND A FOUR *MON* MONTHLY *BELL TAX* LEVIED ON EVERY LANDLORD AND HOMEOWNER IN THE CITY BROUGHT IN ENORMOUS WEALTH, MORE THAN ENOUGH TO SUPPORT ALL THE WARDEN'S STAFF AND LEAVE A FORTUNE TO SPARE.

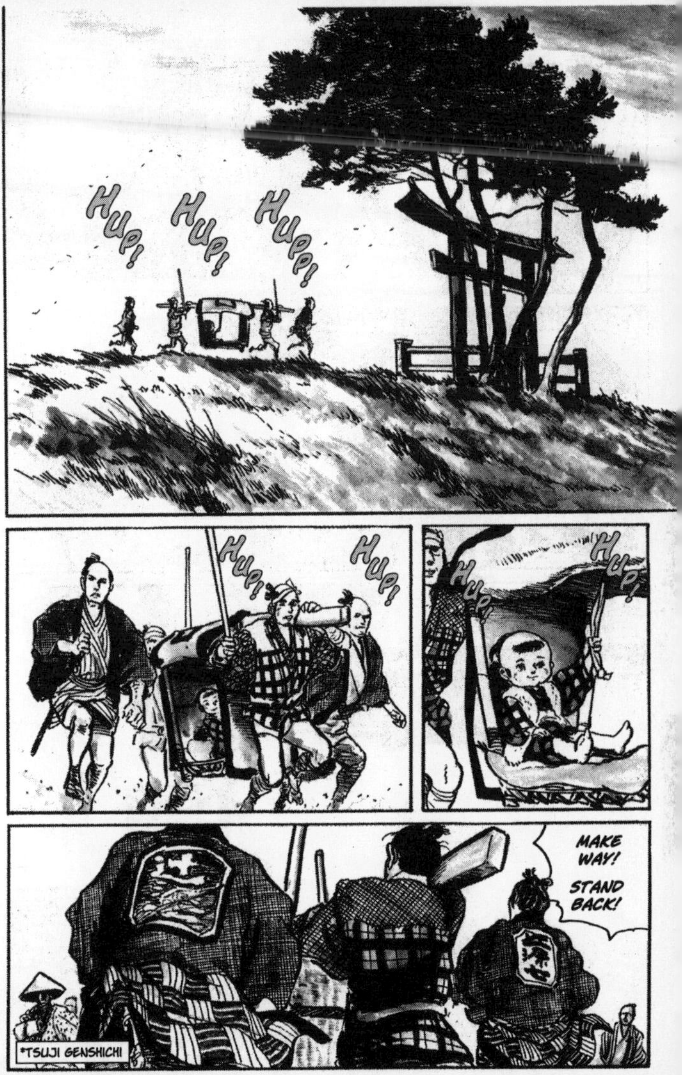
HUPP!
HUP!
HUP!
HUP!
HUP!
HUP!
HUP!
MAKE WAY!
STAND BACK!
*TSUJI GENSHICHI

HUUN    HUUN

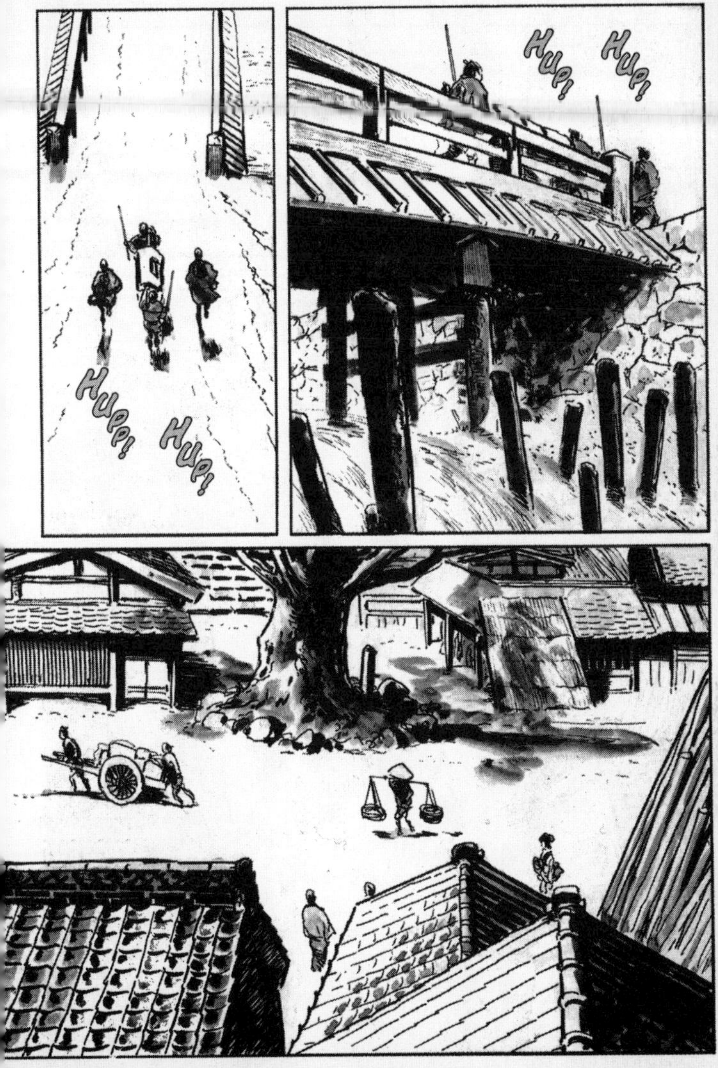
HUP! HUP!
HUP! HUP!

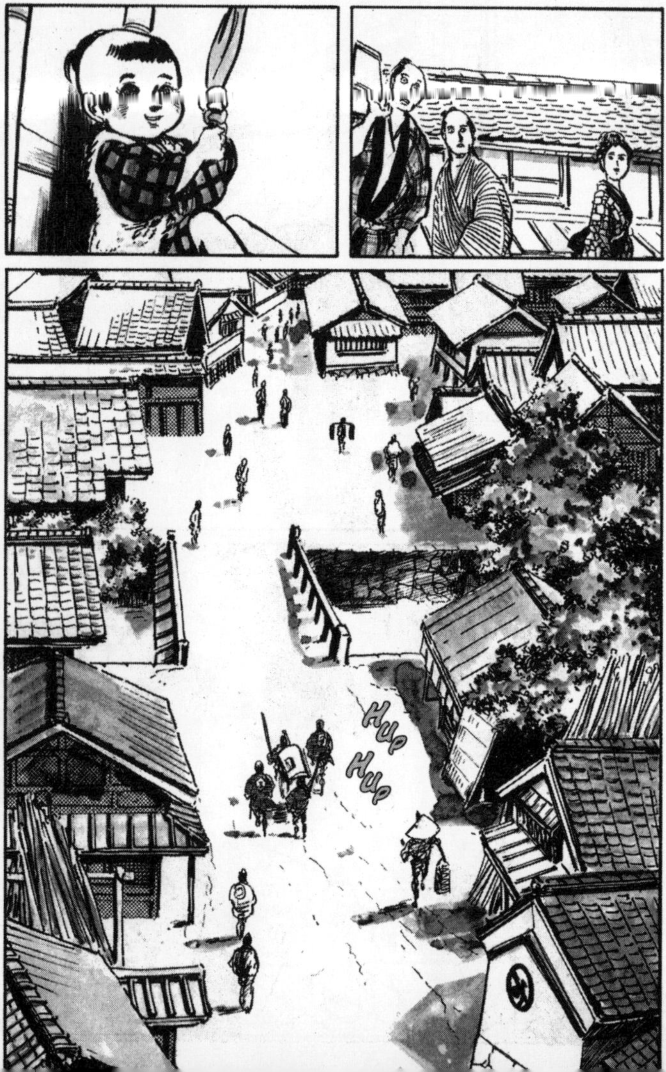
HUP HUP

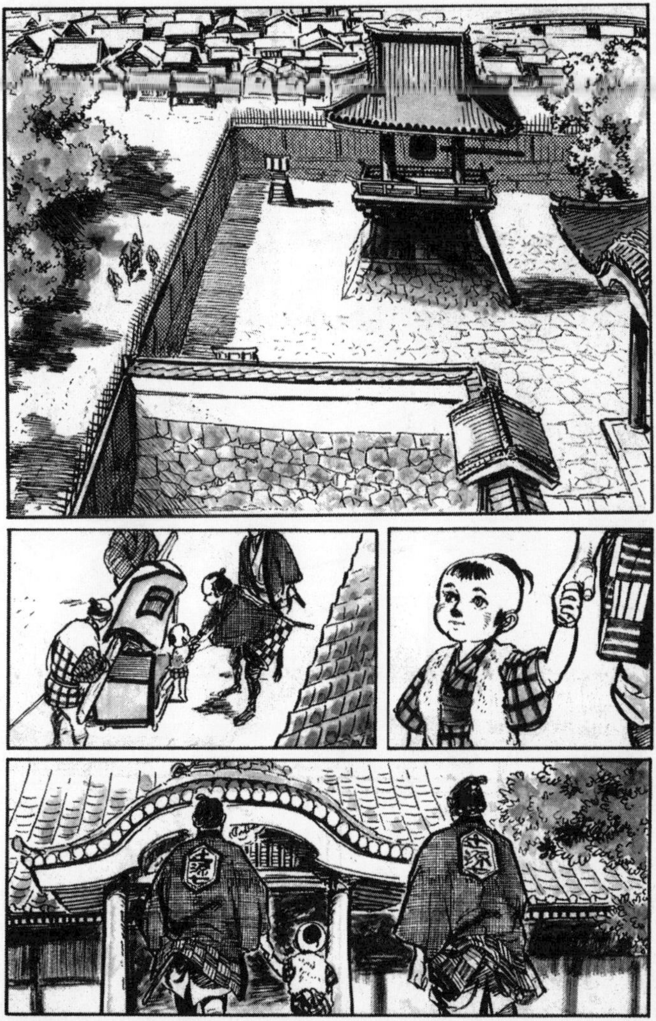

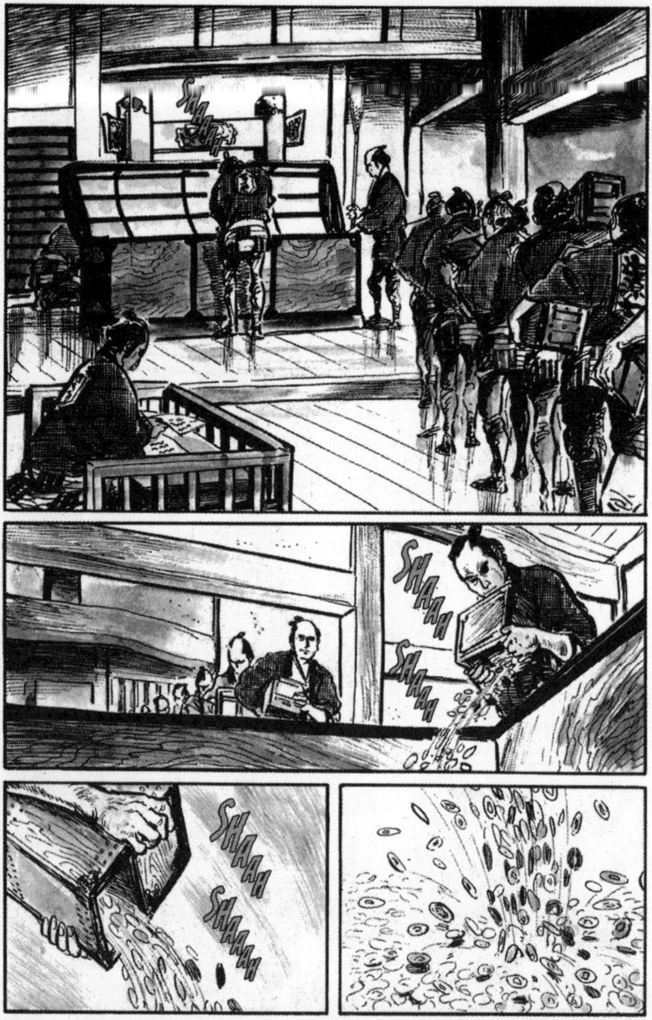
SHAAAH
SHAAAH
SHAAAH
SHAAAH
SHAAAAH

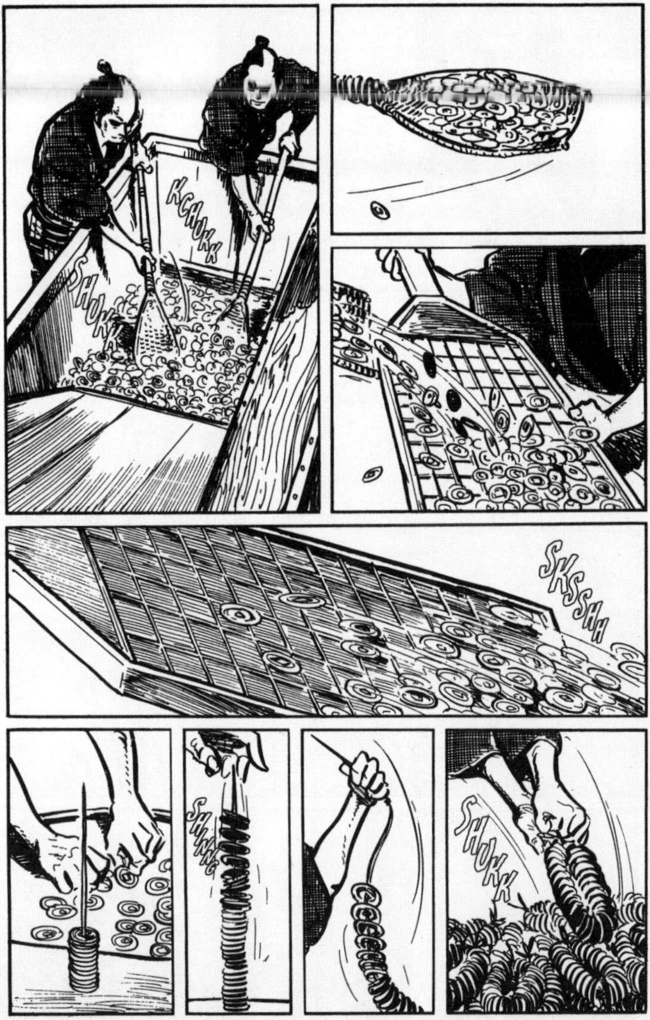
KCHUKK
SHUKK
SKSSHH
SHUKK
SHING

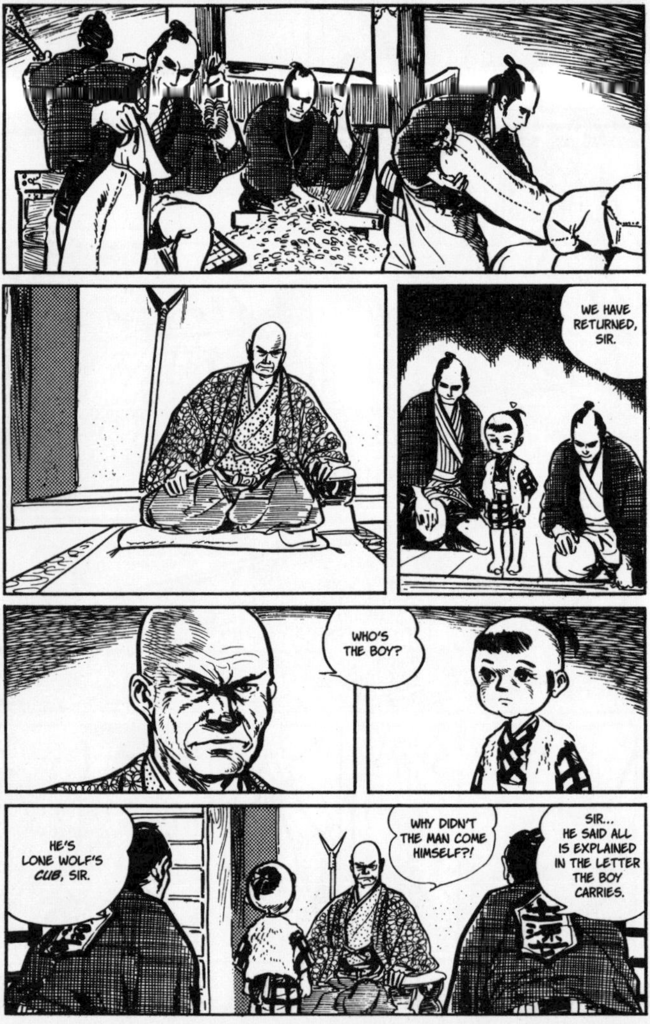
WE HAVE RETURNED, SIR.
WHO'S THE BOY?
HE'S LONE WOLF'S *CUB*, SIR.
WHY DIDN'T THE MAN COME HIMSELF?!
SIR... HE SAID ALL IS EXPLAINED IN THE LETTER THE BOY CARRIES.

?!

MNN...?

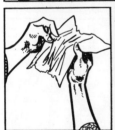

"BY PLEDGE OF HONOR, I AM UNABLE TO SET FOOT IN *KUROBIKI* EDO. I MUST ASK YOU TO MEET ME ON MACHIYA MIKAWA ISLAND ON THE *SHUBIKI* BORDERLINE. FORGIVE THIS UNREASONABLE REQUEST. ŌGAMI.

HMM...

PREPARE A PALANQUIN!

YES, SIR!!

SO THIS BOY IS TO BE MY GUIDE. HE SEEMS A STRONG, *FEARLESS* LAD.

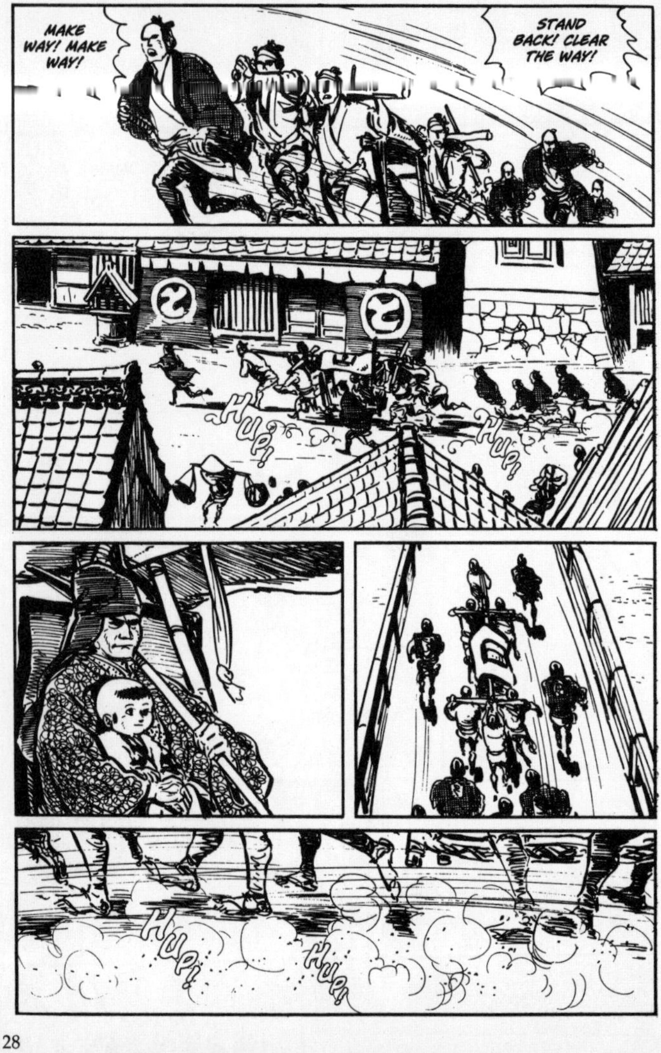
STAND BACK! CLEAR THE WAY!
MAKE WAY! MAKE WAY!
HUP!
HUP!
HUP!
HUP!

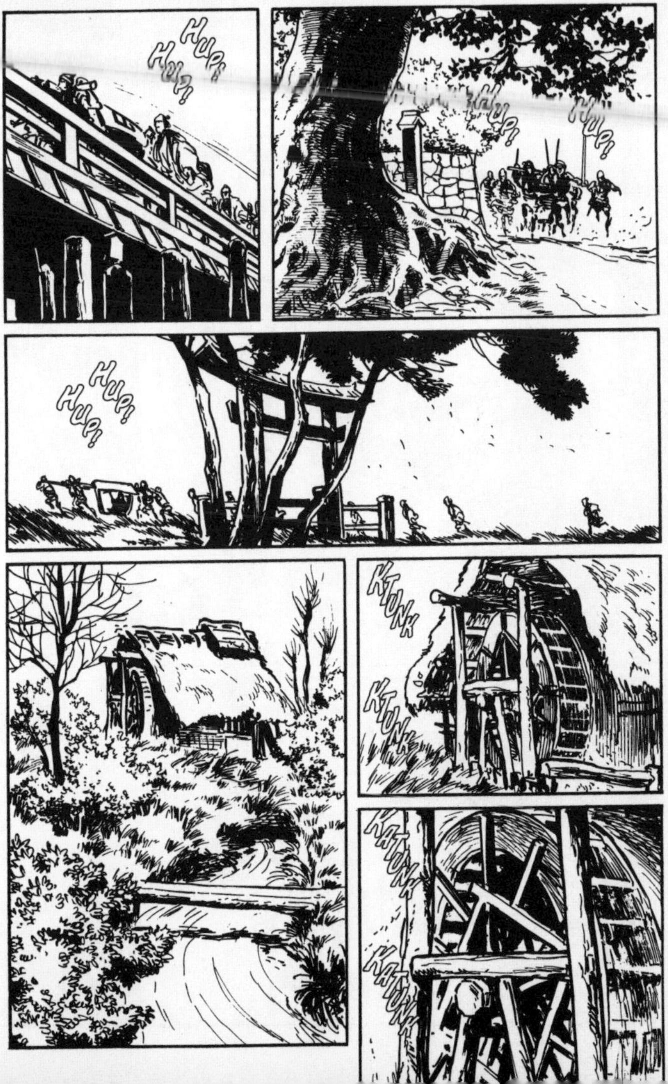
HUP!
HUP!
HUP!
HUP!
HUP!
HUP!
KTUNK
KTUNK
KATUNK
KATUNK

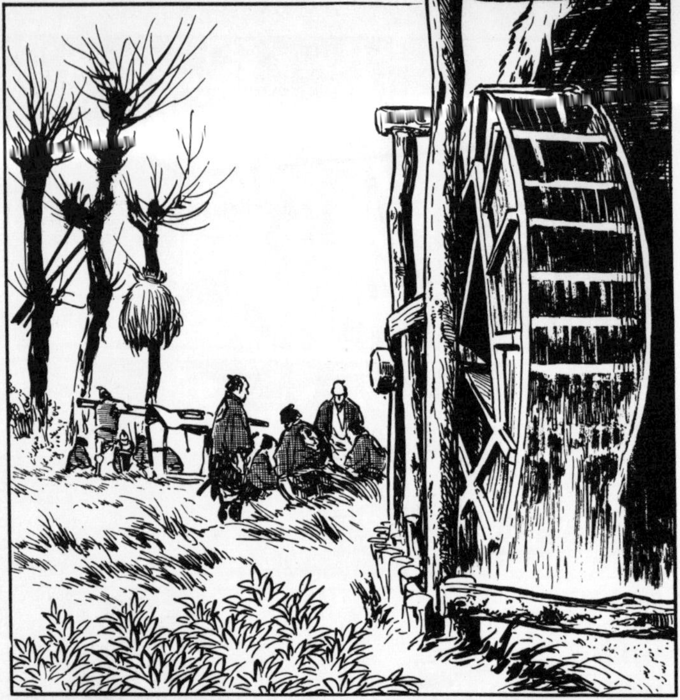
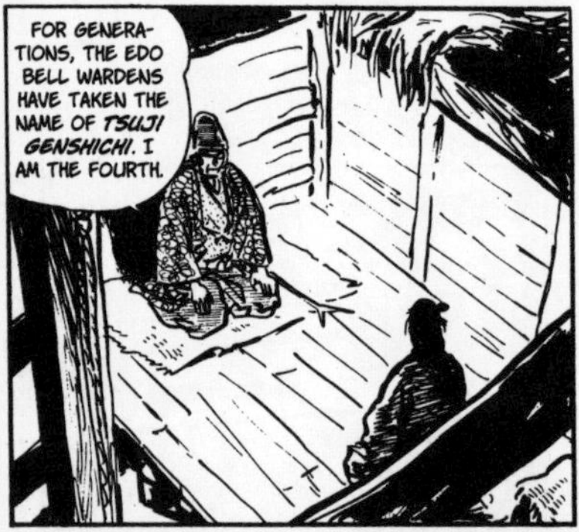
FOR GENERATIONS, THE EDO BELL WARDENS HAVE TAKEN THE NAME OF *TSUJI GENSHICHI*. I AM THE FOURTH.
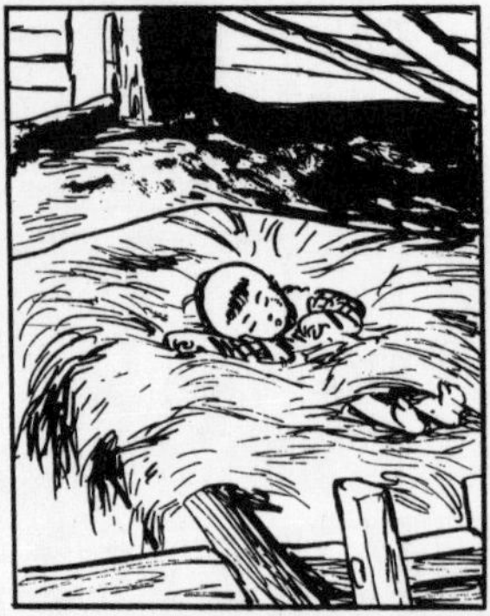

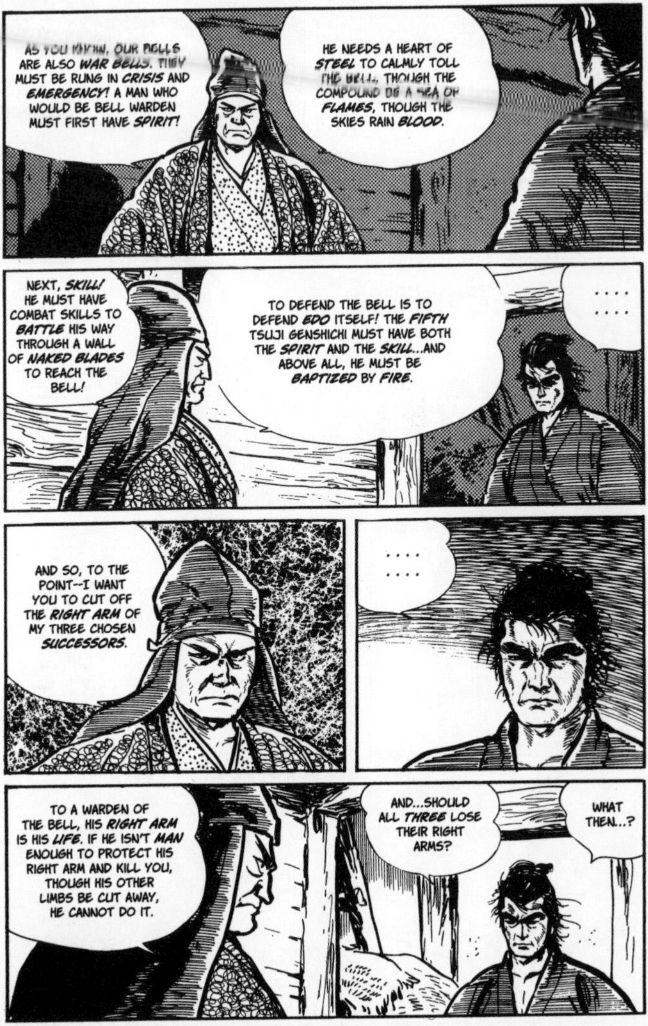
AS YOU KNOW, OUR BELLS ARE ALSO WAR BELLS. THEY MUST BE RUNG IN CRISIS AND EMERGENCY! A MAN WHO WOULD BE BELL WARDEN MUST FIRST HAVE SPIRIT!
HE NEEDS A HEART OF STEEL TO CALMLY TOLL THE BELL, THOUGH THE COMPOUND BE A SEA OF FLAMES, THOUGH THE SKIES RAIN BLOOD.
NEXT, SKILL! HE MUST HAVE COMBAT SKILLS TO BATTLE HIS WAY THROUGH A WALL OF NAKED BLADES TO REACH THE BELL!
TO DEFEND THE BELL IS TO DEFEND EDO ITSELF! THE FIFTH TSUJI GENSHICHI MUST HAVE BOTH THE SPIRIT AND THE SKILL...AND ABOVE ALL, HE MUST BE BAPTIZED BY FIRE.
.... ....
AND SO, TO THE POINT--I WANT YOU TO CUT OFF THE RIGHT ARM OF MY THREE CHOSEN SUCCESSORS.
.... ....
TO A WARDEN OF THE BELL, HIS RIGHT ARM IS HIS LIFE. IF HE ISN'T MAN ENOUGH TO PROTECT HIS RIGHT ARM AND KILL YOU, THOUGH HIS OTHER LIMBS BE CUT AWAY, HE CANNOT DO IT.
AND...SHOULD ALL THREE LOSE THEIR RIGHT ARMS?
WHAT THEN...?

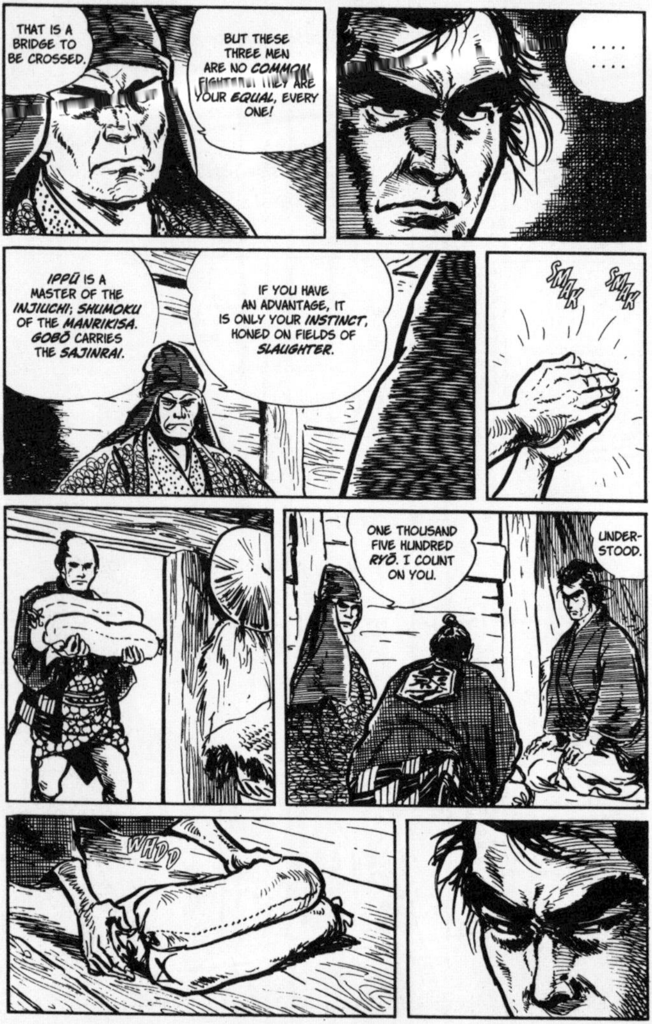
THAT IS A BRIDGE TO BE CROSSED.
BUT THESE THREE MEN ARE NO COMMON FIGHTERS. THEY ARE YOUR EQUAL, EVERY ONE!
....
....
IPPŪ IS A MASTER OF THE INJIUCHI; SHUMOKU OF THE MANRIKISA. GOBŌ CARRIES THE SAJINRAI.
IF YOU HAVE AN ADVANTAGE, IT IS ONLY YOUR INSTINCT, HONED ON FIELDS OF SLAUGHTER.
SMAK
SMAK
ONE THOUSAND FIVE HUNDRED RYŌ. I COUNT ON YOU.
UNDER-STOOD.
WHDD

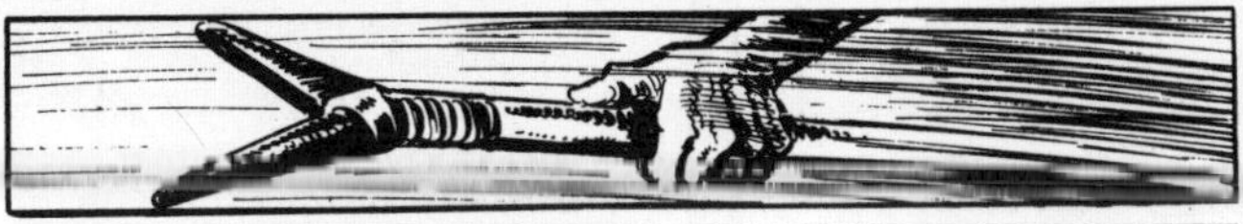

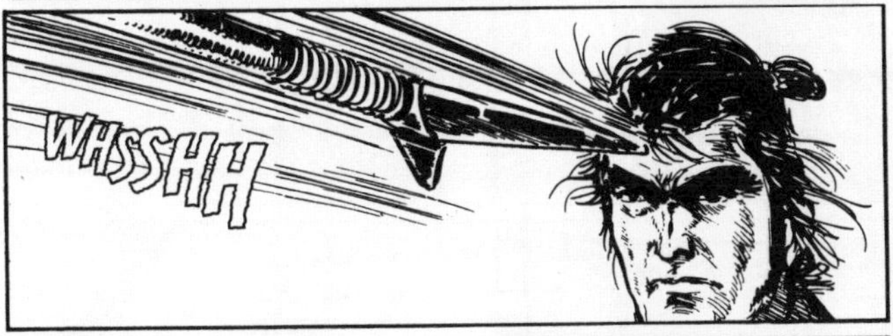
WHSSHH

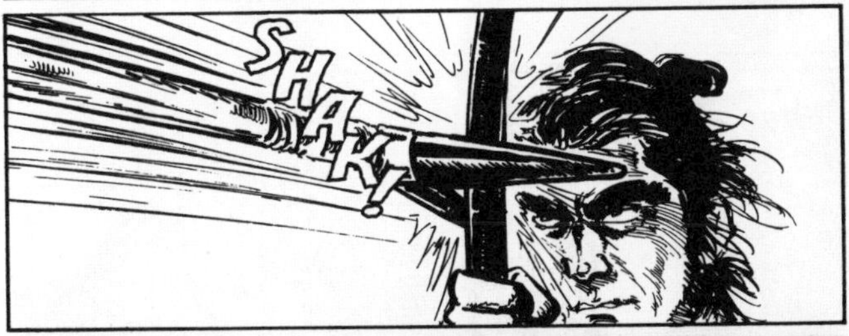
SHAK!

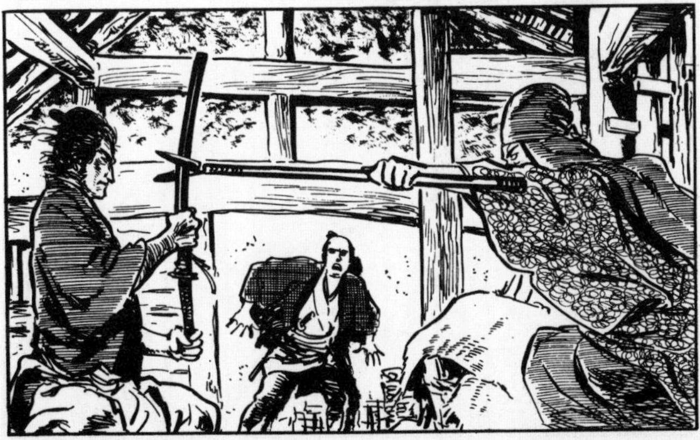

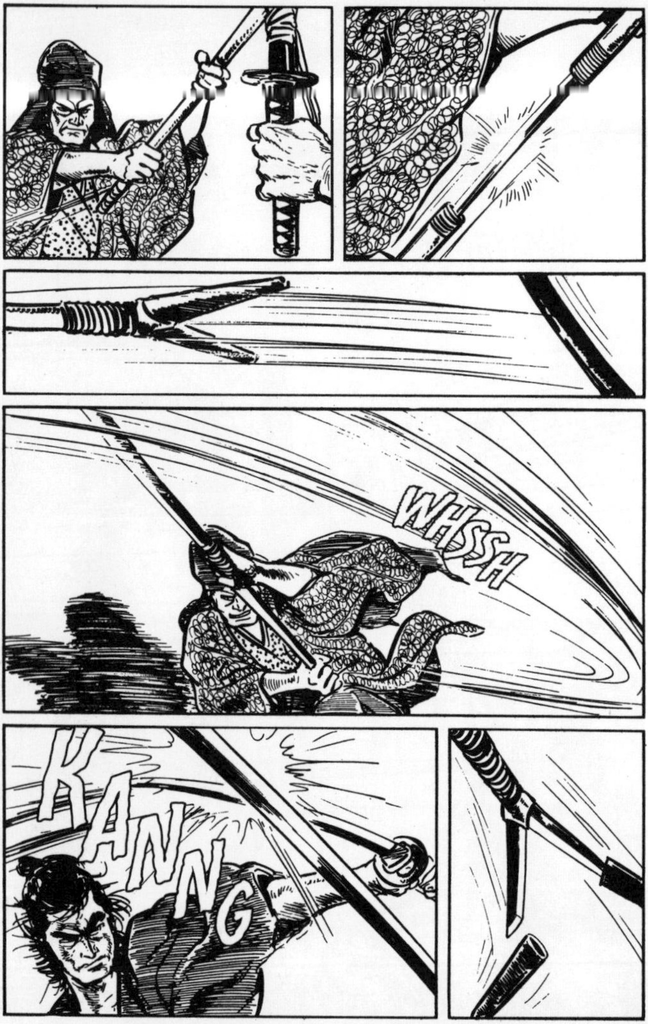
WHSSH
KANNG

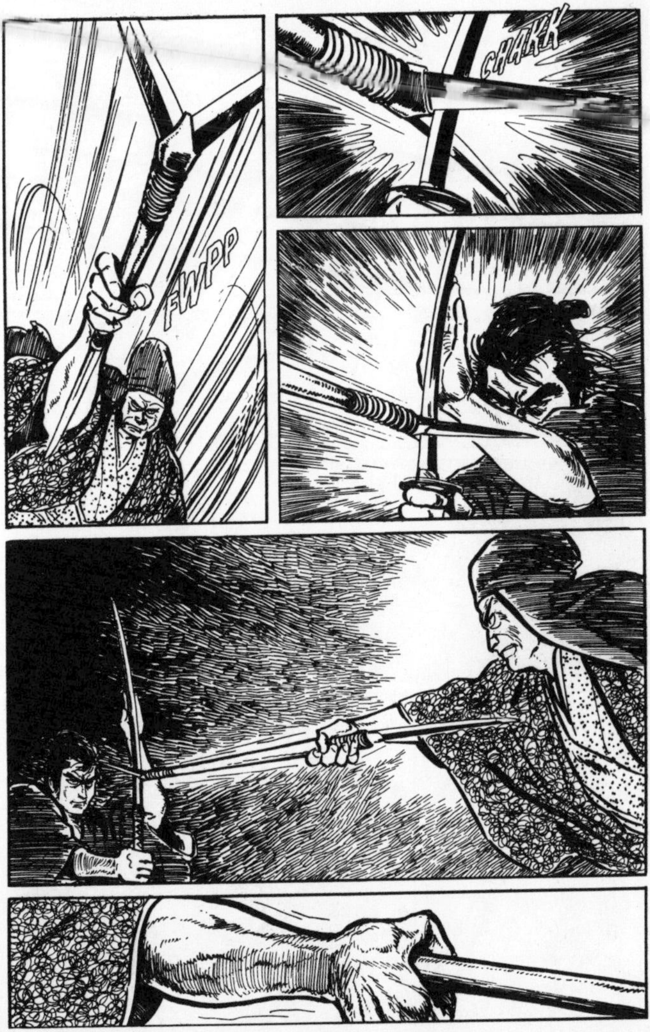
CHAKK
FWIPP

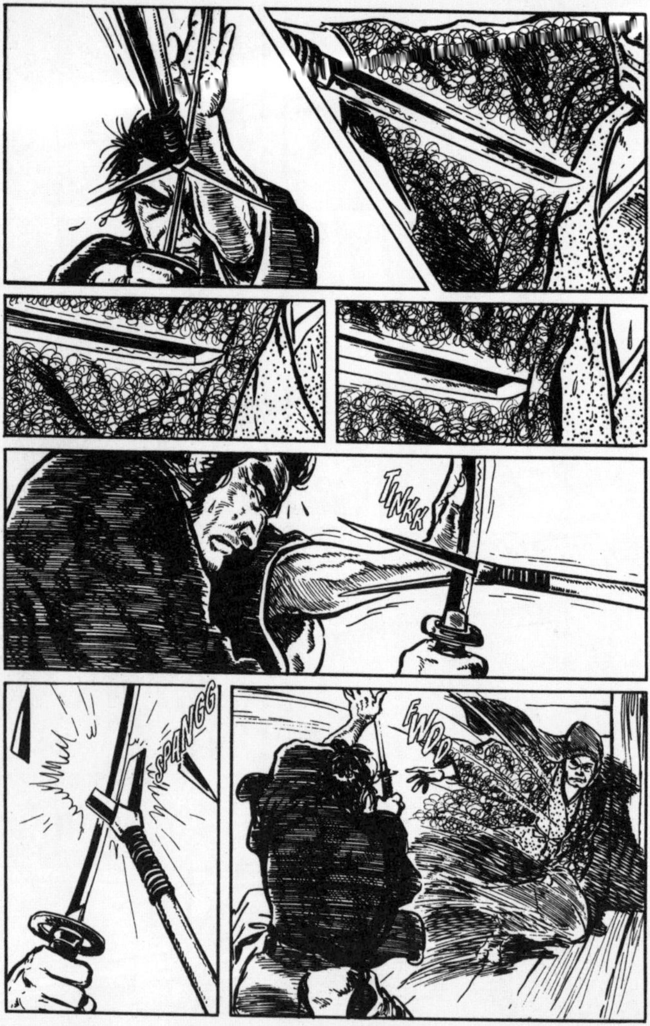
TINKK
FWDD
SPANGG

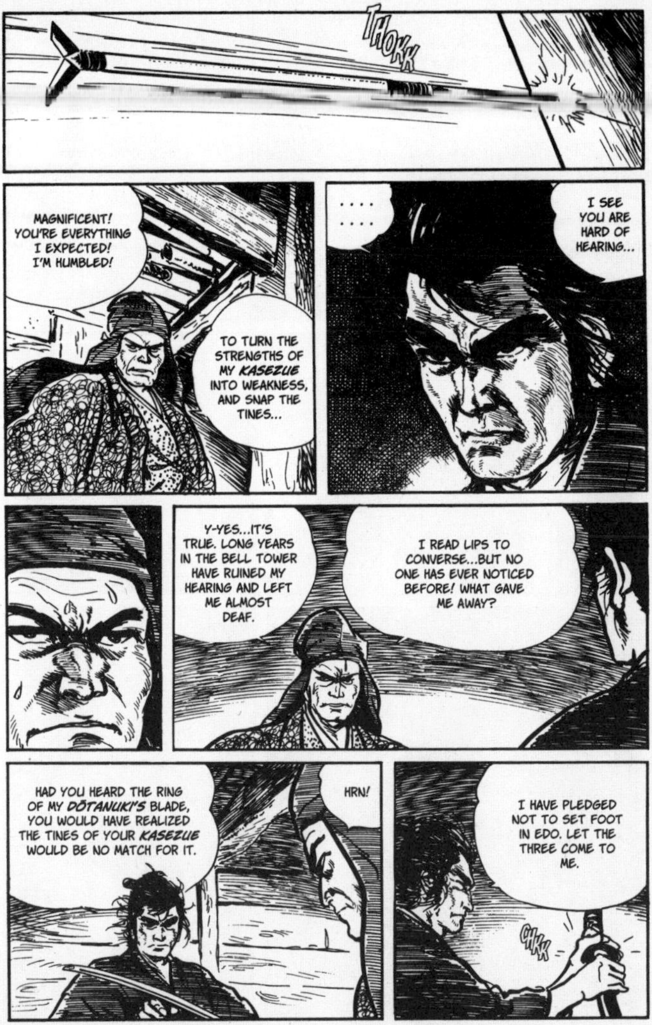
THOKK
MAGNIFICENT! YOU'RE EVERYTHING I EXPECTED! I'M HUMBLED!
TO TURN THE STRENGTHS OF MY *KASEZUE* INTO WEAKNESS, AND SNAP THE TINES...
....
....
I SEE YOU ARE HARD OF HEARING...
Y-YES...IT'S TRUE. LONG YEARS IN THE BELL TOWER HAVE RUINED MY HEARING AND LEFT ME ALMOST DEAF.
I READ LIPS TO CONVERSE...BUT NO ONE HAS EVER NOTICED BEFORE! WHAT GAVE ME AWAY?
HAD YOU HEARD THE RING OF MY *DŌTANUKI'S* BLADE, YOU WOULD HAVE REALIZED THE TINES OF YOUR *KASEZUE* WOULD BE NO MATCH FOR IT.
HRN!
I HAVE PLEDGED NOT TO SET FOOT IN EDO. LET THE THREE COME TO ME.
CHKK

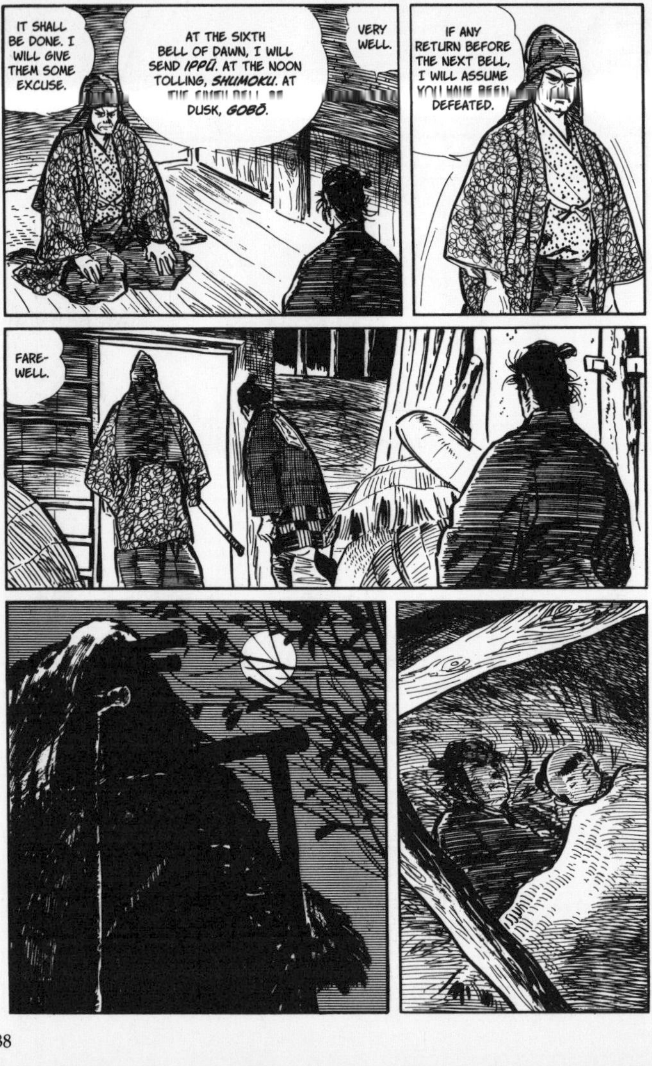
IT SHALL BE DONE. I WILL GIVE THEM SOME EXCUSE.
AT THE SIXTH BELL OF DAWN, I WILL SEND *IPPŪ*. AT THE NOON TOLLING, ***SHUMOKU***. AT THE SIXTH BELL OF DUSK, ***GOBŌ***.
VERY WELL.
IF ANY RETURN BEFORE THE NEXT BELL, I WILL ASSUME YOU HAVE BEEN DEFEATED.
FARE-WELL.

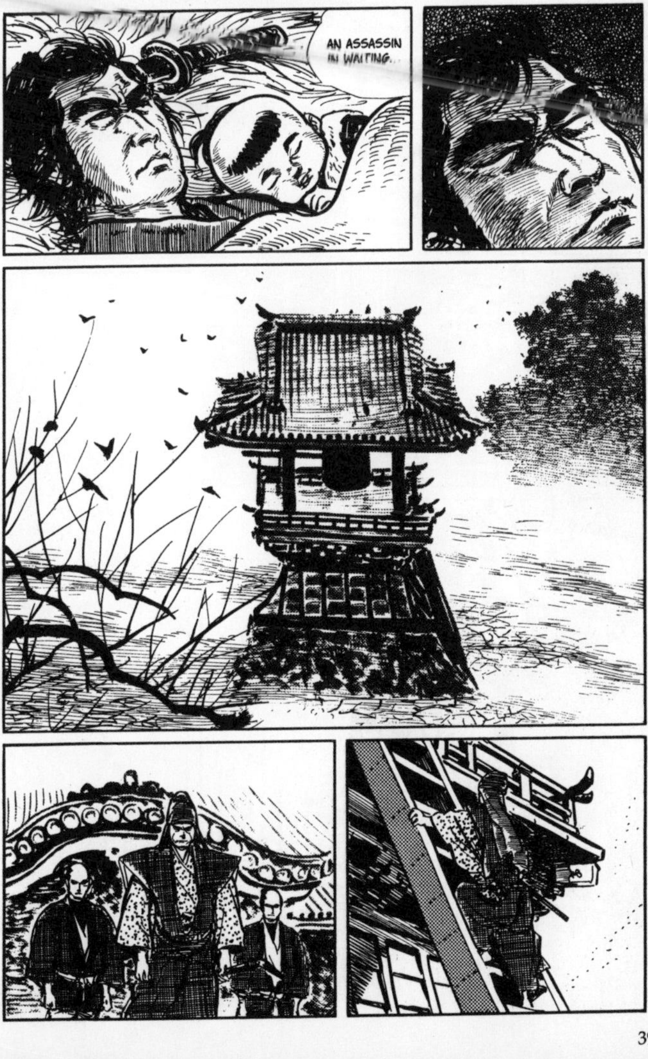
AN ASSASSIN IN WAITING...

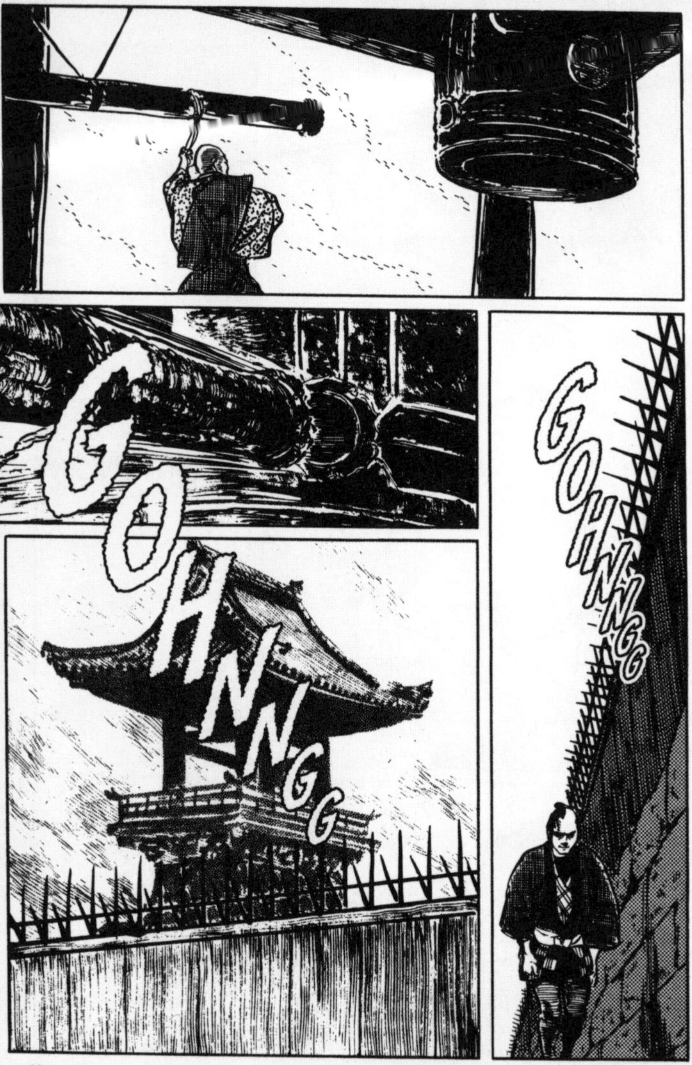
GOHNNGG
GOHNNGG

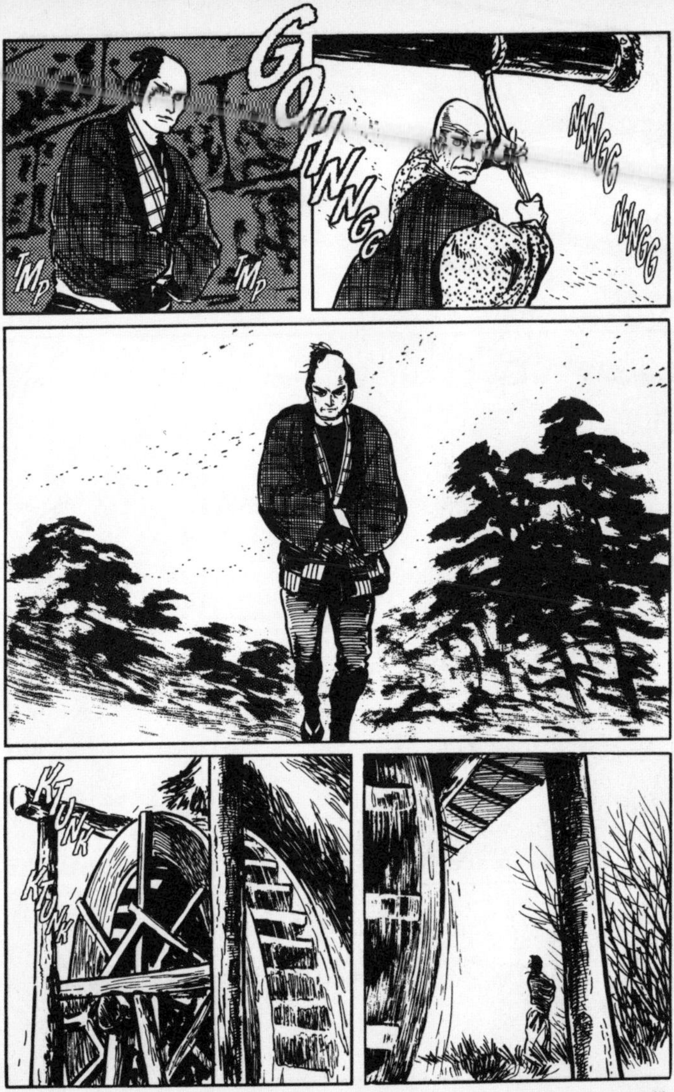
GOHNNNGG
NNNGG
NNNGG
TMP
TMP
KTUNK
KTUNK

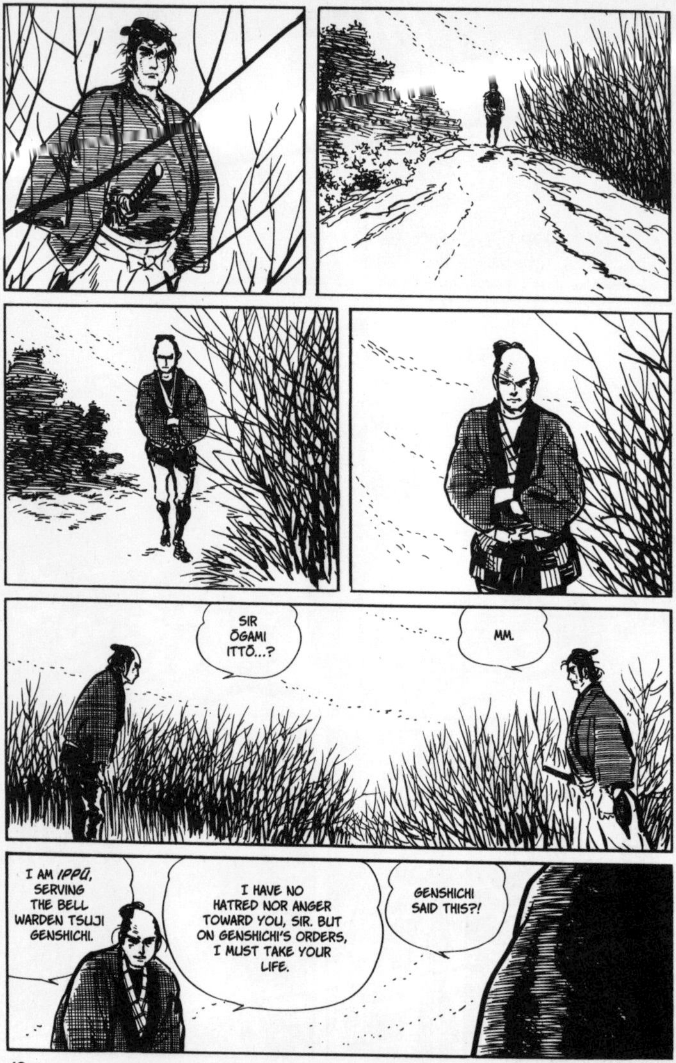
SIR ŌGAMI ITTŌ...?
MM.
I AM *IPPŪ*, SERVING THE BELL WARDEN TSUJI GENSHICHI.
I HAVE NO HATRED NOR ANGER TOWARD YOU, SIR. BUT ON GENSHICHI'S ORDERS, I MUST TAKE YOUR LIFE.
GENSHICHI SAID THIS?!

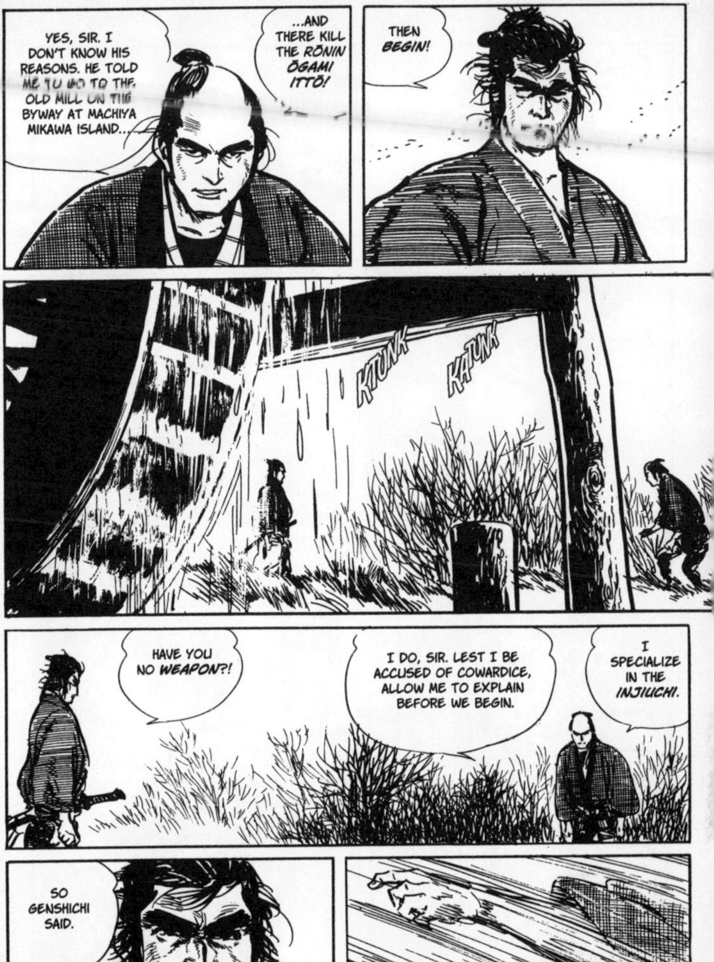
YES, SIR. I DON'T KNOW HIS REASONS. HE TOLD ME TO GO TO THE OLD MILL ON THE BYWAY AT MACHIYA MIKAWA ISLAND...
...AND THERE KILL THE *RŌNIN* *ŌGAMI ITTŌ!*
THEN *BEGIN!*
KATUNK
KATUNK
HAVE YOU NO *WEAPON?!*
I DO, SIR. LEST I BE ACCUSED OF COWARDICE, ALLOW ME TO EXPLAIN BEFORE WE BEGIN.
I SPECIALIZE IN THE *INJIUCHI*.
SO GENSHICHI SAID.

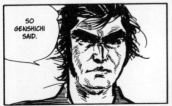

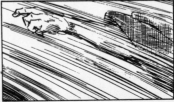

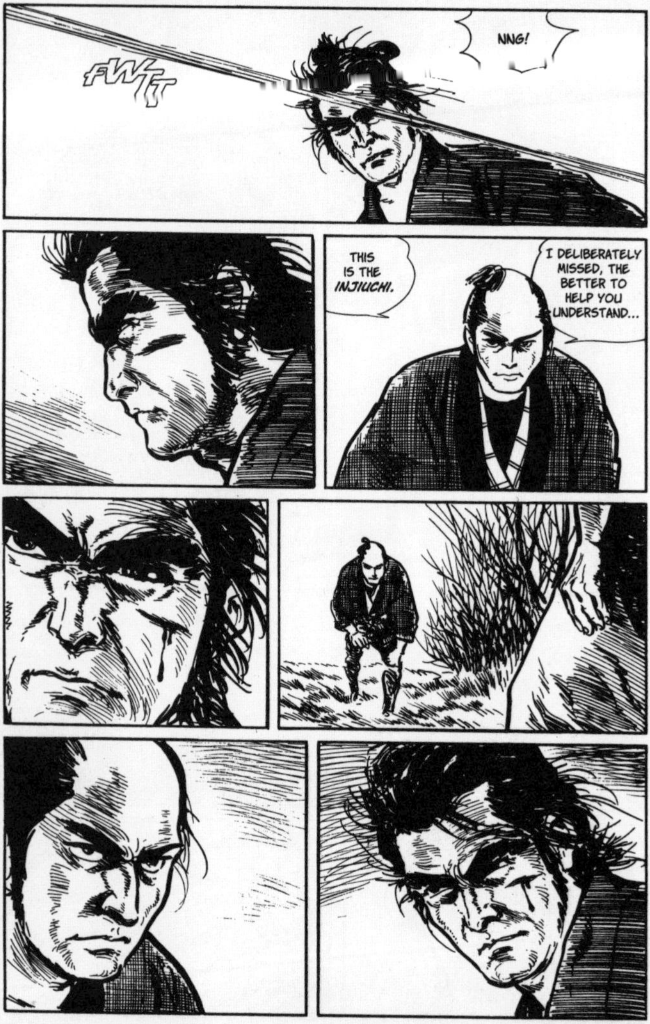
NNG!
FWTT
I DELIBERATELY MISSED, THE BETTER TO HELP YOU UNDERSTAND...
THIS IS THE *INJIUCHI.*

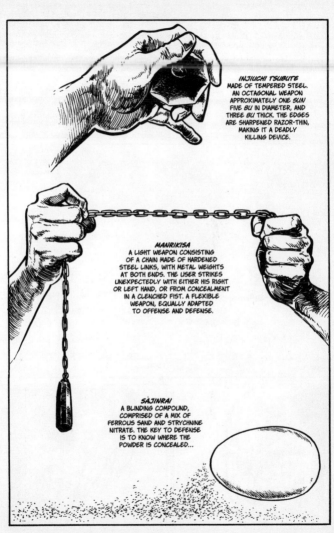

**INJIUCHI TSUBUTE**
MADE OF TEMPERED STEEL.
AN OCTAGONAL WEAPON
APPROXIMATELY ONE *SUN*
FIVE *BU* IN DIAMETER, AND
THREE *BU* THICK. THE EDGES
ARE SHARPENED RAZOR-THIN,
MAKING IT A DEADLY
KILLING DEVICE.

**MANRIKISA**
A LIGHT WEAPON CONSISTING
OF A CHAIN MADE OF HARDENED
STEEL LINKS, WITH METAL WEIGHTS
AT BOTH ENDS. THE USER STRIKES
UNEXPECTEDLY WITH EITHER HIS RIGHT
OR LEFT HAND, OR FROM CONCEALMENT
IN A CLENCHED FIST. A FLEXIBLE
WEAPON, EQUALLY ADAPTED
TO OFFENSE AND DEFENSE.

**SAJINRAI**
A BLINDING COMPOUND,
COMPRISED OF A MIX OF
FERROUS SAND AND STRYCHNINE
NITRATE. THE KEY TO DEFENSE
IS TO KNOW WHERE THE
POWDER IS CONCEALED...

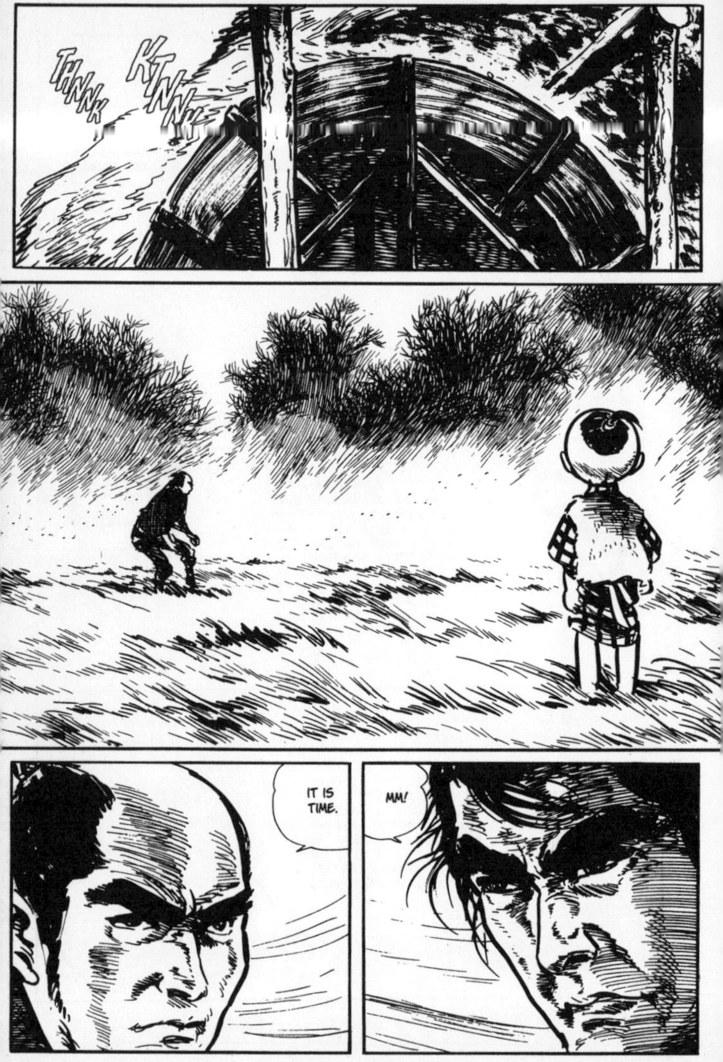
THNNK
KTNNNK
IT IS TIME.
MM!

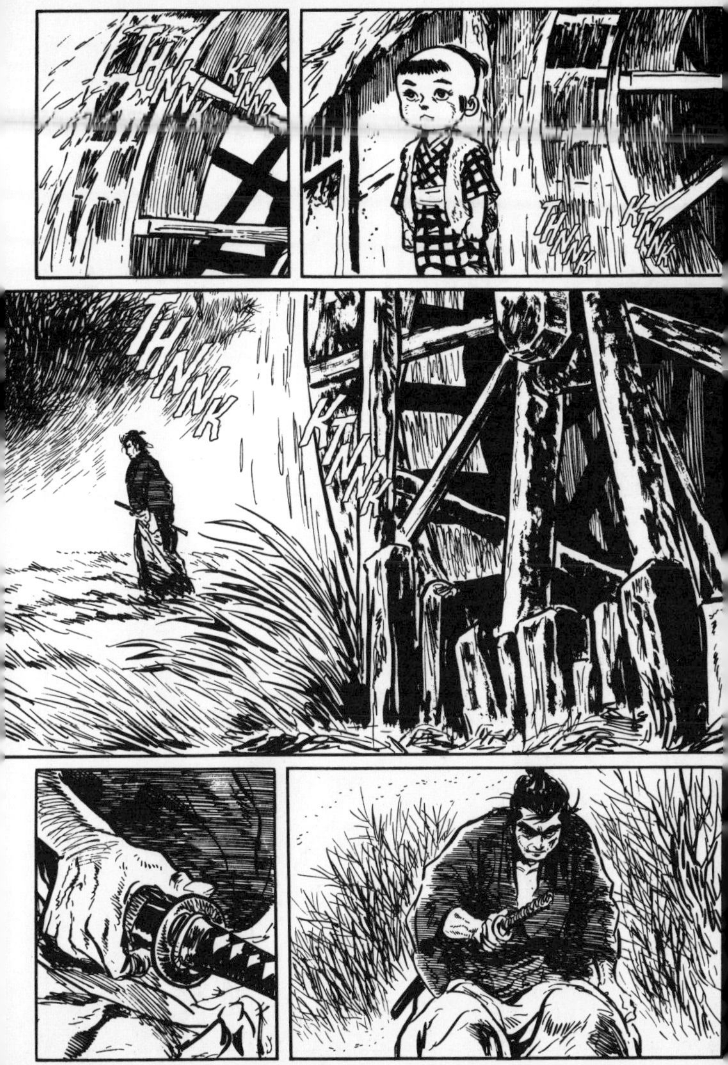
THNNK
KTNNK
THNN
KTNN
THNNK
KTNNK

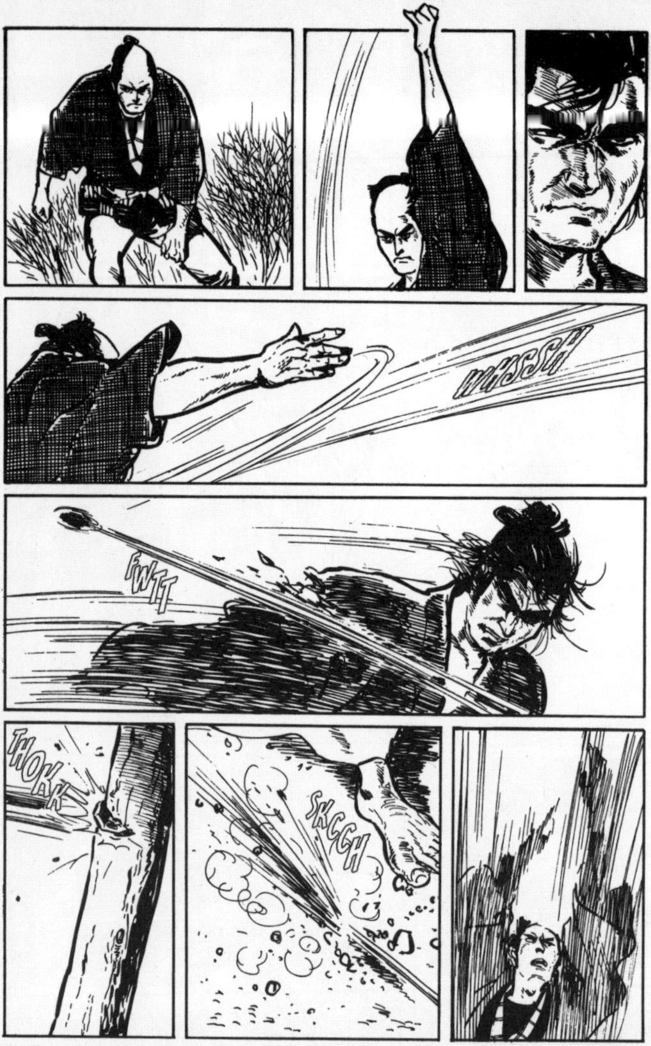
WHSSH
FWTT
SKCCH
THOKK

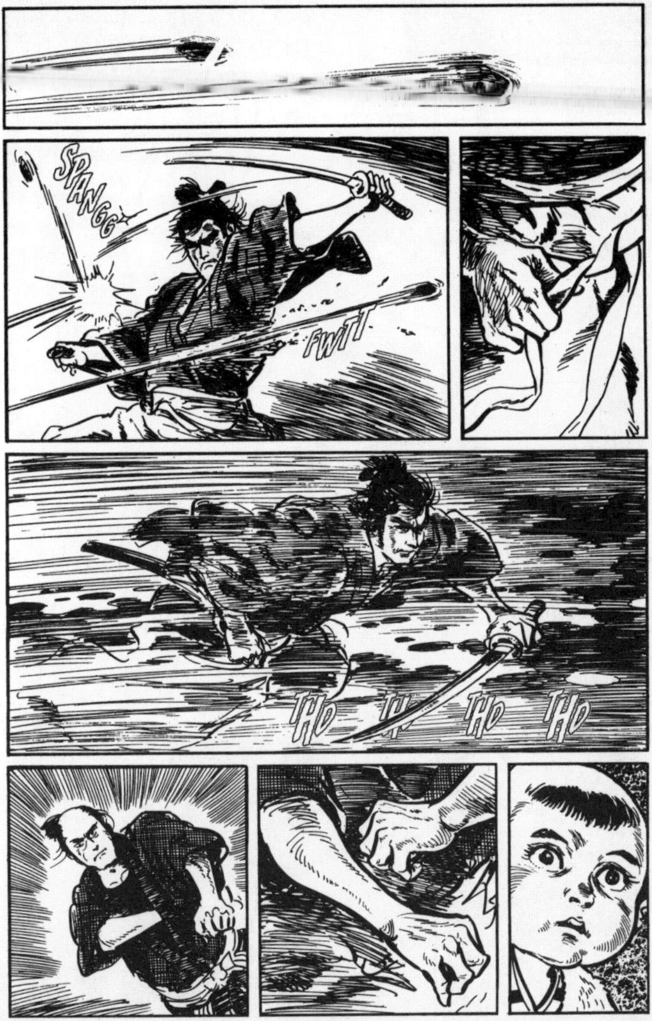
SPANGG
FWITT
THD THD THD THD

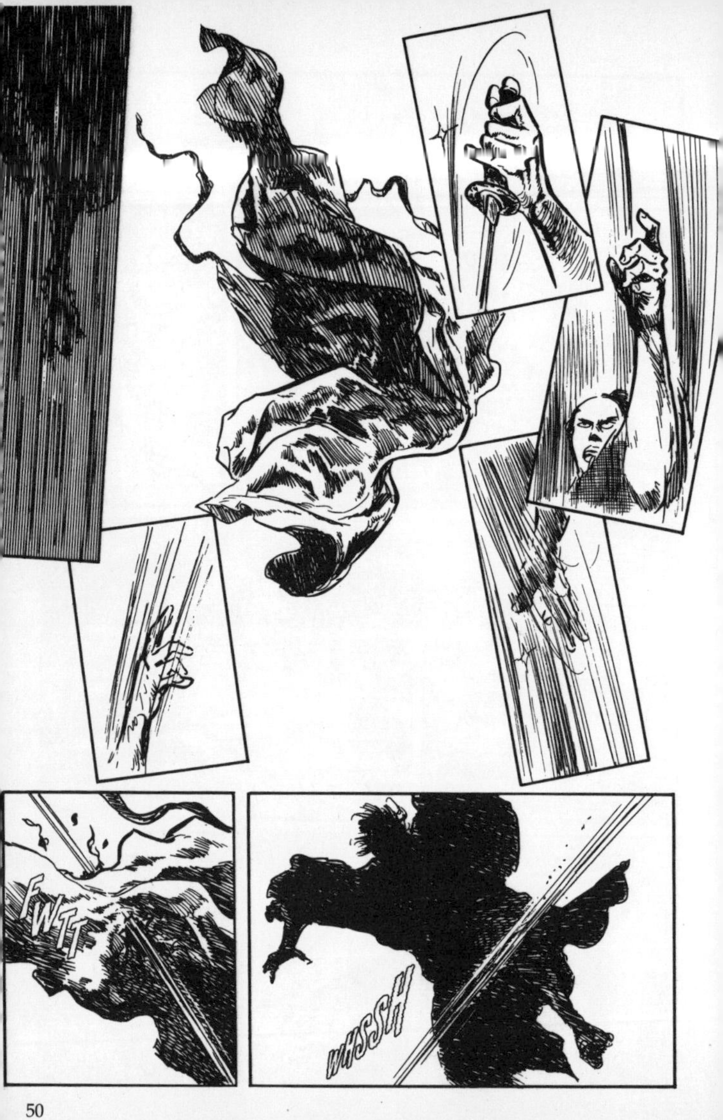
WHSSH
FWTT

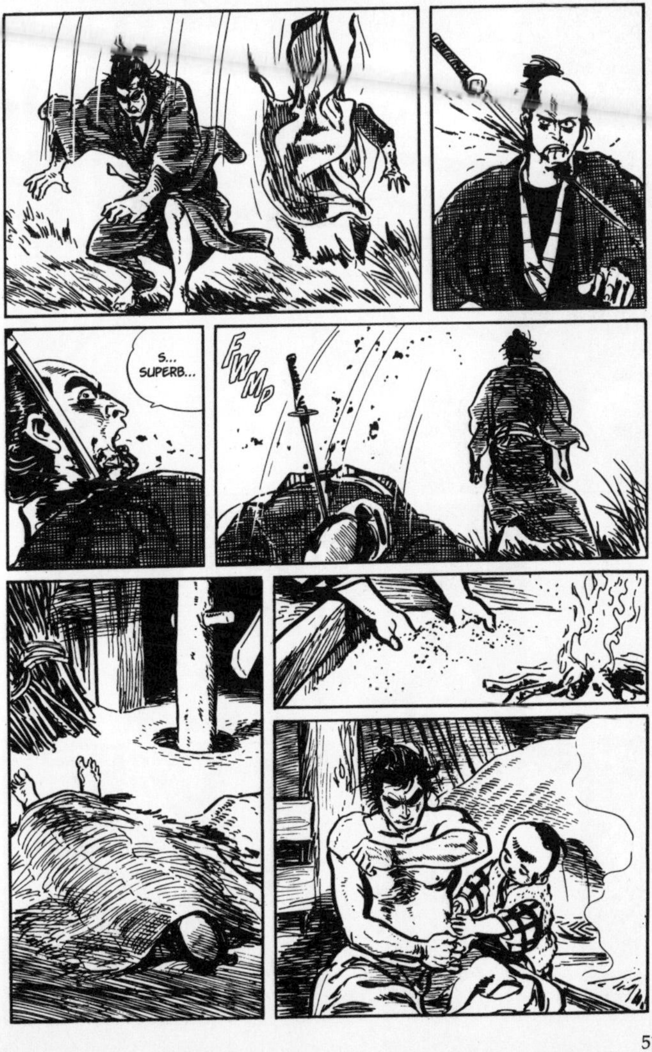
FWMP
S... SUPERB...

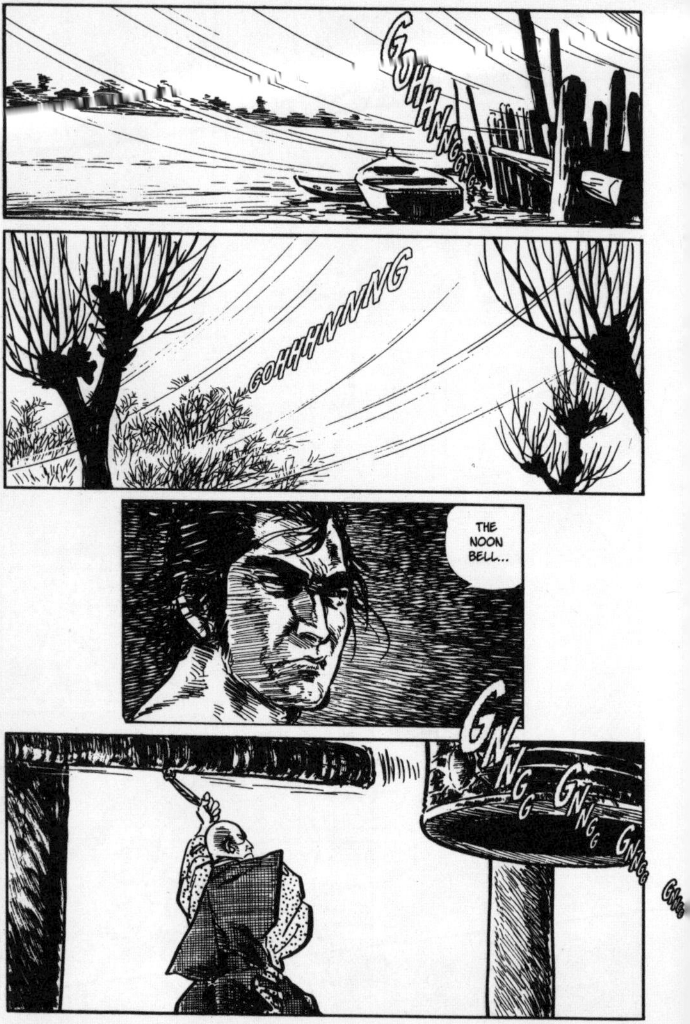
GOHHNNGGNG
GOHHHNNNNG
THE NOON BELL...
GNNGG
GNNGG
GNNGG
GNNG

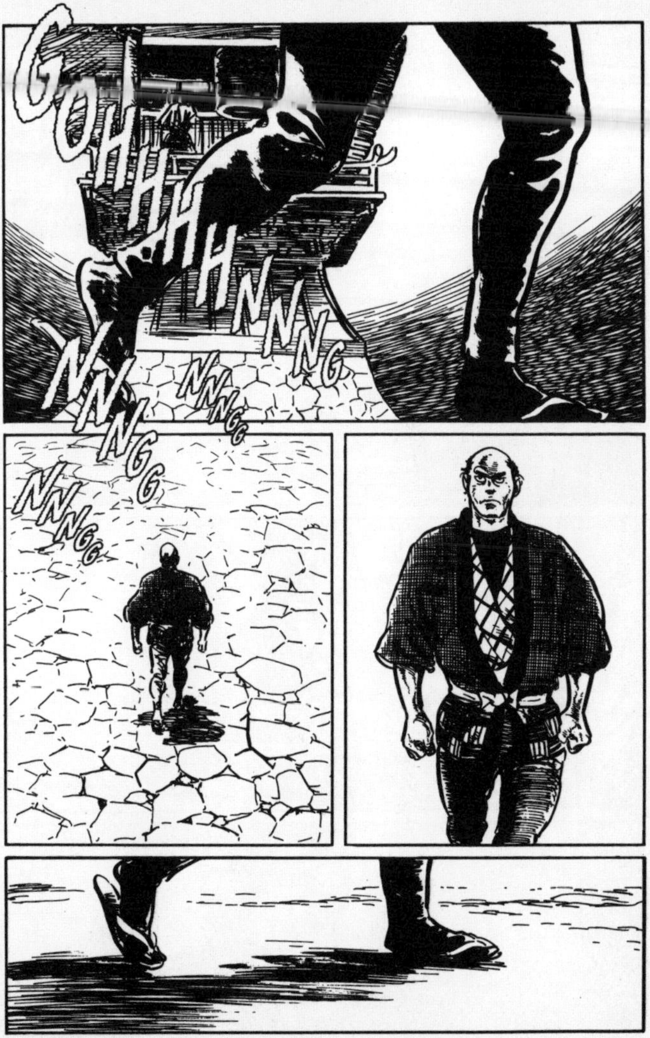
GOHHHHNNNG
NNNGG
NNNGG
NNNGG

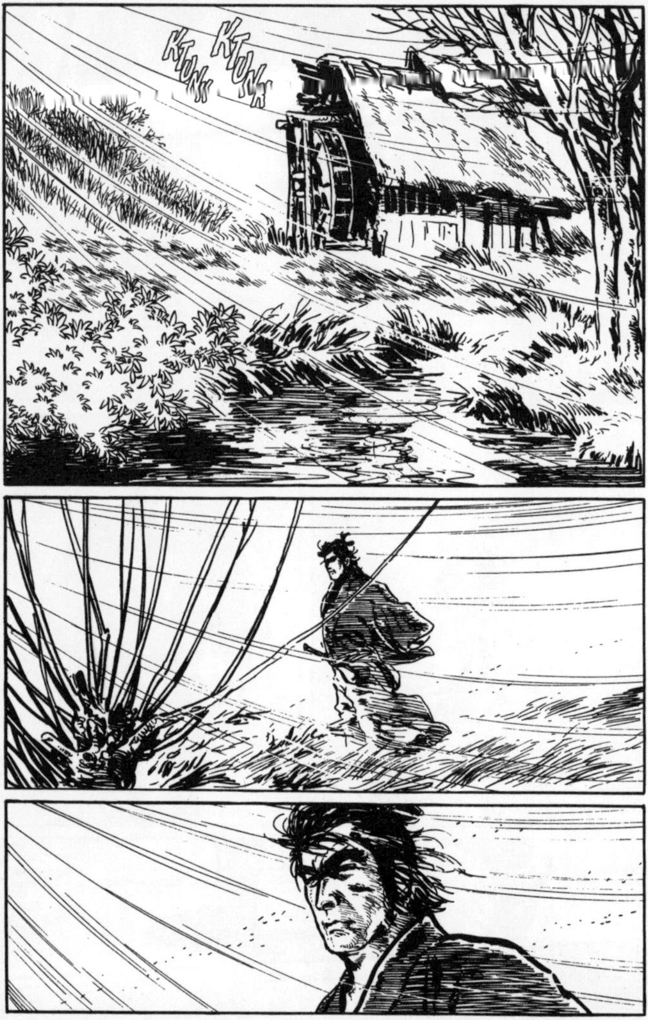
KTUNK
KTUNK

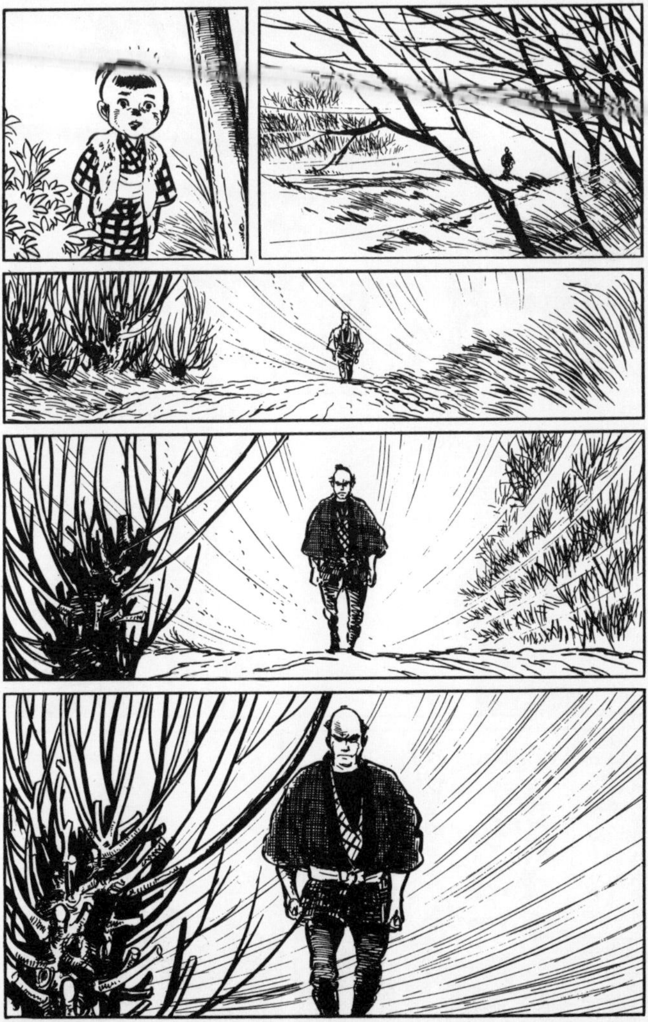

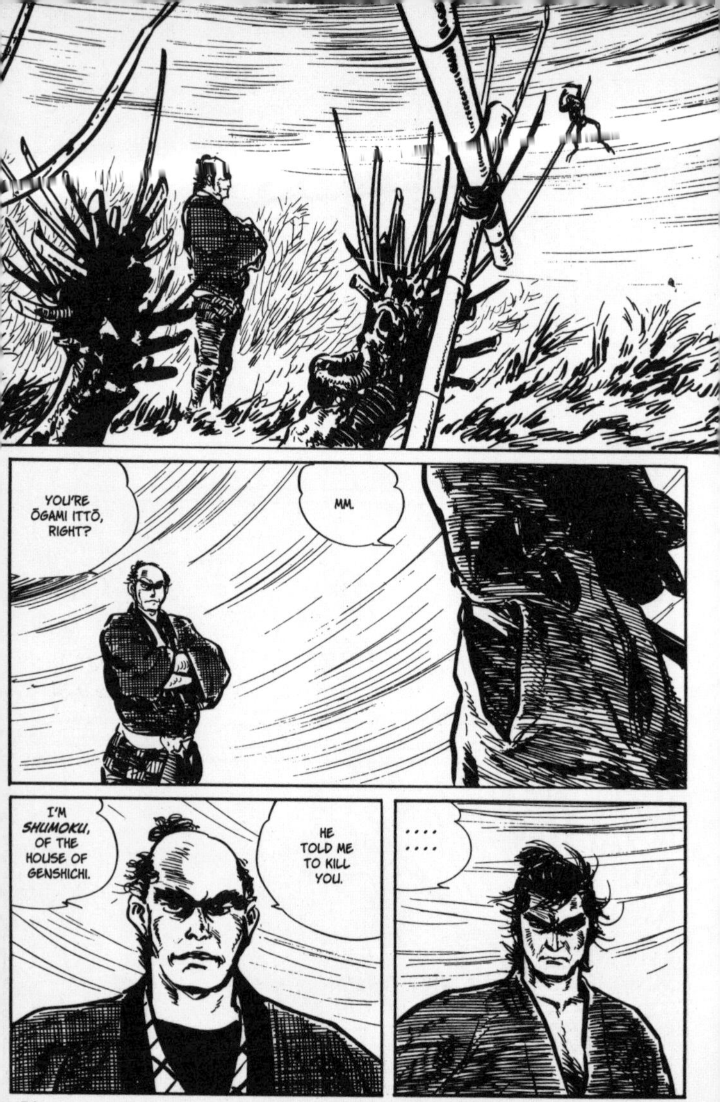
YOU'RE ŌGAMI ITTŌ, RIGHT?
MM.
I'M *SHUMOKU*, OF THE HOUSE OF GENSHICHI.
HE TOLD ME TO KILL YOU.
....
....

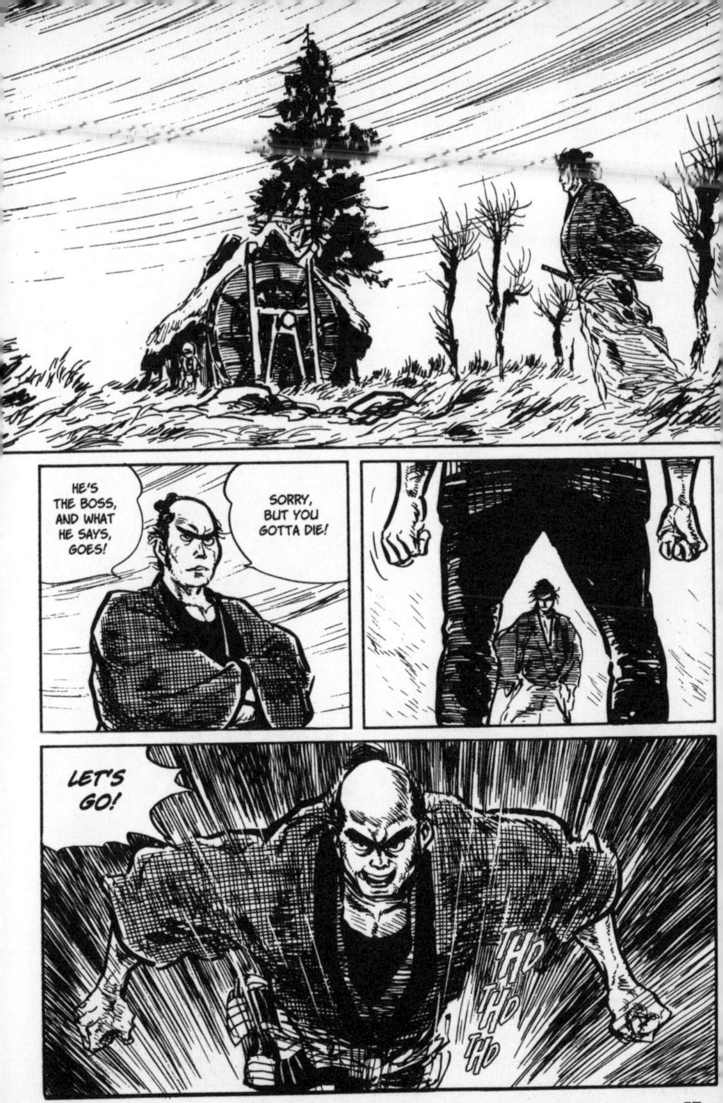
HE'S THE BOSS, AND WHAT HE SAYS, GOES!
SORRY, BUT YOU GOTTA DIE!
LET'S GO!
THD
THD
THD

THO-THO-THO-TH

HYAAHH!

EWAHSSSHH

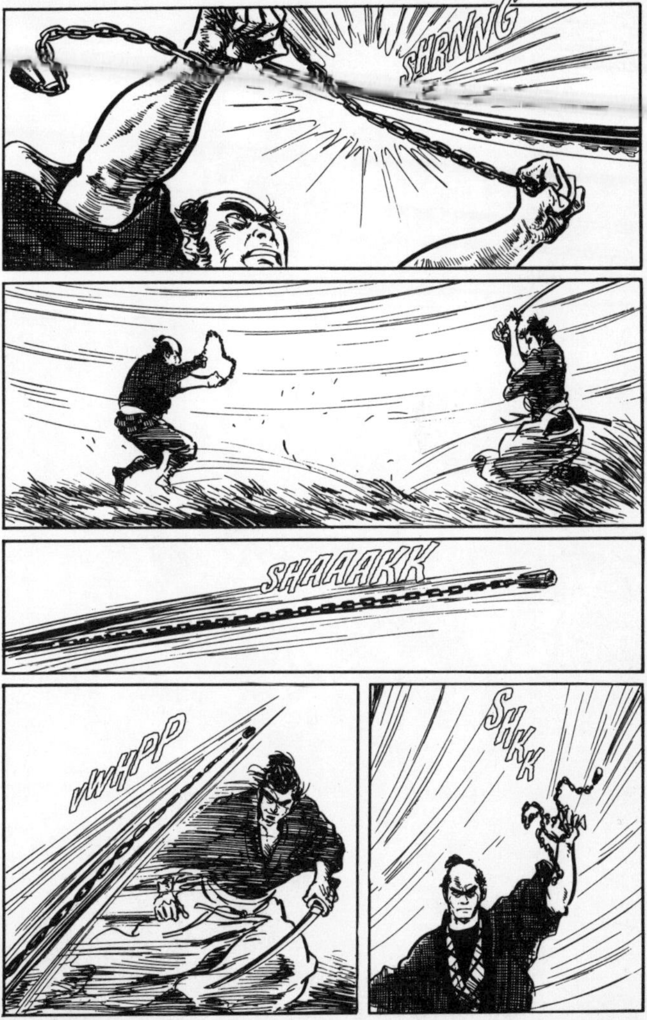
SHRNNG
SHAAAKK
SHKK
VWHPP

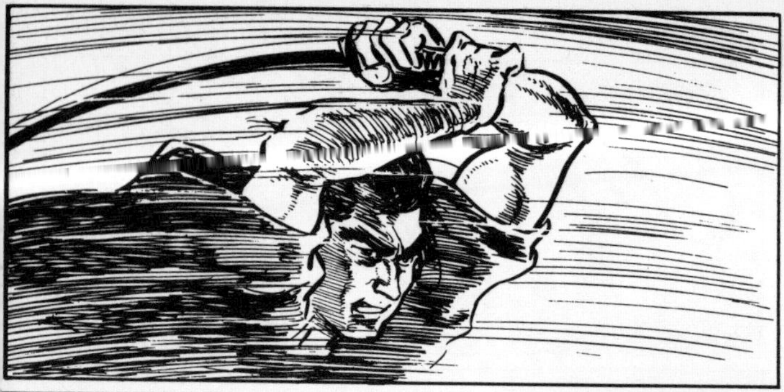
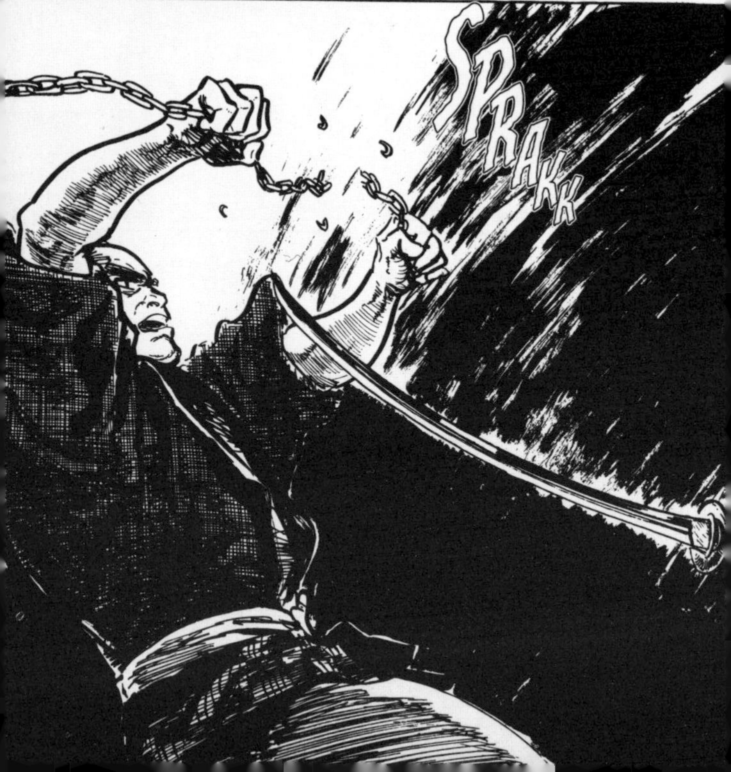
SPRAKK

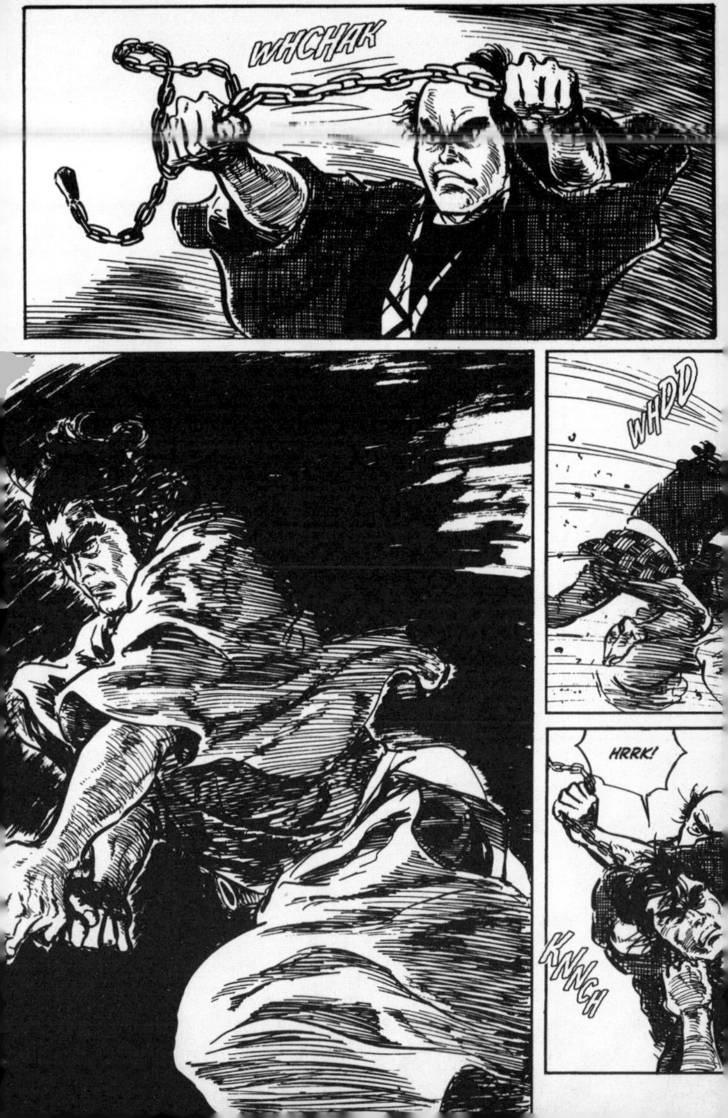
WHCHAK
WHDD
HRRK!
KNNCH

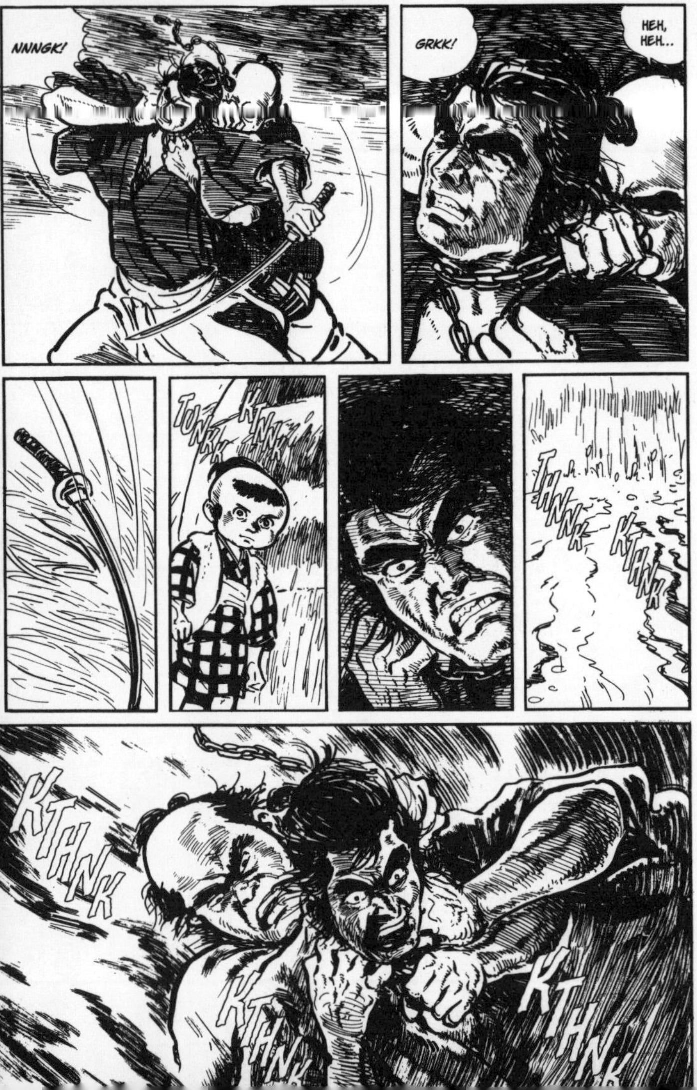
HEH, HEH..
GRKK!
NNNGK!
THNNK
KTHNK
KTNNK
TUNKK
KTHNK
KTHNK
KTHNK

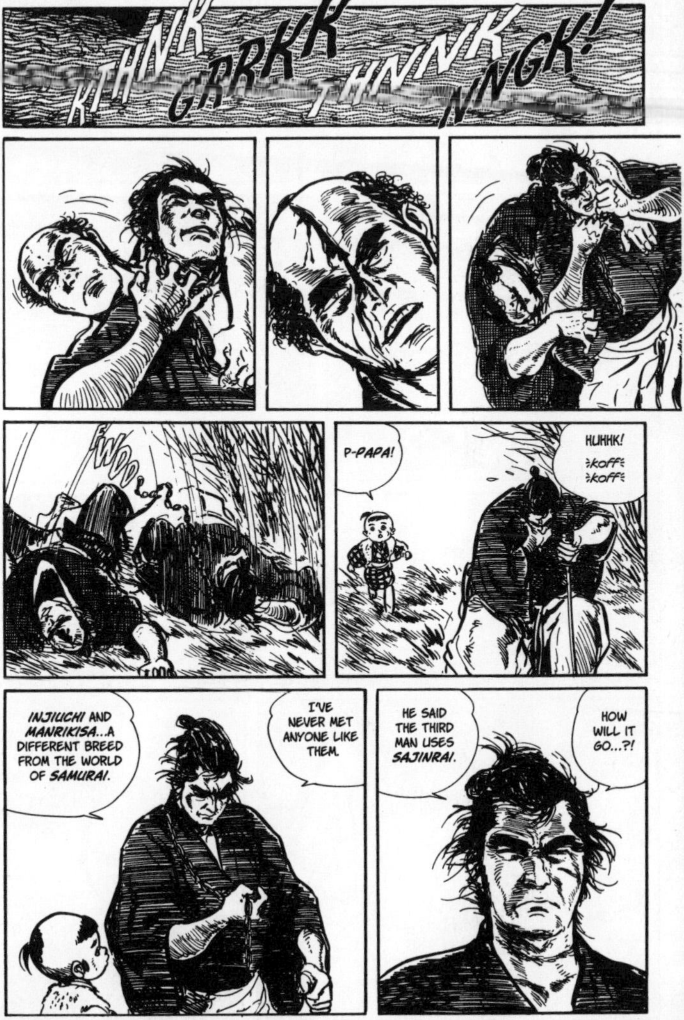
KTHNK
GRRKK
THNNK
NNGK!
FWOO
P-PAPA!
HUHHK!
koff koff
INJIUCHI AND MANRIKISA...A DIFFERENT BREED FROM THE WORLD OF SAMURAI.
I'VE NEVER MET ANYONE LIKE THEM.
HE SAID THE THIRD MAN USES SAJINRAI.
HOW WILL IT GO...?!

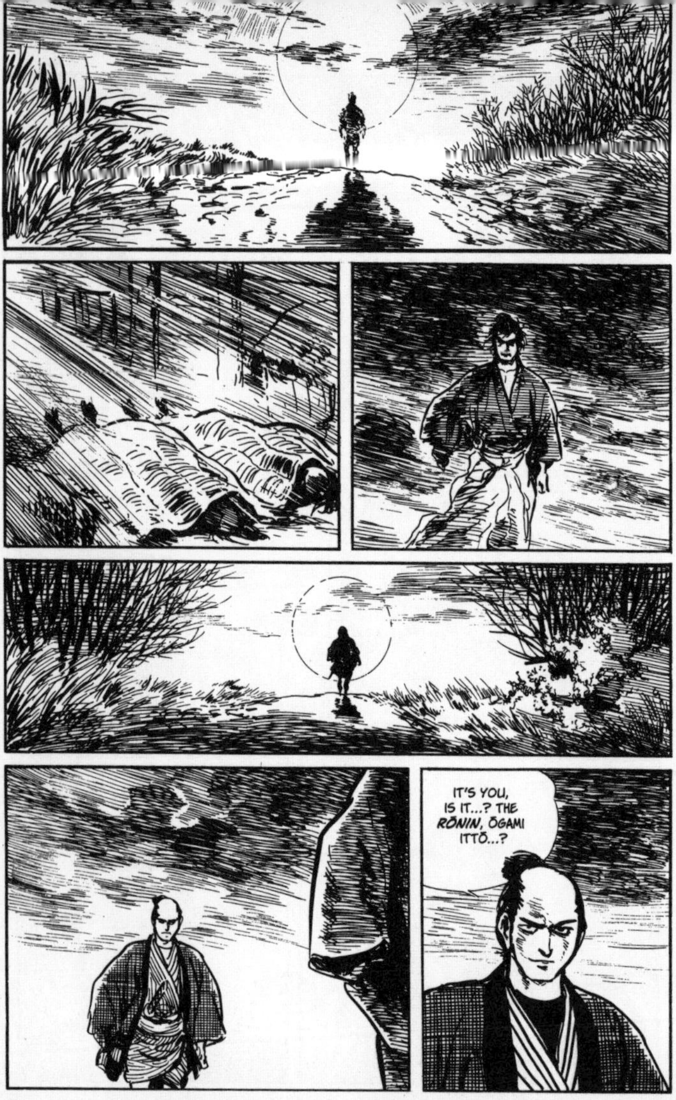
IT'S YOU, IS IT...? THE *RŌNIN*, ŌGAMI ITTŌ...?

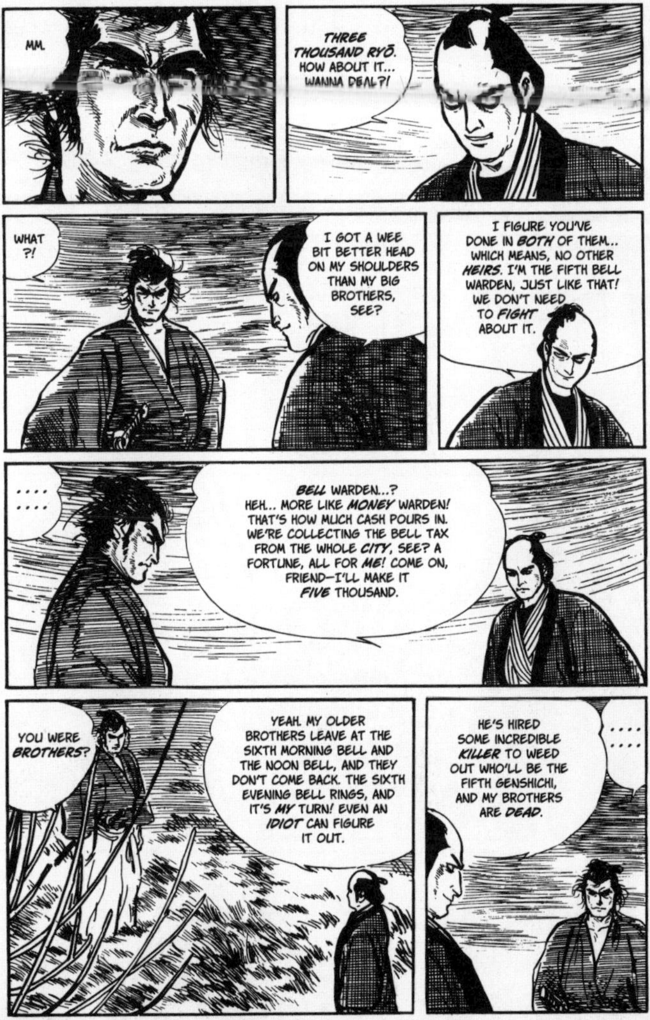
MM.
THREE THOUSAND RYŌ. HOW ABOUT IT... WANNA DEAL?!
WHAT ?!
I GOT A WEE BIT BETTER HEAD ON MY SHOULDERS THAN MY BIG BROTHERS, SEE?
I FIGURE YOU'VE DONE IN BOTH OF THEM.. WHICH MEANS, NO OTHER HEIRS. I'M THE FIFTH BELL WARDEN, JUST LIKE THAT! WE DON'T NEED TO FIGHT ABOUT IT.
.... ....
BELL WARDEN...? HEH... MORE LIKE MONEY WARDEN! THAT'S HOW MUCH CASH POURS IN. WE'RE COLLECTING THE BELL TAX FROM THE WHOLE CITY, SEE? A FORTUNE, ALL FOR ME! COME ON, FRIEND—I'LL MAKE IT FIVE THOUSAND.
YOU WERE BROTHERS?
YEAH. MY OLDER BROTHERS LEAVE AT THE SIXTH MORNING BELL AND THE NOON BELL, AND THEY DON'T COME BACK. THE SIXTH EVENING BELL RINGS, AND IT'S MY TURN! EVEN AN IDIOT CAN FIGURE IT OUT.
HE'S HIRED SOME INCREDIBLE KILLER TO WEED OUT WHO'LL BE THE FIFTH GENSHICHI, AND MY BROTHERS ARE DEAD.
.... ....

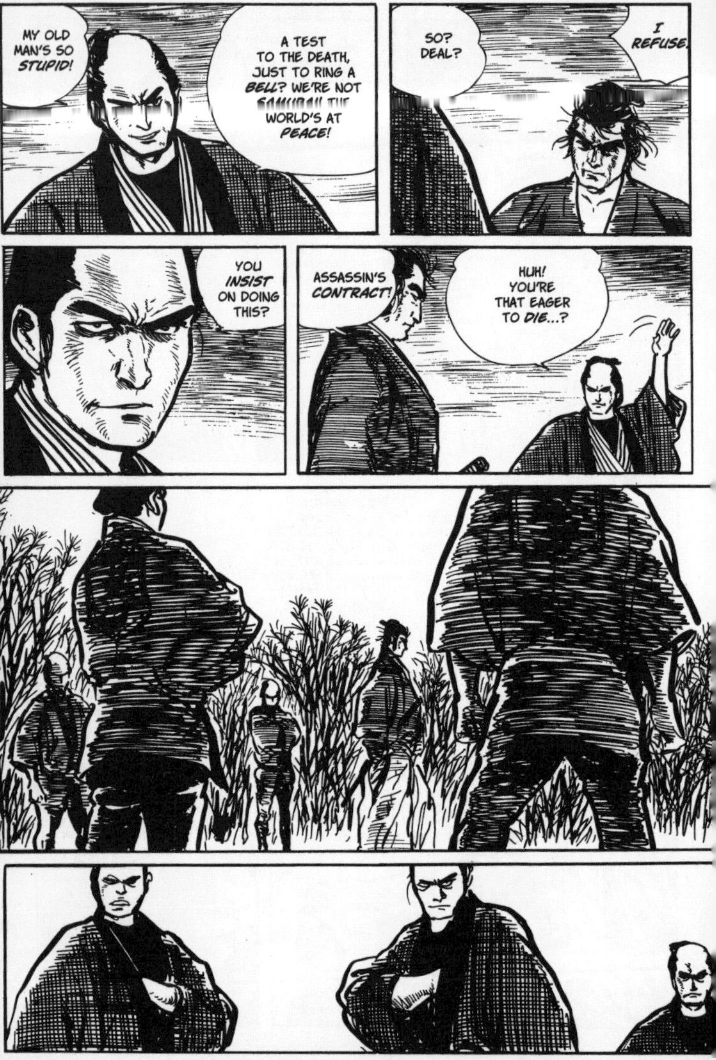
MY OLD MAN'S SO STUPID!
A TEST TO THE DEATH, JUST TO RING A BELL? WE'RE NOT SAMURAI! THE WORLD'S AT PEACE!
SO? DEAL?
I REFUSE.
YOU INSIST ON DOING THIS?
ASSASSIN'S CONTRACT!
HUH! YOU'RE THAT EAGER TO DIE...?

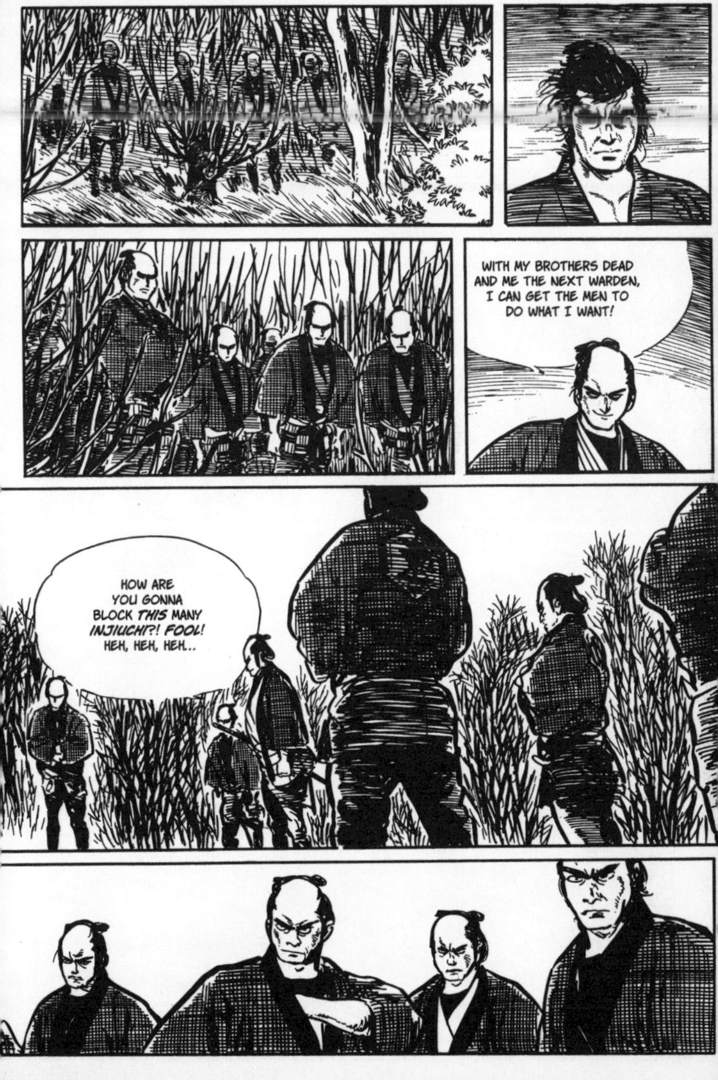
WITH MY BROTHERS DEAD AND ME THE NEXT WARDEN, I CAN GET THE MEN TO DO WHAT I WANT!
HOW ARE YOU GONNA BLOCK *THIS* MANY *INJIUCHI?! FOOL!* HEH, HEH, HEH...

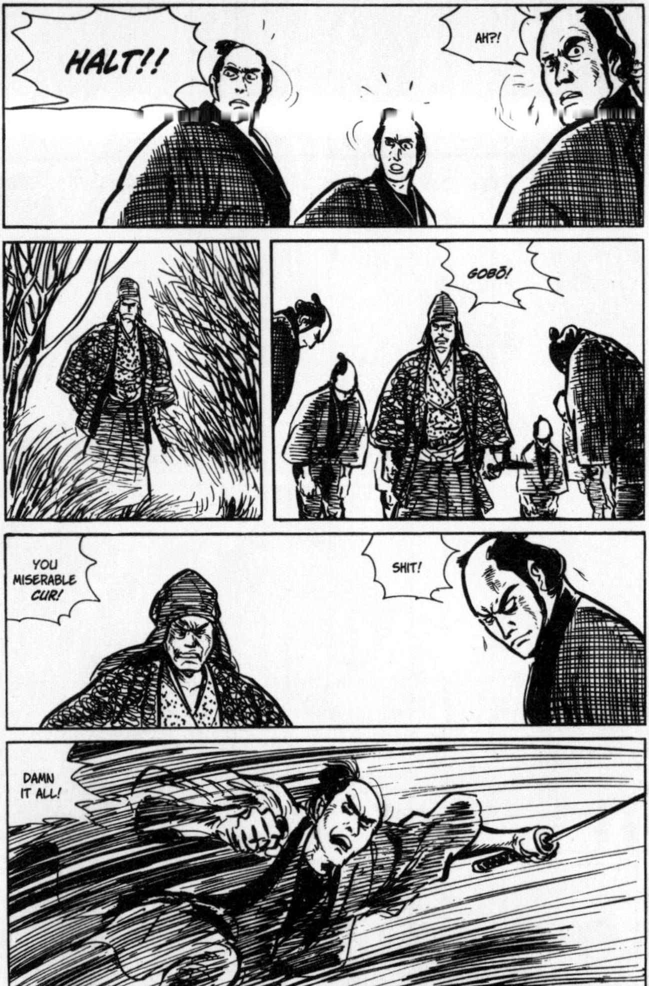
HALT!!
AH?!
GOBŌ!
YOU MISERABLE CUR!
SHIT!
DAMN IT ALL!

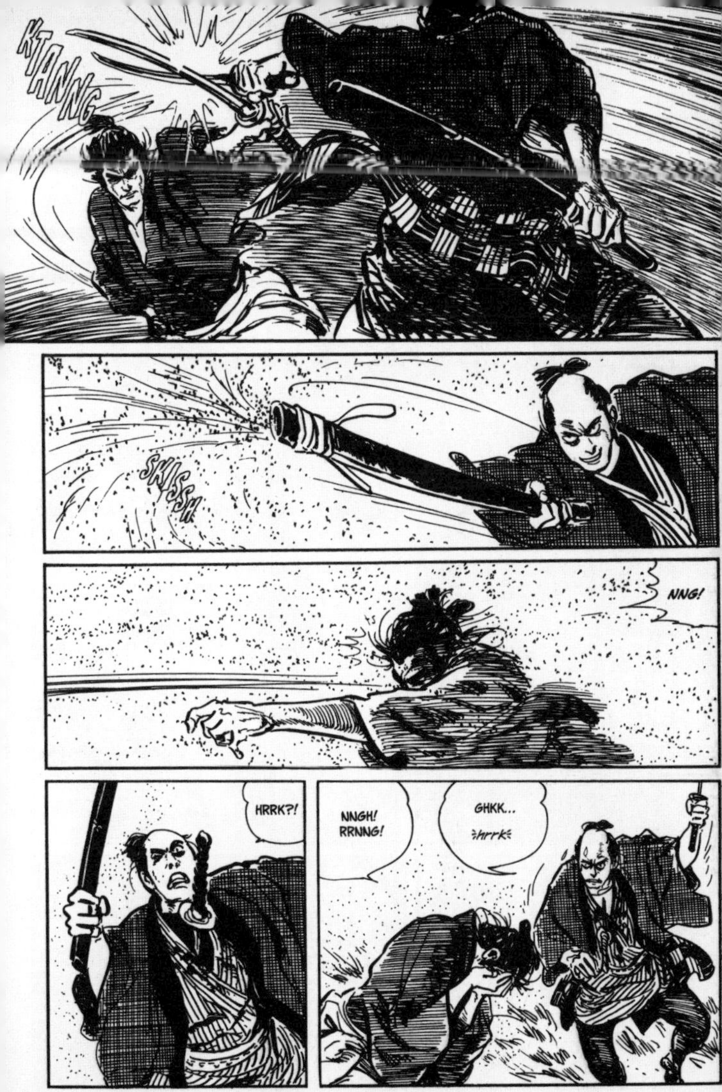
KTANNG
SKISSH
NNG!
GHKK...
hrrk
NNGH! RRNNG!
HRRK?!

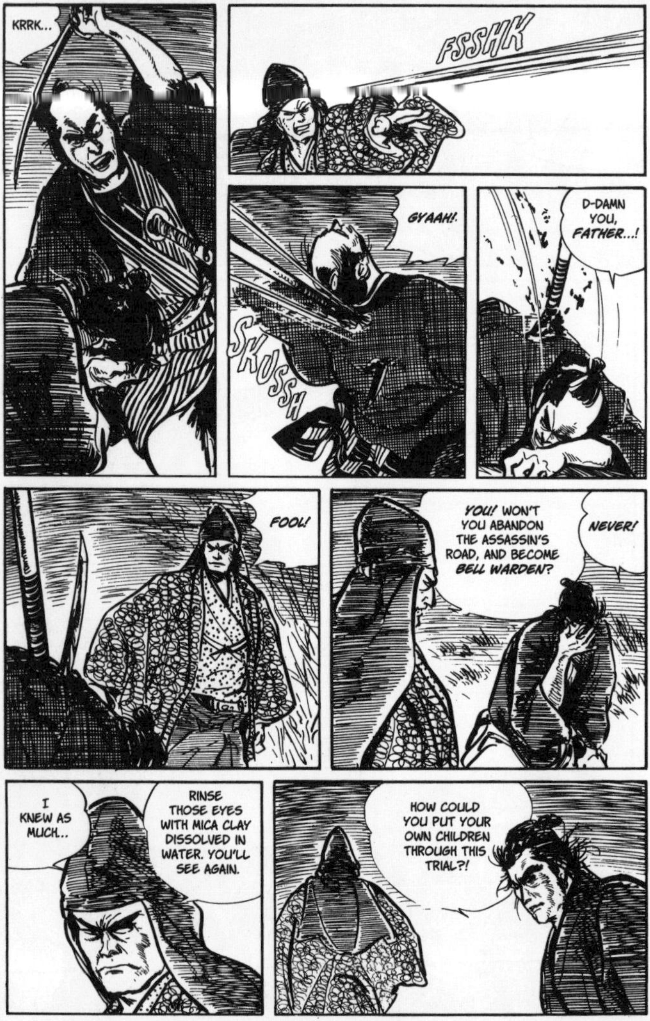
KRRK...
FSSHK
GYAAH!
SKUSSH
D-DAMN YOU, FATHER...!
FOOL!
YOU! WON'T YOU ABANDON THE ASSASSIN'S ROAD, AND BECOME BELL WARDEN?
NEVER!
I KNEW AS MUCH...
RINSE THOSE EYES WITH MICA CLAY DISSOLVED IN WATER. YOU'LL SEE AGAIN.
HOW COULD YOU PUT YOUR OWN CHILDREN THROUGH THIS TRIAL?!

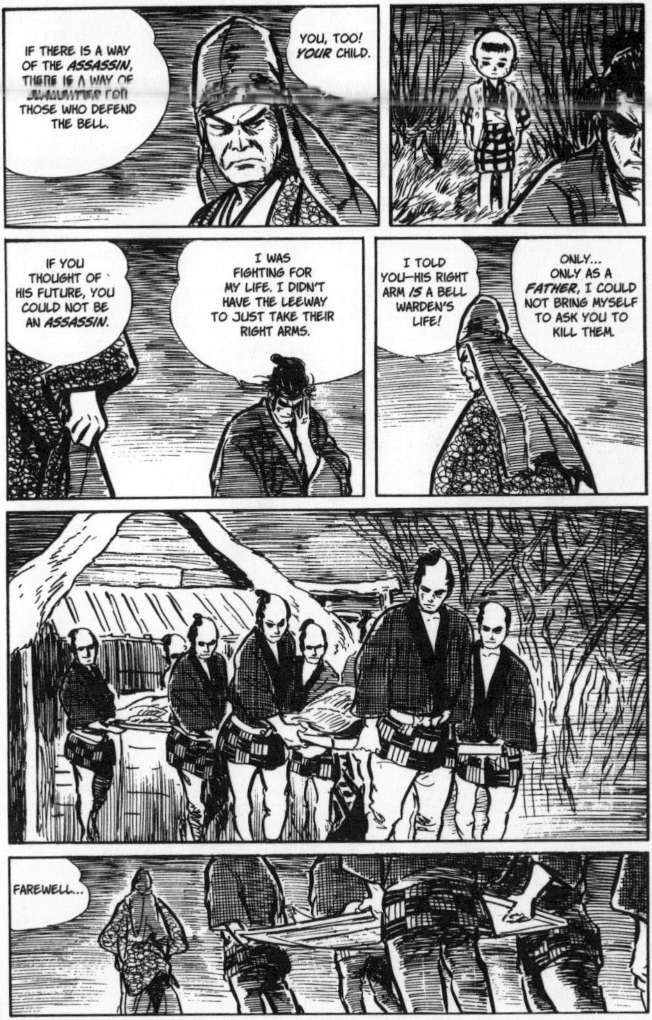

IF THERE IS A WAY OF THE ASSASSIN, THERE IS A WAY OF FOR THOSE WHO DEFEND THE BELL.
YOU, TOO! YOUR CHILD.
IF YOU THOUGHT OF HIS FUTURE, YOU COULD NOT BE AN ASSASSIN.
I WAS FIGHTING FOR MY LIFE. I DIDN'T HAVE THE LEEWAY TO JUST TAKE THEIR RIGHT ARMS.
I TOLD YOU—HIS RIGHT ARM IS A BELL WARDEN'S LIFE!
ONLY... ONLY AS A FATHER, I COULD NOT BRING MYSELF TO ASK YOU TO KILL THEM.
FAREWELL...

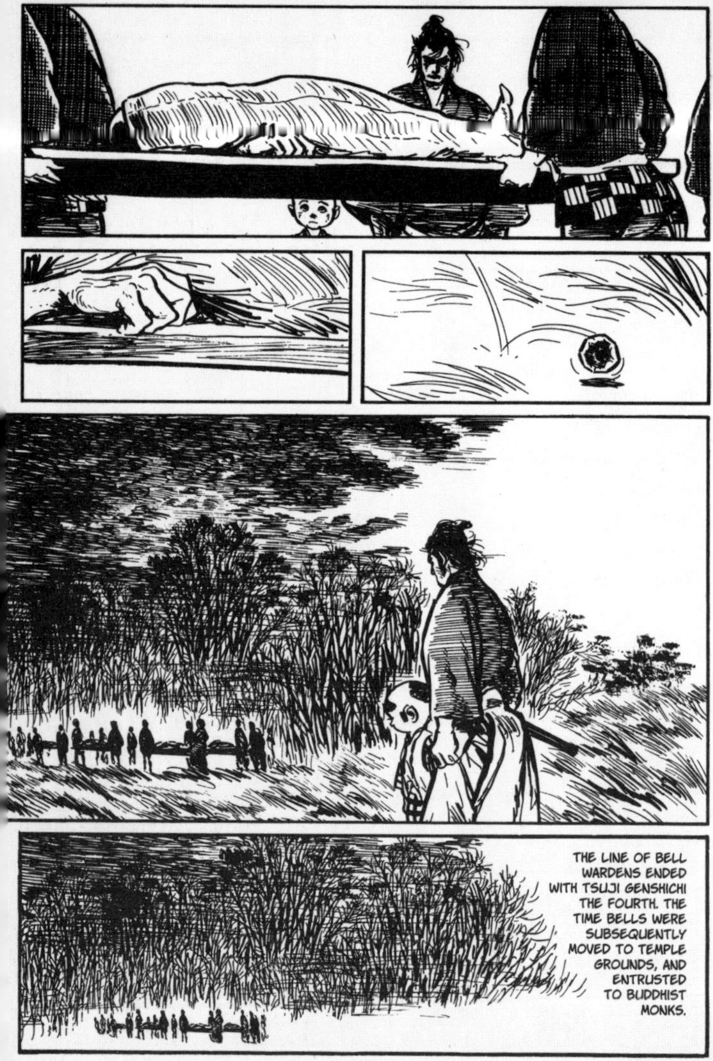
THE LINE OF BELL WARDENS ENDED WITH TSUJI GENSHICHI THE FOURTH. THE TIME BELLS WERE SUBSEQUENTLY MOVED TO TEMPLE GROUNDS, AND ENTRUSTED TO BUDDHIST MONKS.

the twenty-first

# Unfaithful Retainers

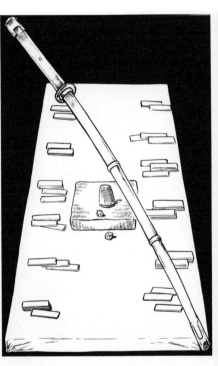

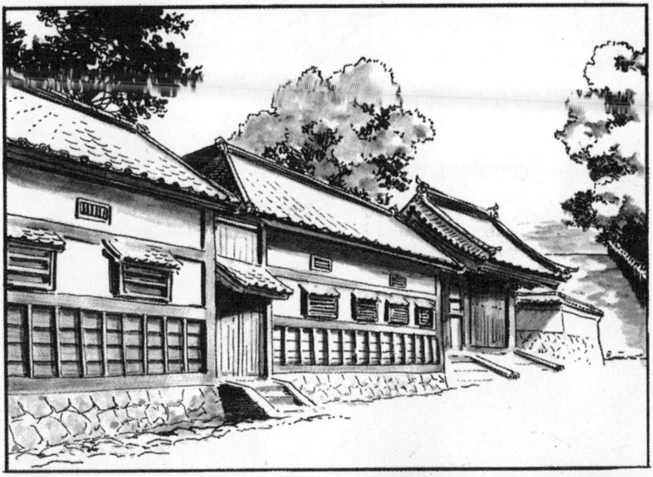

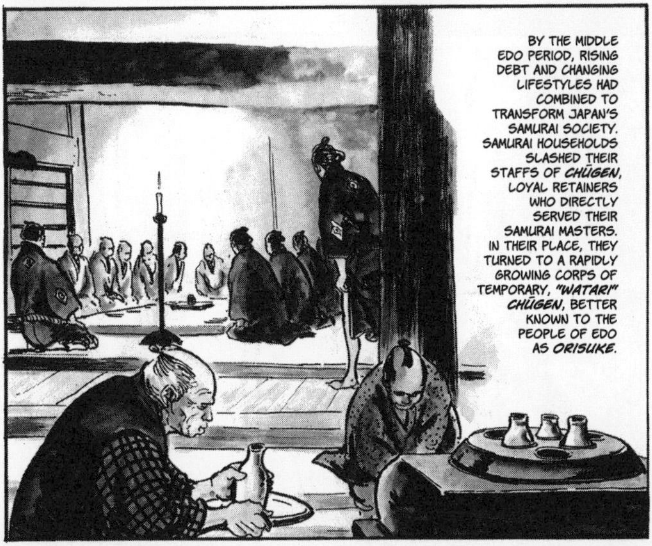
BY THE MIDDLE EDO PERIOD, RISING DEBT AND CHANGING LIFESTYLES HAD COMBINED TO TRANSFORM JAPAN'S SAMURAI SOCIETY. SAMURAI HOUSEHOLDS SLASHED THEIR STAFFS OF *CHŪGEN*, LOYAL RETAINERS WHO DIRECTLY SERVED THEIR SAMURAI MASTERS. IN THEIR PLACE, THEY TURNED TO A RAPIDLY GROWING CORPS OF TEMPORARY, *"WATARI"* *CHŪGEN*, BETTER KNOWN TO THE PEOPLE OF EDO AS *ORISUKE*.

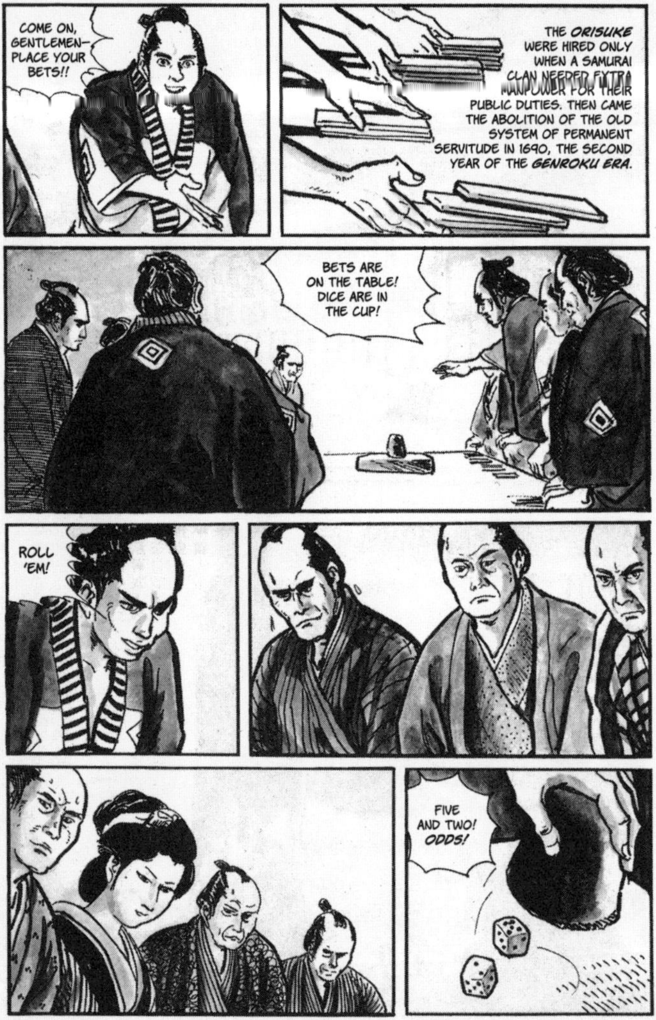
COME ON, GENTLEMEN— PLACE YOUR BETS!!
THE *ORISUKE* WERE HIRED ONLY WHEN A SAMURAI CLAN NEEDED EXTRA MANPOWER FOR THEIR PUBLIC DUTIES. THEN CAME THE ABOLITION OF THE OLD SYSTEM OF PERMANENT SERVITUDE IN 1690, THE SECOND YEAR OF THE *GENROKU ERA*.
BETS ARE ON THE TABLE! DICE ARE IN THE CUP!
ROLL 'EM!
FIVE AND TWO! *ODDS!*

THE *CHŪGEN-GASHIRA*, PERMANENTLY EMPLOYED *BOSSES* WHO OVERSAW A SAMURAI HOUSEHOLD'S *CHŪGEN* STAFF, GAINED THE POWER TO HIRE AND FIRE *ORISUKE* AT THEIR OWN DISCRETION...

...AND THE ENTIRE SYSTEM VEERED TOWARD...

HEY! *HEY!* YOU'RE BLOCKING THE LIGHT!

OUTTA THE WAY, *SANPIN!*

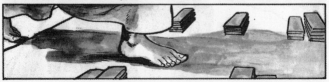

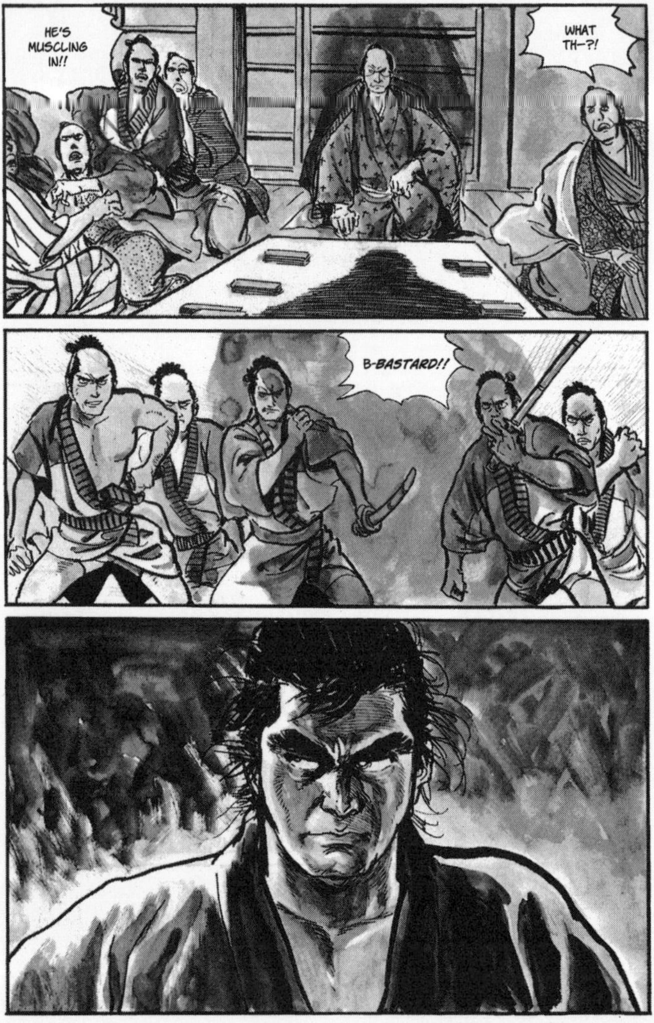
WHAT TH—?!
HE'S MUSCLING IN!!
B-BASTARD!!

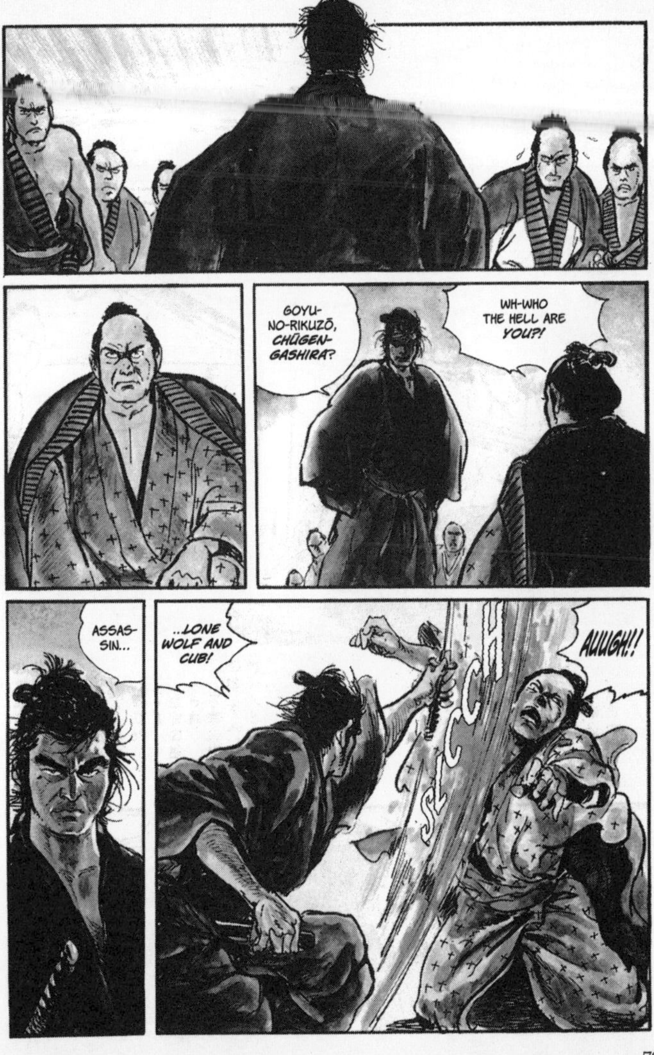
GOYU-NO-RIKUZŌ, CHŪGEN-GASHIRA?
WH-WHO THE HELL ARE YOU?!
ASSAS-SIN...
..LONE WOLF AND CUB!
AUUGH!!

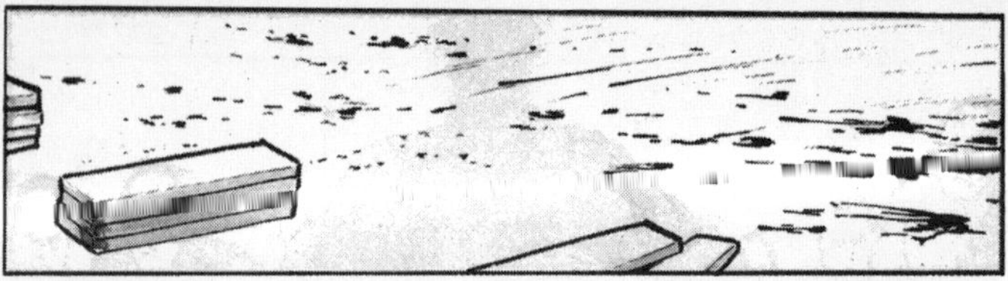

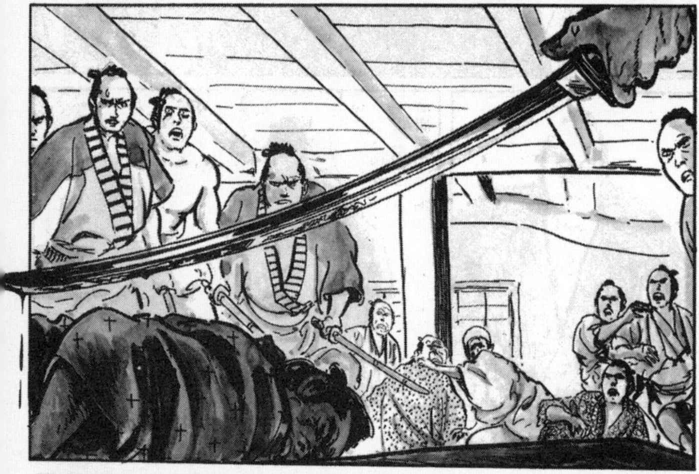

THE *ORISUKE* WERE A NEW BREED. THEY SERVED THE SAMURAI FAMILIES, YET SHARED NONE OF THE *VALUES* OF SAMURAI SOCIETY—NO *LOYALTY*, NO *SELF-SACRIFICE*, NO CONCERN FOR THE *FACE* AND *HONOR* OF THEIR MASTERS. THE *BOND* BETWEEN MASTER AND RETAINER HAD BEEN *SEVERED* COMPLETELY.

SAMURAI SERVANTS HAD TRADITIONALLY FOLLOWED THE CODES OF SAMURAI SOCIETY, LOYAL TO MASTERS WITH THE SAMURAI LICENSE TO KILL—THE RIGHT OF *SEISATSU YODATSU*. BUT NOW THE *ORISUKE* TURNED THE FUNCTIONS OF SAMURAI SOCIETY ON THEIR HEAD.

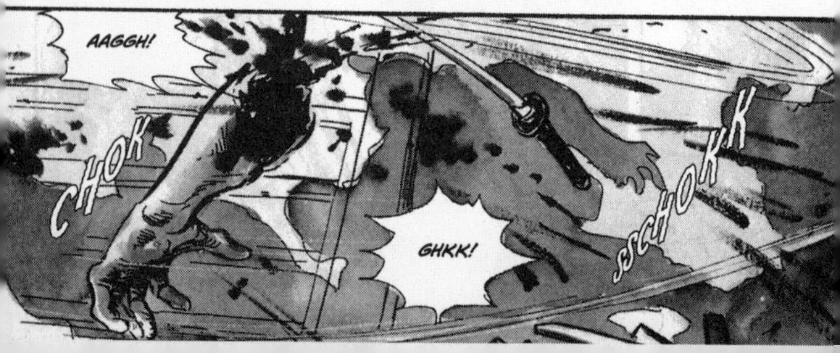
SSCHOKK
AAGGH!
GHKK!
CHOK

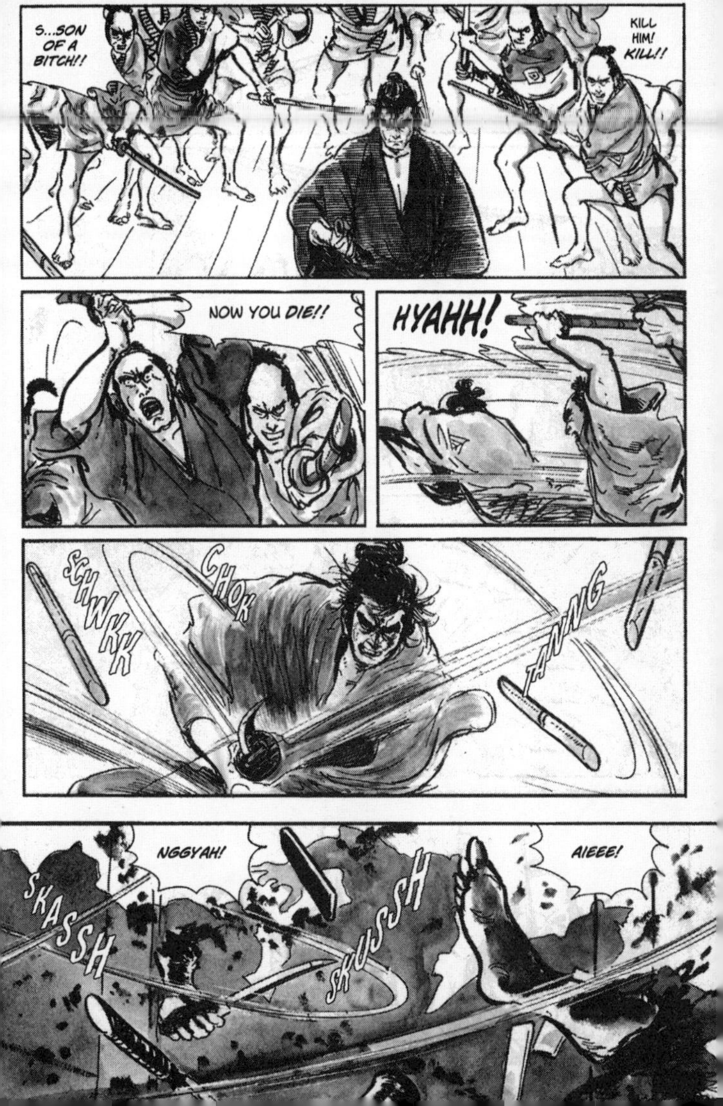
KILL HIM! KILL!!
S...SON OF A BITCH!!
HYAHH!
NOW YOU DIE!!
TANNG
CHOK
SCHWKK
AIEEE!
SKUSSH
NGGYAH!
SKASSH

THEY WERE, AFTER ALL, ONLY ***MERCENARIES***. AND WHILE THEIR SAMURAI MASTERS FOOTED THE BILL, THEY OWED THEIR ***TRUE*** ALLEGIANCE TO THE ***CHŪGEN-GASHIRA*** THAT HIRED THEM. IT WAS THESE *ORISUKE* BOSSES, HEADING UP GANGS THAT SHARED THE *SEISATSU YODATSU* RIGHTS OF SAMURAI SOCIETY AND WERE ALREADY SYSTEMATICALLY ORGANIZED BY HOUSEHOLD, THAT QUICKLY TURNED MANY *ORISUKE* TO A LIFE OF ***GAMBLING*** AND ***CRIME***.

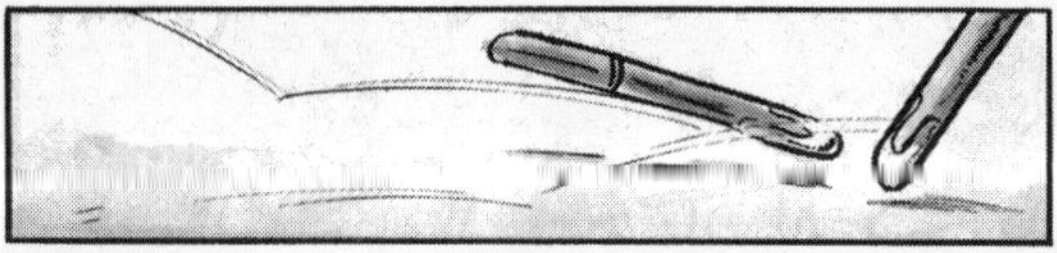

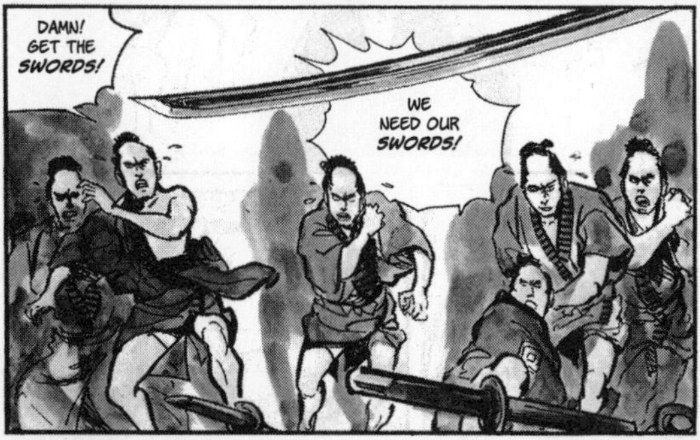
DAMN! GET THE SWORDS!
WE NEED OUR SWORDS!

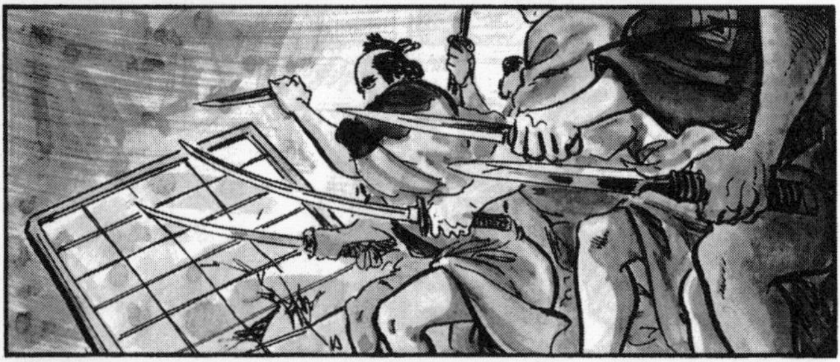

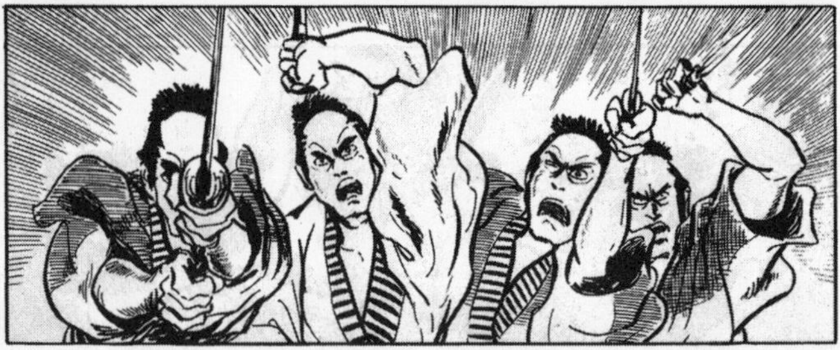

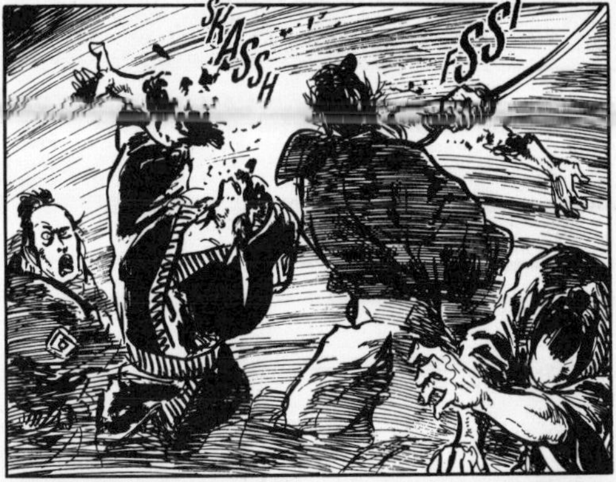
SKASSH
FSST

THE AUTHORITIES WERE HELPLESS TO INTERVENE. IF THEY *SUPPRESSED* THE *ORISUKE*, THEY WOULDN'T BE ABLE TO MOBILIZE MAN-POWER ON COMMAND. AND THUS THE *ORISUKE* SYNDICATES GREW EVER LARGER AND COCKIER, WITH THE TACIT APPROVAL OF THE *DAIMYŌ* AND THE *HATAMOTO* SAMURAI FAMILIES WHO NOW RELIED UPON THEM.

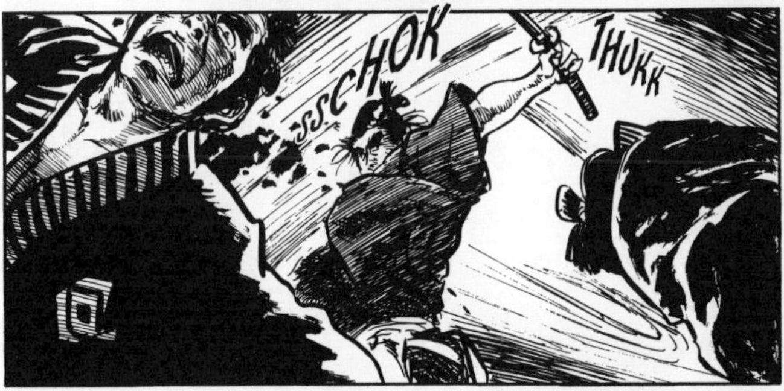
THUKK
SSCHOK

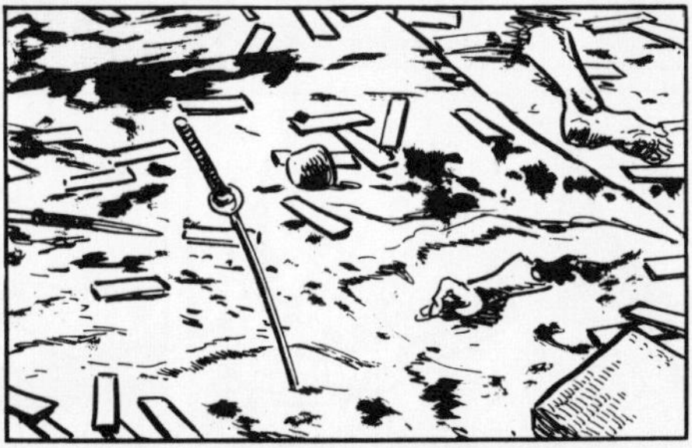

MOREOVER, THE BARRACKS IN THE SAMURAI FAMILY COMPOUNDS WHERE THE *ORISUKE* LIVED WERE BEYOND THE REACH OF THE LAW, AND THUS TAILOR-MADE FOR ILLEGAL GAMBLING. SOON MANY BARRACKS BOSSES, THE *HEYA-GASHIRA*, WERE PRESIDING OVER GANGS OF UNRULY GAMBLERS. THE *ORISUKE* WERE TRULY THE TWISTED OFFSPRING OF SAMURAI SOCIETY ITSELF.

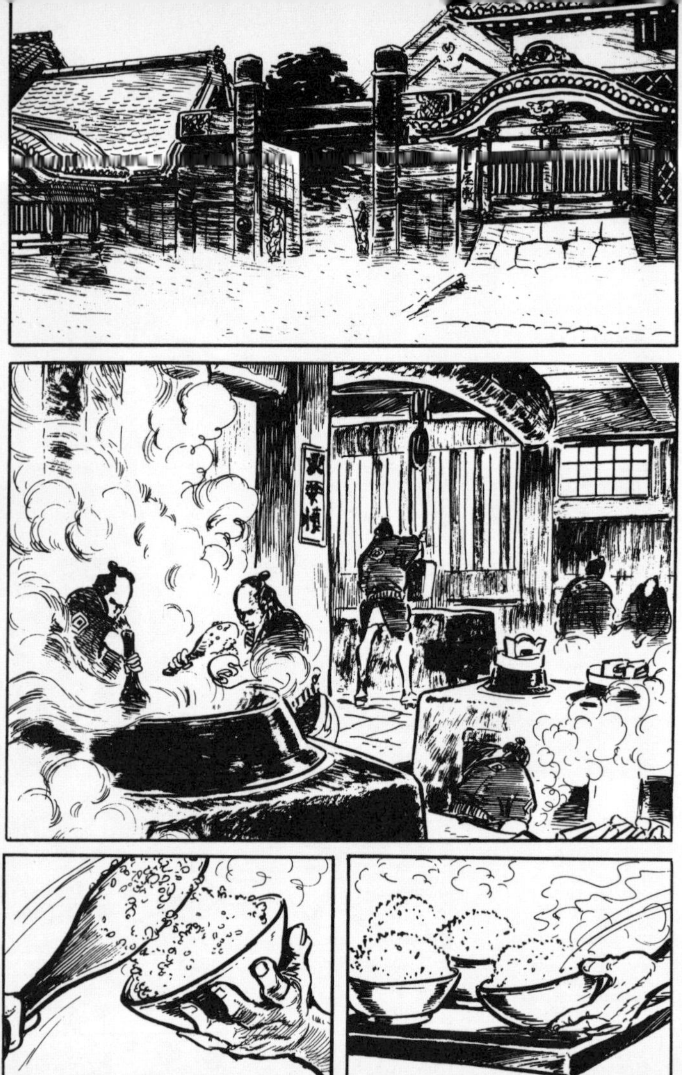

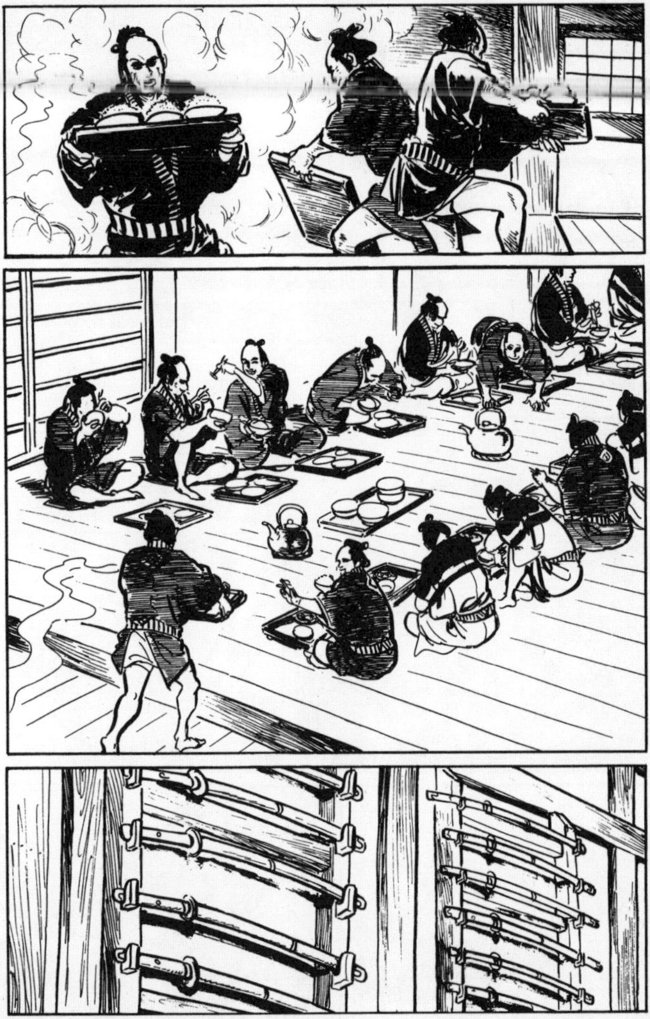

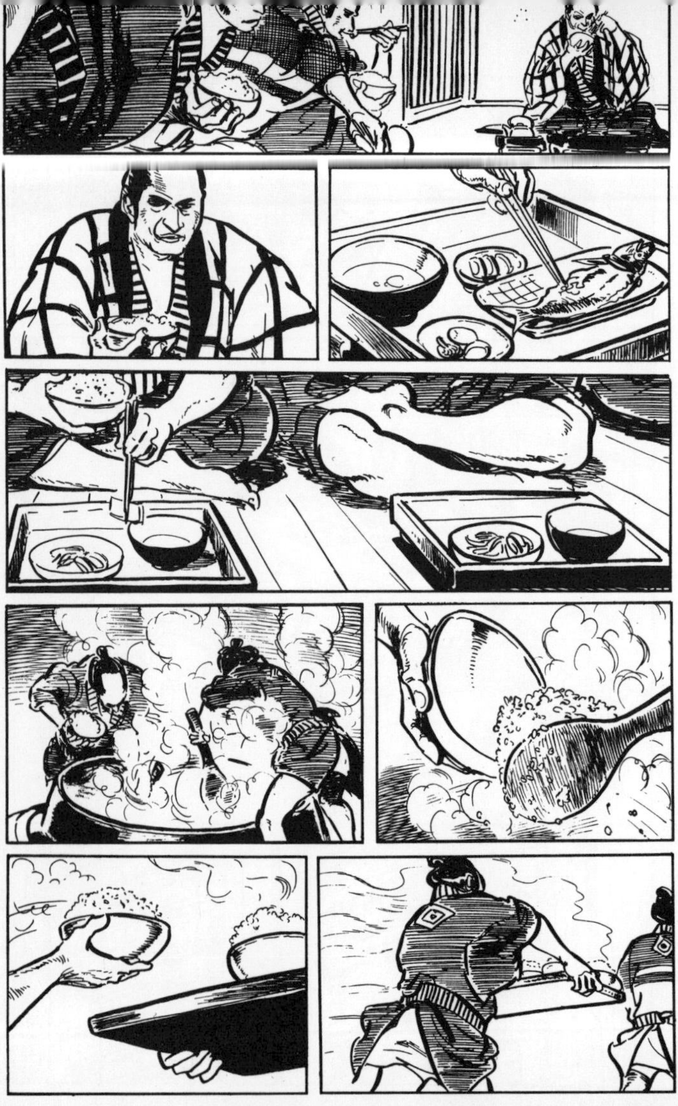

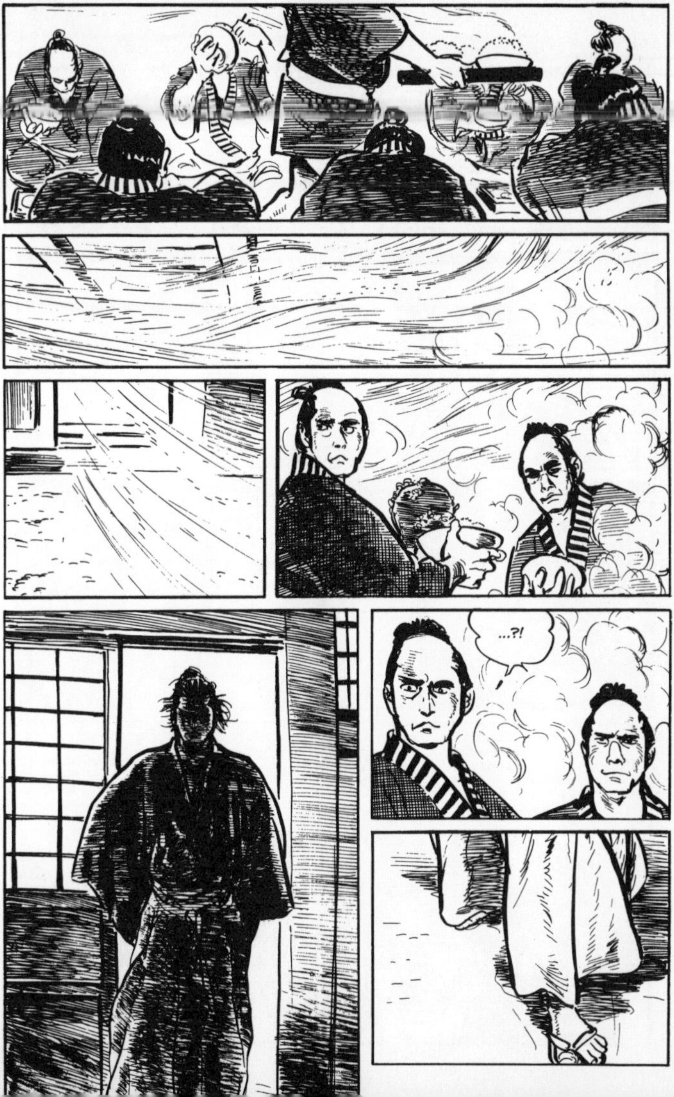
...?!

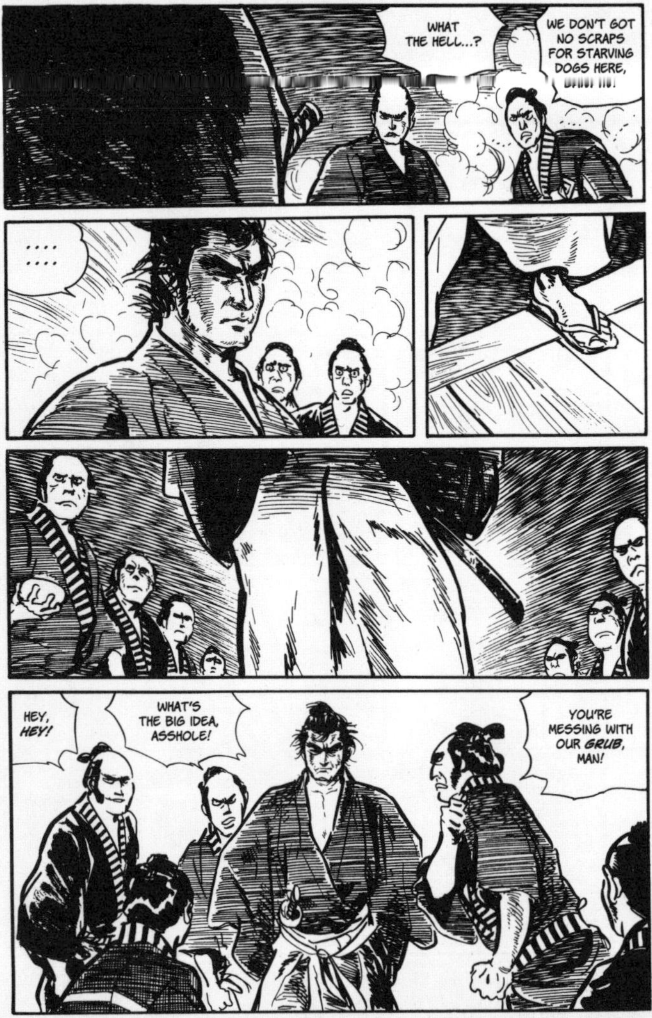
WHAT THE HELL...?
WE DON'T GOT NO SCRAPS FOR STARVING DOGS HERE,
....
....
....
HEY, *HEY!*
WHAT'S THE BIG IDEA, ASSHOLE!
YOU'RE MESSING WITH OUR *GRUB*, MAN!

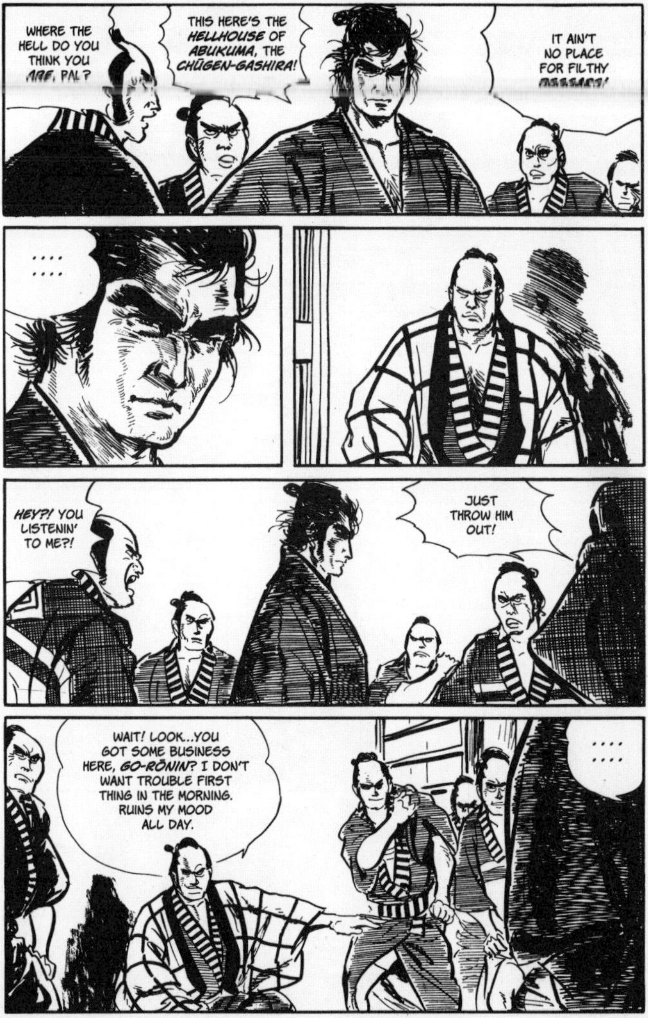
WHERE THE HELL DO YOU THINK YOU ARE, PAL?
THIS HERE'S THE *HELLHOUSE* OF *ABUKUMA*, THE *CHŪGEN-GASHIRA!*
IT AIN'T NO PLACE FOR FILTHY
....
....
*HEY?!* YOU LISTENIN' TO ME?!
JUST THROW HIM OUT!
WAIT! LOOK...YOU GOT SOME BUSINESS HERE, *GO-RŌNIN?* I DON'T WANT TROUBLE FIRST THING IN THE MORNING. RUINS MY MOOD ALL DAY.
....
....

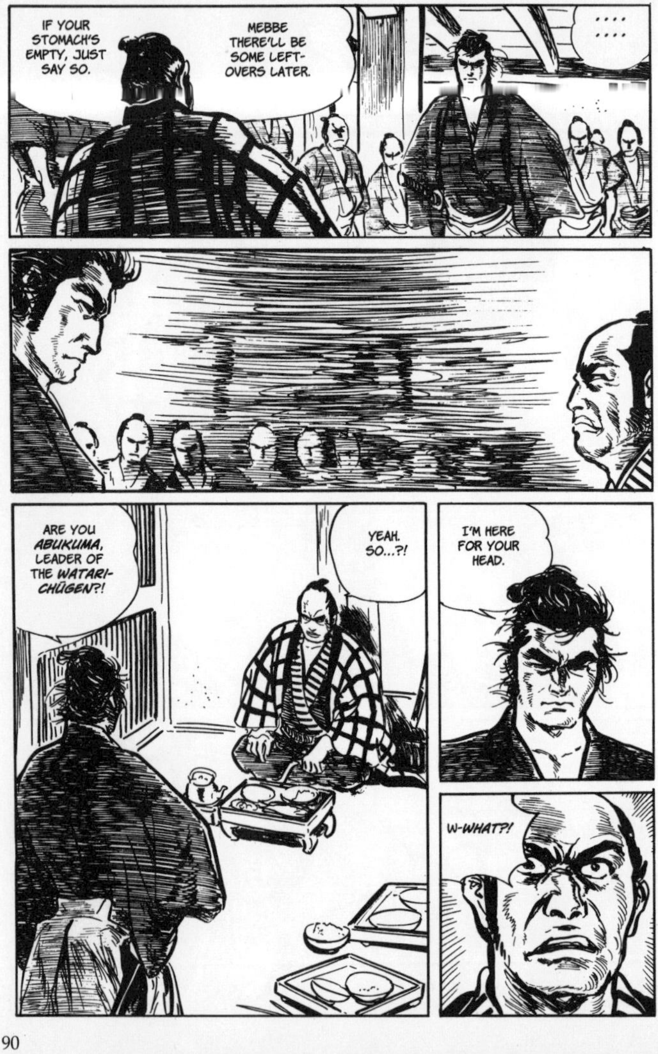
IF YOUR STOMACH'S EMPTY, JUST SAY SO.
MEBBE THERE'LL BE SOME LEFT-OVERS LATER.
....
....
ARE YOU *ABUKUMA*, LEADER OF THE *WATARI-CHŪGEN*?!
YEAH. SO...?!
I'M HERE FOR YOUR HEAD.
W-*WHAT*?!

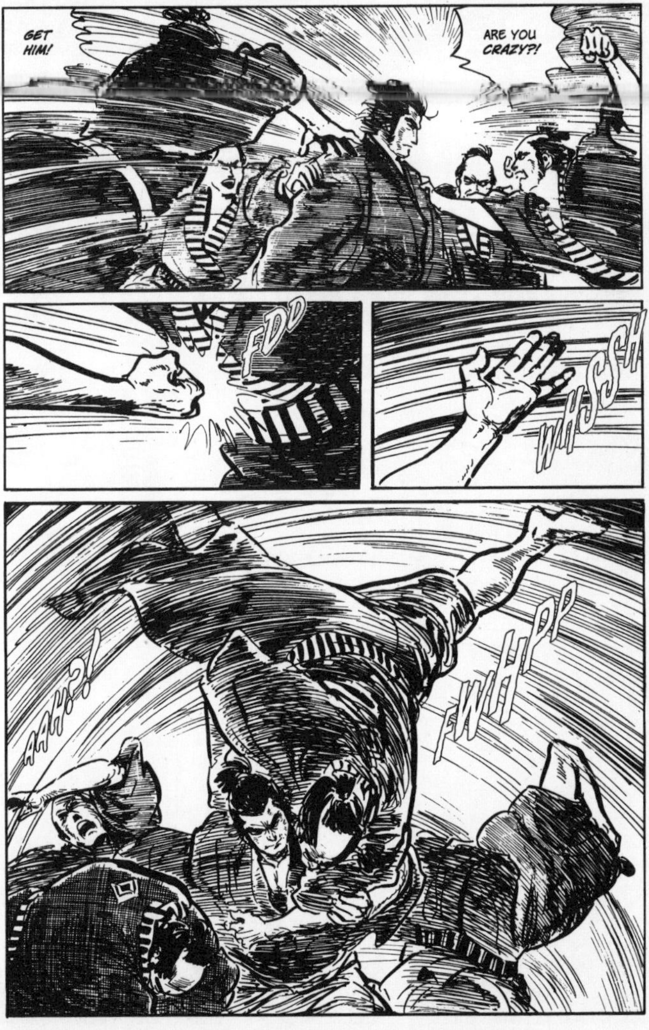

GET HIM!
ARE YOU CRAZY?!
FDD
WHSSSH
AAH?!
FWHIPP

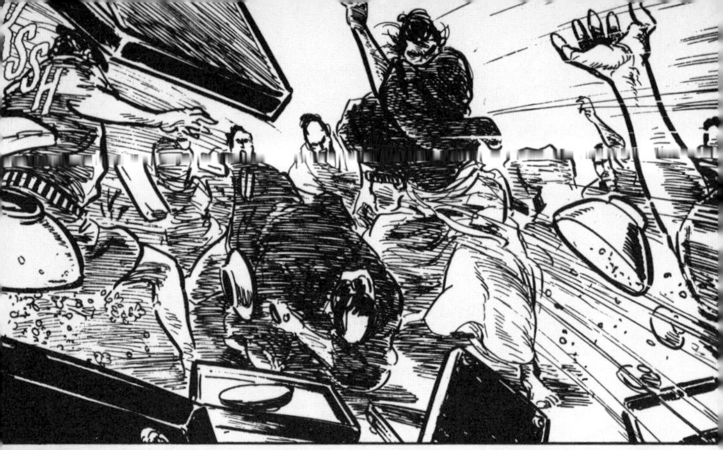
SSH
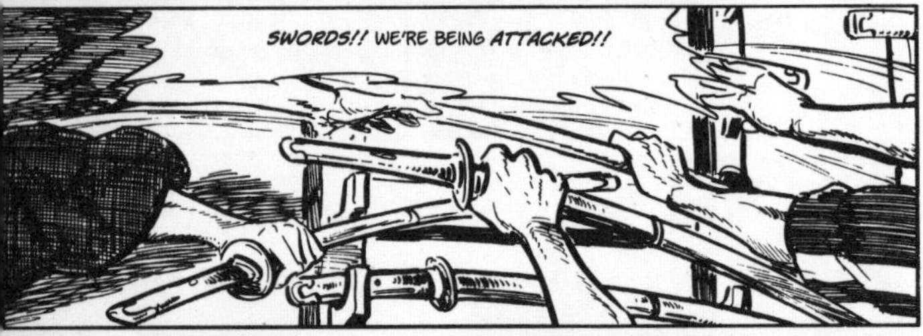
SWORDS!! WE'RE BEING ATTACKED!!
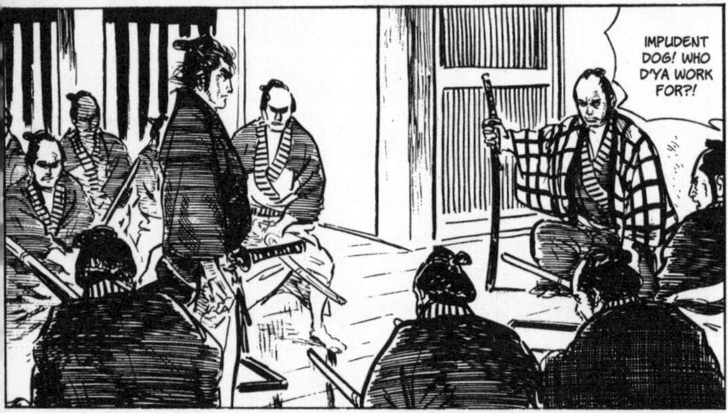
IMPUDENT DOG! WHO D'YA WORK FOR?!

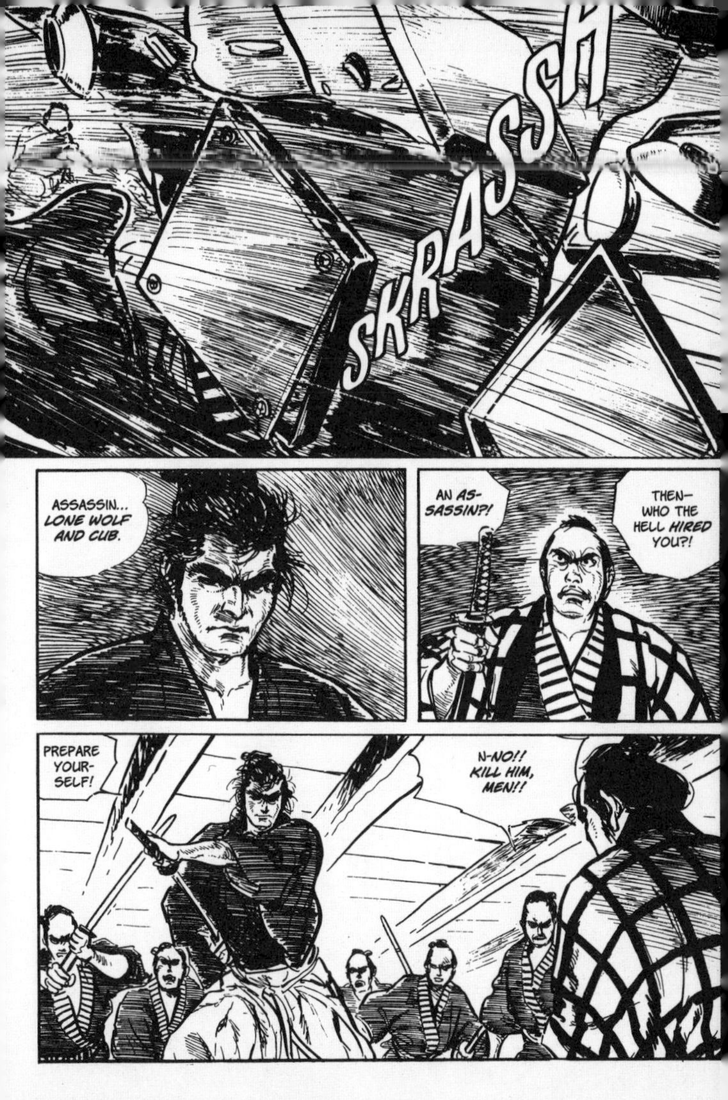
SKRASSH
ASSASSIN... LONE WOLF AND CUB.
AN AS-SASSIN?!
THEN— WHO THE HELL HIRED YOU?!
PREPARE YOUR-SELF!
N-NO!! KILL HIM, MEN!!

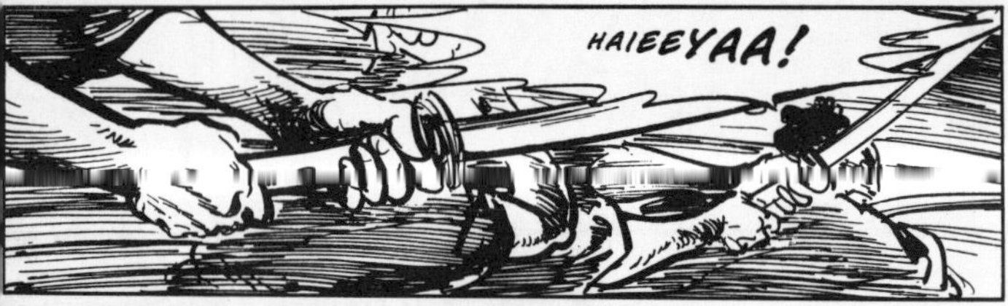
HAIEEYAA!
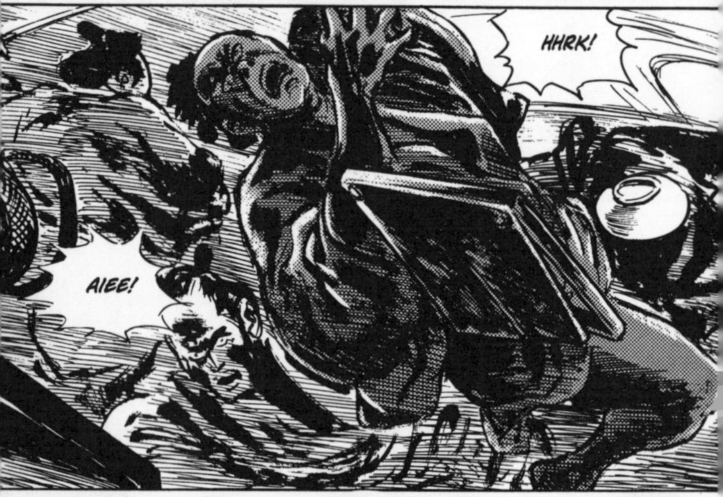
HHRK!
AIEE!
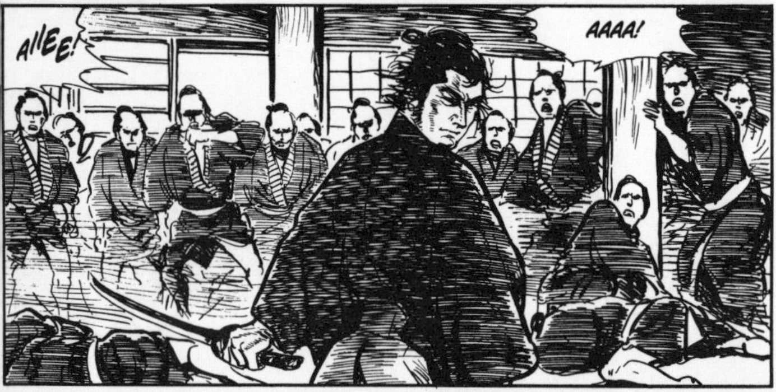
AAAA!
AIEE!

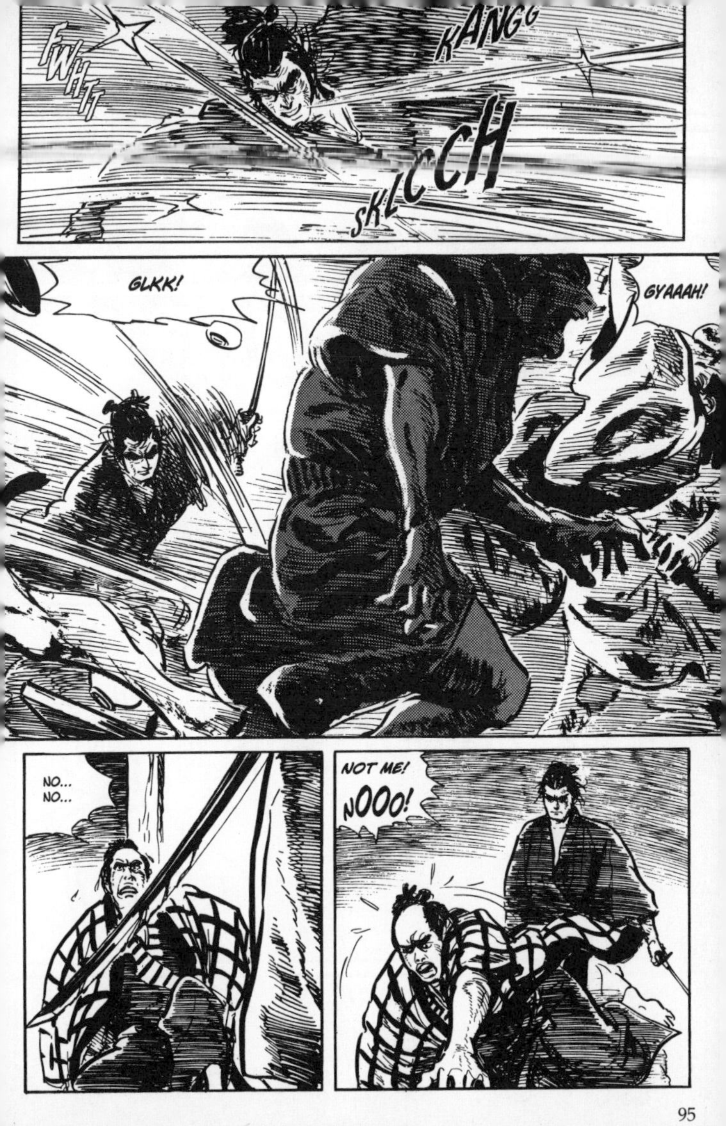
KANGG
FWHTT
SKLCCH
GYAAAH!
GLKK!
NOT ME!
NOOO!
NO...
NO...

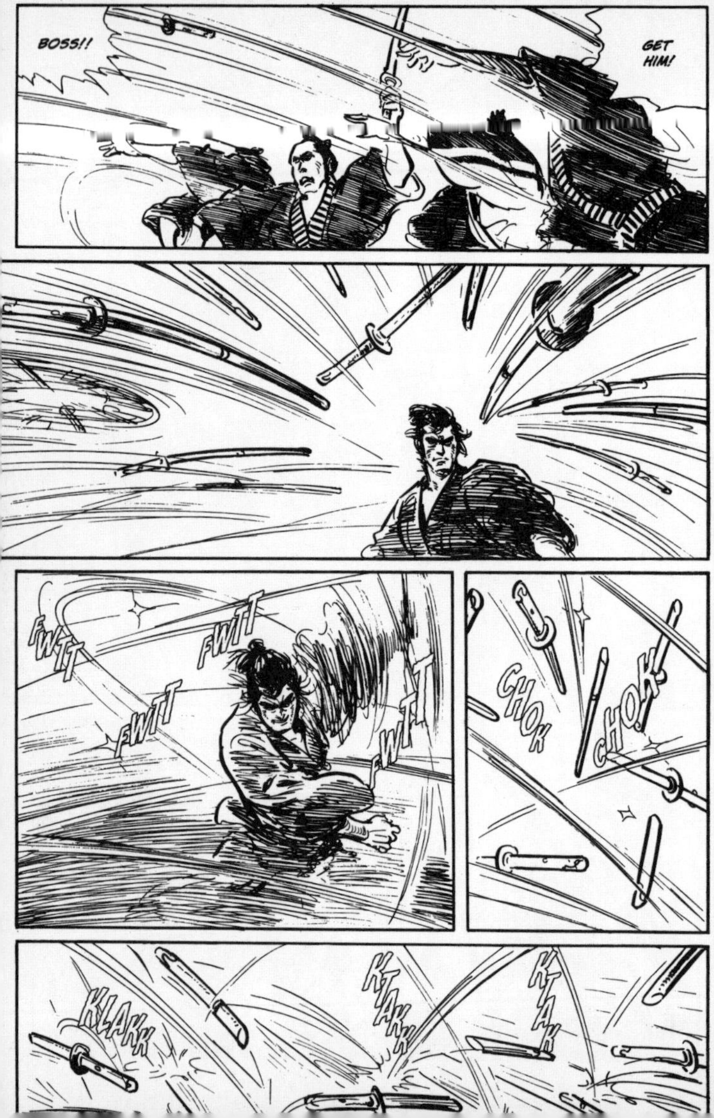
GET HIM!
BOSS!!
CHOK
CHOK
FWTT
FWTT
FWTT
FWTT
KTAK
KTAKK
KLAKK

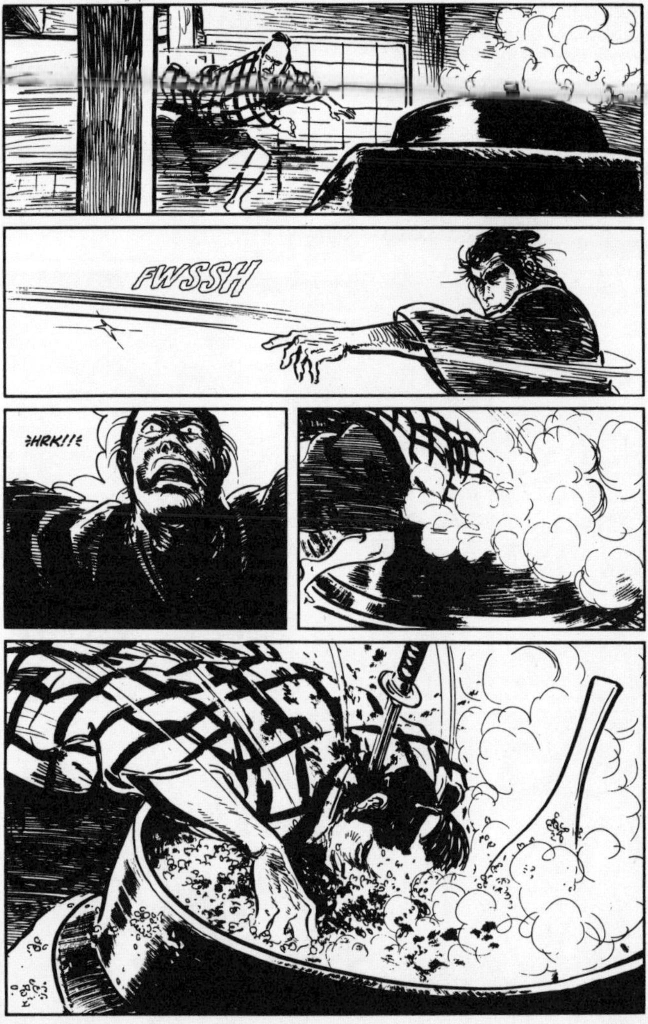
FWSSH
HRK!!

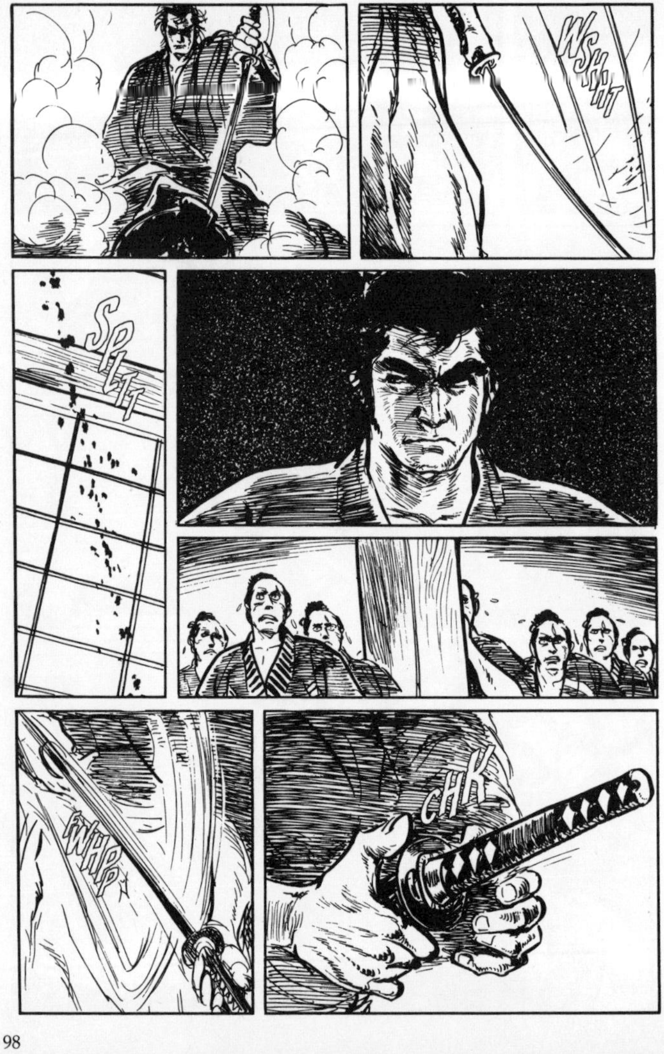
WSHIT
SPLTT
CHK
FWHPP

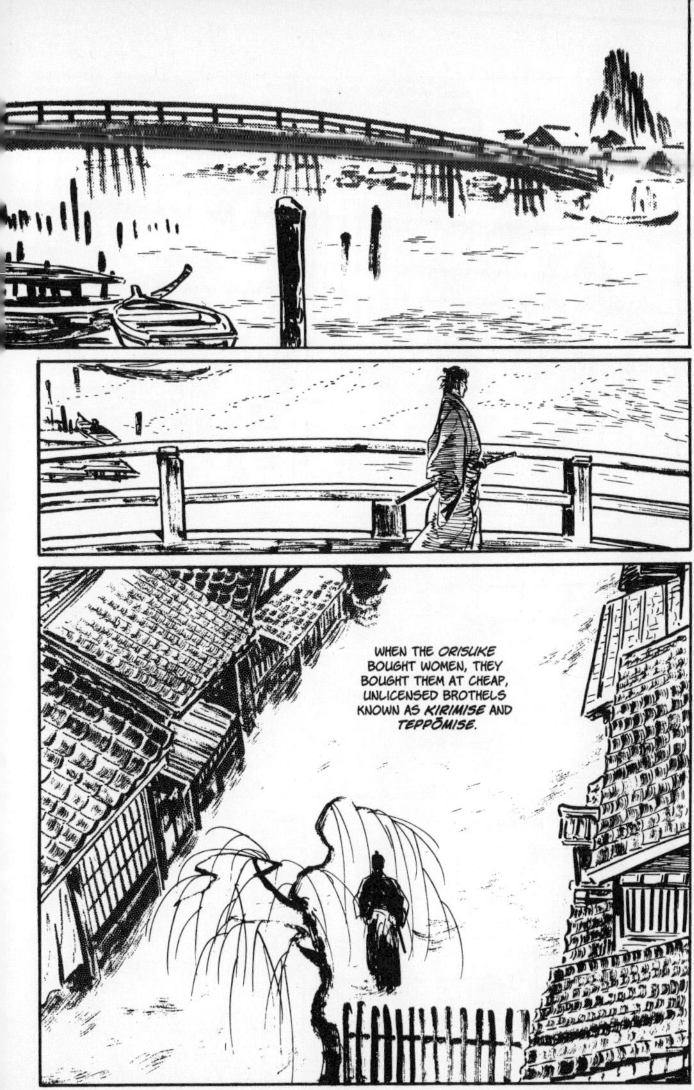
WHEN THE ORISUKE BOUGHT WOMEN, THEY BOUGHT THEM AT CHEAP, UNLICENSED BROTHELS KNOWN AS KIRIMISE AND TEPPŌMISE.

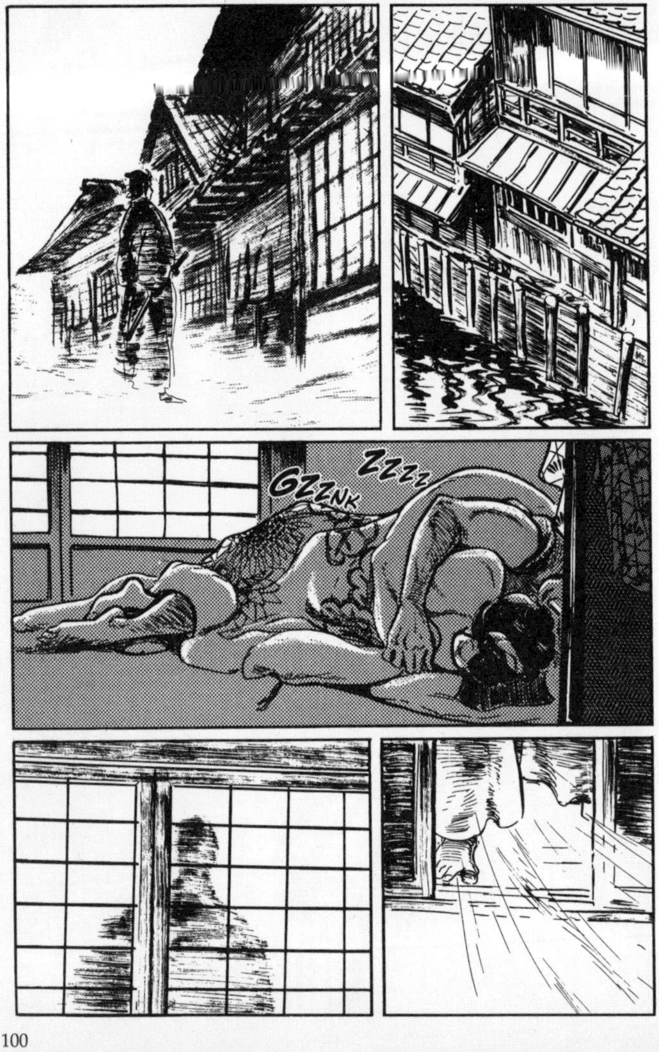
ZZZZ
GZZZNK

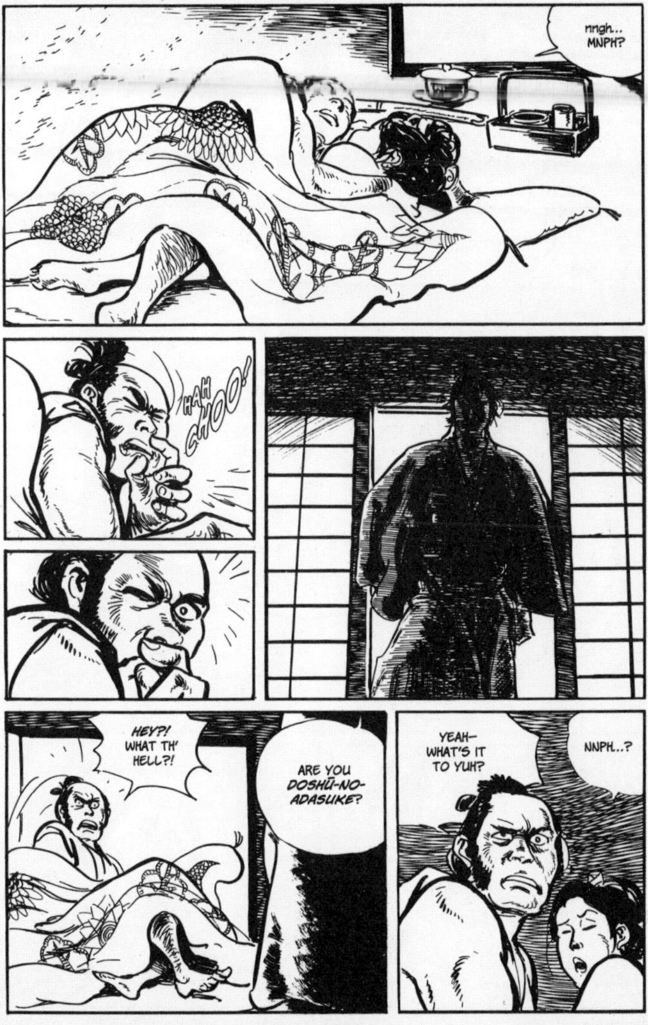
nngh... MNPH?
HAH CHOO!
HEY?! WHAT TH' HELL?!
ARE YOU DOSHŪ-NO-ADASUKE?
YEAH— WHAT'S IT TO YUH?
NNPH...?

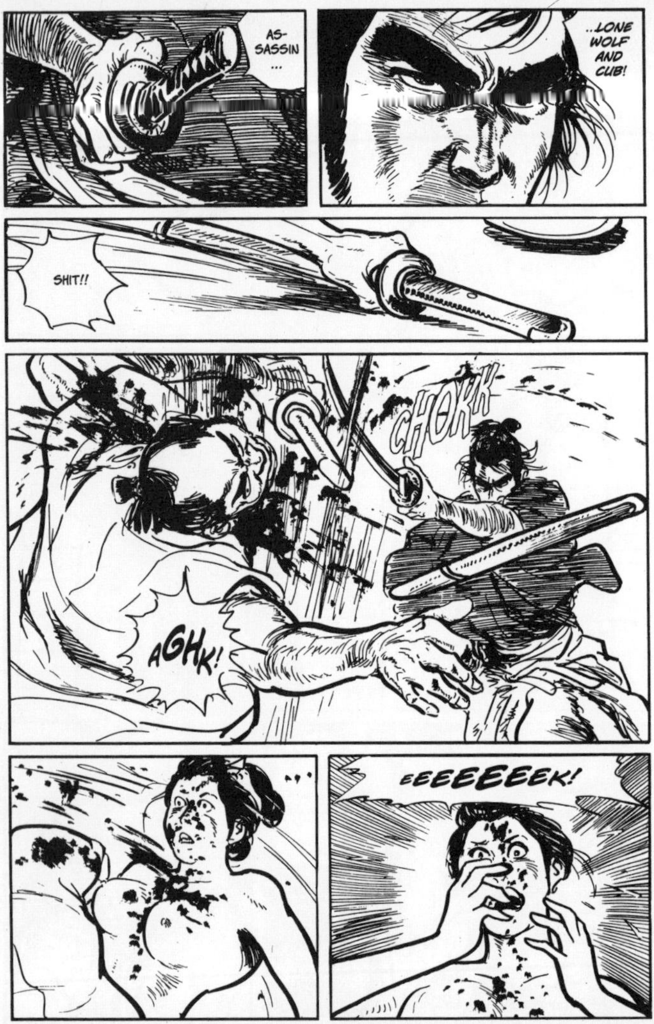
AS-SASSIN ...
..LONE WOLF AND CUB!
SHIT!!
CHORK
AGHK!
EEEEEEEEK!

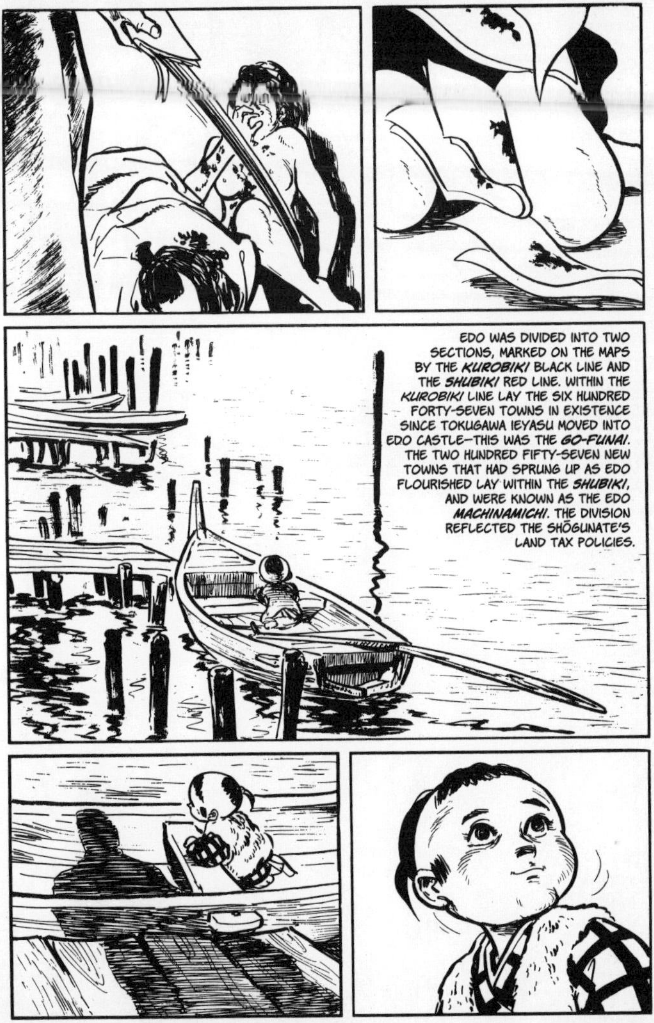
EDO WAS DIVIDED INTO TWO SECTIONS, MARKED ON THE MAPS BY THE KUROBIKI BLACK LINE AND THE SHUBIKI RED LINE. WITHIN THE KUROBIKI LINE LAY THE SIX HUNDRED FORTY-SEVEN TOWNS IN EXISTENCE SINCE TOKUGAWA IEYASU MOVED INTO EDO CASTLE—THIS WAS THE GO-FUNAI. THE TWO HUNDRED FIFTY-SEVEN NEW TOWNS THAT HAD SPRUNG UP AS EDO FLOURISHED LAY WITHIN THE SHUBIKI, AND WERE KNOWN AS THE EDO MACHINAMICHI. THE DIVISION REFLECTED THE SHŌGUNATE'S LAND TAX POLICIES.

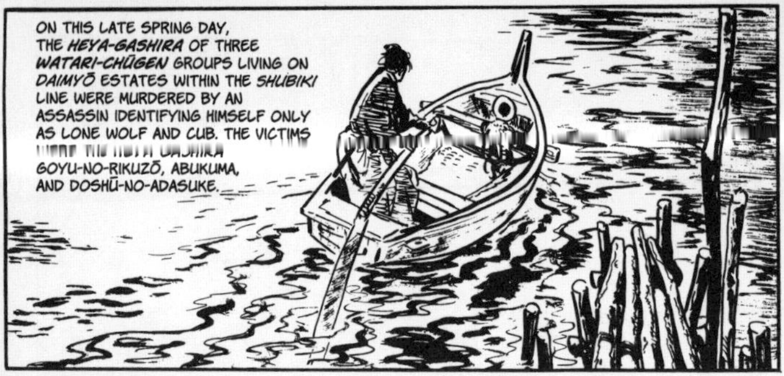
ON THIS LATE SPRING DAY, THE *HEYA-GASHIRA* OF THREE *WATARI-CHŪGEN* GROUPS LIVING ON *DAIMYŌ* ESTATES WITHIN THE *SHUBIKI* LINE WERE MURDERED BY AN ASSASSIN IDENTIFYING HIMSELF ONLY AS LONE WOLF AND CUB. THE VICTIMS WERE THE *HEYA-GASHIRA* GOYU-NO-RIKUZŌ, ABUKUMA, AND DOSHŪ-NO-ADASUKE.

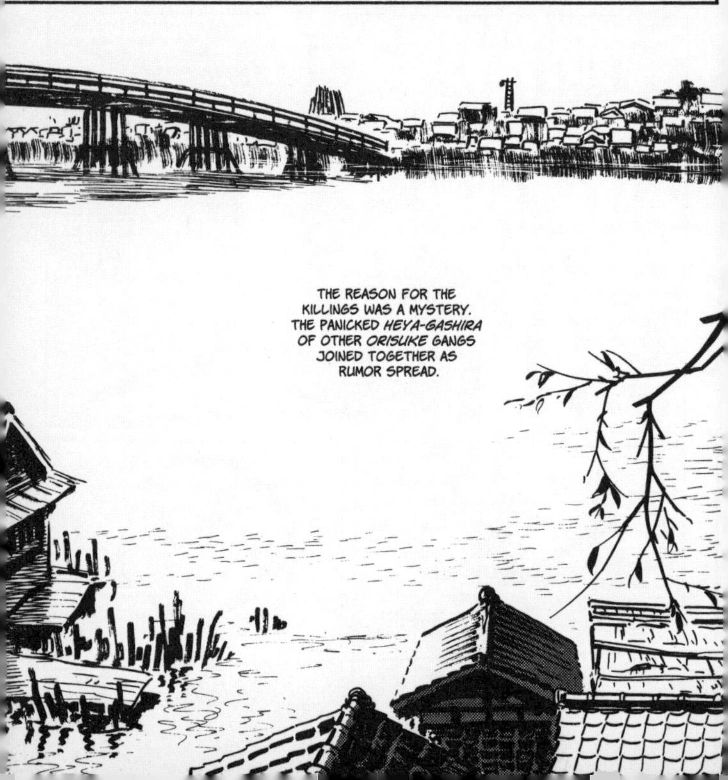
THE REASON FOR THE KILLINGS WAS A MYSTERY. THE PANICKED *HEYA-GASHIRA* OF OTHER *ORISUKE* GANGS JOINED TOGETHER AS RUMOR SPREAD.

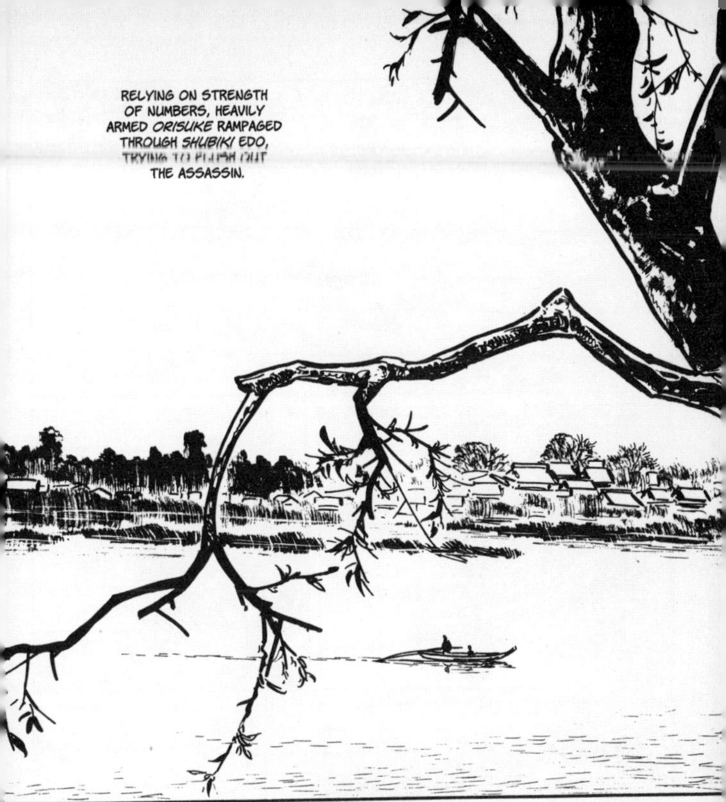
RELYING ON STRENGTH OF NUMBERS, HEAVILY ARMED *ORISUKE* RAMPAGED THROUGH *SHUBIKI* EDO, TRYING TO FLUSH OUT THE ASSASSIN.

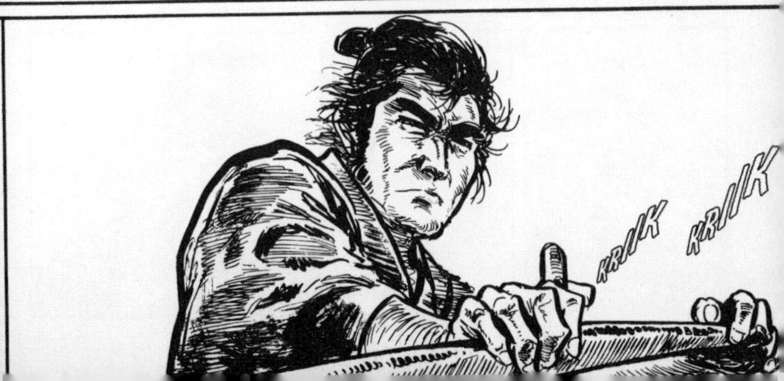
KRIIK
KRIIK

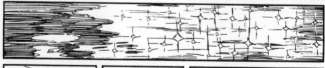

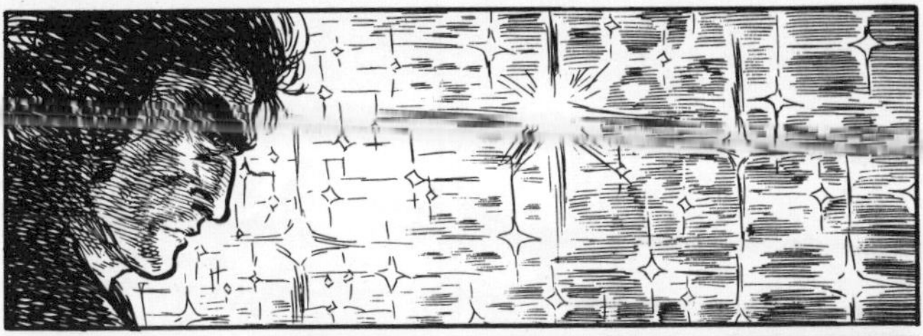
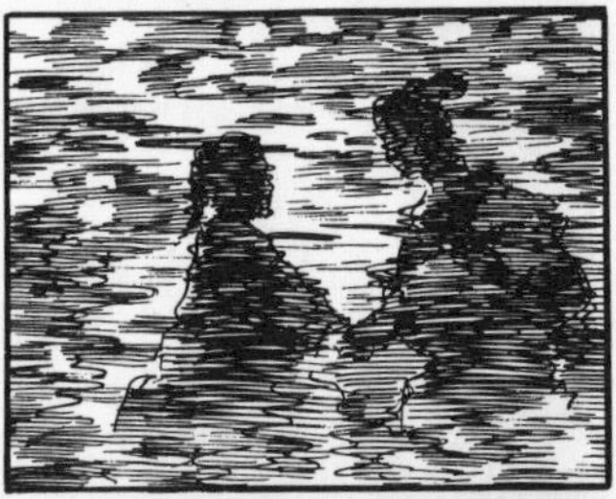
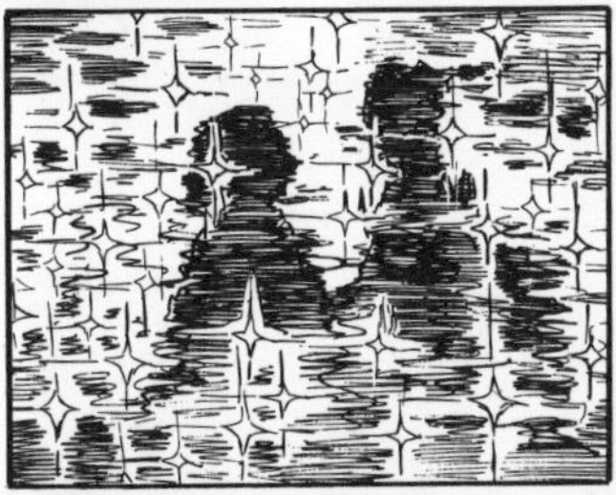
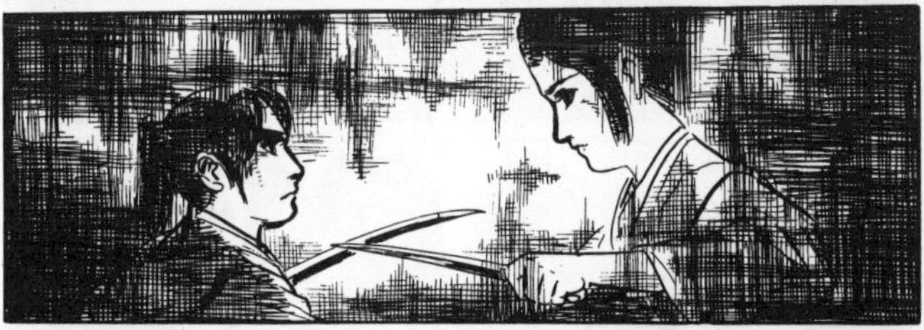
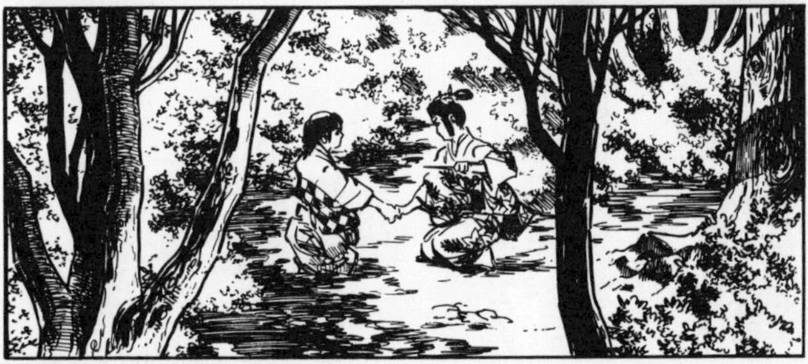

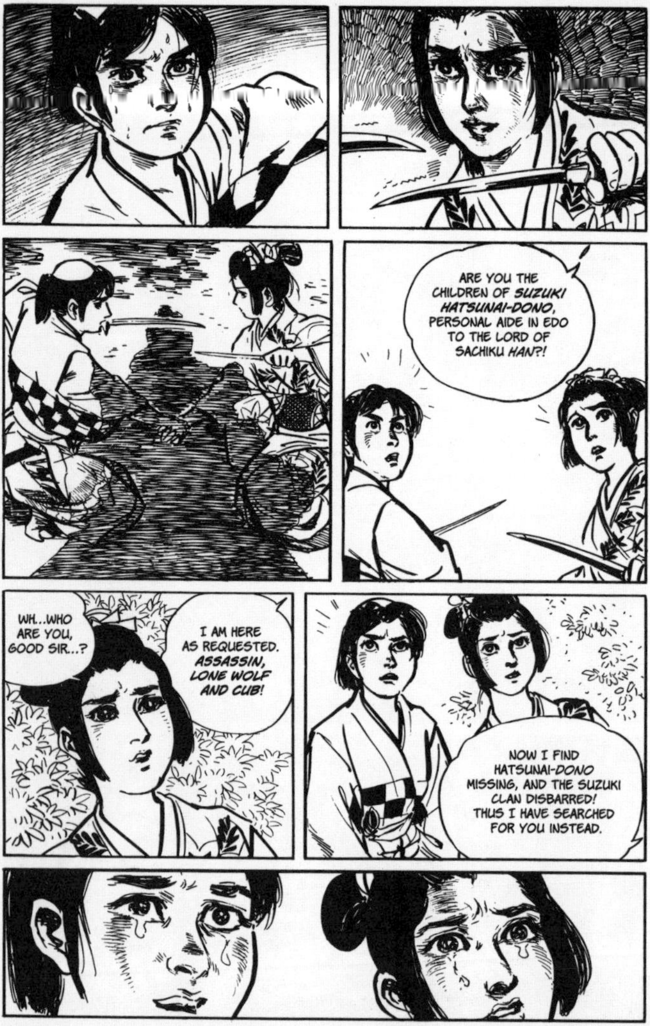
ARE YOU THE CHILDREN OF *SUZUKI HATSUNAI-DONO*, PERSONAL AIDE IN EDO TO THE LORD OF SACHIKU *HAN*?!
WH...WHO ARE YOU, GOOD SIR...?
I AM HERE AS REQUESTED. ***ASSASSIN, LONE WOLF AND CUB!***
NOW I FIND HATSUNAI-*DONO* MISSING, AND THE SUZUKI CLAN DISBARRED! THUS I HAVE SEARCHED FOR YOU INSTEAD.

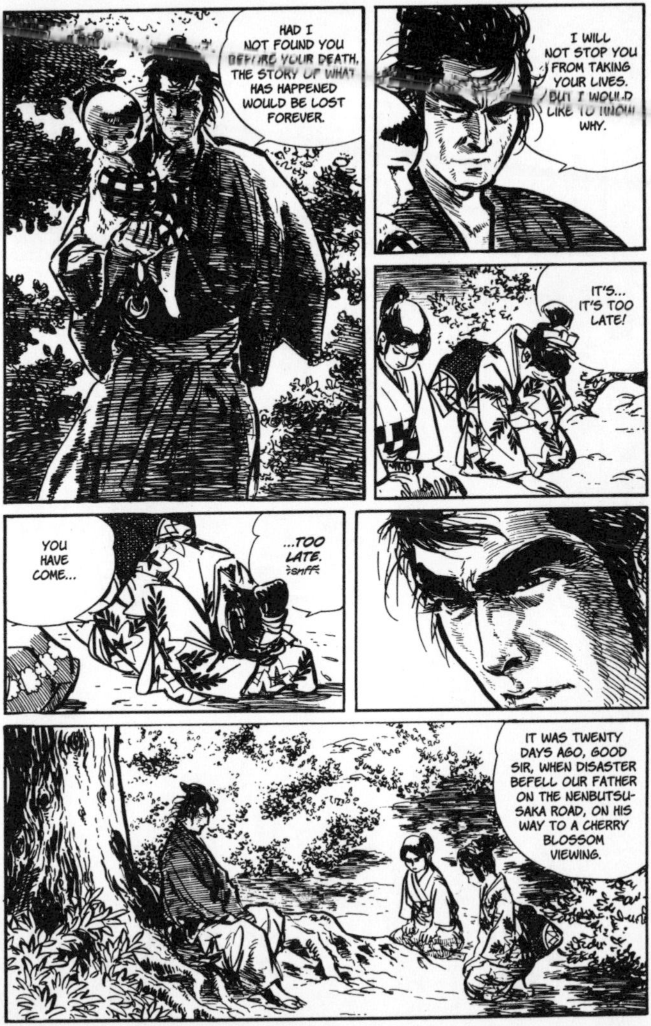
HAD I NOT FOUND YOU BEFORE YOUR DEATH, THE STORY OF WHAT HAS HAPPENED WOULD BE LOST FOREVER.
I WILL NOT STOP YOU FROM TAKING YOUR LIVES. BUT I WOULD LIKE TO KNOW WHY.
IT'S... IT'S TOO LATE!
YOU HAVE COME...
...TOO LATE.
snff
IT WAS TWENTY DAYS AGO, GOOD SIR, WHEN DISASTER BEFELL OUR FATHER ON THE NENBUTSU-SAKA ROAD, ON HIS WAY TO A CHERRY BLOSSOM VIEWING.

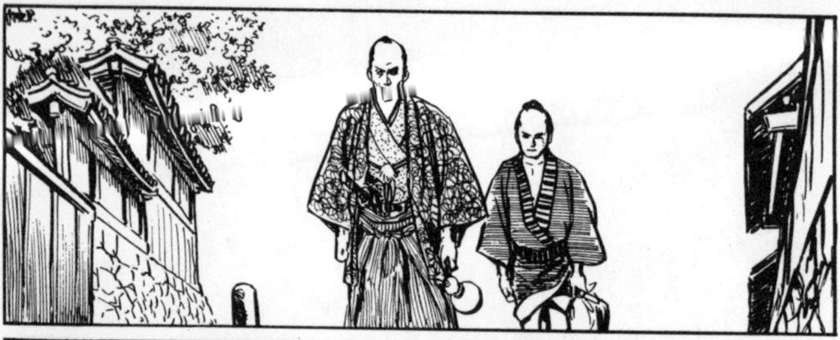

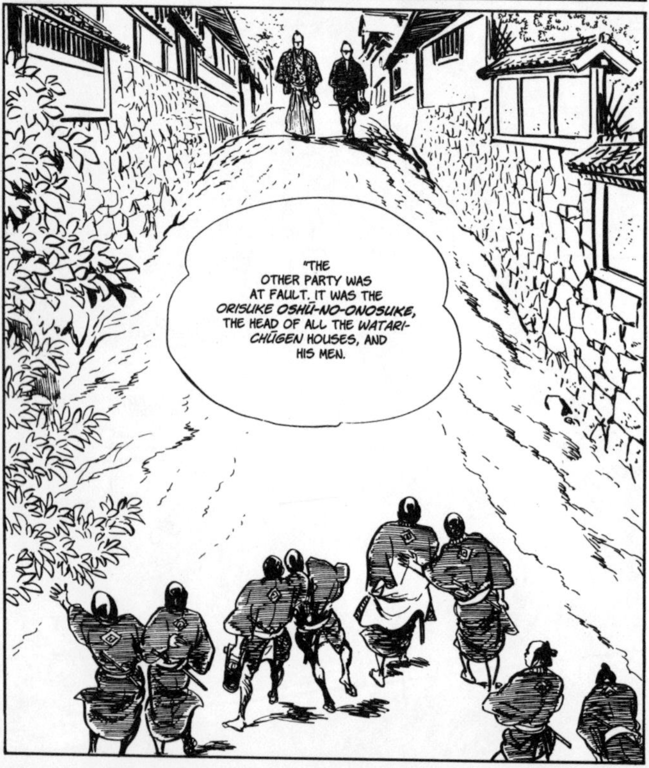
"THE OTHER PARTY WAS AT FAULT. IT WAS THE *ORISUKE OSHŪ-NO-ONOSUKE*, THE HEAD OF ALL THE *WATARI-CHŪGEN* HOUSES, AND HIS MEN.

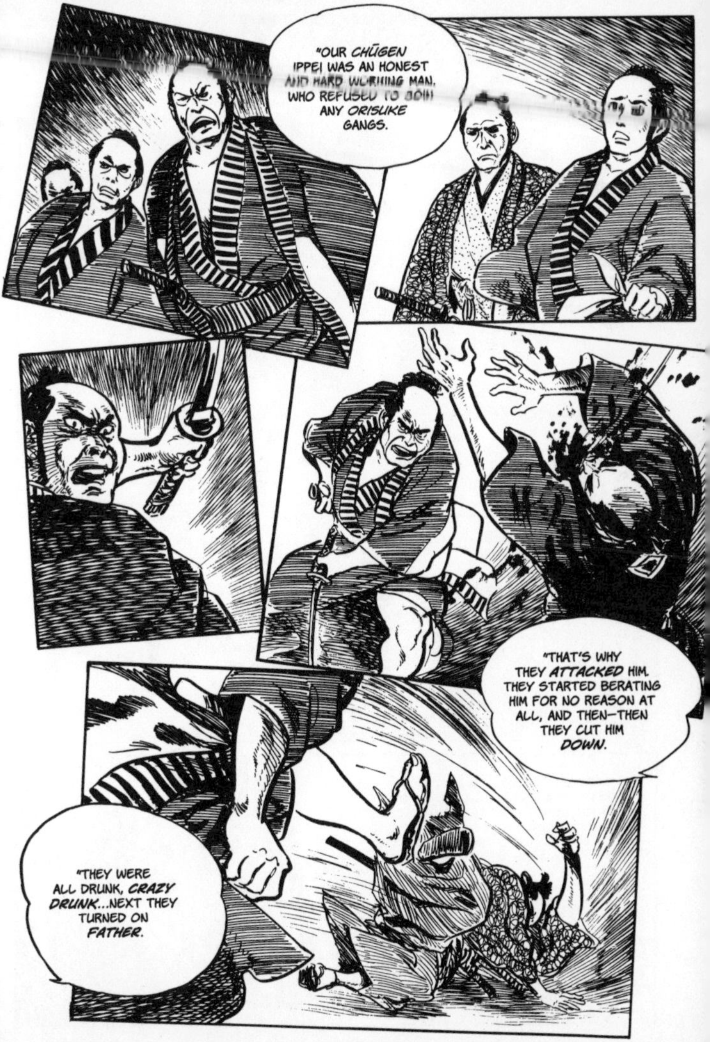
"OUR CHŪGEN IPPEI WAS AN HONEST AND HARD WORKING MAN, WHO REFUSED TO JOIN ANY ORISUKE GANGS.
"THAT'S WHY THEY ATTACKED HIM. THEY STARTED BERATING HIM FOR NO REASON AT ALL, AND THEN—THEN THEY CUT HIM DOWN.
"THEY WERE ALL DRUNK, CRAZY DRUNK...NEXT THEY TURNED ON FATHER.

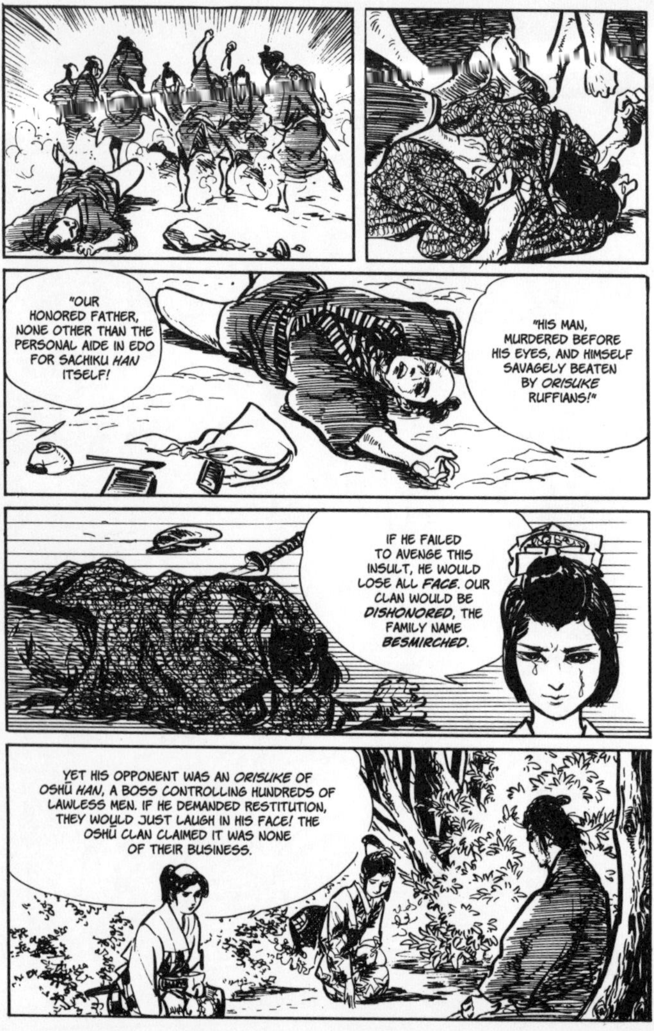
"OUR HONORED FATHER, NONE OTHER THAN THE PERSONAL AIDE IN EDO FOR SACHIKU HAN ITSELF!
"HIS MAN, MURDERED BEFORE HIS EYES, AND HIMSELF SAVAGELY BEATEN BY ORISUKE RUFFIANS!"
IF HE FAILED TO AVENGE THIS INSULT, HE WOULD LOSE ALL FACE. OUR CLAN WOULD BE DISHONORED, THE FAMILY NAME BESMIRCHED.
YET HIS OPPONENT WAS AN ORISUKE OF OSHŪ HAN, A BOSS CONTROLLING HUNDREDS OF LAWLESS MEN. IF HE DEMANDED RESTITUTION, THEY WOULD JUST LAUGH IN HIS FACE! THE OSHŪ CLAN CLAIMED IT WAS NONE OF THEIR BUSINESS.

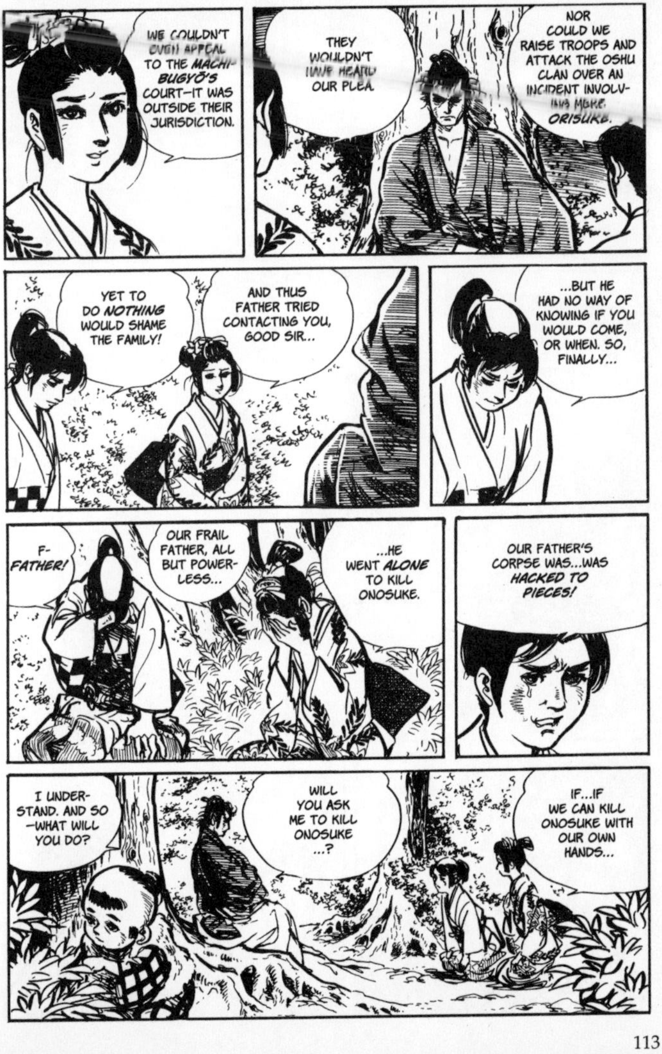
WE COULDN'T EVEN APPEAL TO THE *MACHI-BUGYŌ'S* COURT—IT WAS OUTSIDE THEIR JURISDICTION.
THEY WOULDN'T HAVE HEARD OUR PLEA.
NOR COULD WE RAISE TROOPS AND ATTACK THE OSHU CLAN OVER AN INCIDENT INVOLVING MERE *ORISUKE.*
YET TO DO *NOTHING* WOULD SHAME THE FAMILY!
AND THUS FATHER TRIED CONTACTING YOU, GOOD SIR...
...BUT HE HAD NO WAY OF KNOWING IF YOU WOULD COME, OR WHEN. SO, FINALLY...
F-*FATHER!*
OUR FRAIL FATHER, ALL BUT POWERLESS...
...HE WENT *ALONE* TO KILL ONOSUKE.
OUR FATHER'S CORPSE WAS...WAS *HACKED TO PIECES!*
I UNDERSTAND. AND SO —WHAT WILL YOU DO?
WILL YOU ASK ME TO KILL ONOSUKE ...?
IF...IF WE CAN KILL ONOSUKE WITH OUR OWN HANDS...

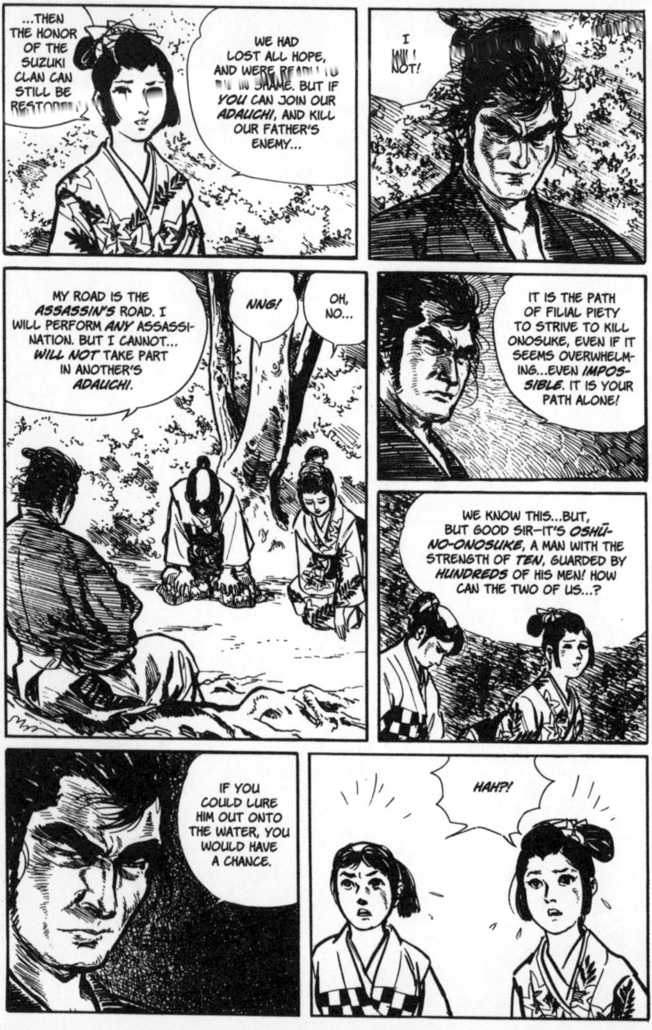
WE HAD LOST ALL HOPE, AND WERE READY TO DIE IN SHAME. BUT IF *YOU* CAN JOIN OUR *ADAUCHI*, AND KILL OUR FATHER'S ENEMY...
...THEN THE HONOR OF THE SUZUKI CLAN CAN STILL BE RESTORED
I WILL NOT!
MY ROAD IS THE *ASSASSIN'S* ROAD. I WILL PERFORM *ANY* ASSASSINATION. BUT I CANNOT... *WILL NOT* TAKE PART IN ANOTHER'S *ADAUCHI*.
*NNG!*
OH, NO...
IT IS THE PATH OF FILIAL PIETY TO STRIVE TO KILL ONOSUKE, EVEN IF IT SEEMS OVERWHELMING...EVEN *IMPOSSIBLE*. IT IS YOUR PATH ALONE!
WE KNOW THIS...BUT, BUT GOOD SIR—IT'S *OSHŪ-NO-ONOSUKE*, A MAN WITH THE STRENGTH OF *TEN*, GUARDED BY *HUNDREDS* OF HIS MEN! HOW CAN THE TWO OF US...?
IF YOU COULD LURE HIM OUT ONTO THE WATER, YOU WOULD HAVE A CHANCE.
*HAH?!*

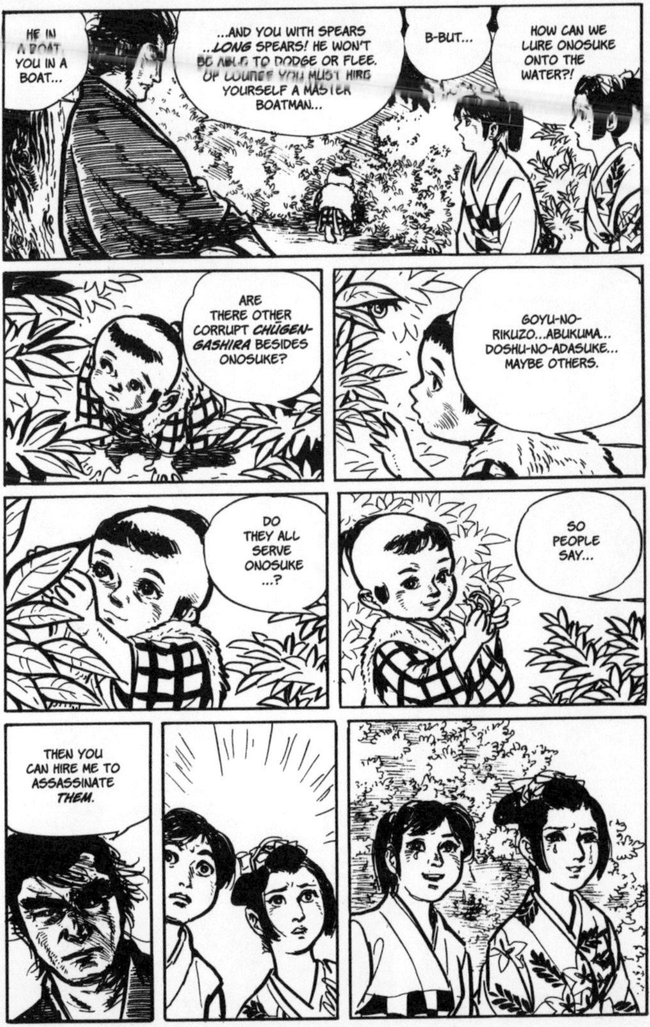
HE IN A BOAT, YOU IN A BOAT...
...AND YOU WITH SPEARS ...LONG SPEARS! HE WON'T BE ABLE TO DODGE OR FLEE. OF COURSE YOU MUST HIRE YOURSELF A MASTER BOATMAN...
B-BUT...
HOW CAN WE LURE ONOSUKE ONTO THE WATER?!
ARE THERE OTHER CORRUPT CHŪGEN-GASHIRA BESIDES ONOSUKE?
GOYU-NO-RIKUZO...ABUKUMA... DOSHU-NO-ADASUKE... MAYBE OTHERS.
DO THEY ALL SERVE ONOSUKE ...?
SO PEOPLE SAY...
THEN YOU CAN HIRE ME TO ASSASSINATE THEM.

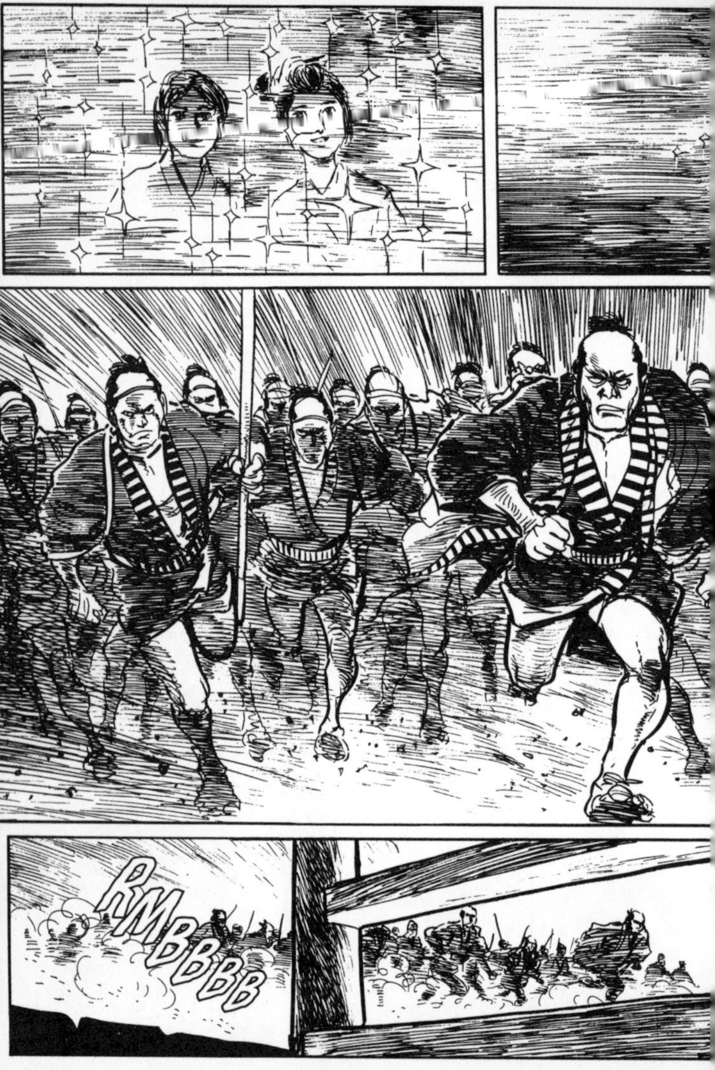
RMBBBB

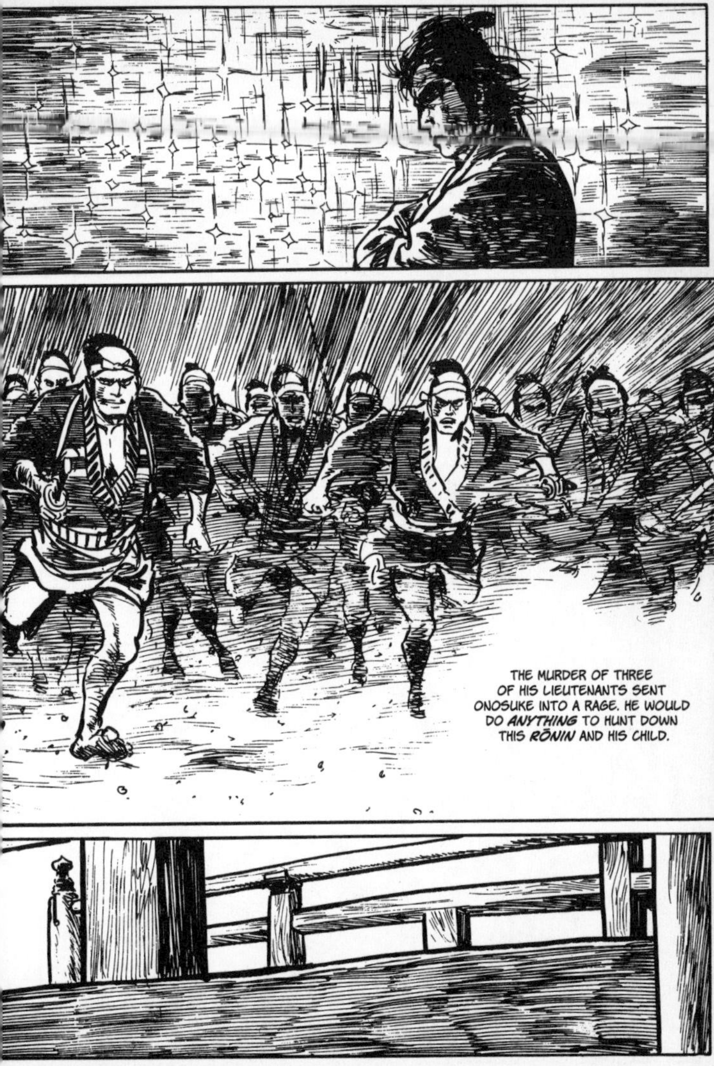
THE MURDER OF THREE OF HIS LIEUTENANTS SENT ONOSUKE INTO A RAGE. HE WOULD DO *ANYTHING* TO HUNT DOWN THIS *RŌNIN* AND HIS CHILD.

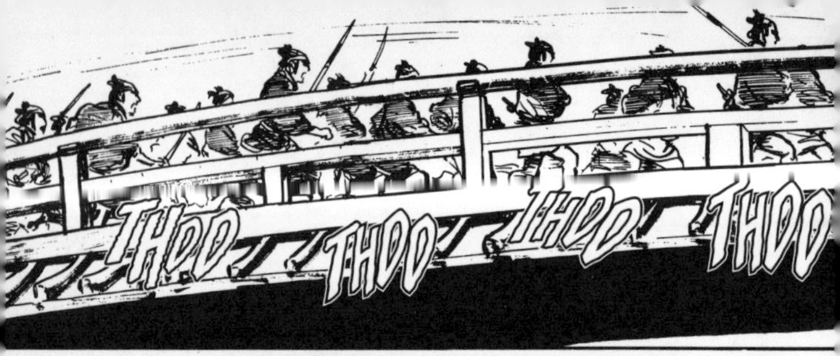
THOO
THOO
THOO
THOO
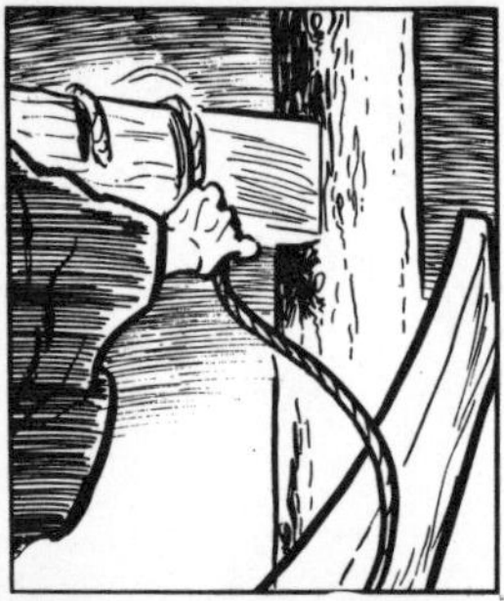
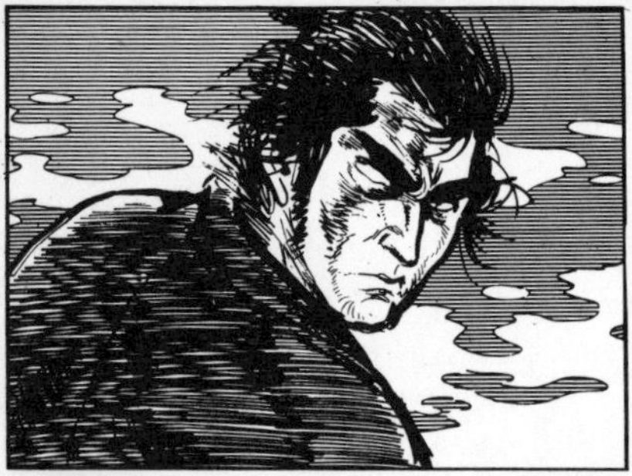
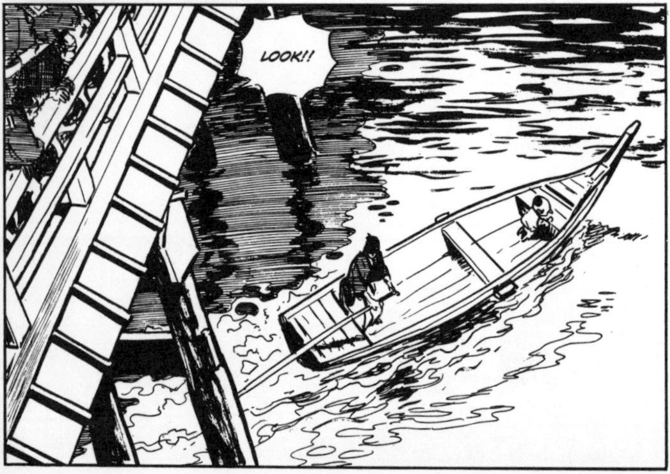
LOOK!!

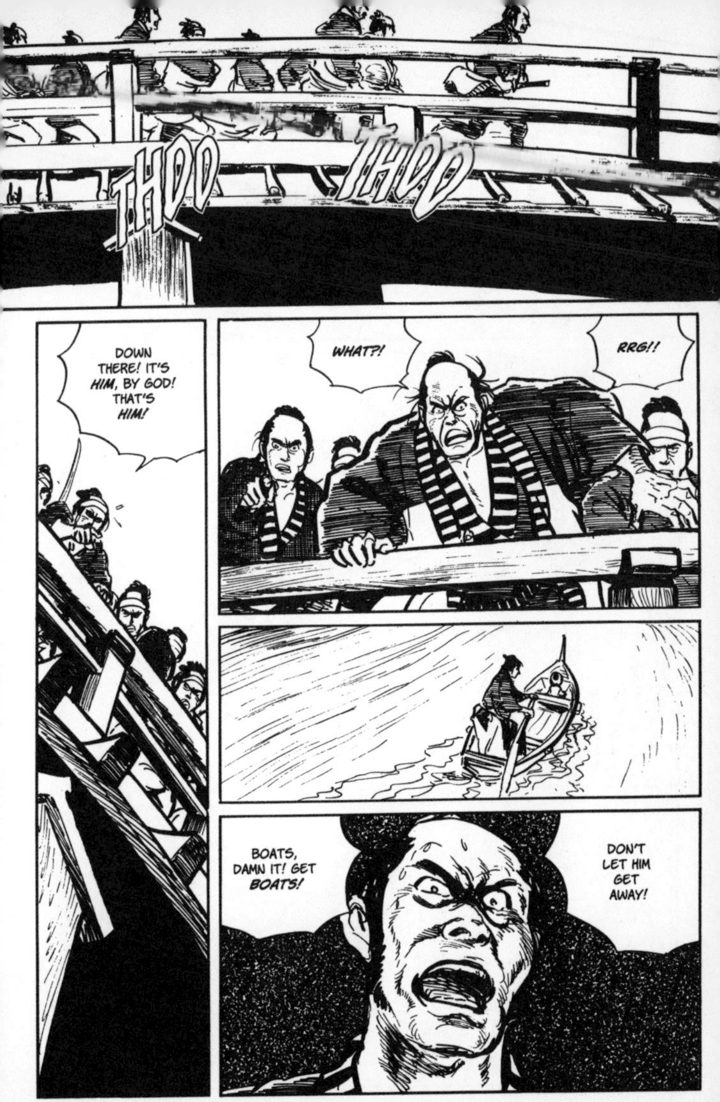
THOO
THOO
RRG!!
WHAT?!
DON'T LET HIM GET AWAY!
BOATS, DAMN IT! GET BOATS!
DOWN THERE! IT'S HIM, BY GOD! THAT'S HIM!

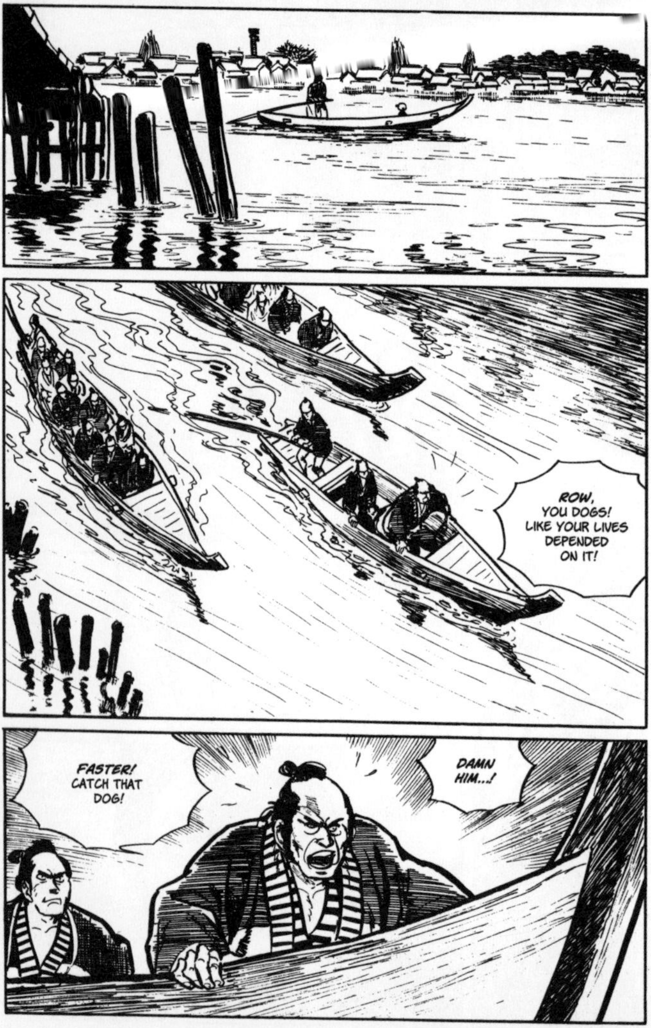
ROW, YOU DOGS! LIKE YOUR LIVES DEPENDED ON IT!
DAMN HIM...!
FASTER! CATCH THAT DOG!

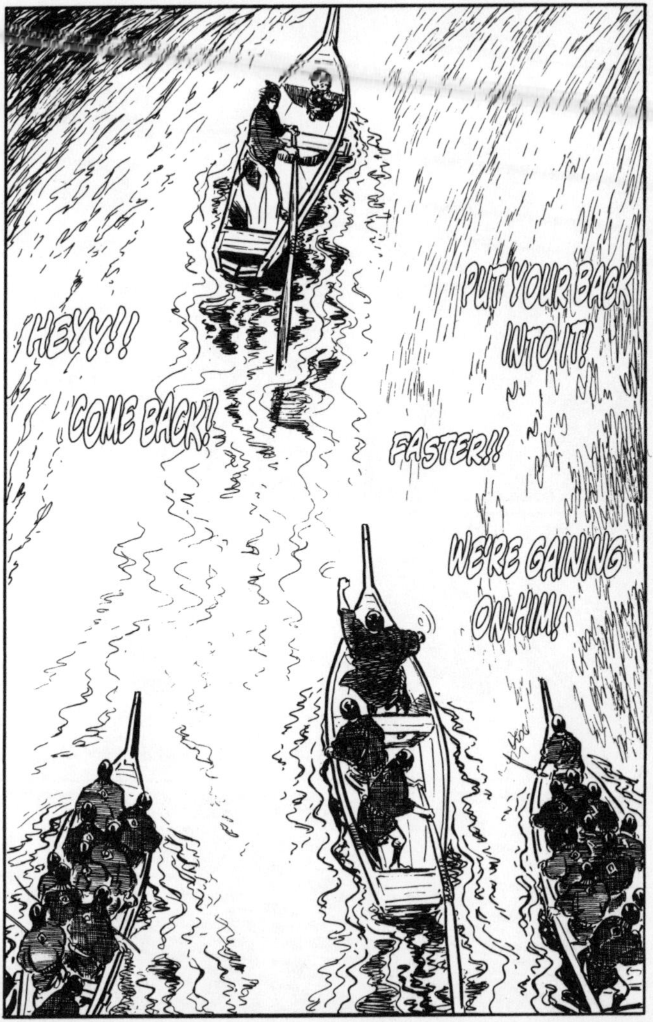
PUT YOUR BACK INTO IT!
HEYY!!
COME BACK!
FASTER!!
WE'RE GAINING ON HIM!

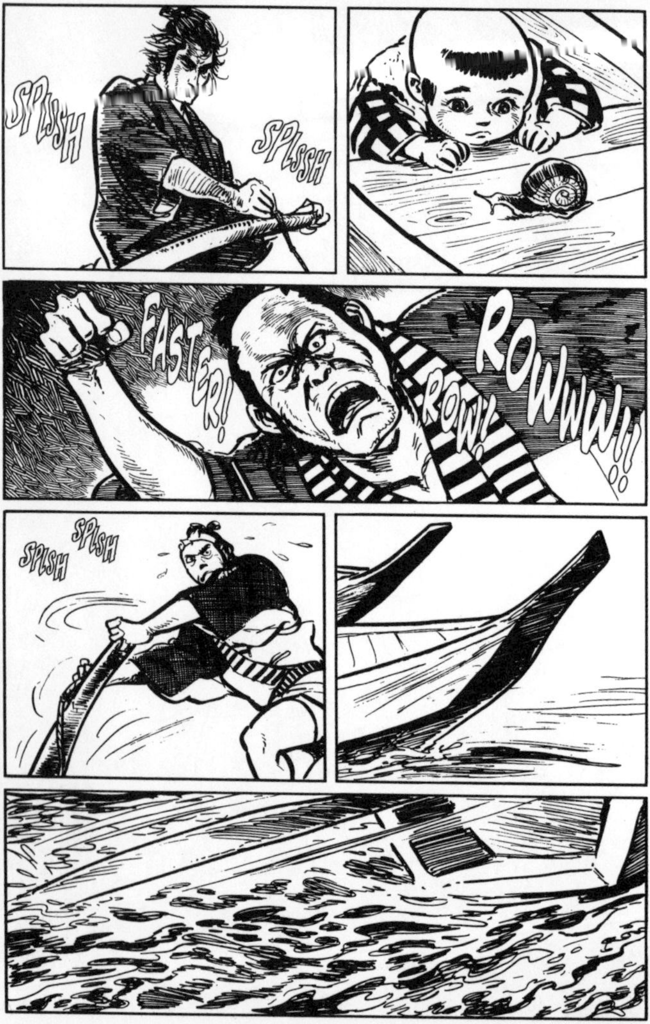
SPLSSH
SPLSSH
ROWWW!!
ROW!
FASTER!
SPLSH
SPLSH

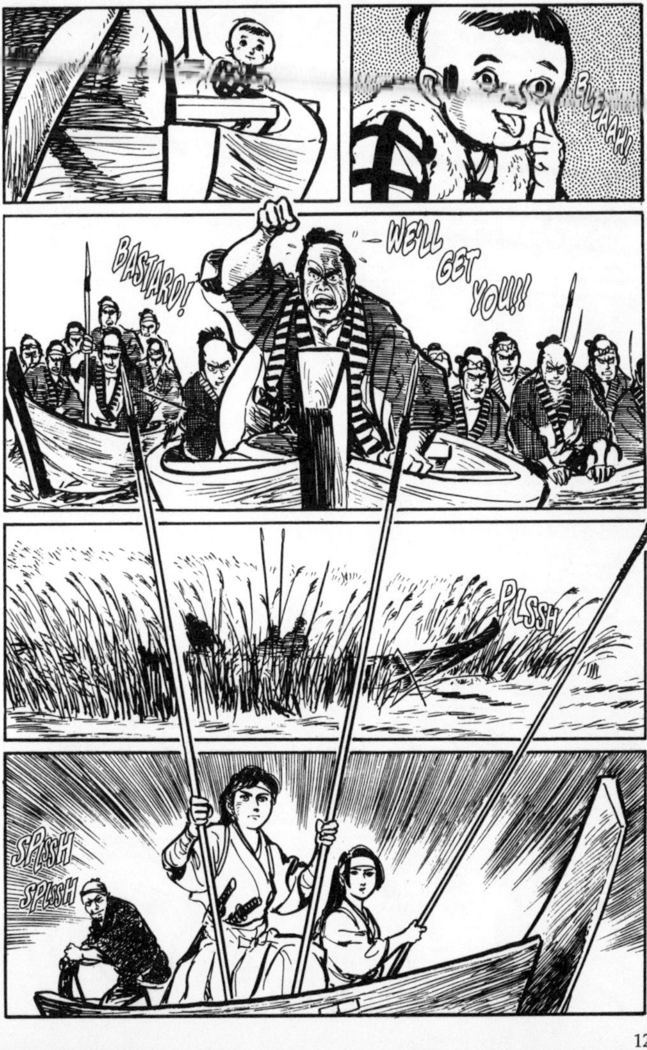
BLLAAAH!!
WE'LL GET YOU!!!
BASTARD!
PLSSH
SPLSSH
SPLSSH

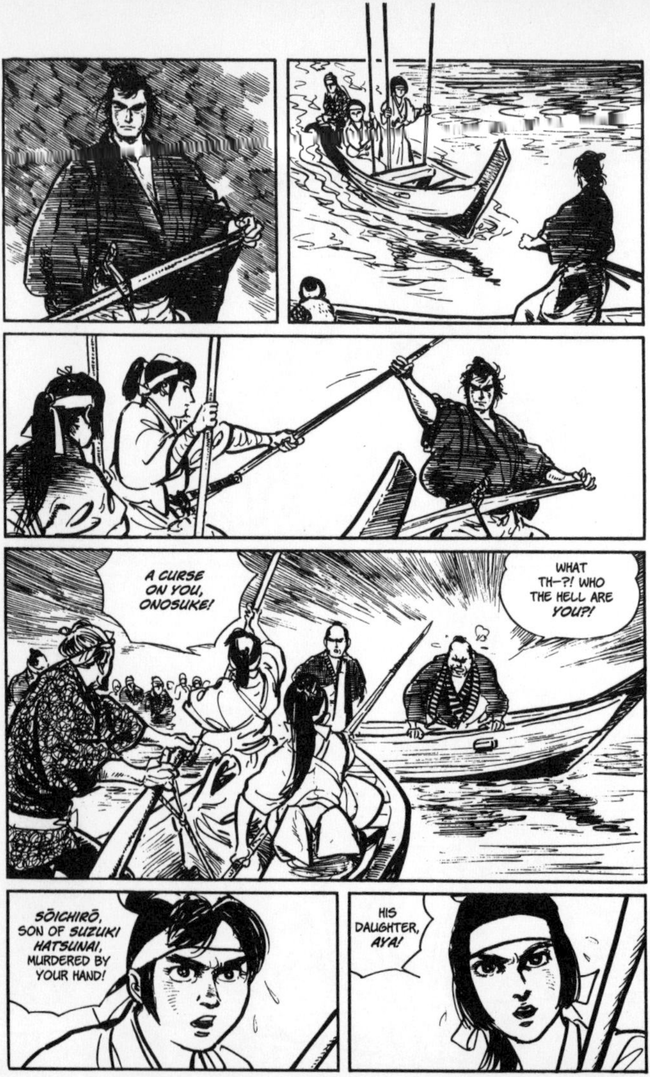
A CURSE ON YOU, ONOSUKE!
WHAT TH–?! WHO THE HELL ARE YOU?!
SŌICHIRŌ, SON OF SUZUKI HATSUNAI, MURDERED BY YOUR HAND!
HIS DAUGHTER, AYA!

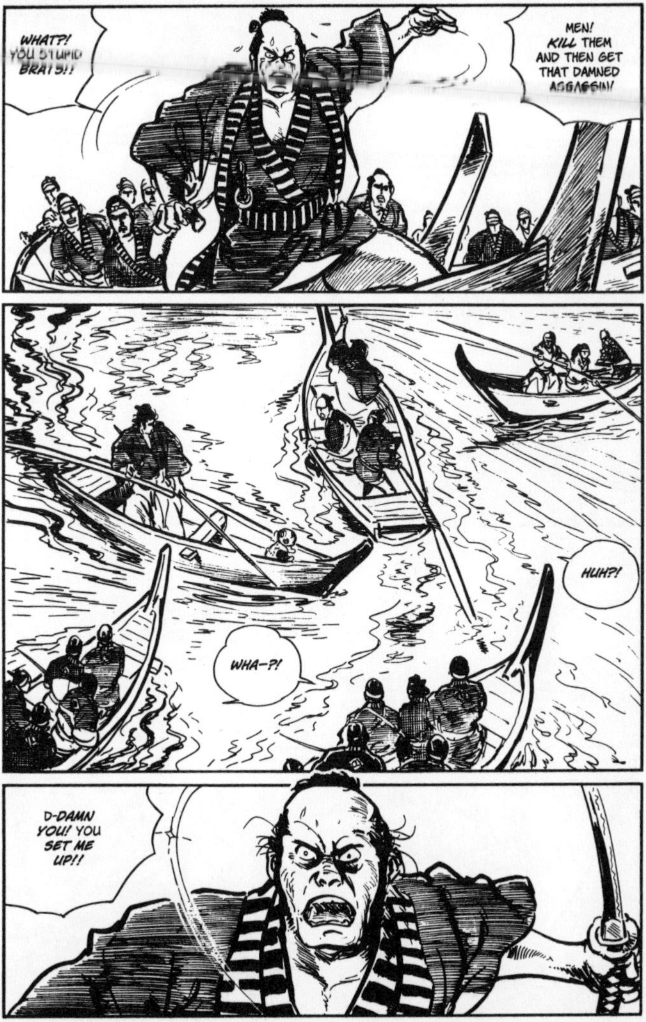
MEN! KILL THEM AND THEN GET THAT DAMNED ASSASSIN!
WHAT?! YOU STUPID BRATS!!
HUH?!
WHA-?!
D-DAMN YOU! YOU SET ME UP!!

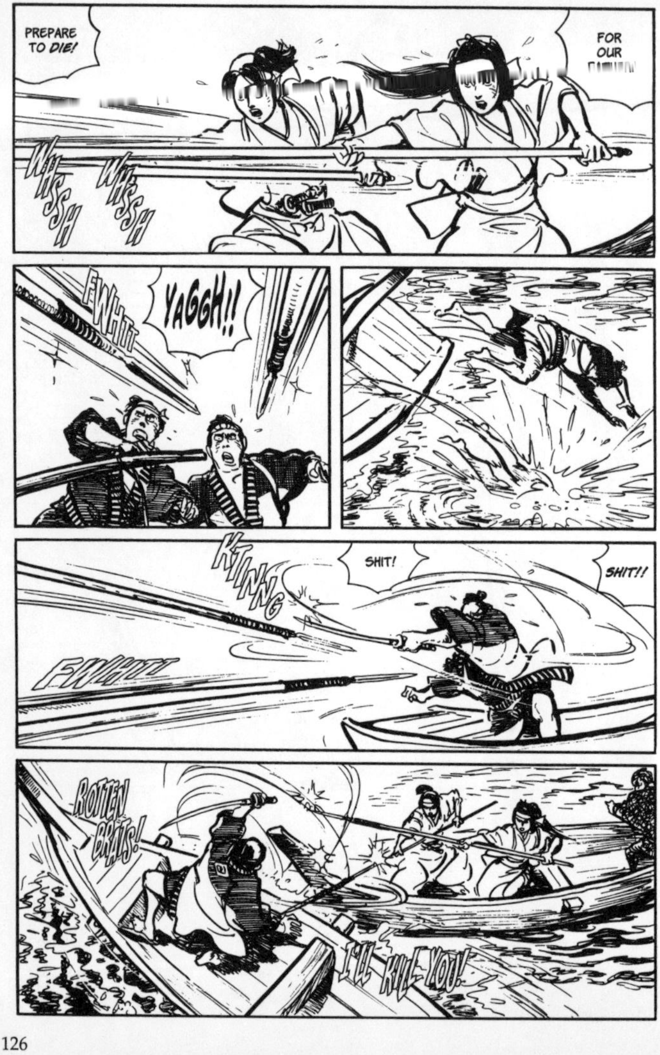
PREPARE TO DIE!
FOR OUR [redacted]
WHSSH
WHSSH
FWHTT
YAGGH!!
KTINNG
SHIT!
SHIT!!
FWHTT
ROTTEN BRATS!
I'LL KILL YOU!

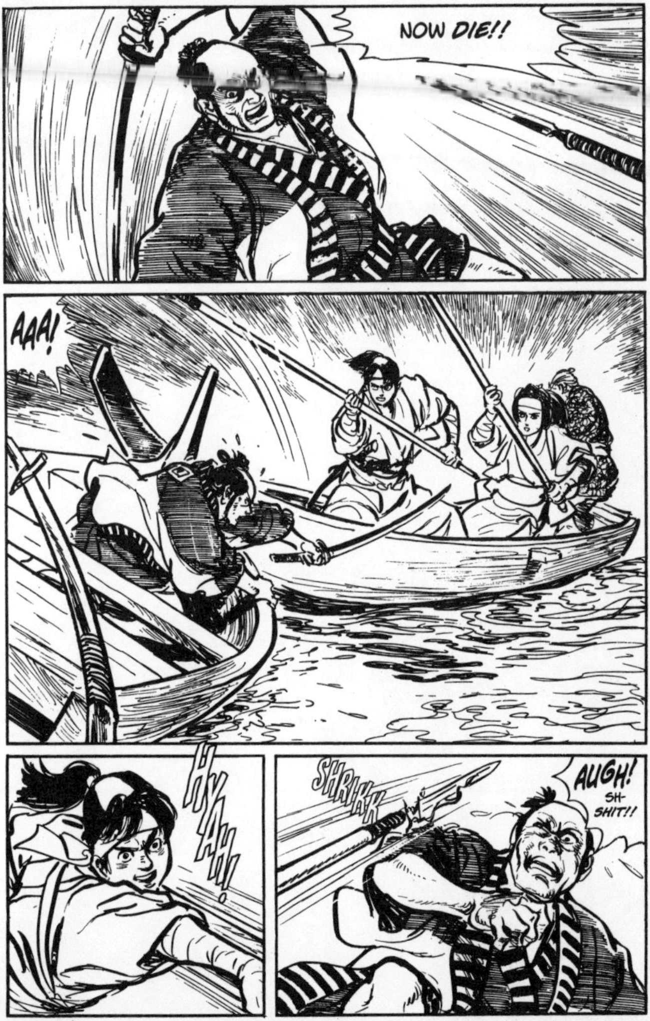
NOW DIE!!
AAA!
HYAAH!
SHRIKK
AUGH!
SH-
SHIT!!

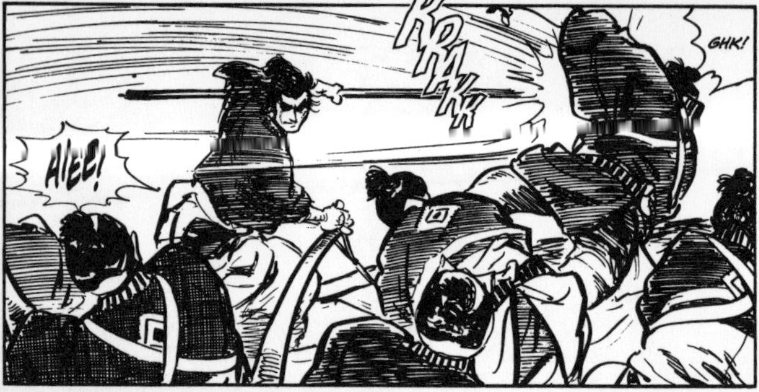
GHK!
KRAKK
AIEE!

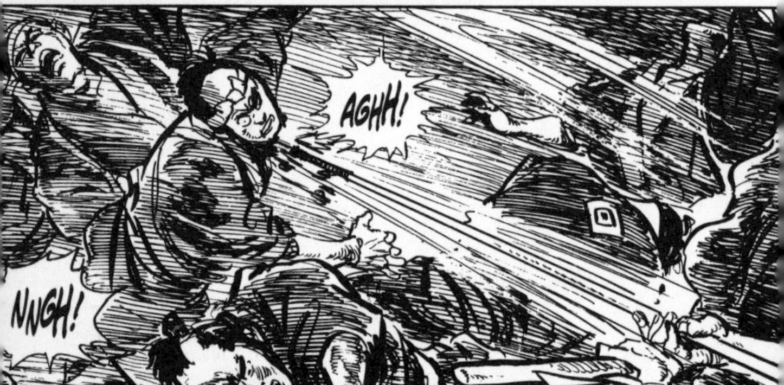
AGHH!
NNGH!

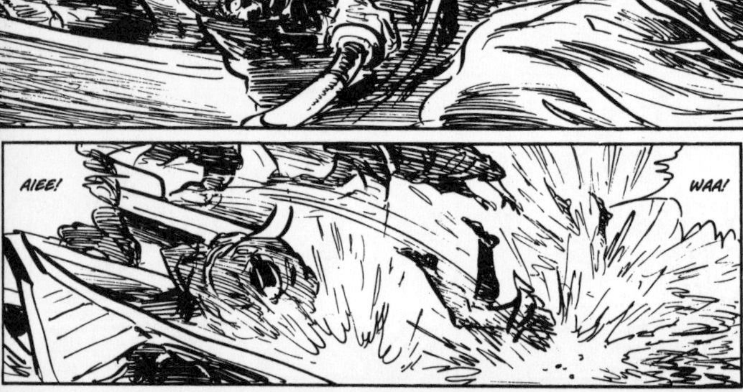
WAA!
AIEE!

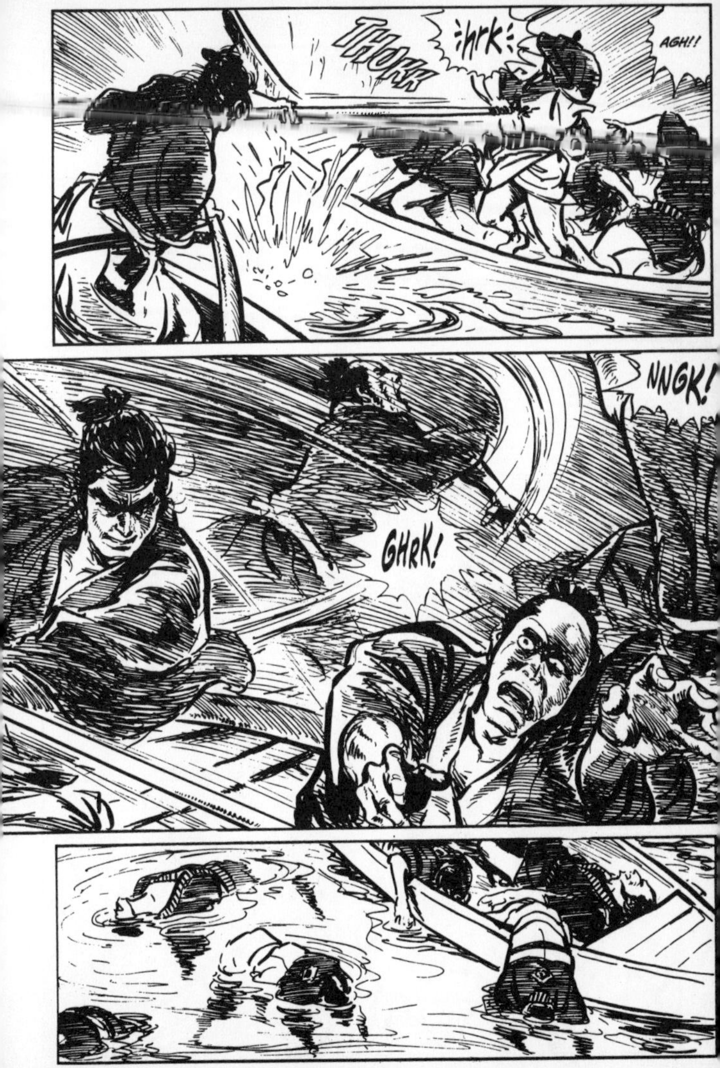
AGH!!
hrk
THOKK
NNGK!
GHRK!

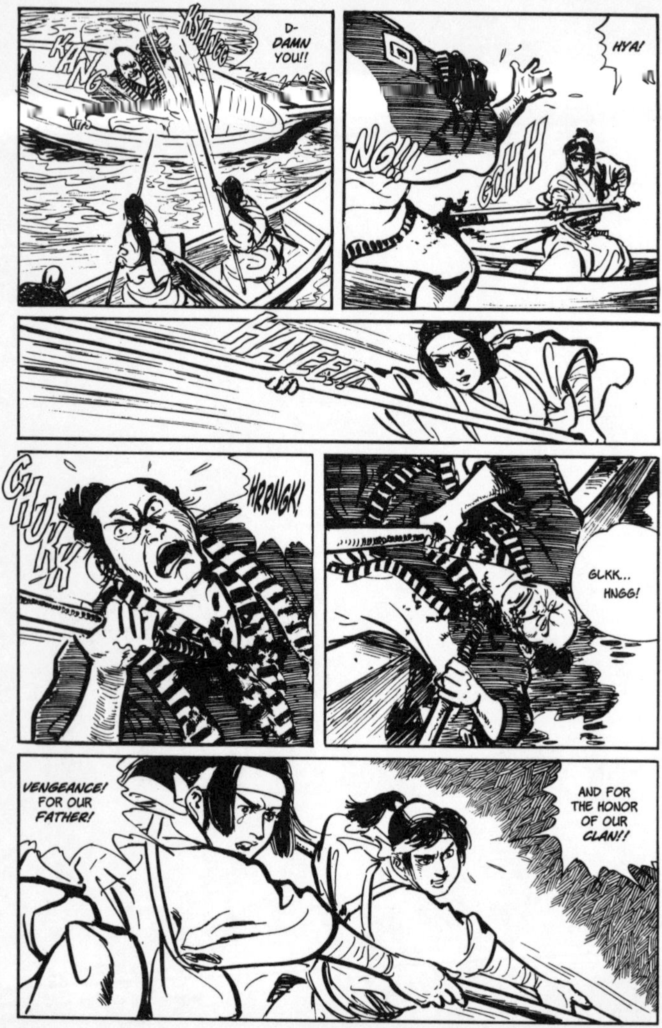
HYA!
NG!!
GCHH
D-DAMN YOU!!
KSHNGG
KANG
HAIEE!!
GLKK... HNGG!
HRRNGK!
CHUKK
VENGEANCE! FOR OUR FATHER!
AND FOR THE HONOR OF OUR CLAN!!

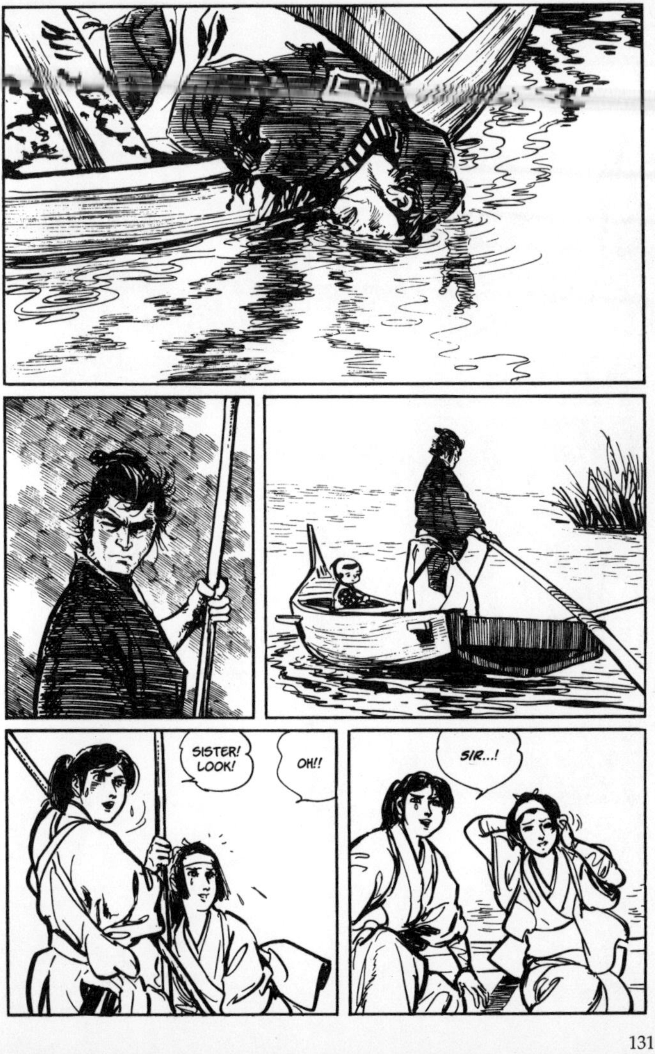
SISTER! LOOK!
OH!!
SIR...!

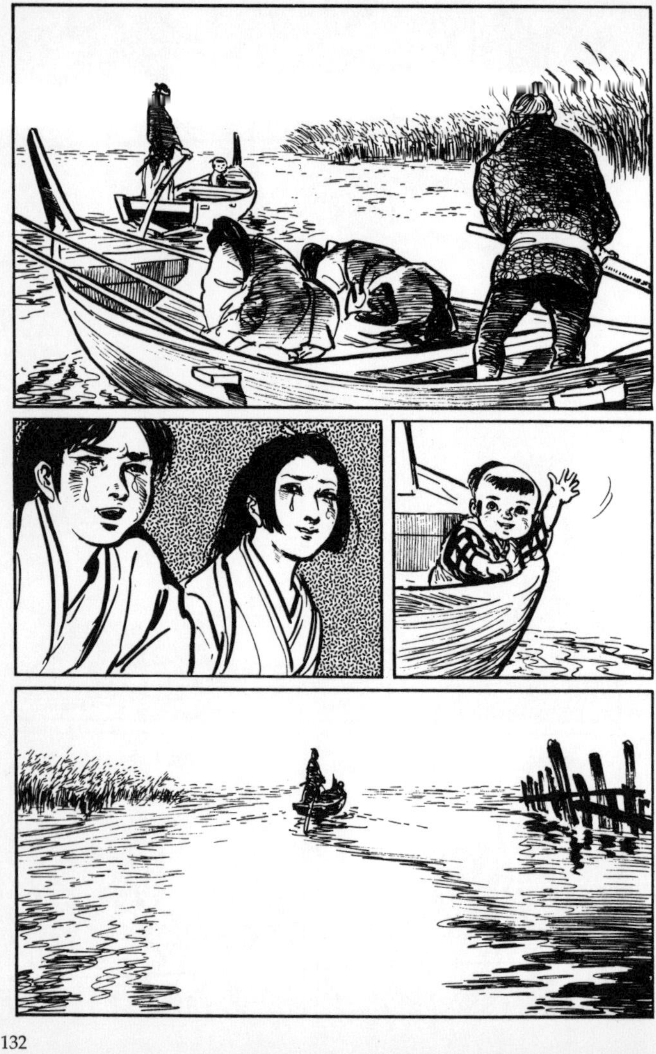

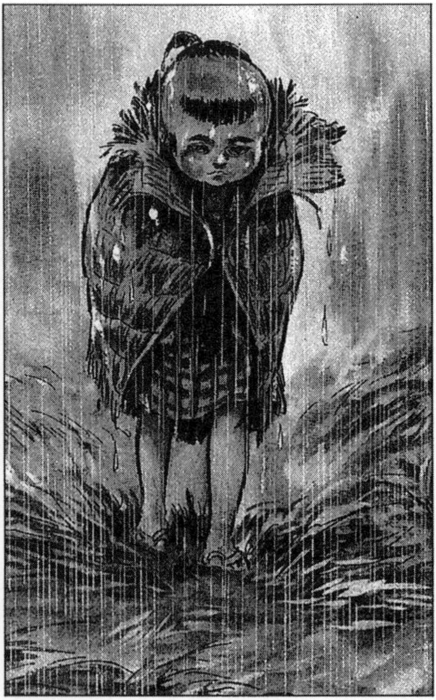

the twenty-second

# Parting Frost

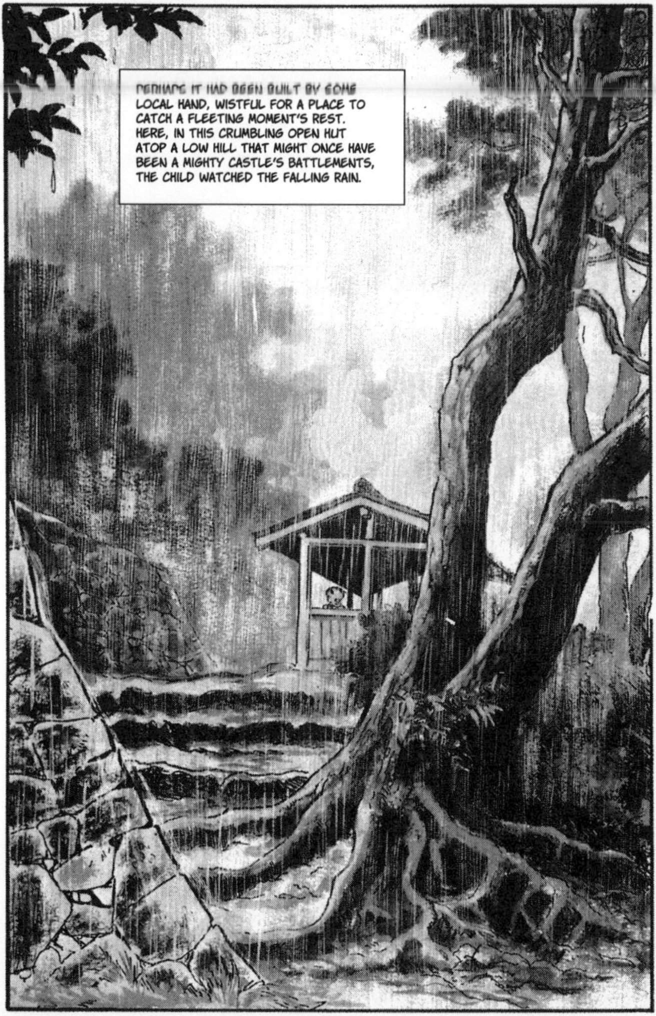
PERHAPS IT HAD BEEN BUILT BY SOME LOCAL HAND, WISTFUL FOR A PLACE TO CATCH A FLEETING MOMENT'S REST. HERE, IN THIS CRUMBLING OPEN HUT ATOP A LOW HILL THAT MIGHT ONCE HAVE BEEN A MIGHTY CASTLE'S BATTLEMENTS, THE CHILD WATCHED THE FALLING RAIN.

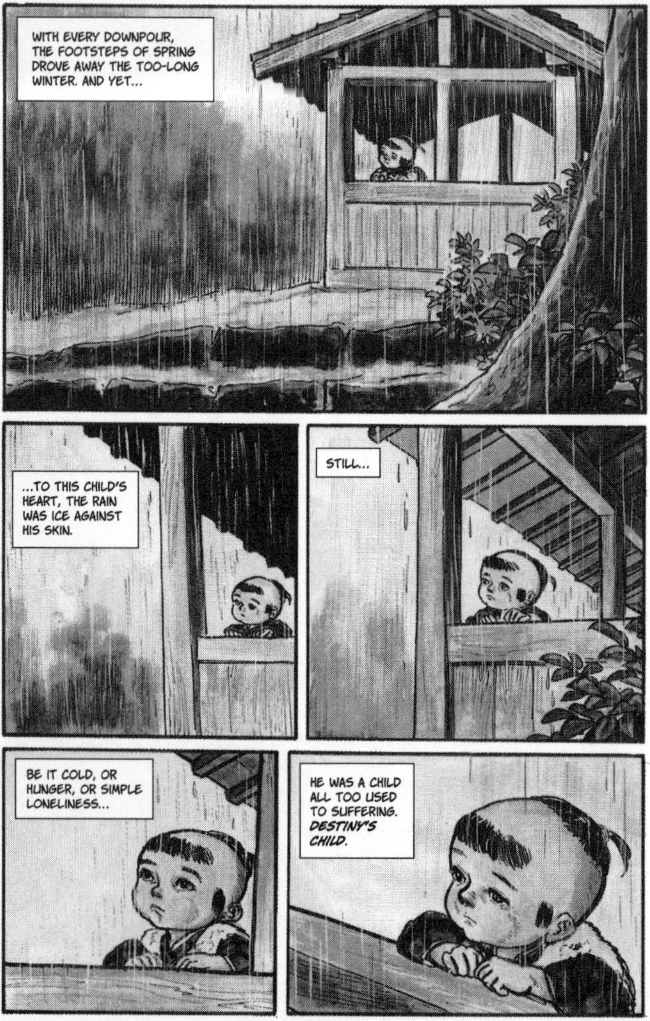
WITH EVERY DOWNPOUR, THE FOOTSTEPS OF SPRING DROVE AWAY THE TOO-LONG WINTER. AND YET...
...TO THIS CHILD'S HEART, THE RAIN WAS ICE AGAINST HIS SKIN.
STILL...
BE IT COLD, OR HUNGER, OR SIMPLE LONELINESS...
HE WAS A CHILD ALL TOO USED TO SUFFERING. *DESTINY'S CHILD.*

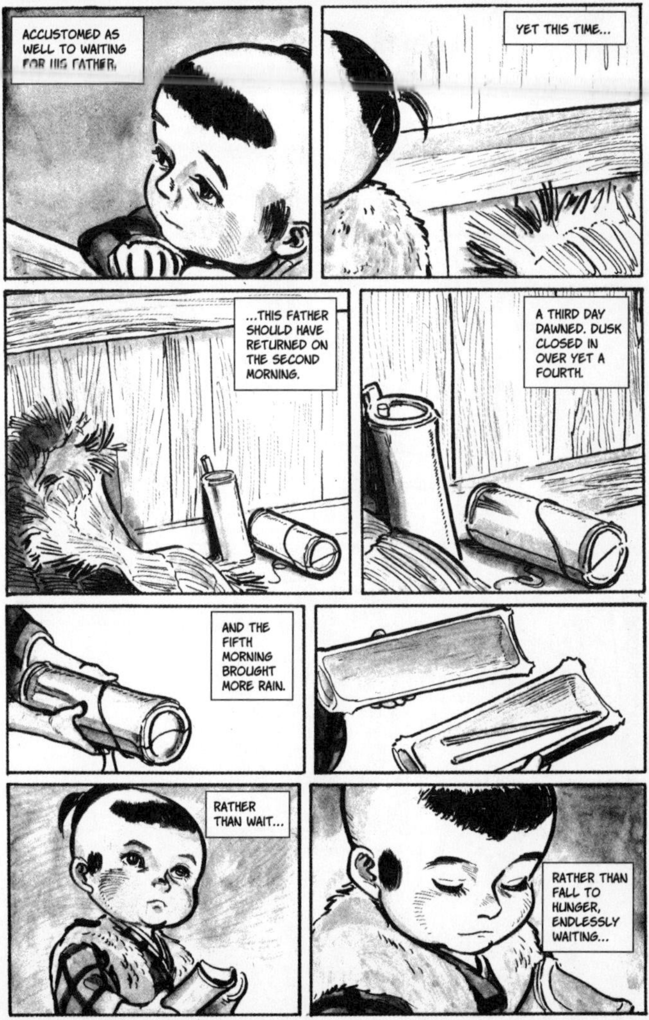
ACCUSTOMED AS WELL TO WAITING FOR HIS FATHER.
YET THIS TIME...
...THIS FATHER SHOULD HAVE RETURNED ON THE SECOND MORNING.
A THIRD DAY DAWNED. DUSK CLOSED IN OVER YET A FOURTH.
AND THE FIFTH MORNING BROUGHT MORE RAIN.
RATHER THAN WAIT...
RATHER THAN FALL TO HUNGER, ENDLESSLY WAITING...

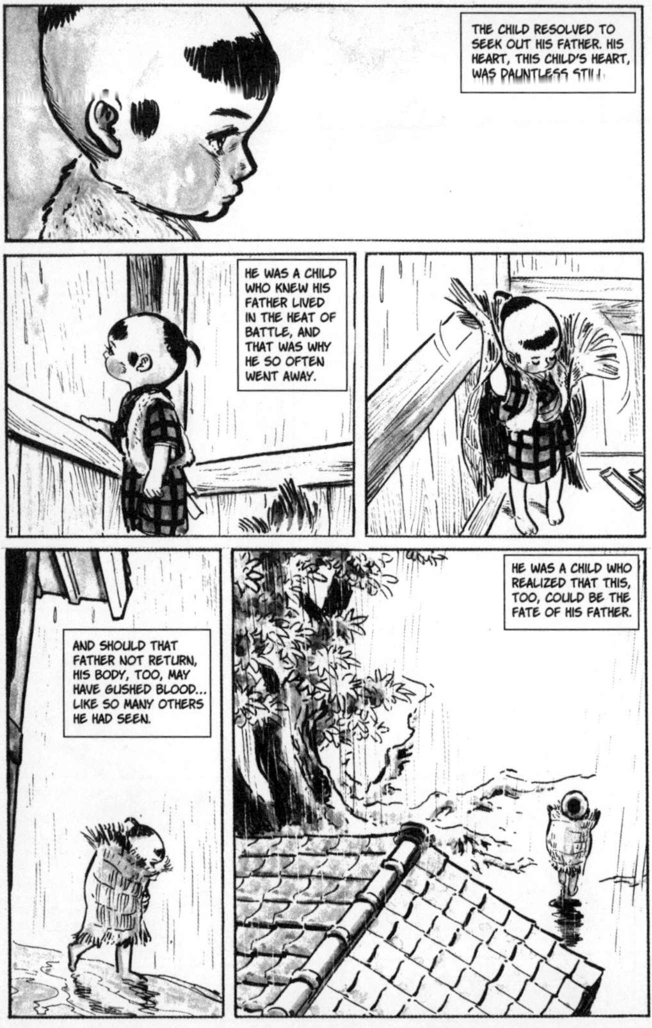
THE CHILD RESOLVED TO SEEK OUT HIS FATHER. HIS HEART, THIS CHILD'S HEART, WAS DAUNTLESS STILL.
HE WAS A CHILD WHO KNEW HIS FATHER LIVED IN THE HEAT OF BATTLE, AND THAT WAS WHY HE SO OFTEN WENT AWAY.
AND SHOULD THAT FATHER NOT RETURN, HIS BODY, TOO, MAY HAVE GUSHED BLOOD... LIKE SO MANY OTHERS HE HAD SEEN.
HE WAS A CHILD WHO REALIZED THAT THIS, TOO, COULD BE THE FATE OF HIS FATHER.

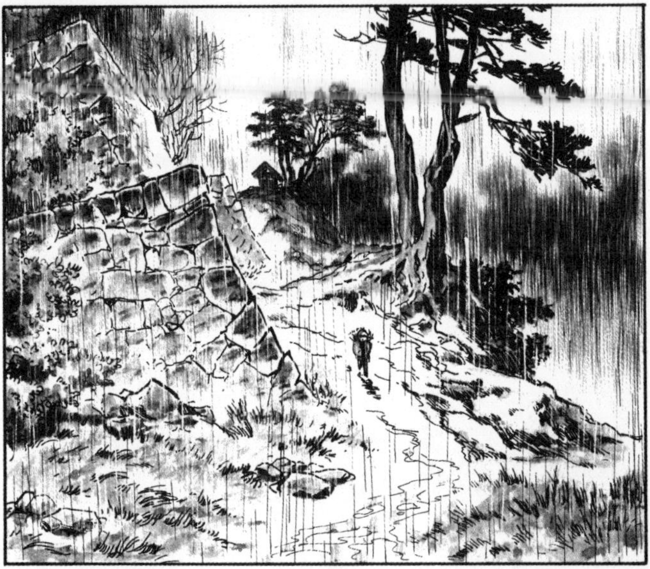
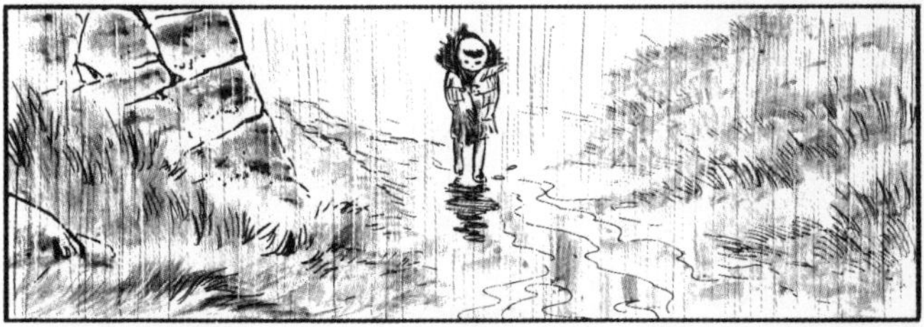
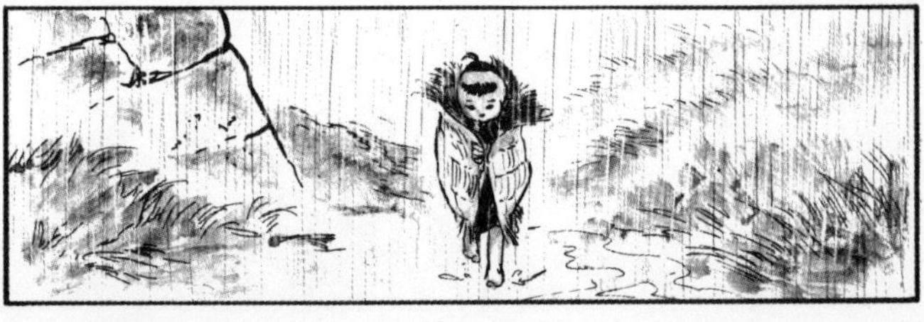

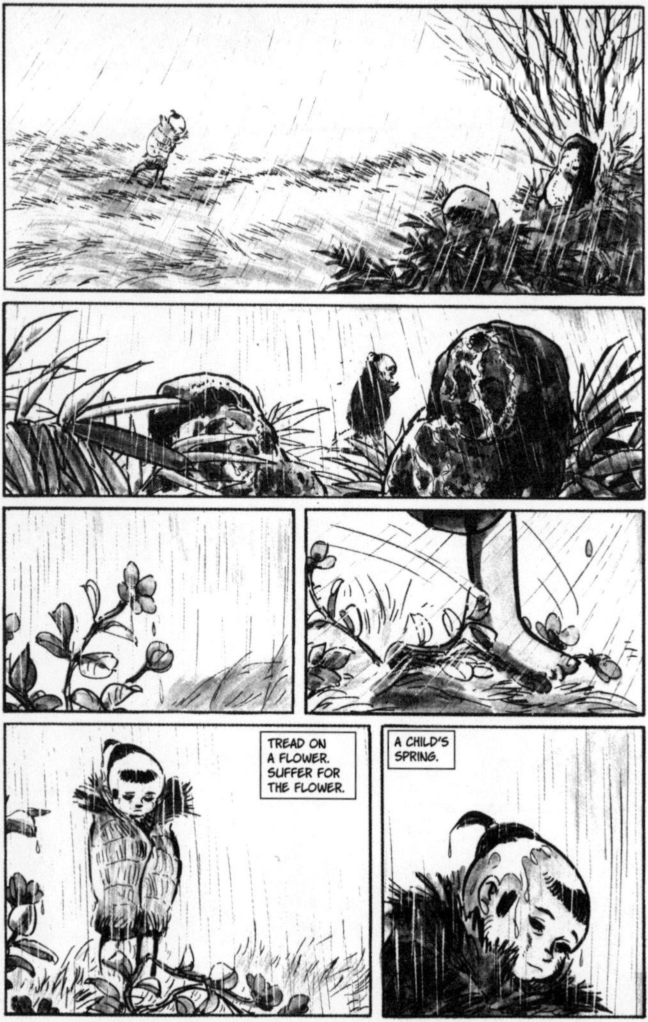
A CHILD'S SPRING.
TREAD ON A FLOWER. SUFFER FOR THE FLOWER.

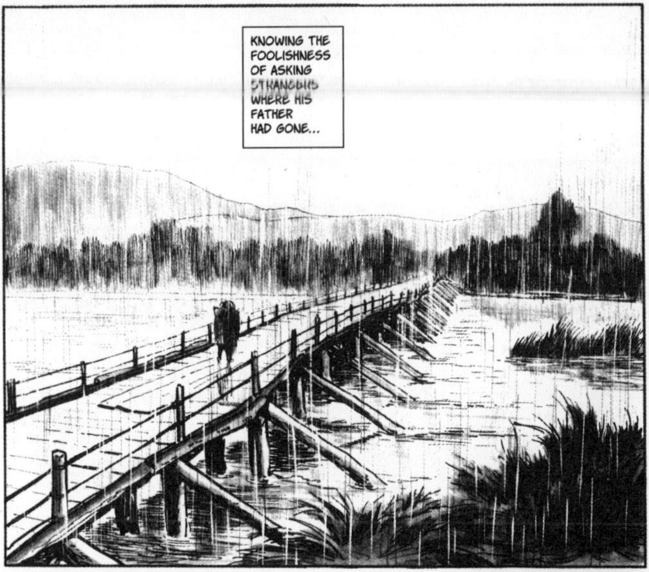
KNOWING THE FOOLISHNESS OF ASKING STRANGERS WHERE HIS FATHER HAD GONE...
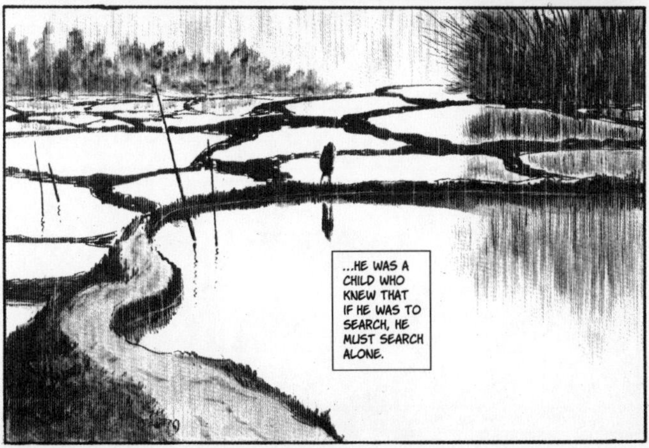
...HE WAS A CHILD WHO KNEW THAT IF HE WAS TO SEARCH, HE MUST SEARCH ALONE.

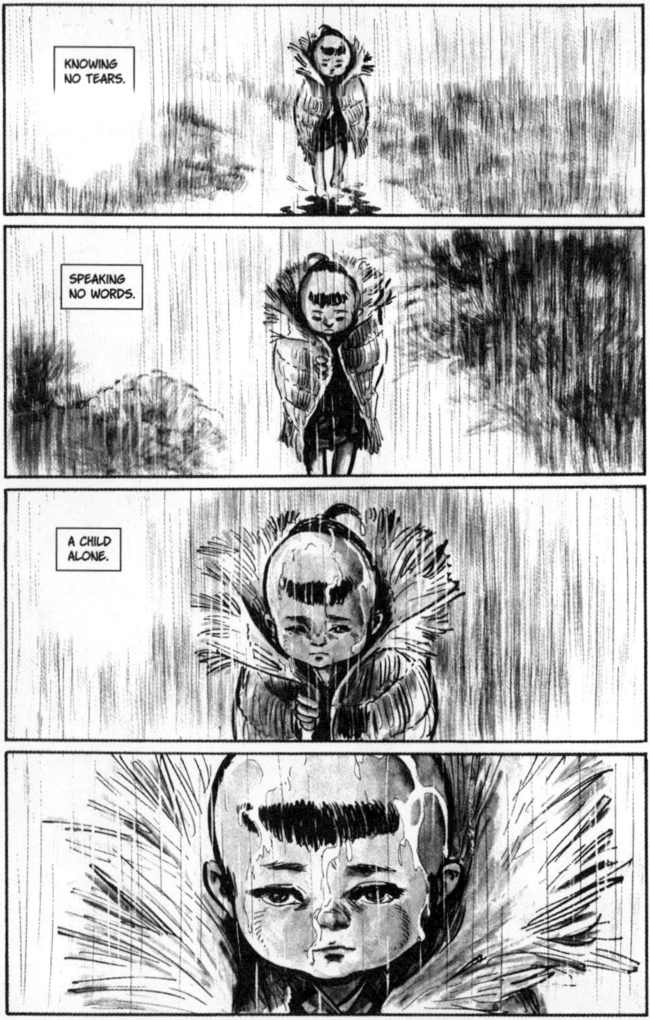
KNOWING NO TEARS.
SPEAKING NO WORDS.
A CHILD ALONE.

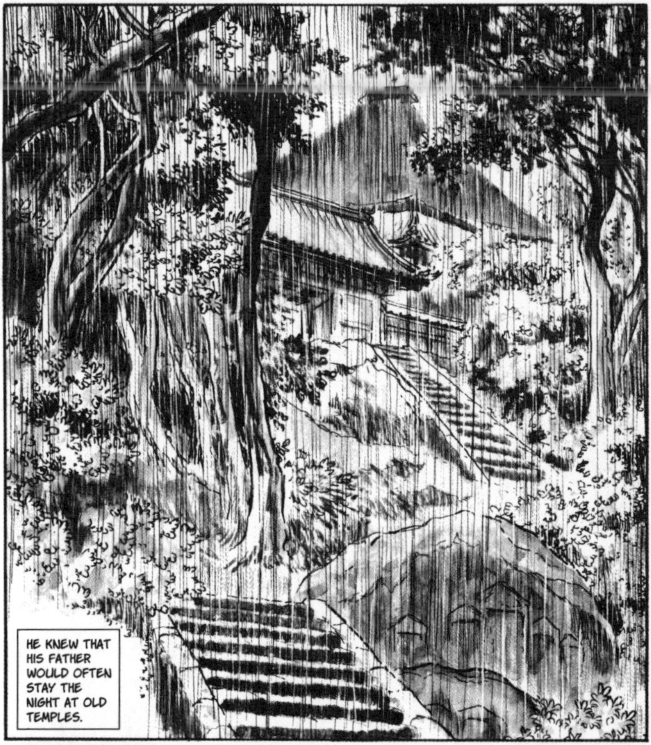
HE KNEW THAT HIS FATHER WOULD OFTEN STAY THE NIGHT AT OLD TEMPLES.
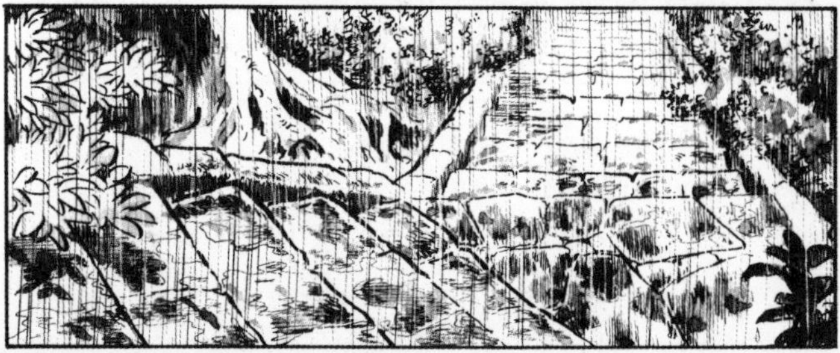

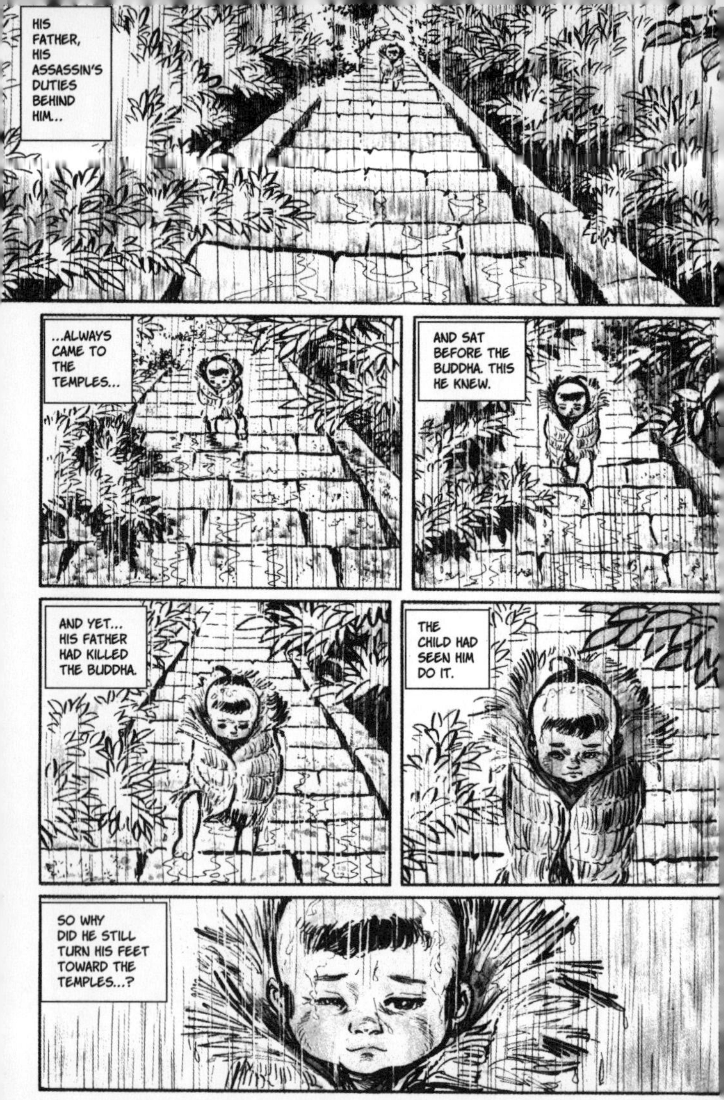
HIS FATHER, HIS ASSASSIN'S DUTIES BEHIND HIM...
...ALWAYS CAME TO THE TEMPLES...
AND SAT BEFORE THE BUDDHA. THIS HE KNEW.
AND YET... HIS FATHER HAD KILLED THE BUDDHA.
THE CHILD HAD SEEN HIM DO IT.
SO WHY DID HE STILL TURN HIS FEET TOWARD THE TEMPLES...?

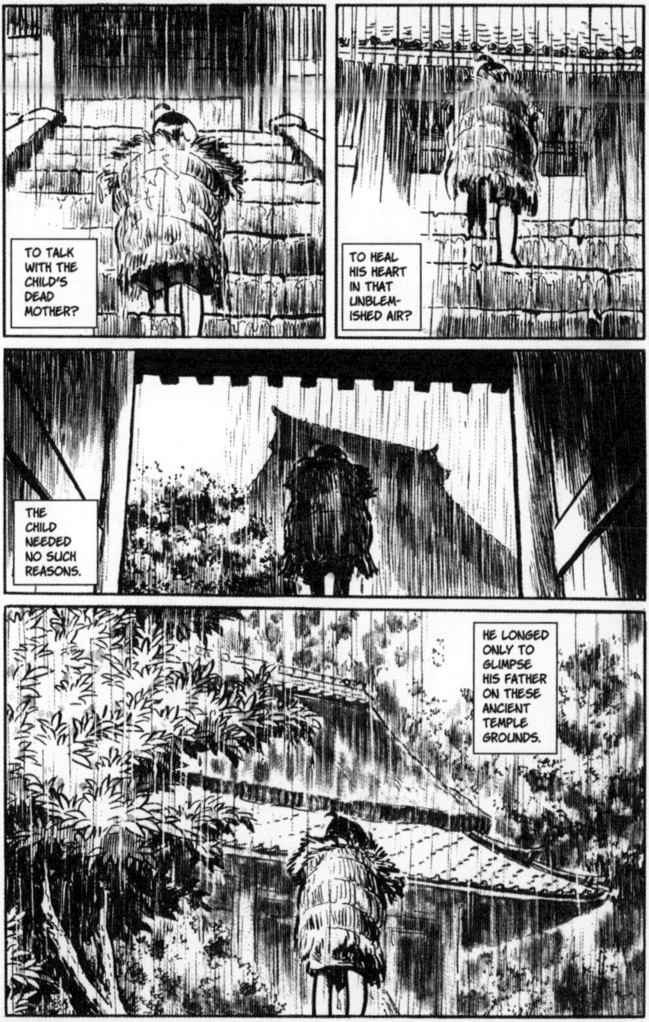
TO TALK WITH THE CHILD'S DEAD MOTHER?
TO HEAL HIS HEART IN THAT UNBLEM-ISHED AIR?
THE CHILD NEEDED NO SUCH REASONS.
HE LONGED ONLY TO GLIMPSE HIS FATHER ON THESE ANCIENT TEMPLE GROUNDS.

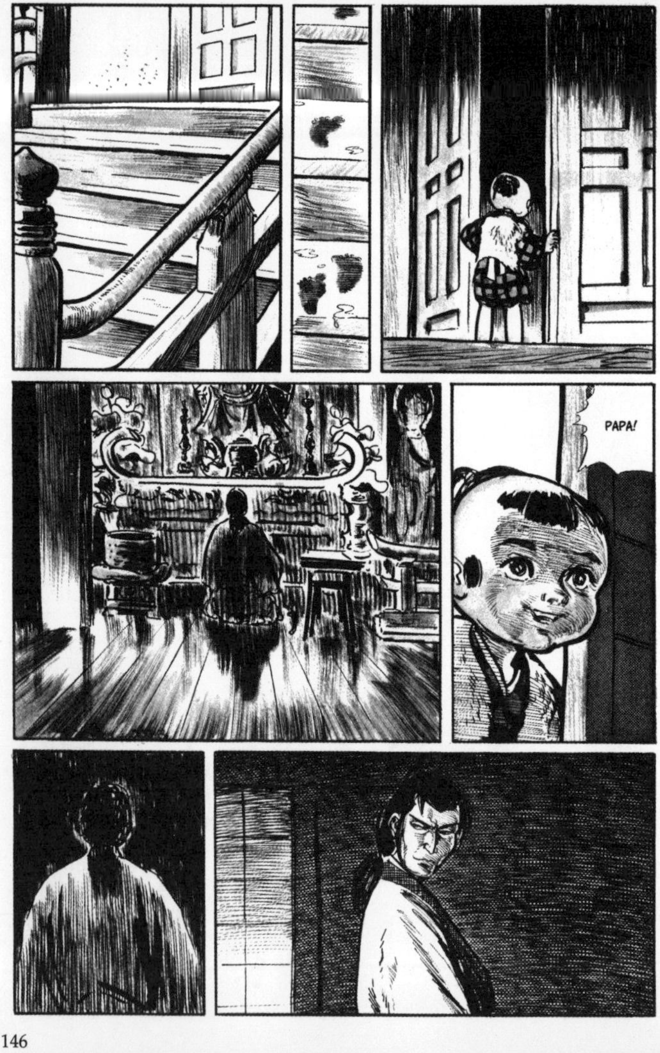
PAPA!

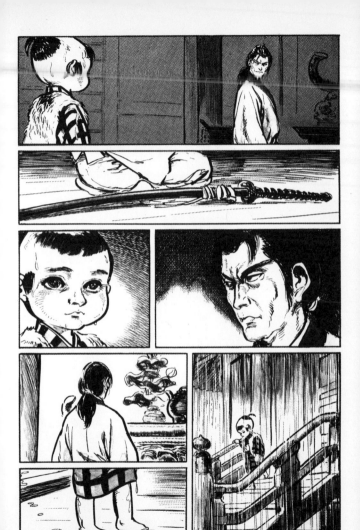

147

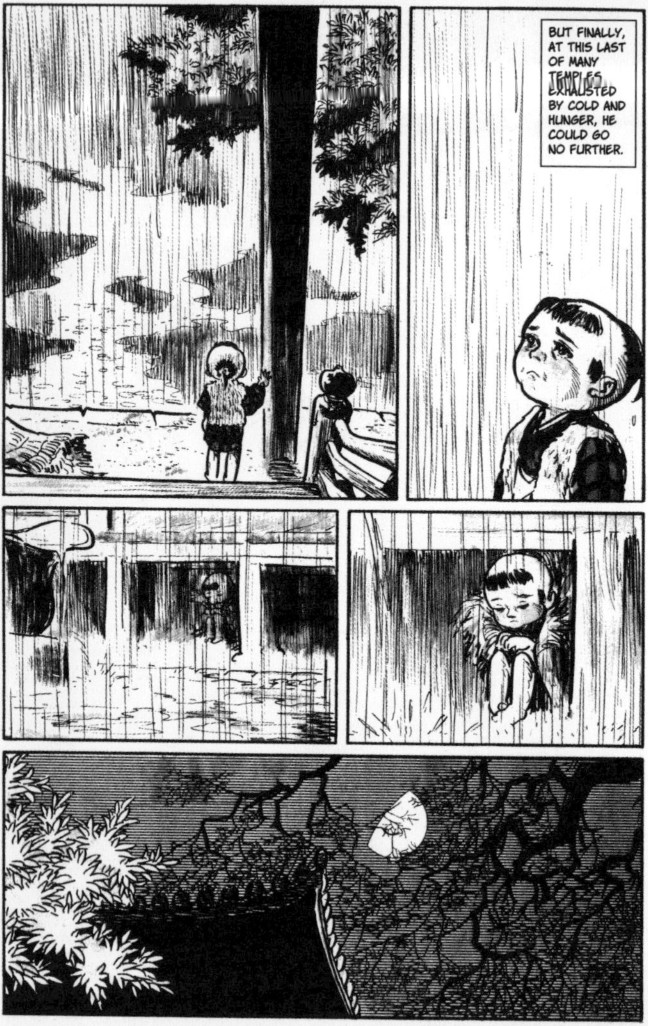
BUT FINALLY, AT THIS LAST OF MANY TEMPLES EXHAUSTED BY COLD AND HUNGER, HE COULD GO NO FURTHER.

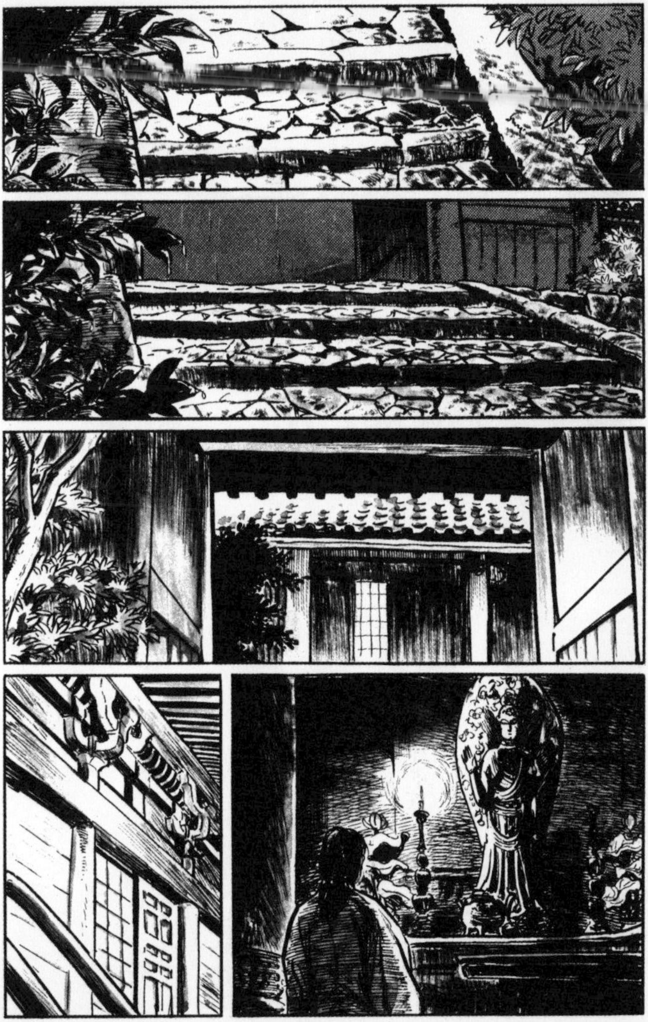

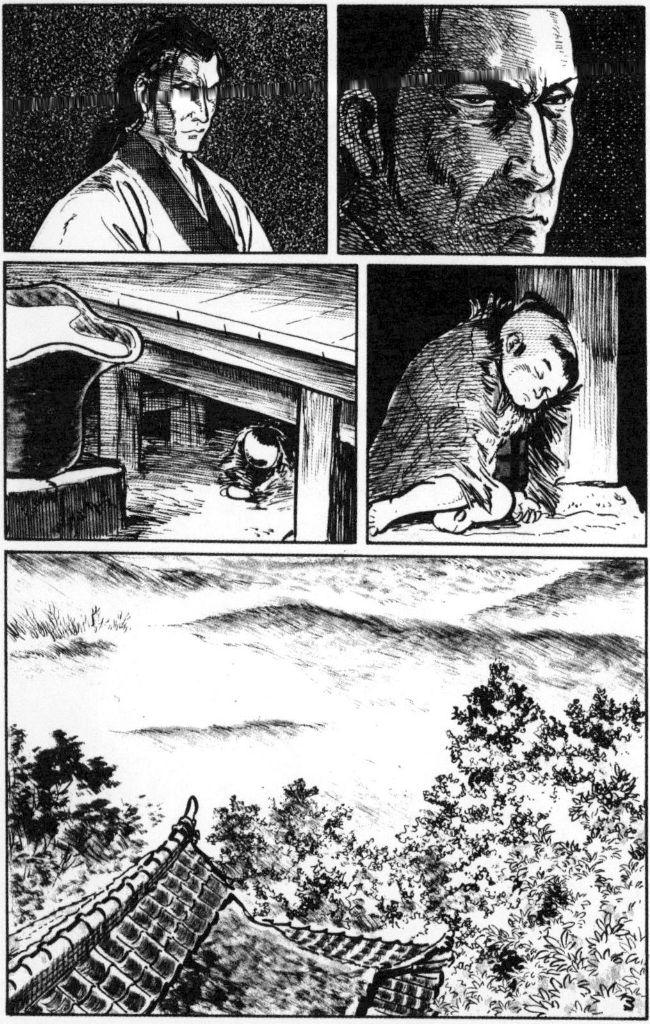

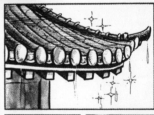

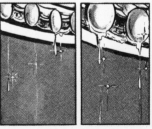

151

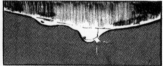

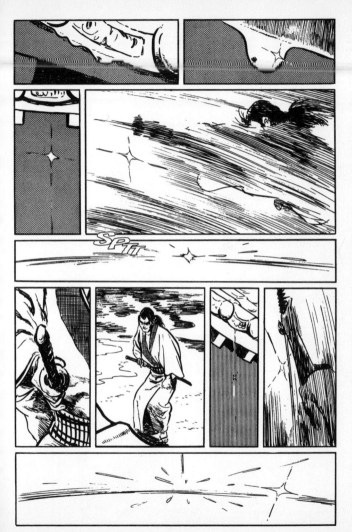

SP
tir

153

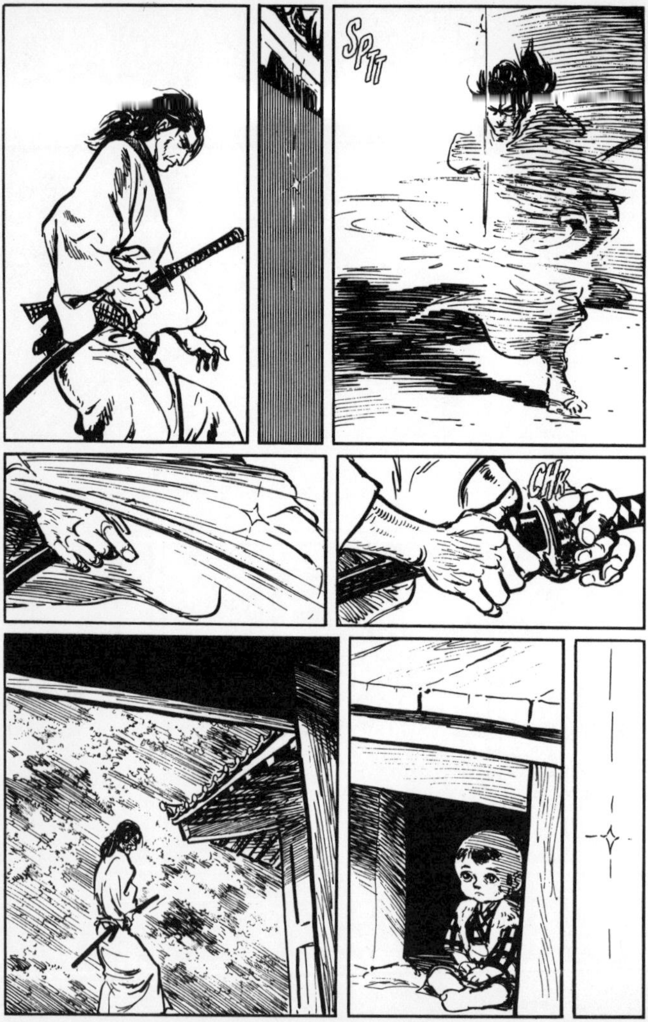
SPTT
CHK

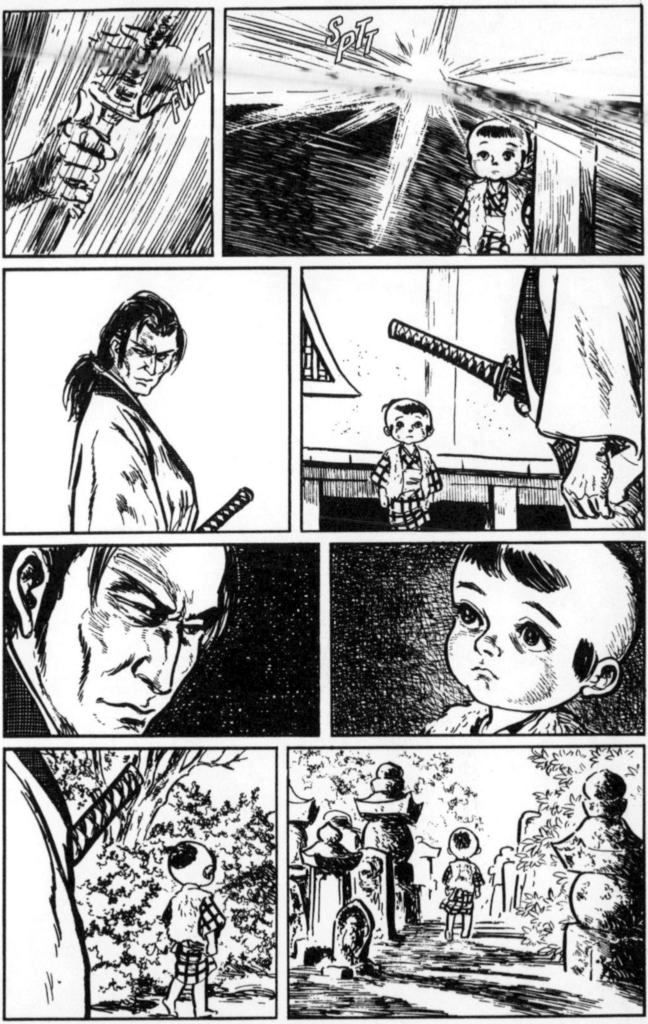
SPTT
FWIT

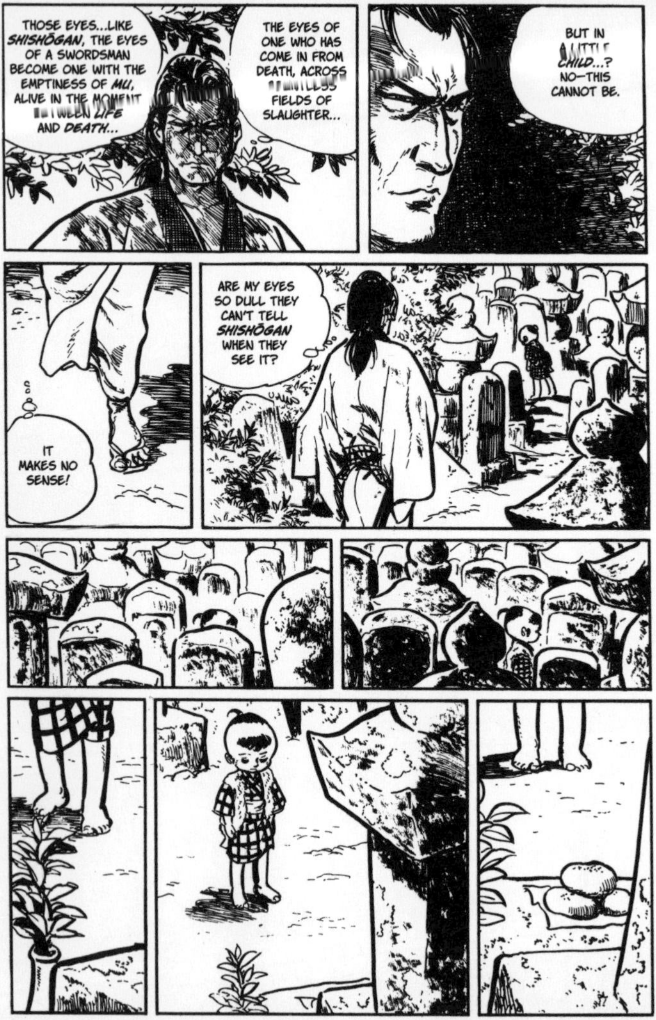
THOSE EYES...LIKE SHISHŌGAN, THE EYES OF A SWORDSMAN BECOME ONE WITH THE EMPTINESS OF MU, ALIVE IN THE MOMENT
LIFE AND DEATH...
THE EYES OF ONE WHO HAS COME IN FROM DEATH, ACROSS
FIELDS OF SLAUGHTER...
BUT IN A
CHILD...? NO—THIS CANNOT BE.
IT MAKES NO SENSE!
ARE MY EYES SO DULL THEY CAN'T TELL SHISHŌGAN WHEN THEY SEE IT?

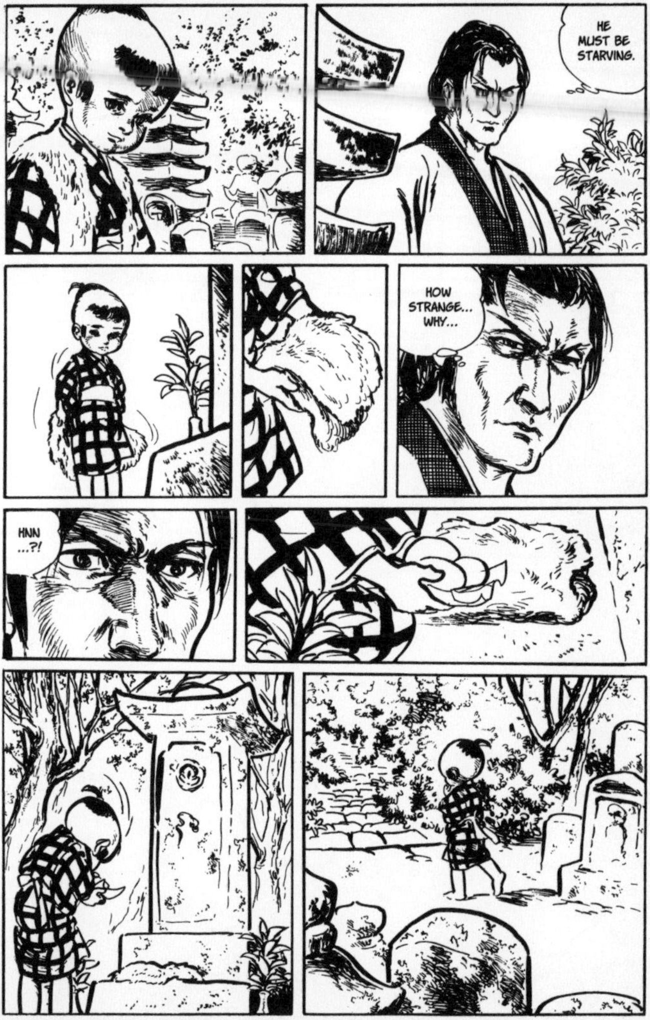
HE MUST BE STARVING.
HOW STRANGE... WHY...
HNN ...?!

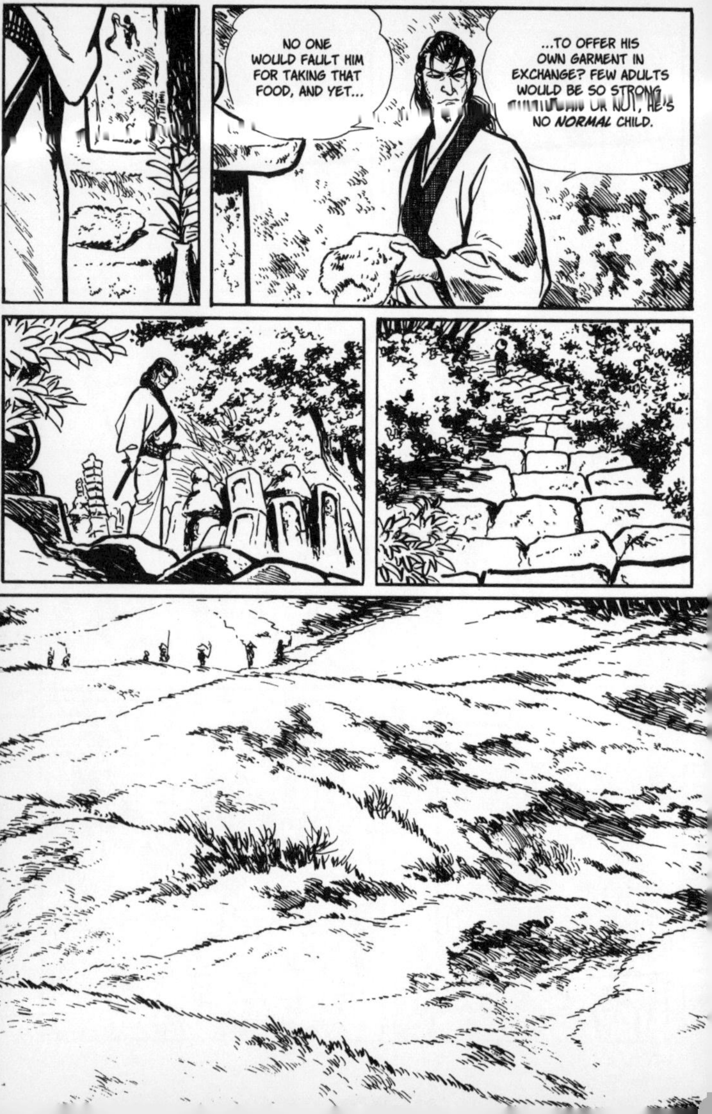
NO ONE WOULD FAULT HIM FOR TAKING THAT FOOD, AND YET...
...TO OFFER HIS OWN GARMENT IN EXCHANGE? FEW ADULTS WOULD BE SO STRONG
OR NOT, HE'S NO NORMAL CHILD.

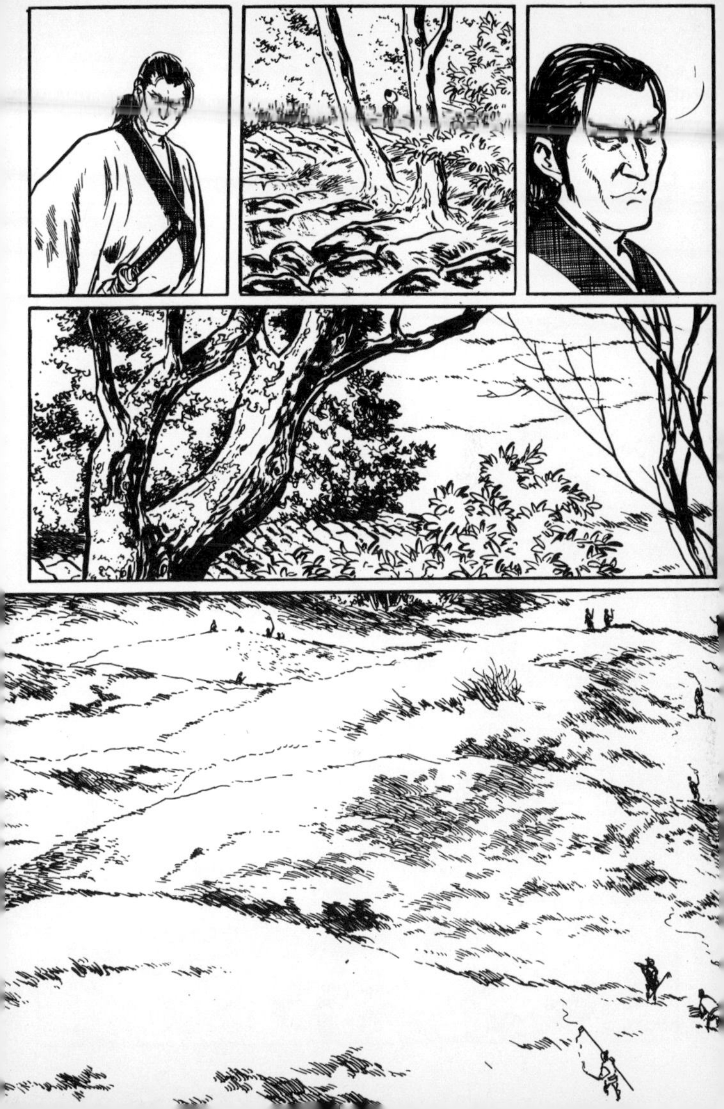

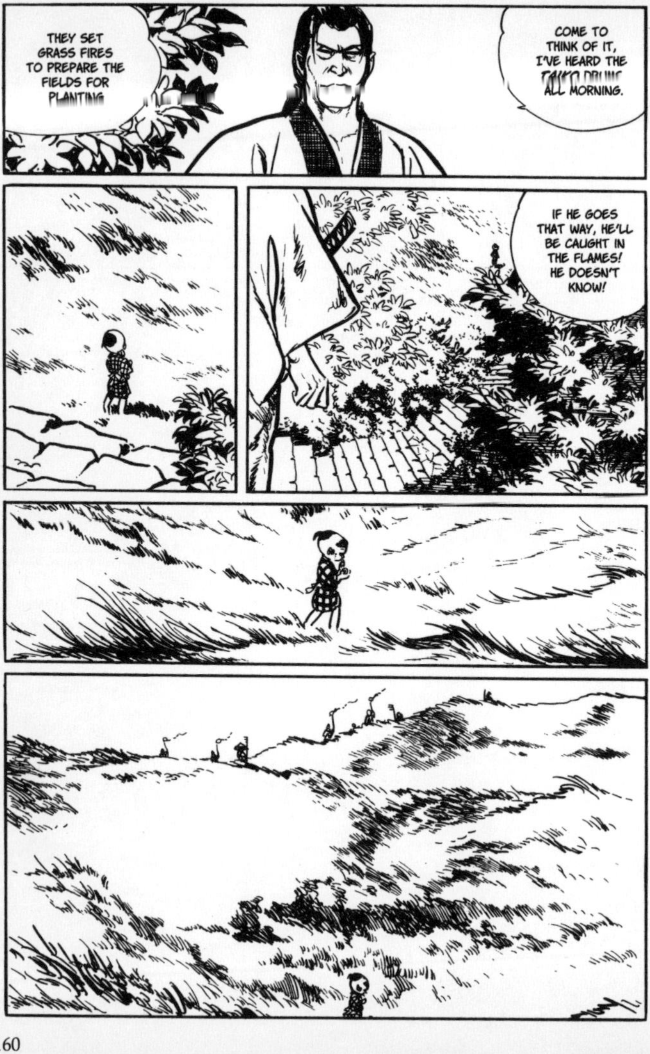
COME TO THINK OF IT, I'VE HEARD THE TAIKO DRUMS ALL MORNING.
THEY SET GRASS FIRES TO PREPARE THE FIELDS FOR PLANTING
IF HE GOES THAT WAY, HE'LL BE CAUGHT IN THE FLAMES! HE DOESN'T KNOW!

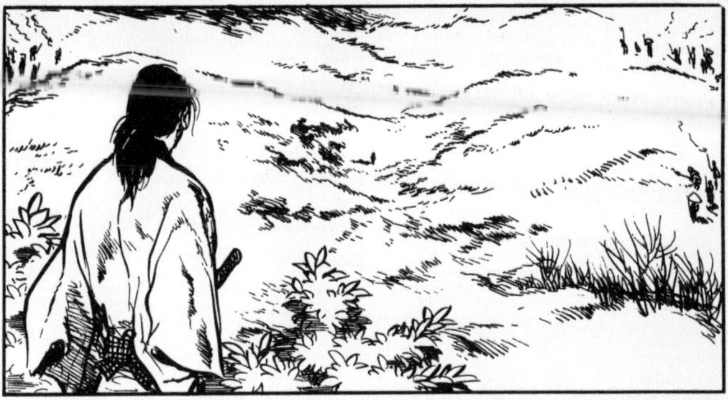
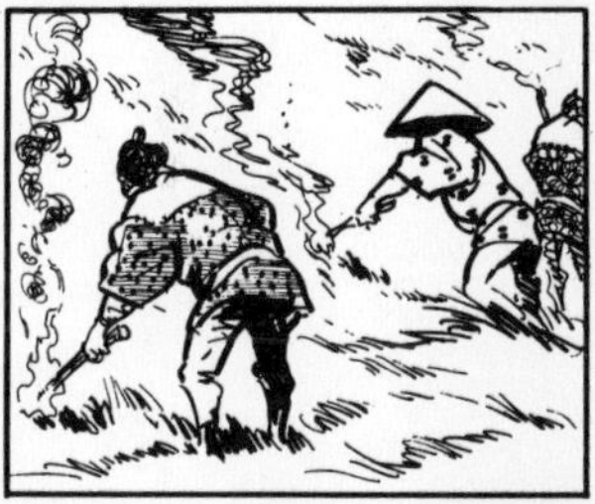
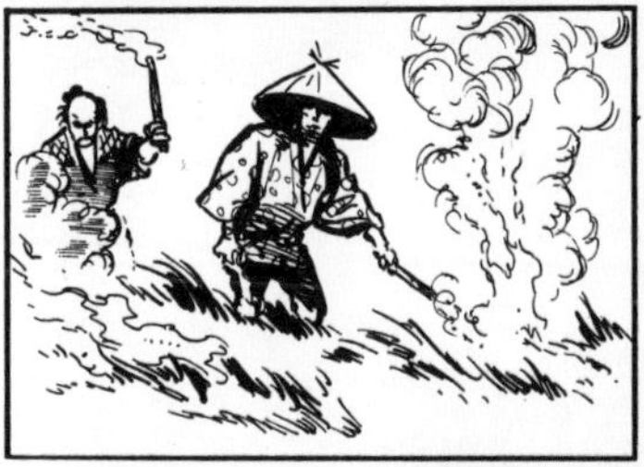
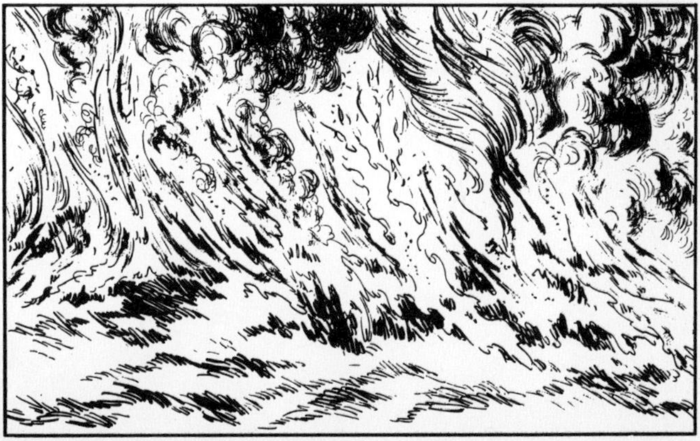

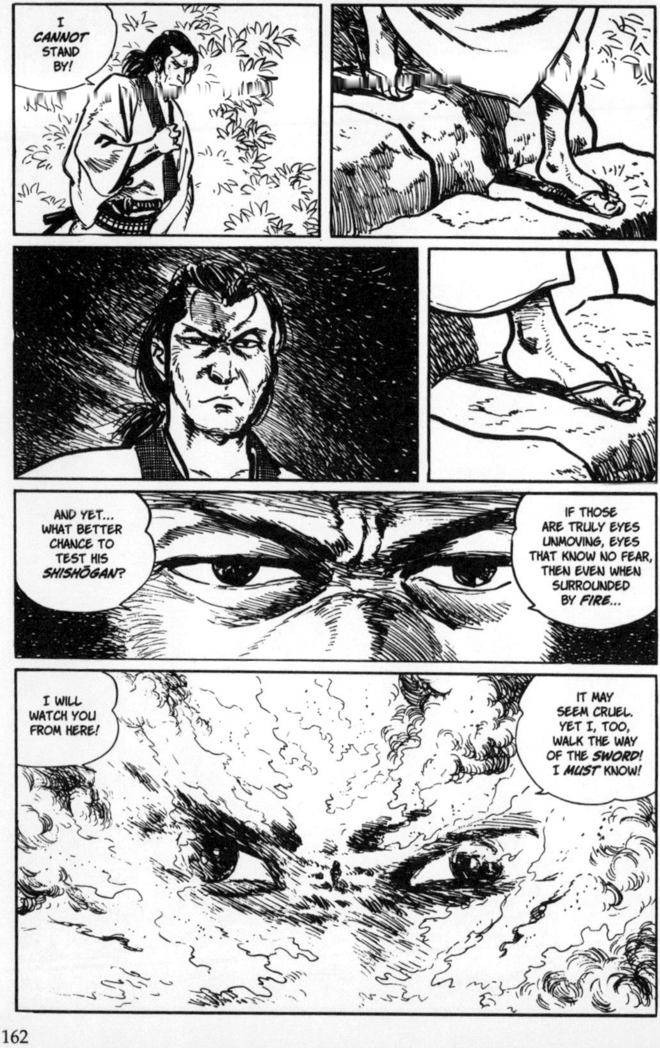
I *CANNOT* STAND BY!
AND YET... WHAT BETTER CHANCE TO TEST HIS *SHISHŌGAN*?
IF THOSE ARE TRULY EYES UNMOVING, EYES THAT KNOW NO FEAR, THEN EVEN WHEN SURROUNDED BY *FIRE*...
I WILL WATCH YOU FROM HERE!
IT MAY SEEM CRUEL. YET I, TOO, WALK THE WAY OF THE *SWORD*! I *MUST* KNOW!

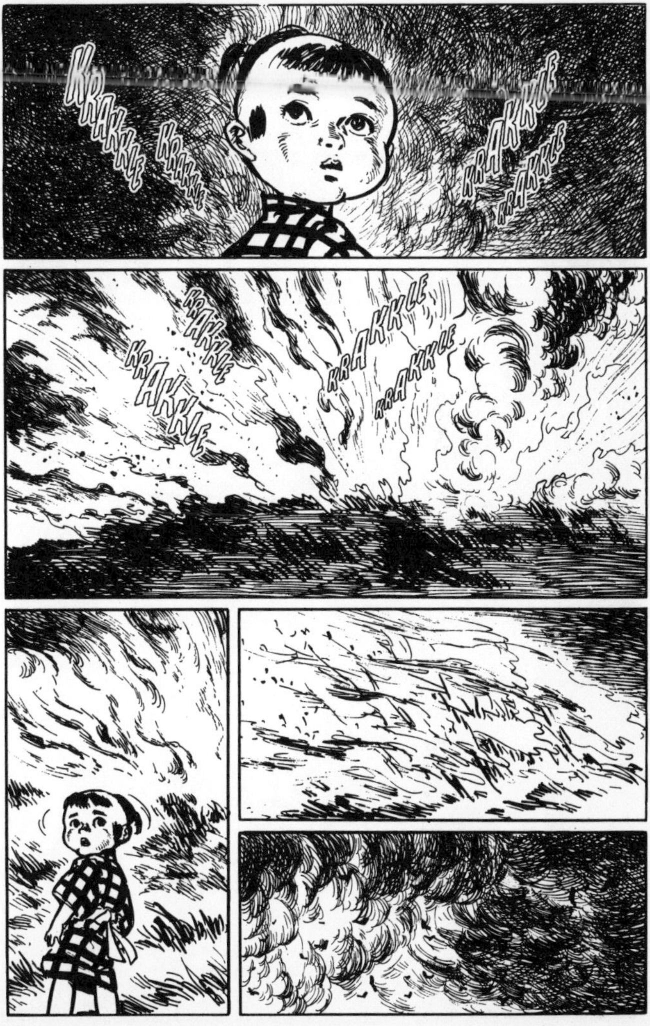
KRAKKLE
KRAKKLE
KRAKKLE
KRAKKLE
KRAKKLE
KRAKKLE
KRAKKLE
KRAKKLE

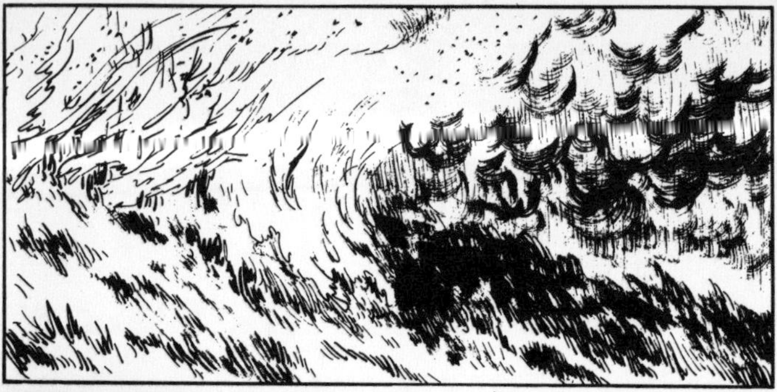
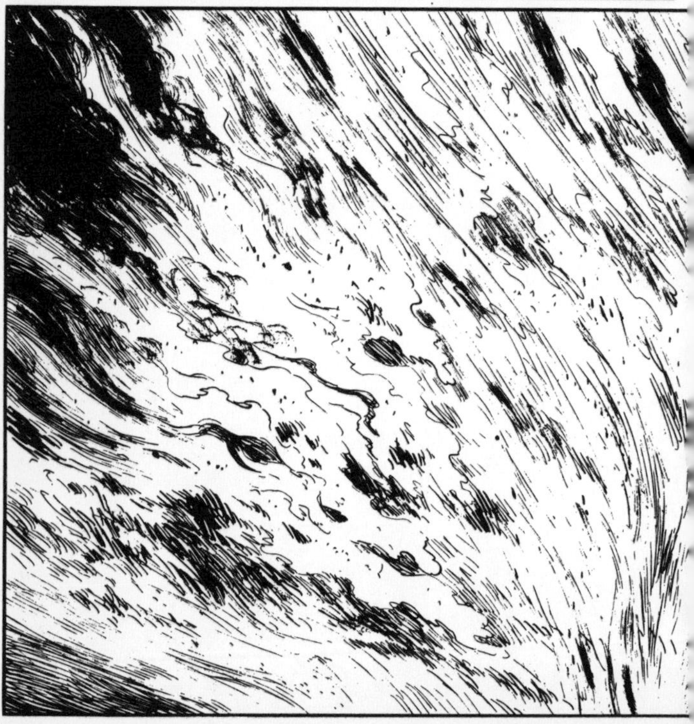

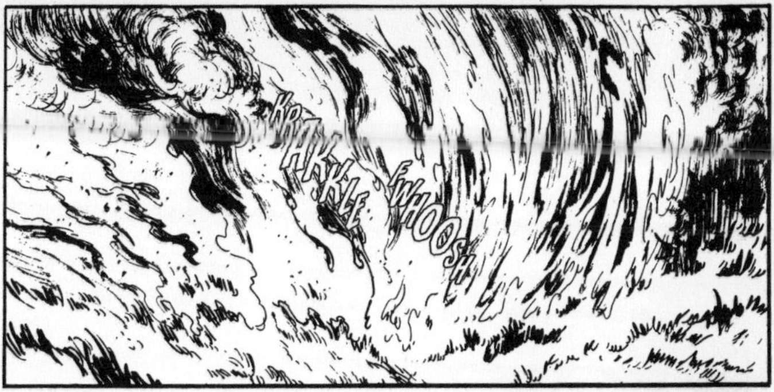
FWHOOSH
KRAKKLE

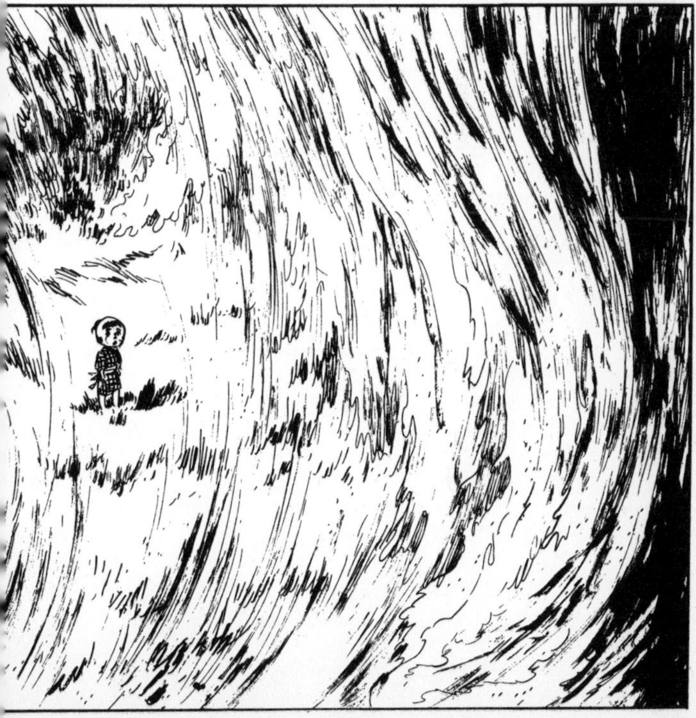

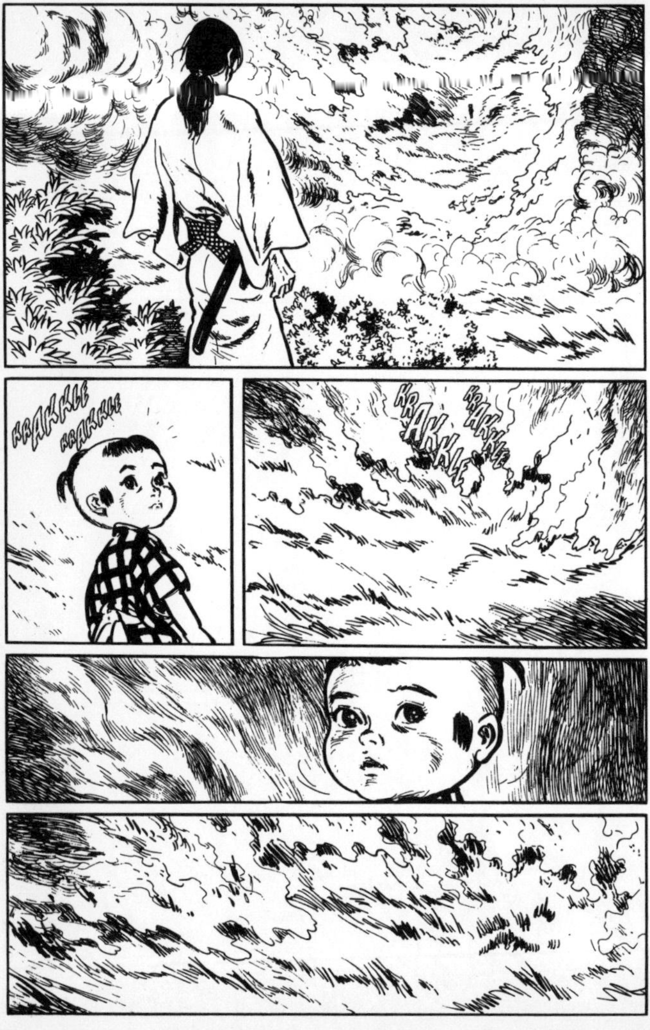
KRAKKLE
KRAKKLE
KRAKKLE
KRAKKLE

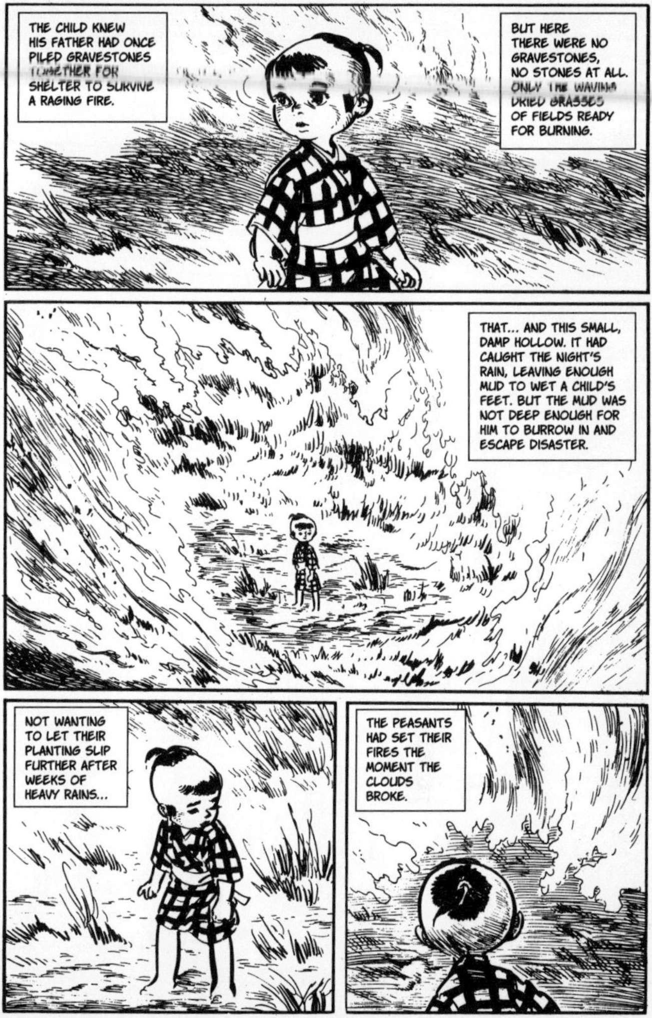
THE CHILD KNEW HIS FATHER HAD ONCE PILED GRAVESTONES TOGETHER FOR SHELTER TO SURVIVE A RAGING FIRE.
BUT HERE THERE WERE NO GRAVESTONES, NO STONES AT ALL. ONLY THE WAVING DRIED GRASSES OF FIELDS READY FOR BURNING.
THAT... AND THIS SMALL, DAMP HOLLOW. IT HAD CAUGHT THE NIGHT'S RAIN, LEAVING ENOUGH MUD TO WET A CHILD'S FEET. BUT THE MUD WAS NOT DEEP ENOUGH FOR HIM TO BURROW IN AND ESCAPE DISASTER.
NOT WANTING TO LET THEIR PLANTING SLIP FURTHER AFTER WEEKS OF HEAVY RAINS...
THE PEASANTS HAD SET THEIR FIRES THE MOMENT THE CLOUDS BROKE.

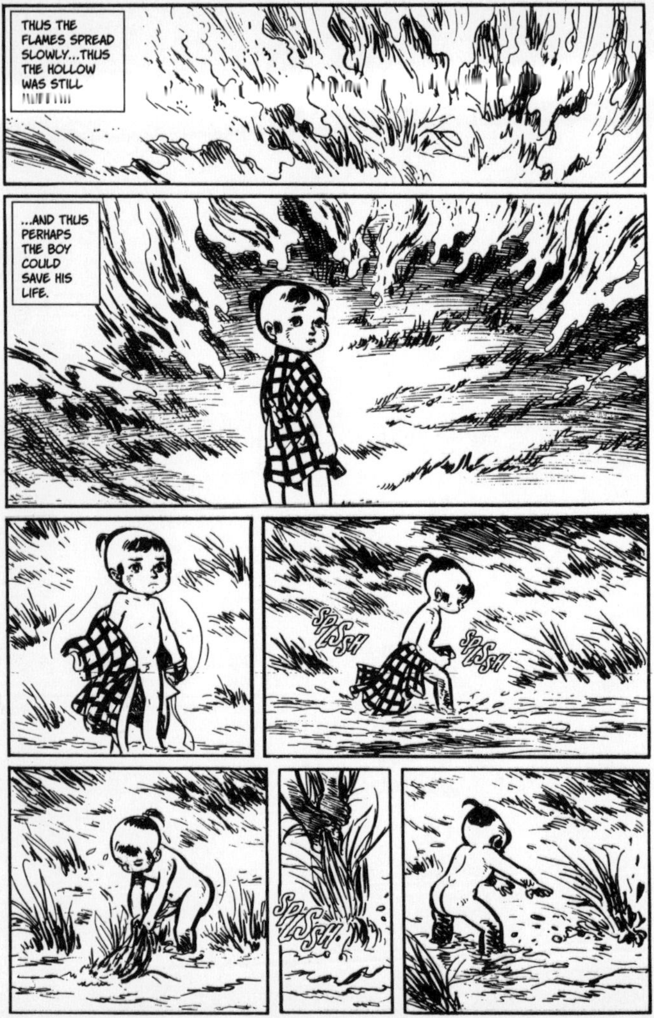
THUS THE FLAMES SPREAD SLOWLY...THUS THE HOLLOW WAS STILL
...AND THUS PERHAPS THE BOY COULD SAVE HIS LIFE.
SPLSSH
SPLSSH
SPLSSH!

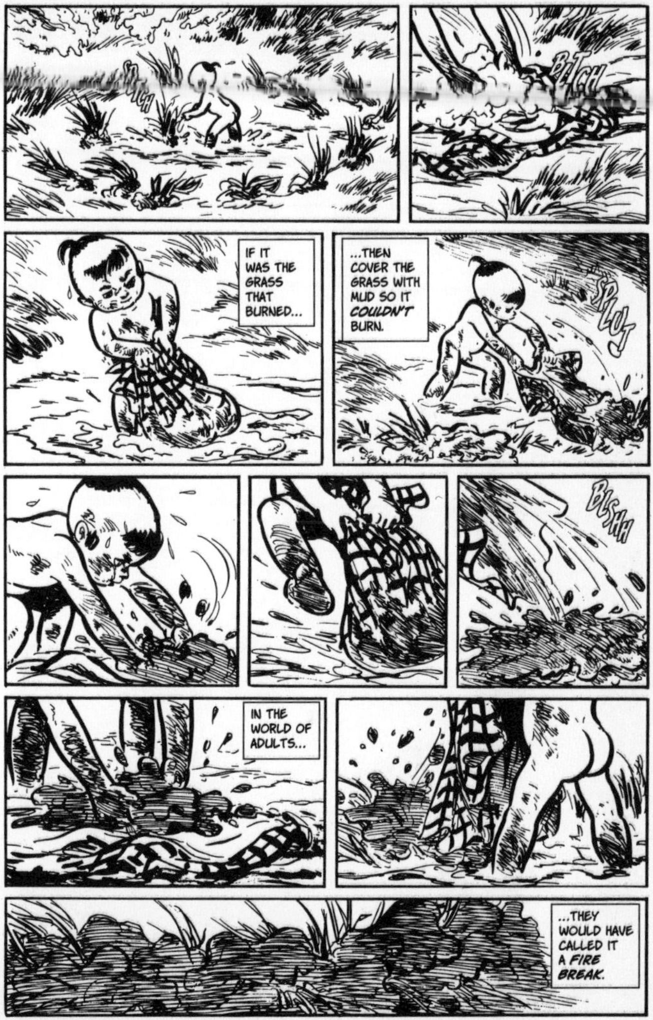
BLTCH
IF IT WAS THE GRASS THAT BURNED...
...THEN COVER THE GRASS WITH MUD SO IT *COULDN'T* BURN.
SPLUT
BLSHH
IN THE WORLD OF ADULTS...
...THEY WOULD HAVE CALLED IT A *FIRE BREAK.*

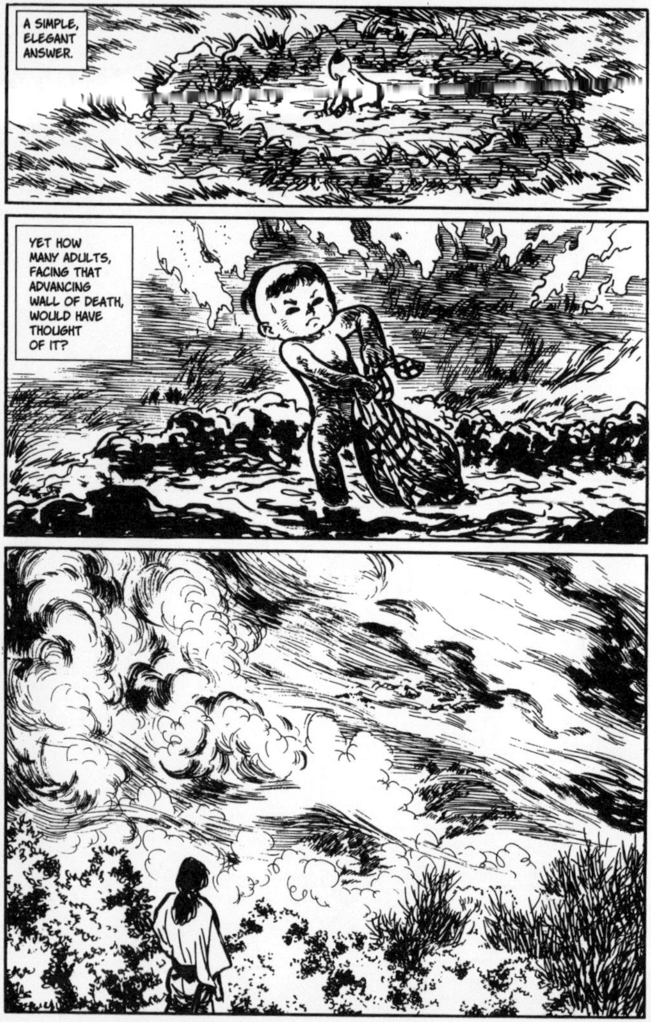
A SIMPLE, ELEGANT ANSWER.
YET HOW MANY ADULTS, FACING THAT ADVANCING WALL OF DEATH, WOULD HAVE THOUGHT OF IT?

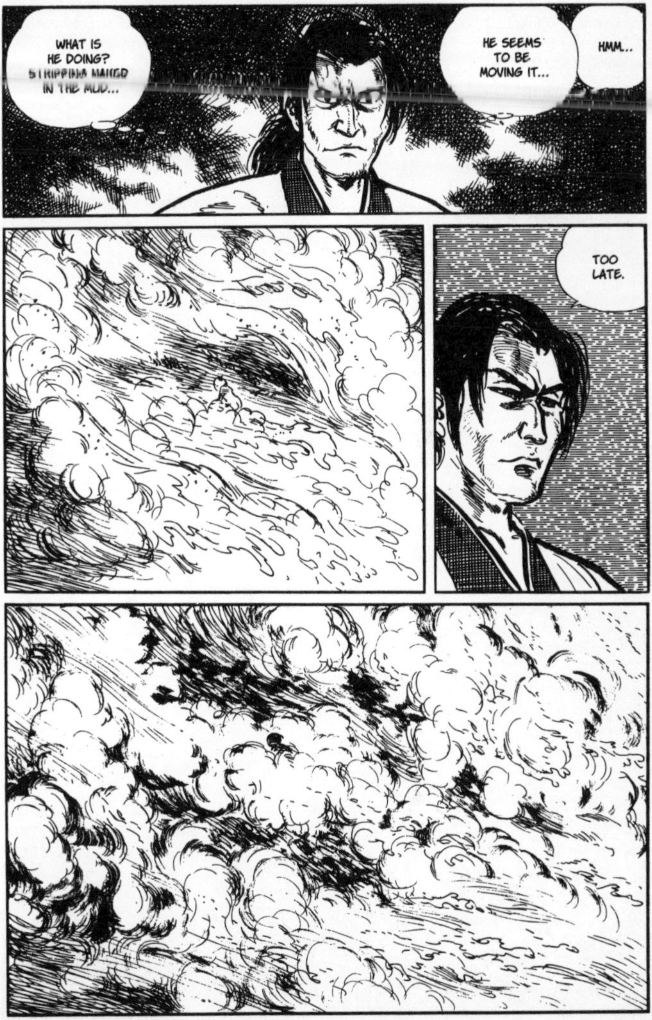
WHAT IS HE DOING? STRIPPING NAKED IN THE MUD...
HE SEEMS TO BE MOVING IT...
HMM...
TOO LATE.

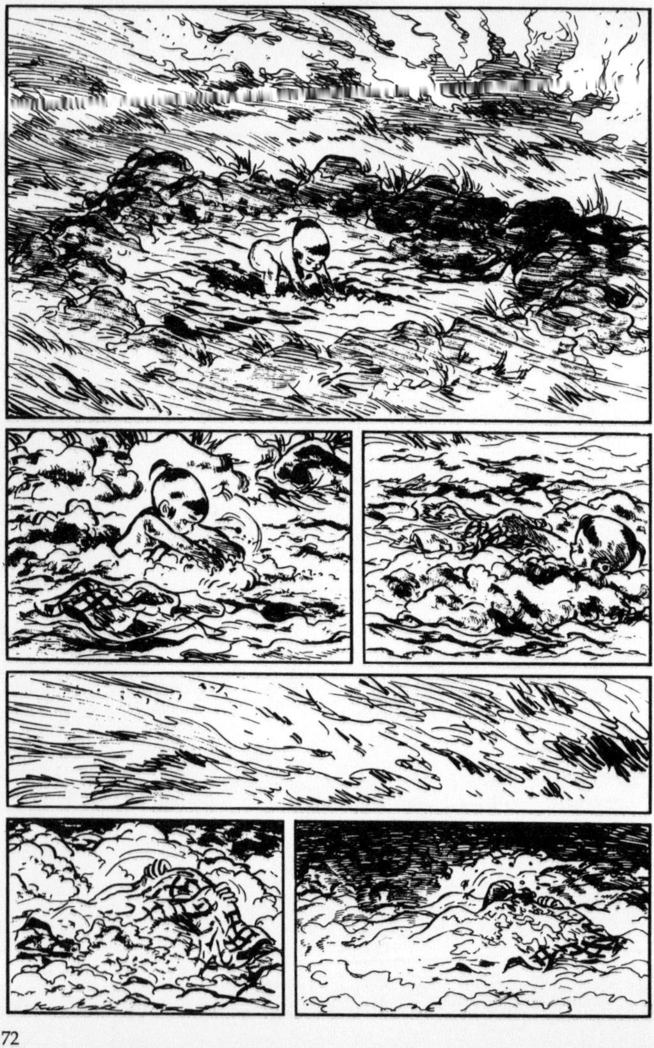

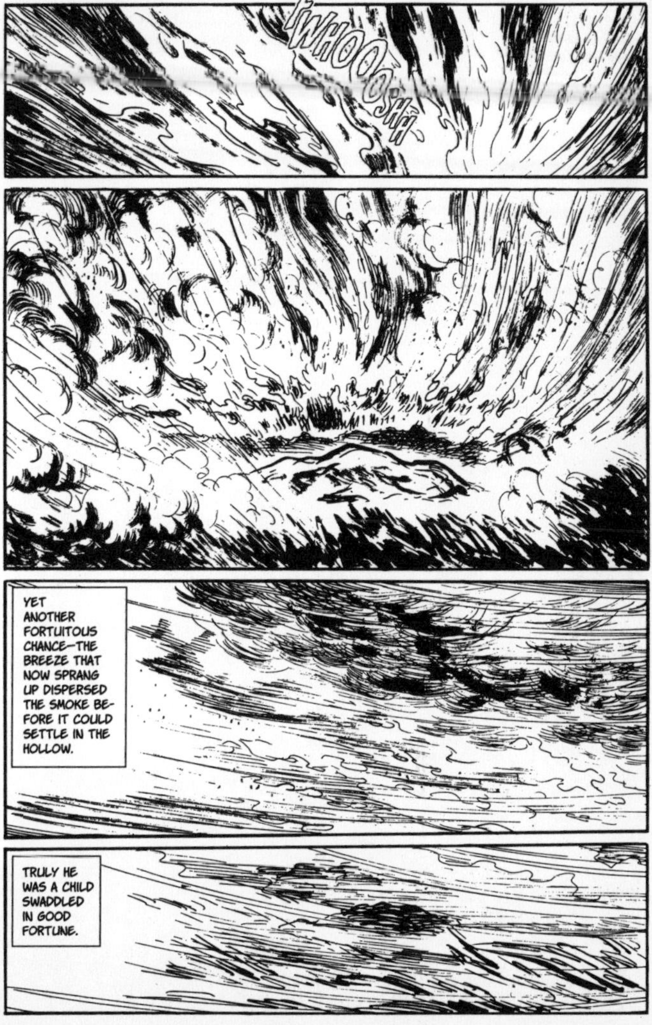
FWHOOOSHH
YET ANOTHER FORTUITOUS CHANCE—THE BREEZE THAT NOW SPRANG UP DISPERSED THE SMOKE BE- FORE IT COULD SETTLE IN THE HOLLOW.
TRULY HE WAS A CHILD SWADDLED IN GOOD FORTUNE.

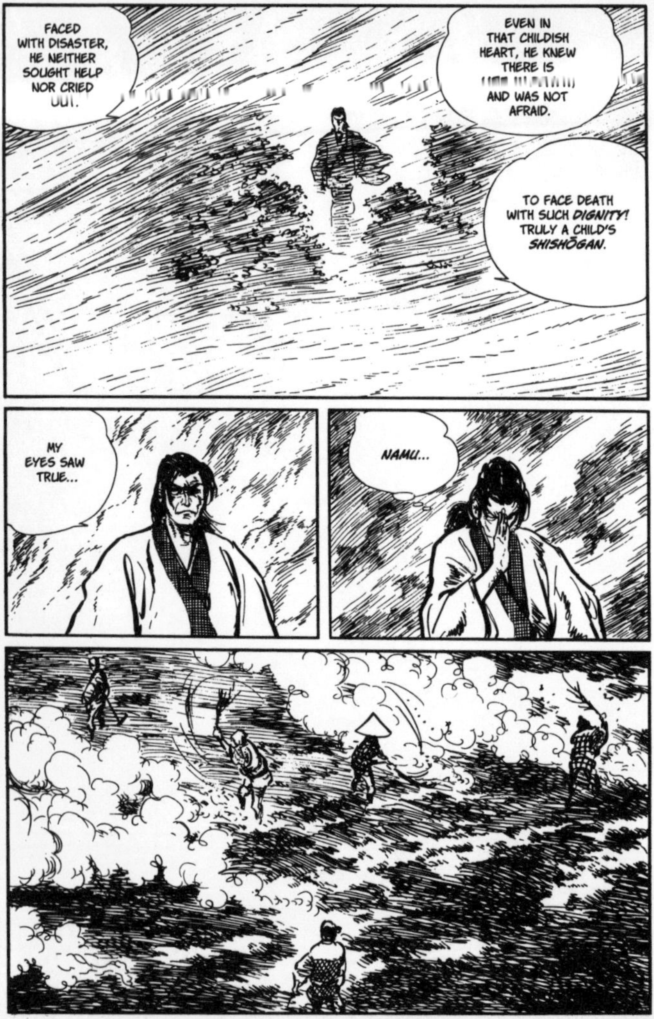
FACED WITH DISASTER, HE NEITHER SOUGHT HELP NOR CRIED
EVEN IN THAT CHILDISH HEART, HE KNEW THERE IS
AND WAS NOT AFRAID.
TO FACE DEATH WITH SUCH *DIGNITY*! TRULY A CHILD'S *SHISHŌGAN*.
MY EYES SAW TRUE...
*NAMU...*

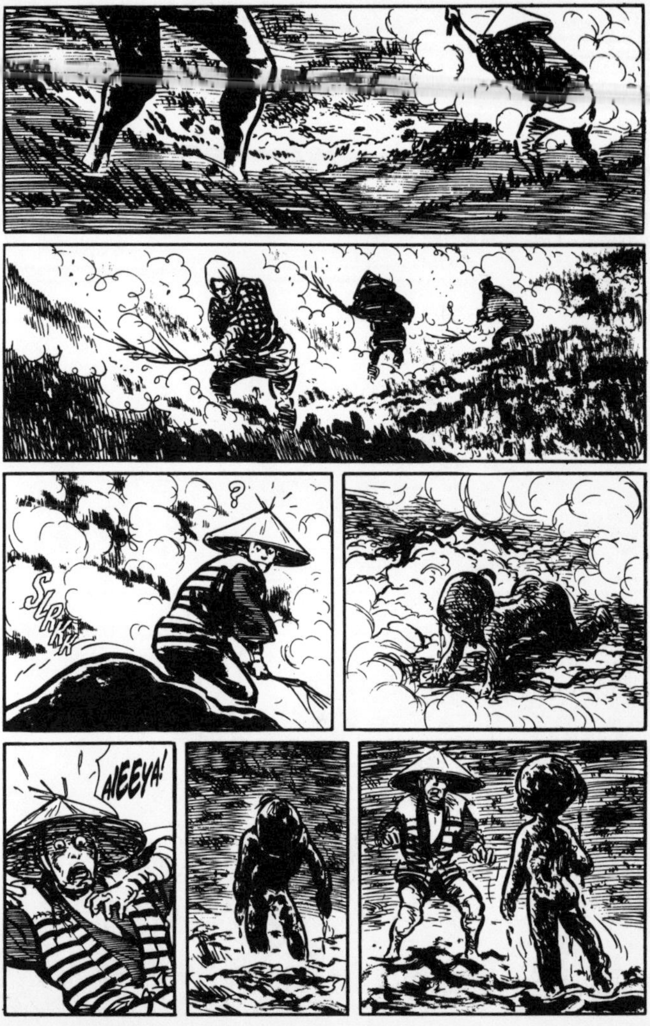
?
SLRKK
AIEEYA!

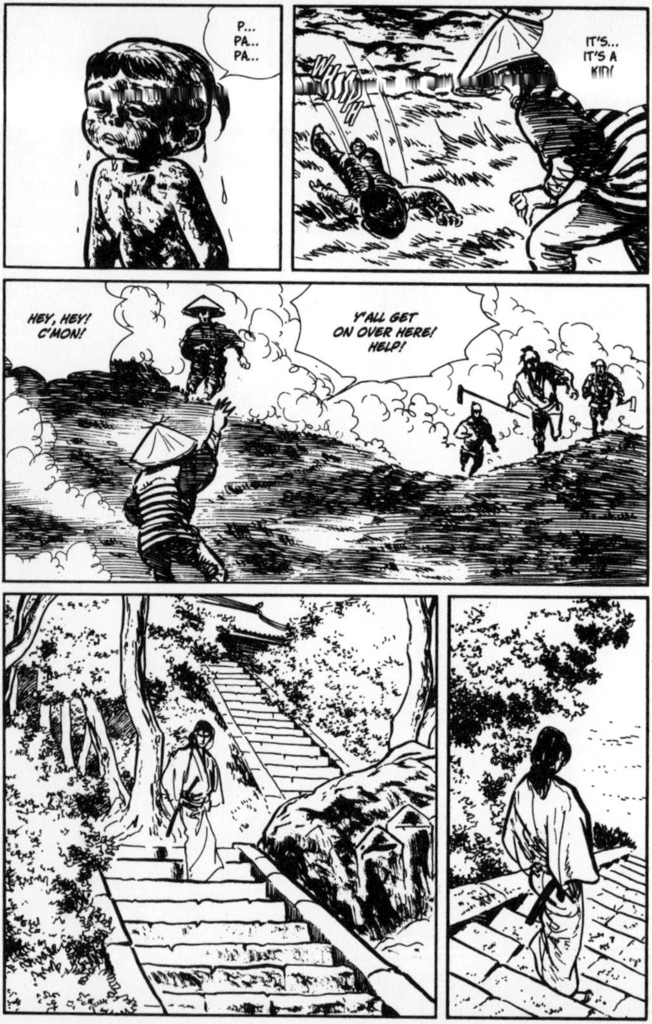
P... PA... PA...
IT'S... IT'S A KID!
HEY, HEY! C'MON!
Y'ALL GET ON OVER HERE! HELP!

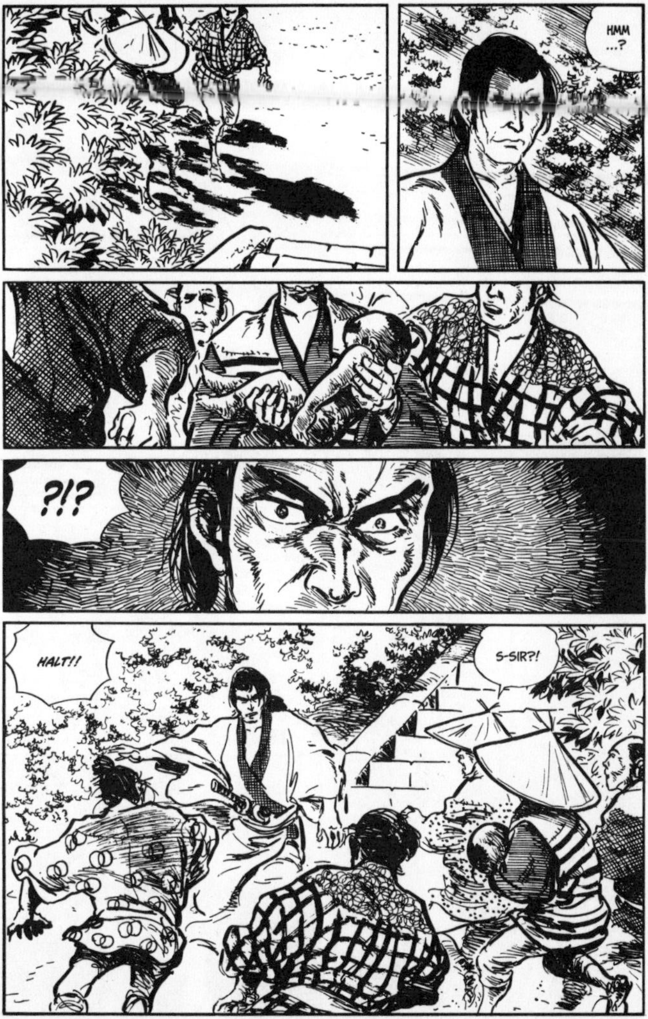
HMM ...?
?!?
HALT!!
S-SIR?!

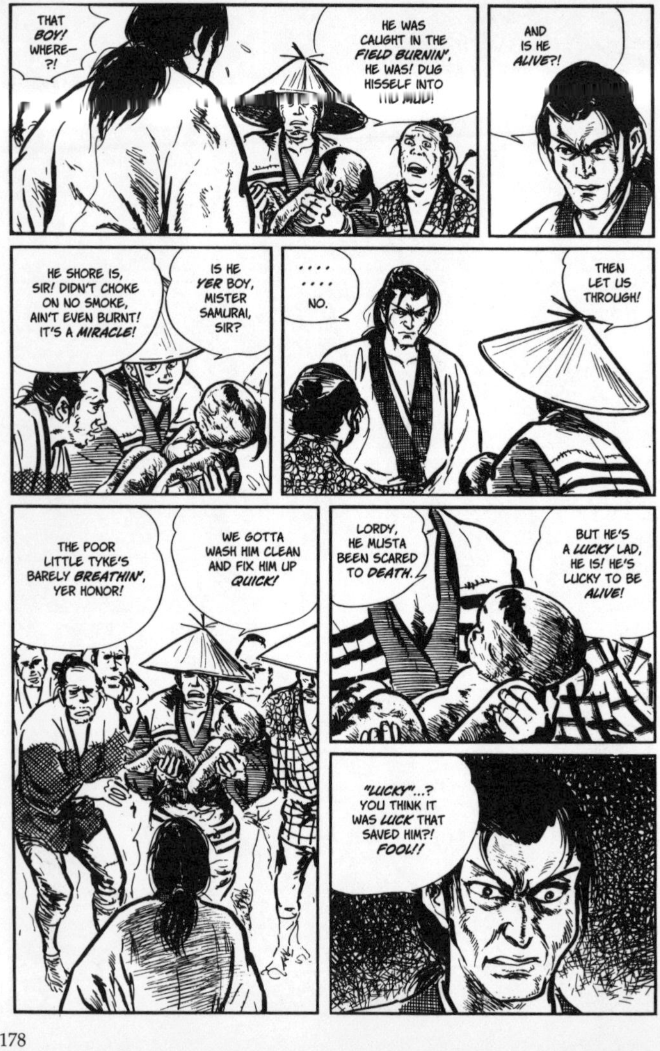
THAT BOY! WHERE—?!
HE WAS CAUGHT IN THE FIELD BURNIN', HE WAS! DUG HISSELF INTO THE MUD!
AND IS HE ALIVE?!
HE SHORE IS, SIR! DIDN'T CHOKE ON NO SMOKE, AIN'T EVEN BURNT! IT'S A MIRACLE!
IS HE YER BOY, MISTER SAMURAI, SIR?
.... .... NO.
THEN LET US THROUGH!
THE POOR LITTLE TYKE'S BARELY BREATHIN', YER HONOR!
WE GOTTA WASH HIM CLEAN AND FIX HIM UP QUICK!
LORDY, HE MUSTA BEEN SCARED TO DEATH.
BUT HE'S A LUCKY LAD, HE IS! HE'S LUCKY TO BE ALIVE!
"LUCKY"...? YOU THINK IT WAS LUCK THAT SAVED HIM?! FOOL!!

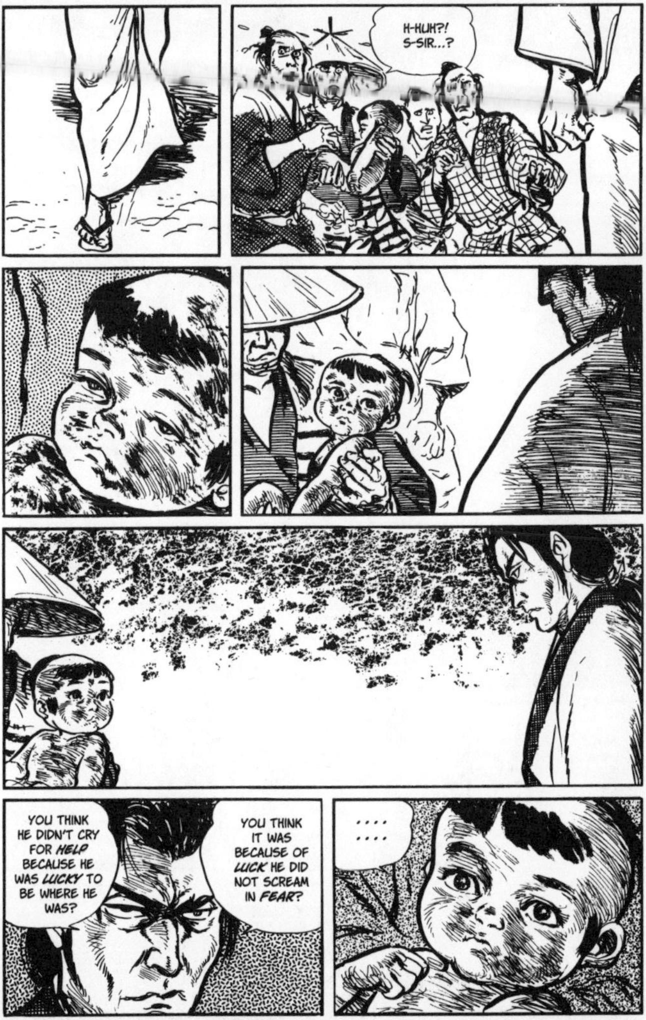
H-HUH?! S-SIR...?
YOU THINK HE DIDN'T CRY FOR HELP BECAUSE HE WAS LUCKY TO BE WHERE HE WAS?
YOU THINK IT WAS BECAUSE OF LUCK HE DID NOT SCREAM IN FEAR?
....
....

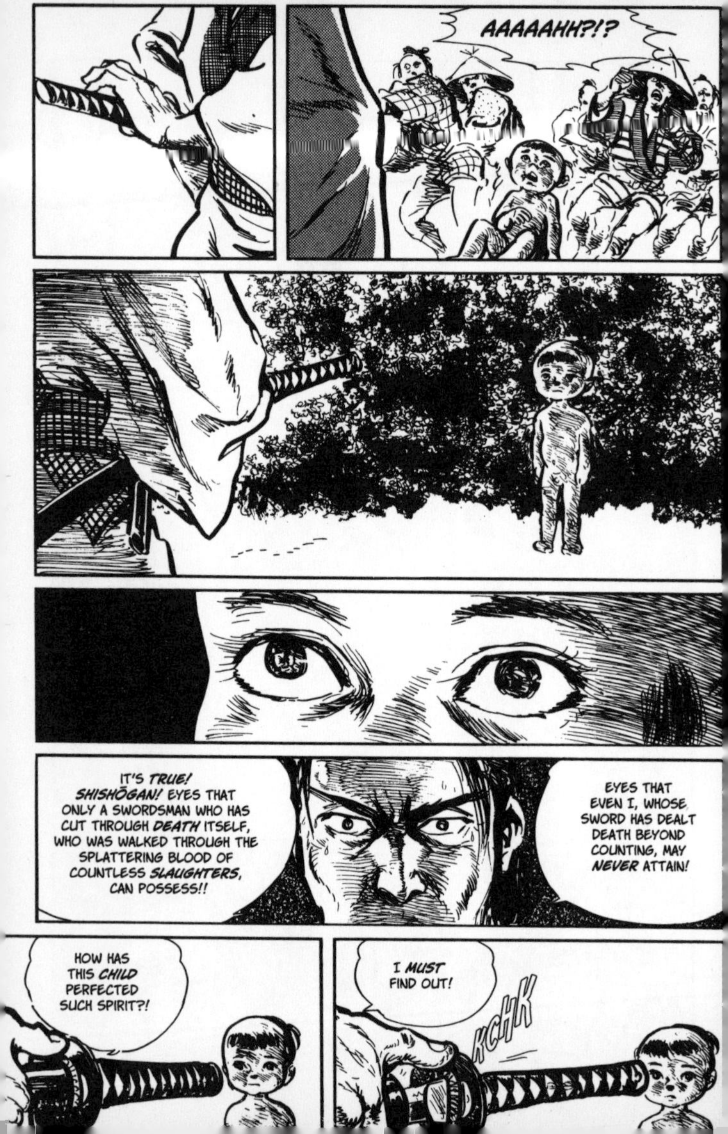
AAAAAHH?!?
IT'S TRUE! SHISHŌGAN! EYES THAT ONLY A SWORDSMAN WHO HAS CUT THROUGH DEATH ITSELF, WHO WAS WALKED THROUGH THE SPLATTERING BLOOD OF COUNTLESS SLAUGHTERS, CAN POSSESS!!
EYES THAT EVEN I, WHOSE SWORD HAS DEALT DEATH BEYOND COUNTING, MAY NEVER ATTAIN!
HOW HAS THIS CHILD PERFECTED SUCH SPIRIT?!
I MUST FIND OUT!
KCHK

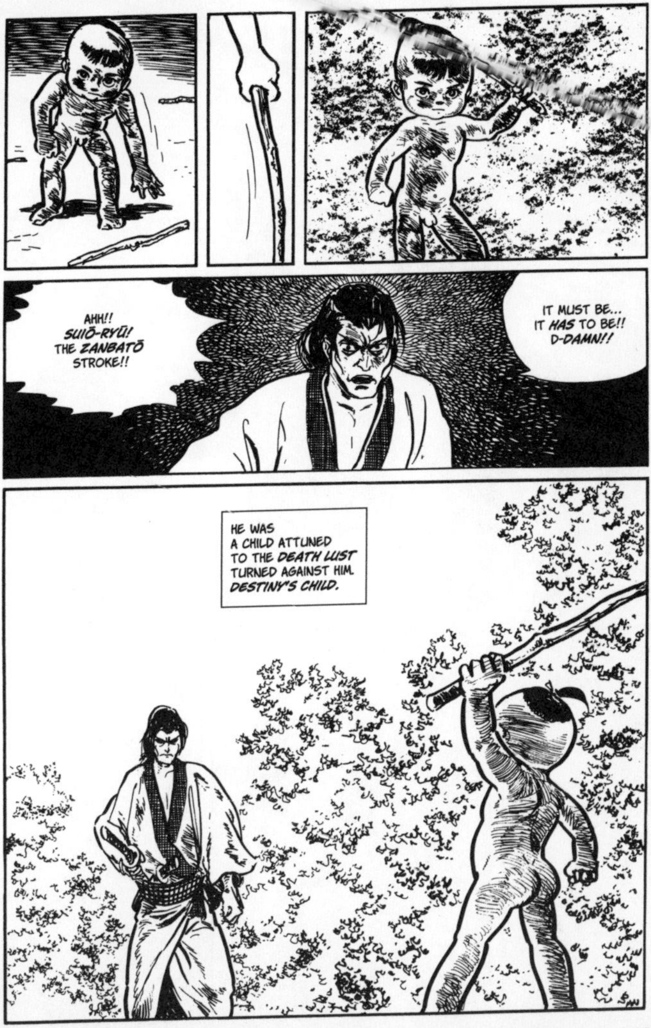
AHH!! SUIŌ-RYŪ! THE ZANBATŌ STROKE!!
IT MUST BE... IT HAS TO BE!! D-DAMN!!
HE WAS A CHILD ATTUNED TO THE DEATH LUST TURNED AGAINST HIM. DESTINY'S CHILD.

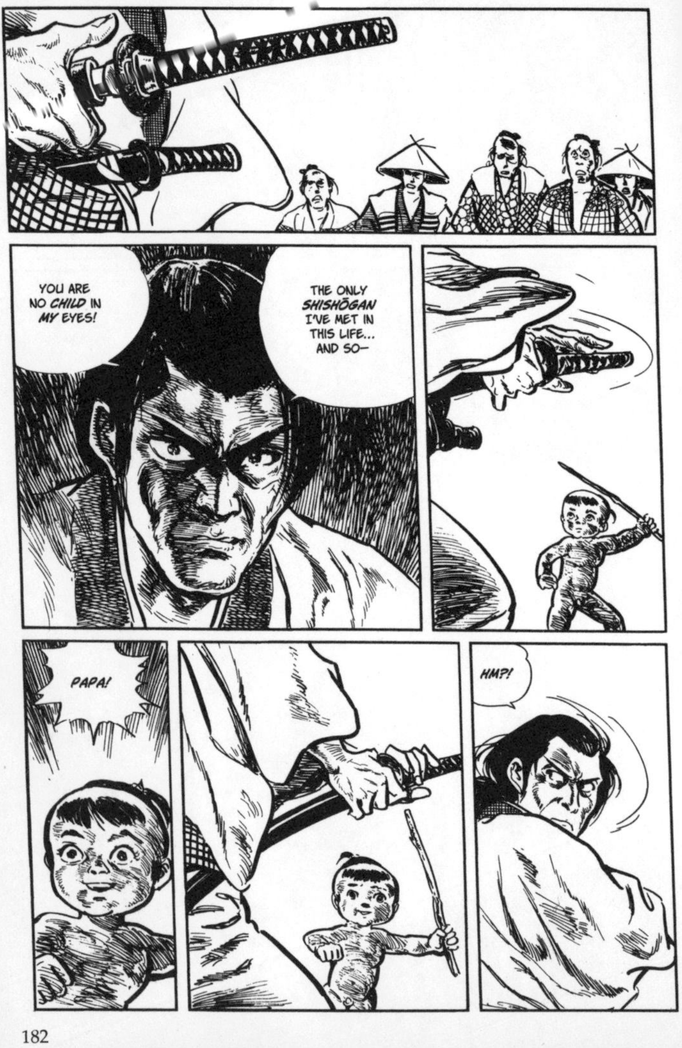
THE ONLY SHISHŌGAN I'VE MET IN THIS LIFE... AND SO—
YOU ARE NO CHILD IN MY EYES!
HM?!
PAPA!

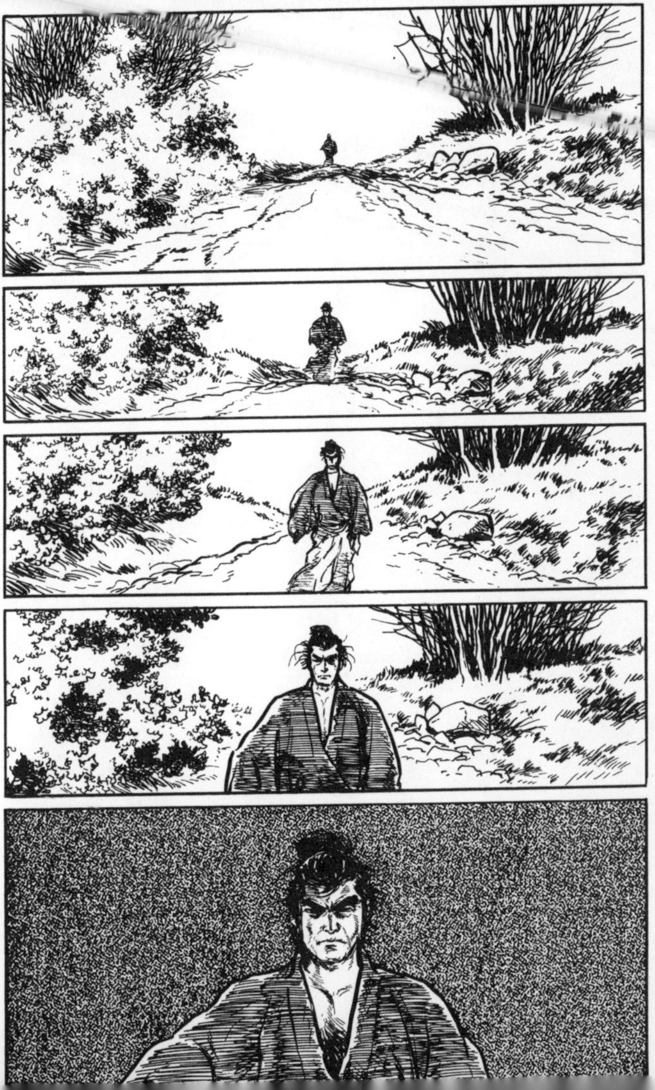

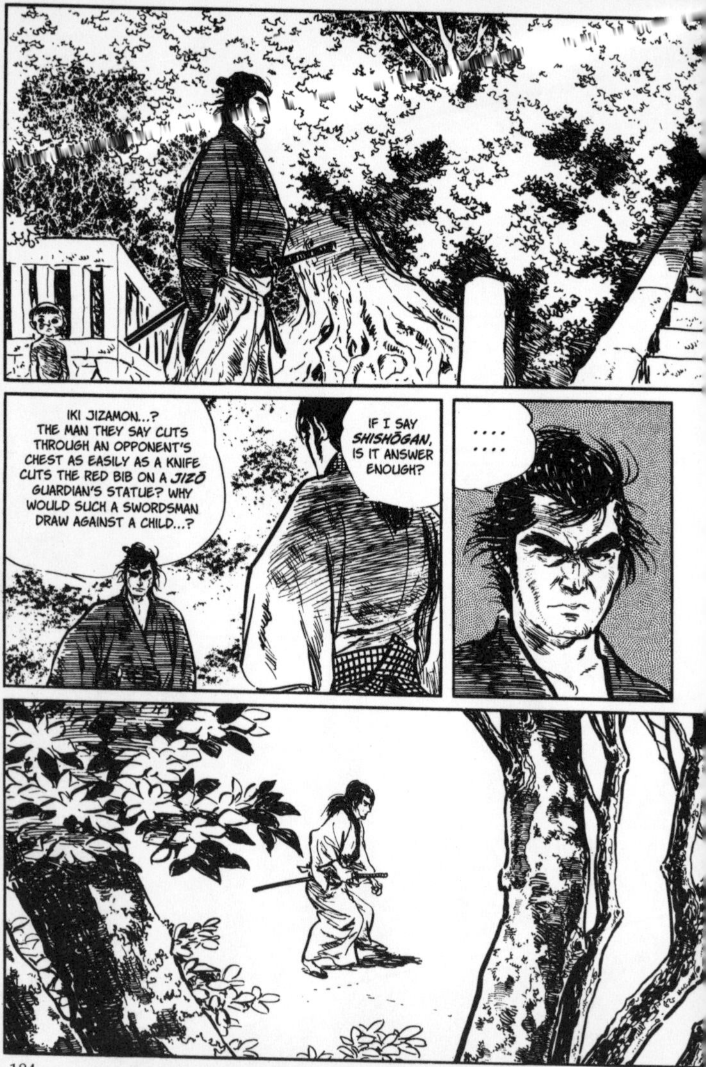
IKI JIZAMON...? THE MAN THEY SAY CUTS THROUGH AN OPPONENT'S CHEST AS EASILY AS A KNIFE CUTS THE RED BIB ON A *JIZŌ* GUARDIAN'S STATUE? WHY WOULD SUCH A SWORDSMAN DRAW AGAINST A CHILD...?
IF I SAY *SHISHŌGAN*, IS IT ANSWER ENOUGH?
....
....

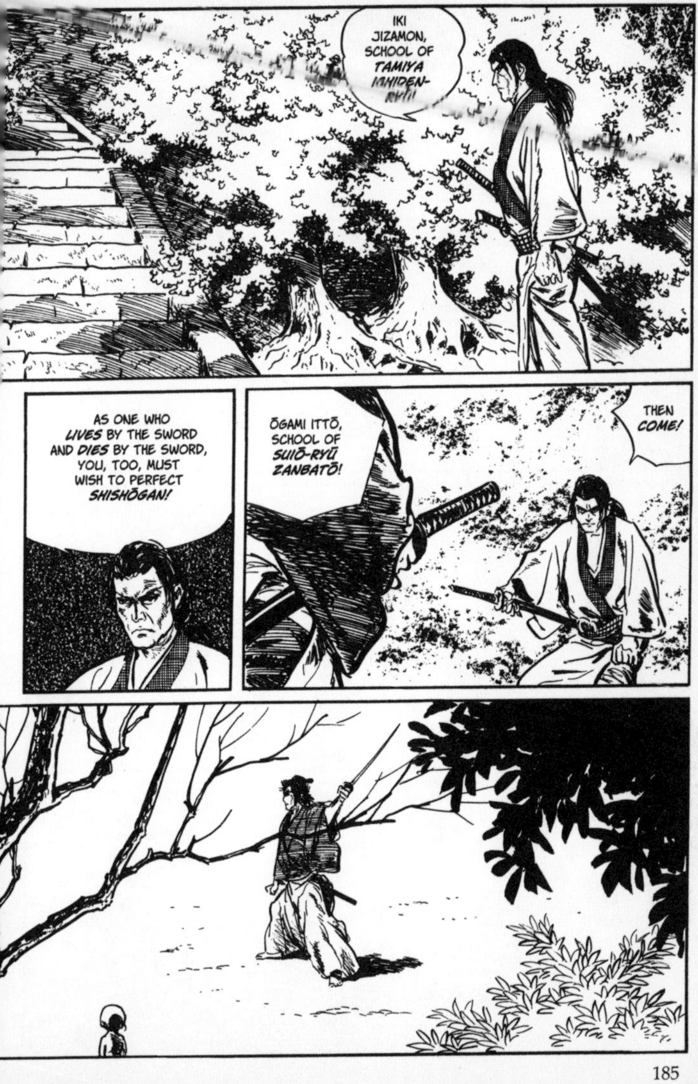
IKI JIZAMON, SCHOOL OF *TAMIYA ICHIDEN-RYŪ!*
THEN *COME!*
ŌGAMI ITTŌ, SCHOOL OF *SUIŌ-RYŪ ZANBATŌ!*
AS ONE WHO *LIVES* BY THE SWORD AND *DIES* BY THE SWORD, YOU, TOO, MUST WISH TO PERFECT *SHISHŌGAN!*

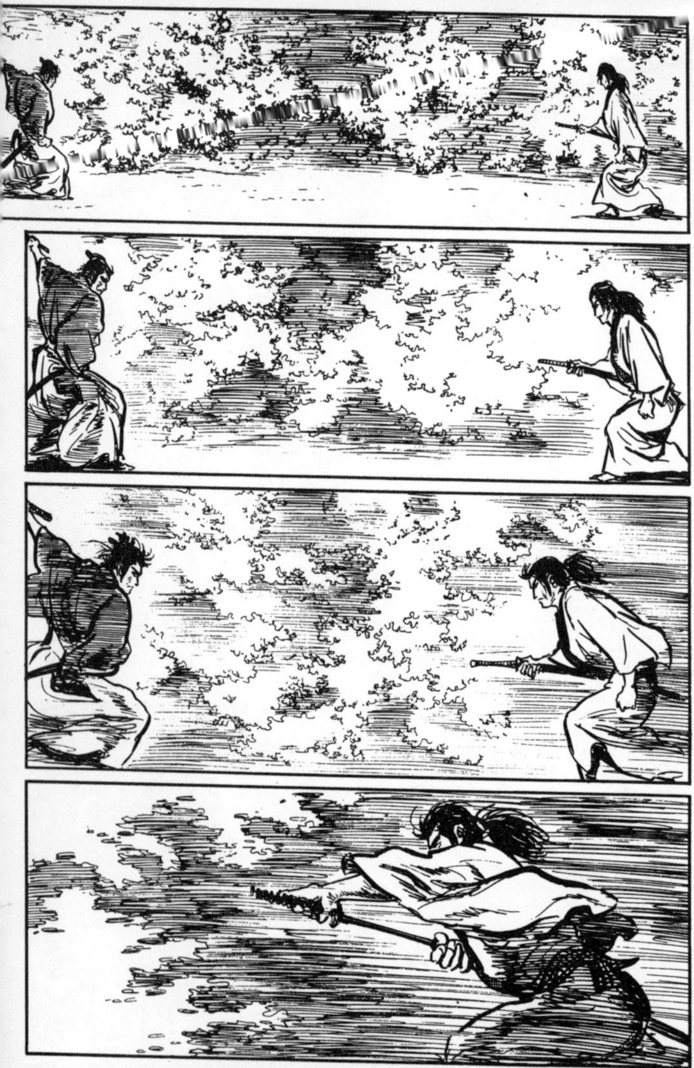

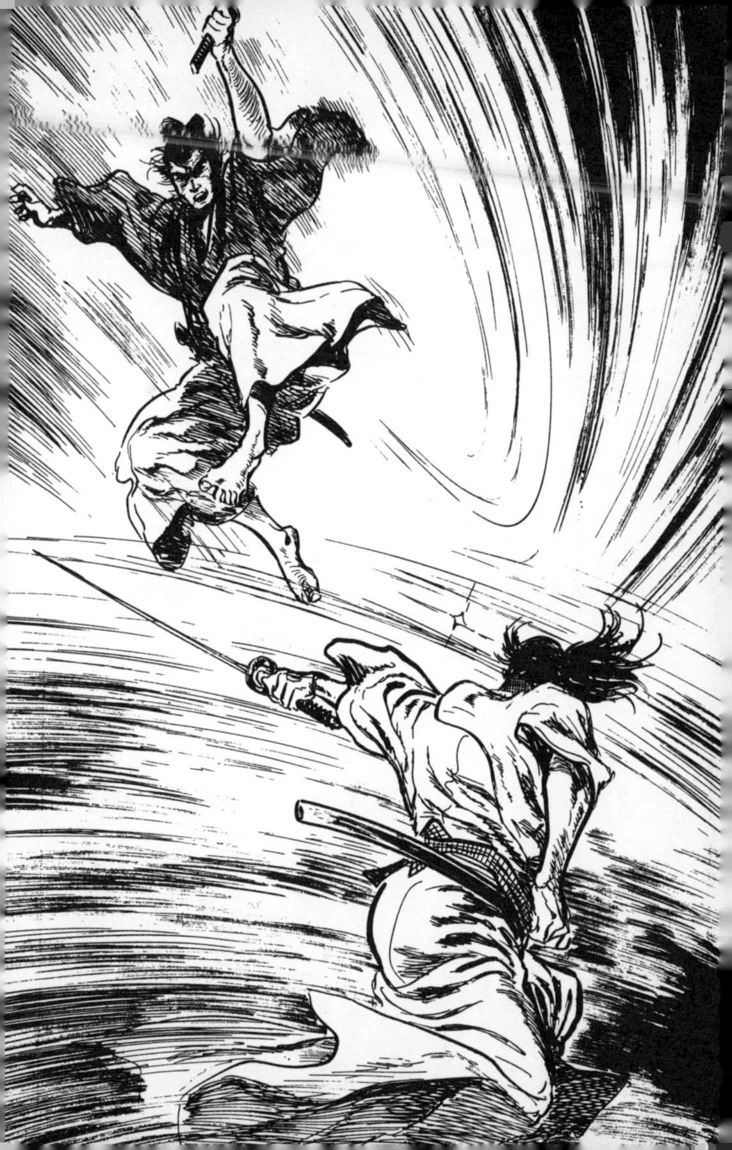

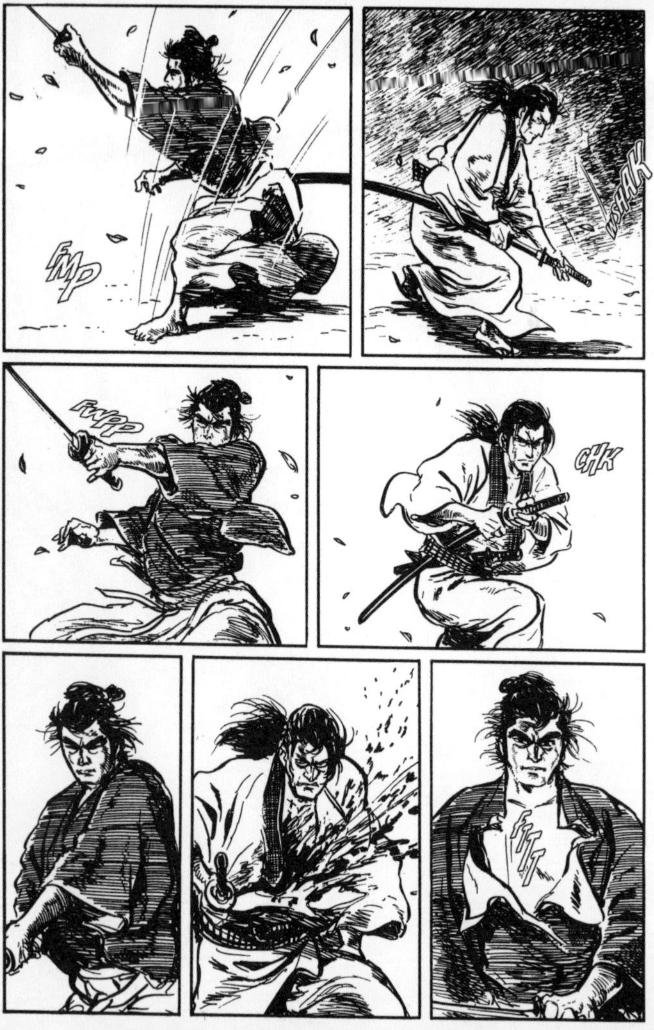
wSHAK
FMP
CHK
FWPP
FTTT

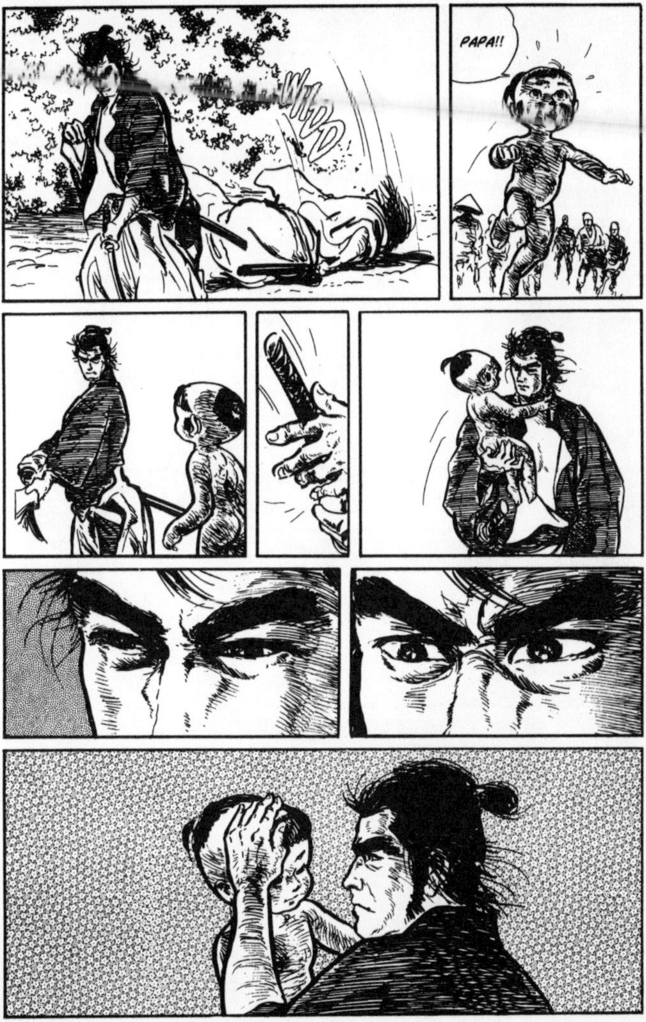
PAPA!!

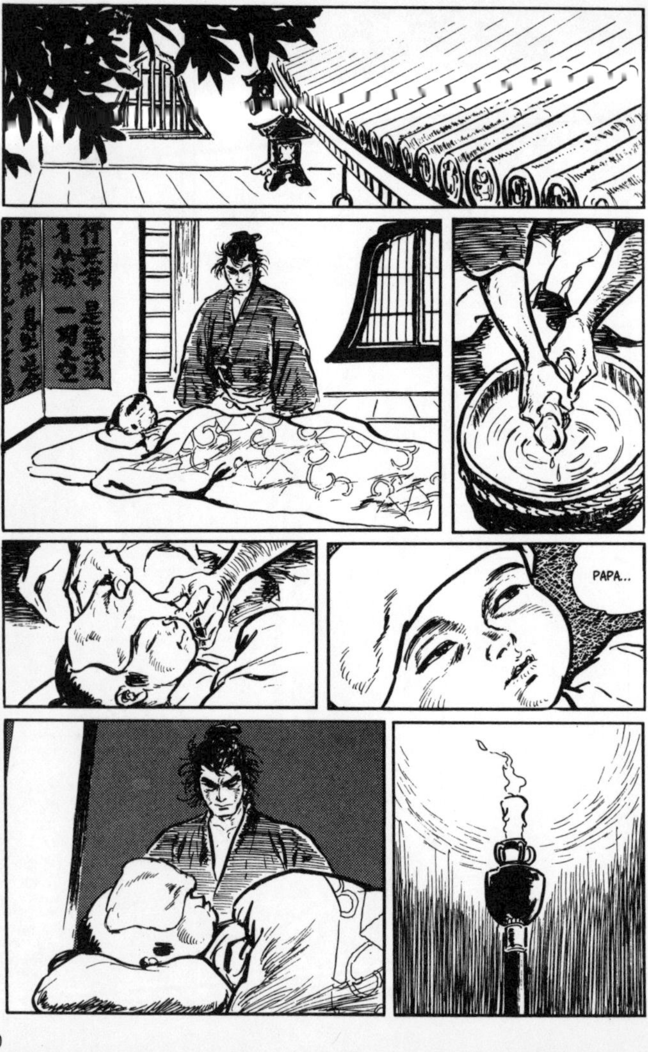
PAPA...

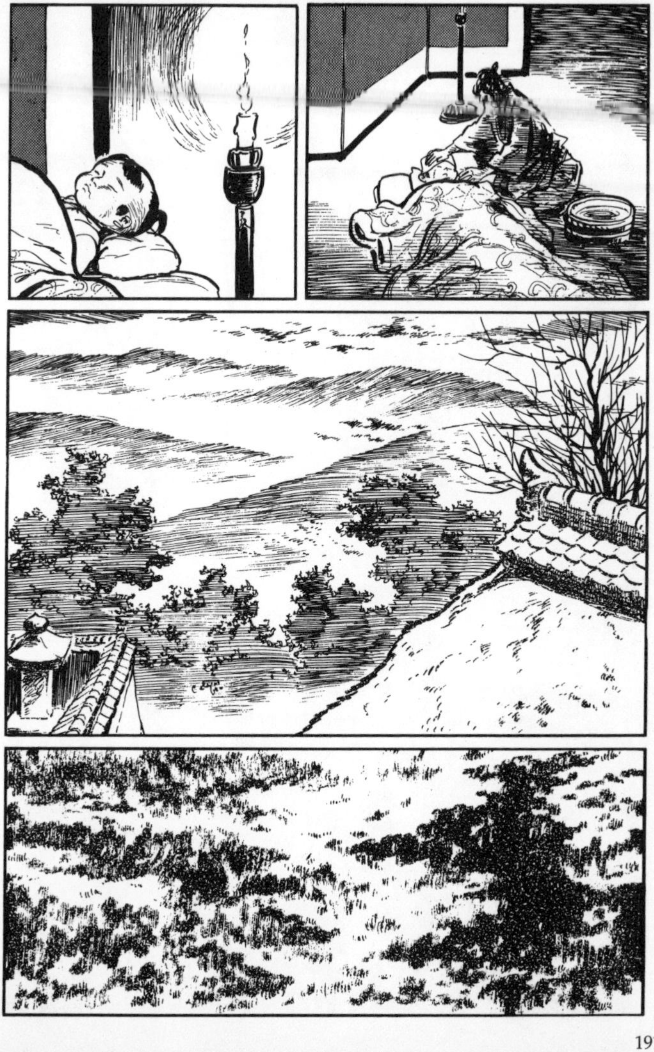

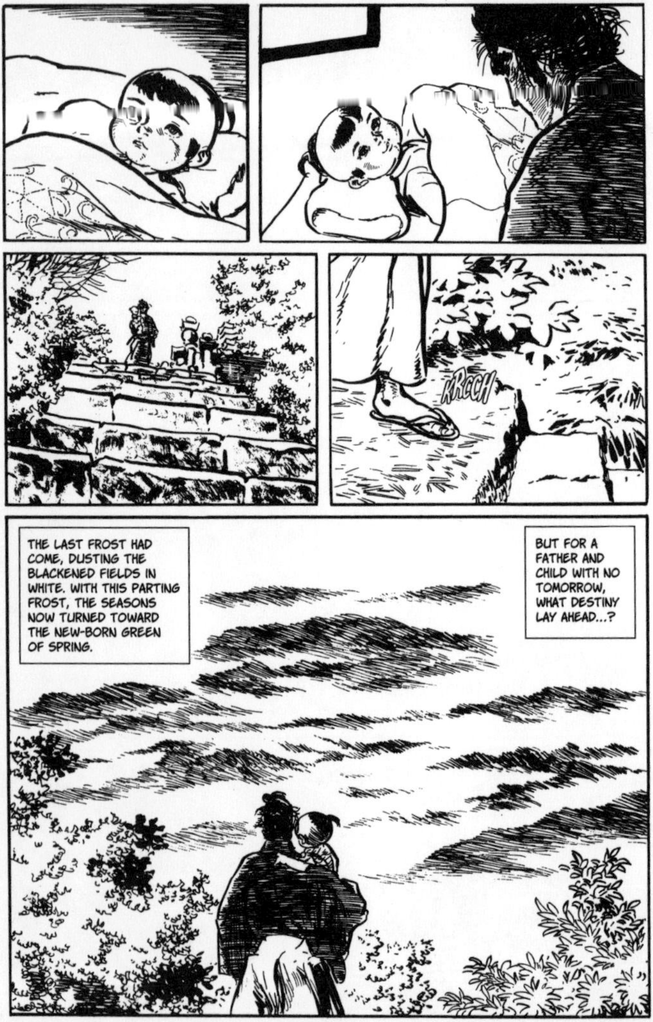
KRCCH
THE LAST FROST HAD COME, DUSTING THE BLACKENED FIELDS IN WHITE. WITH THIS PARTING FROST, THE SEASONS NOW TURNED TOWARD THE NEW-BORN GREEN OF SPRING.
BUT FOR A FATHER AND CHILD WITH NO TOMORROW, WHAT DESTINY LAY AHEAD...?

the twenty-third

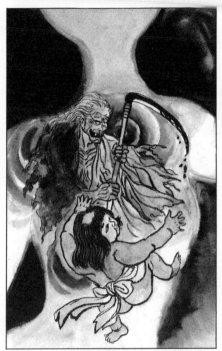

# Performer

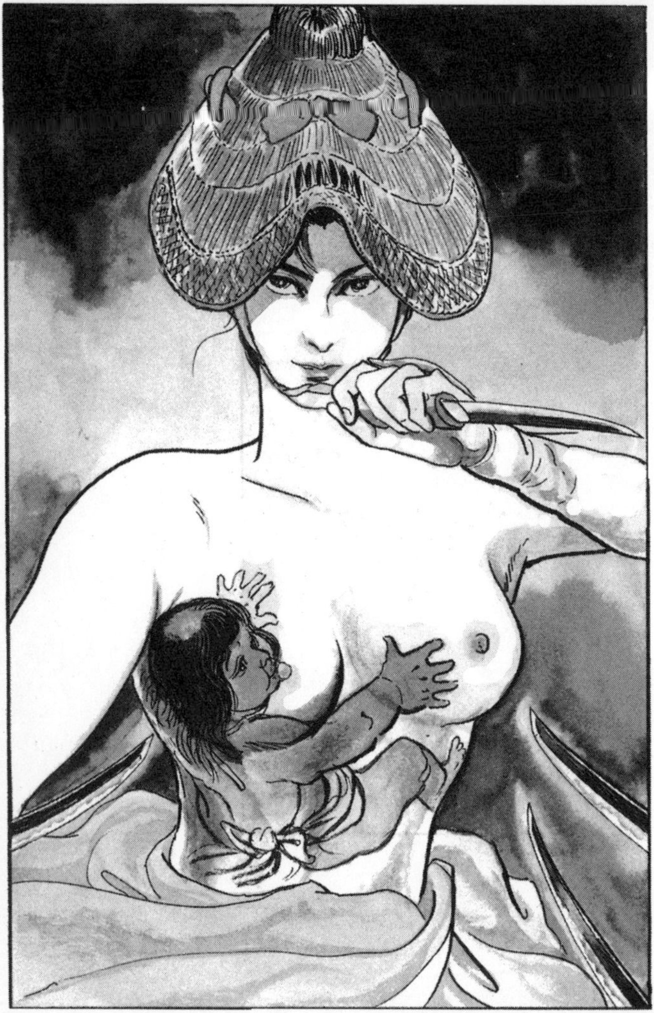

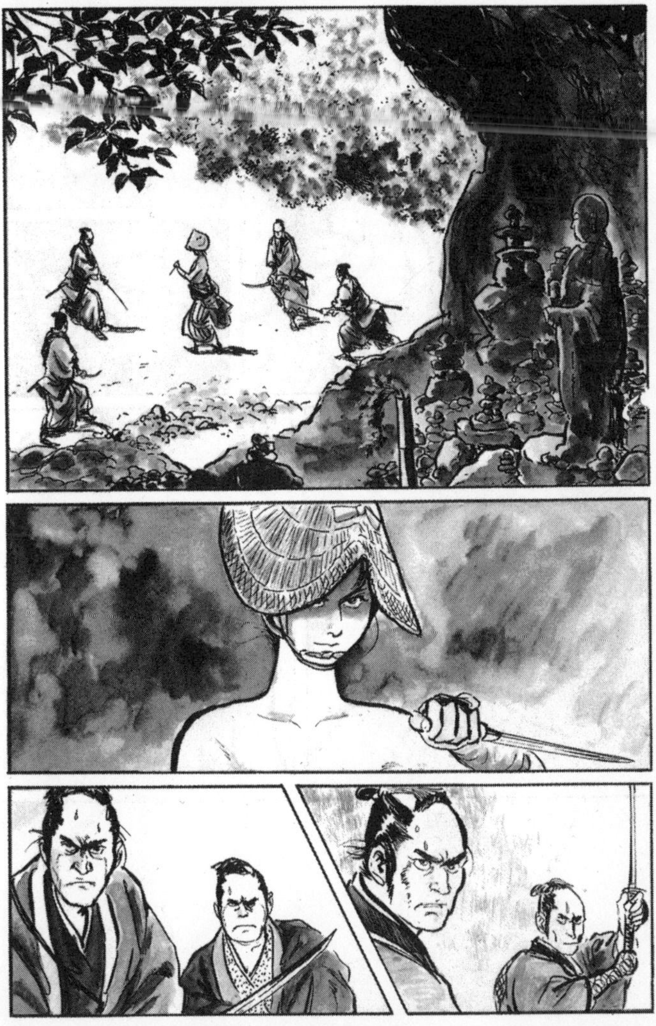

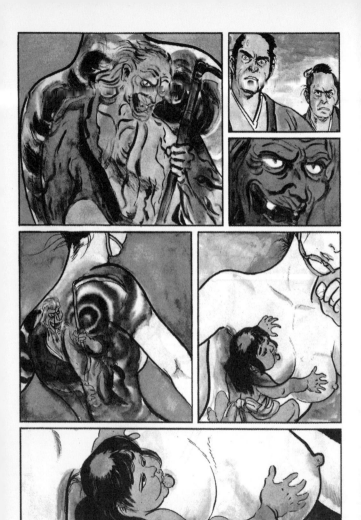

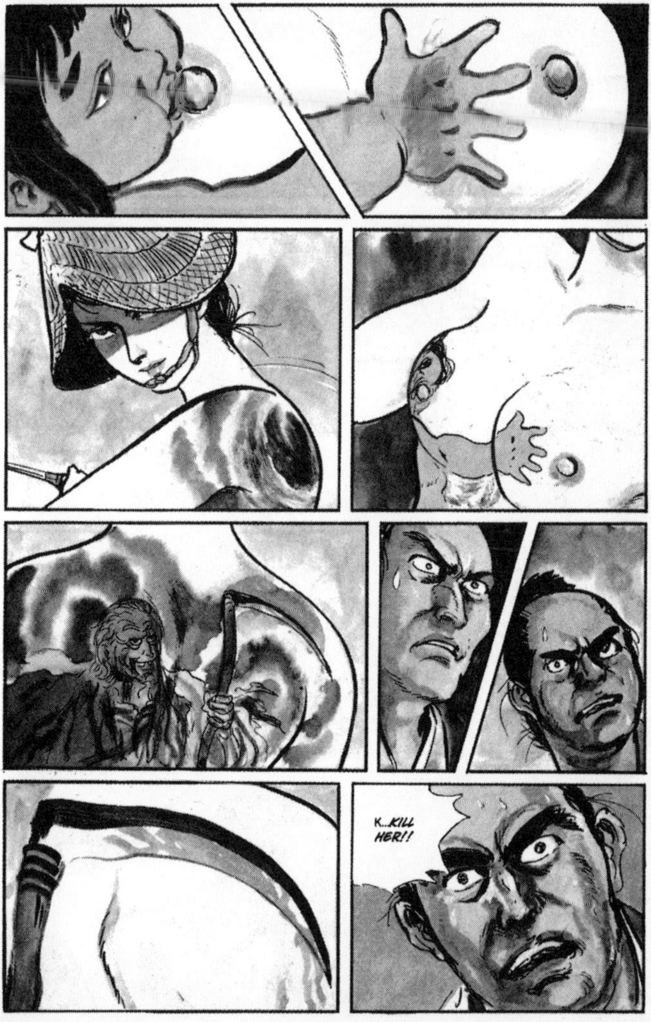
K...KILL HER!!

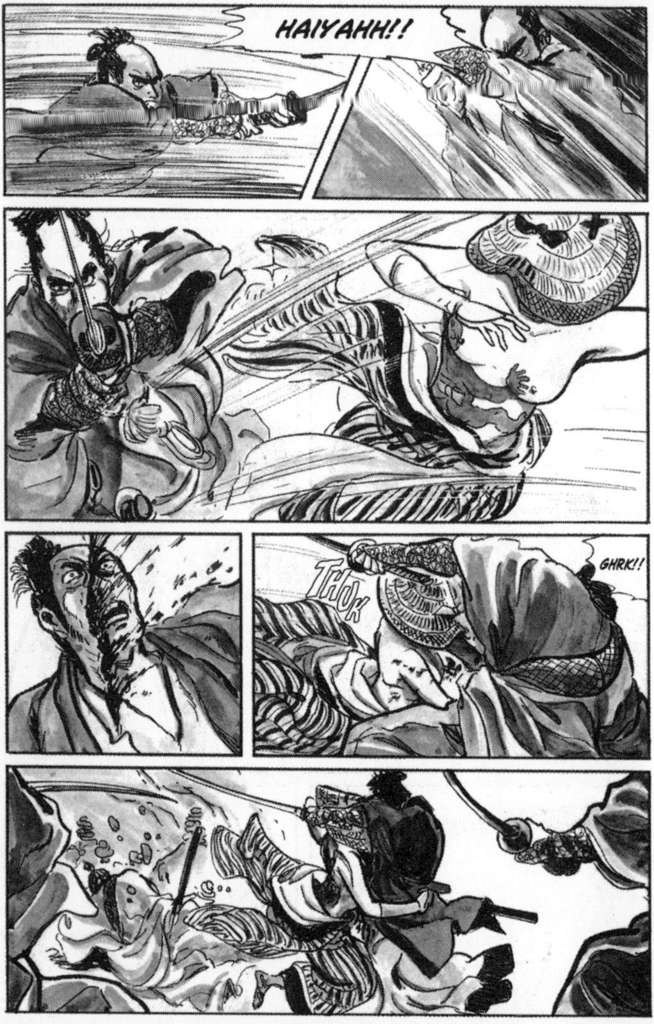
HAIYAHH!!
GHRK!!
THUK

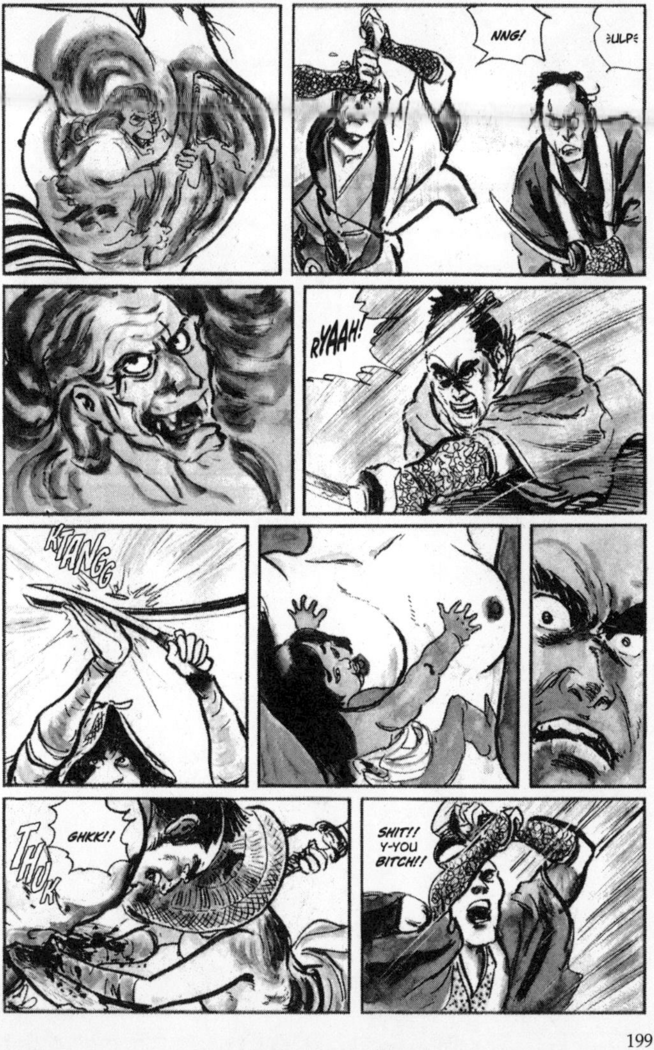
ULP
NNG!
RYAAH!
KTANGG
SHIT!! Y-YOU BITCH!!
GHKK!!
THUK

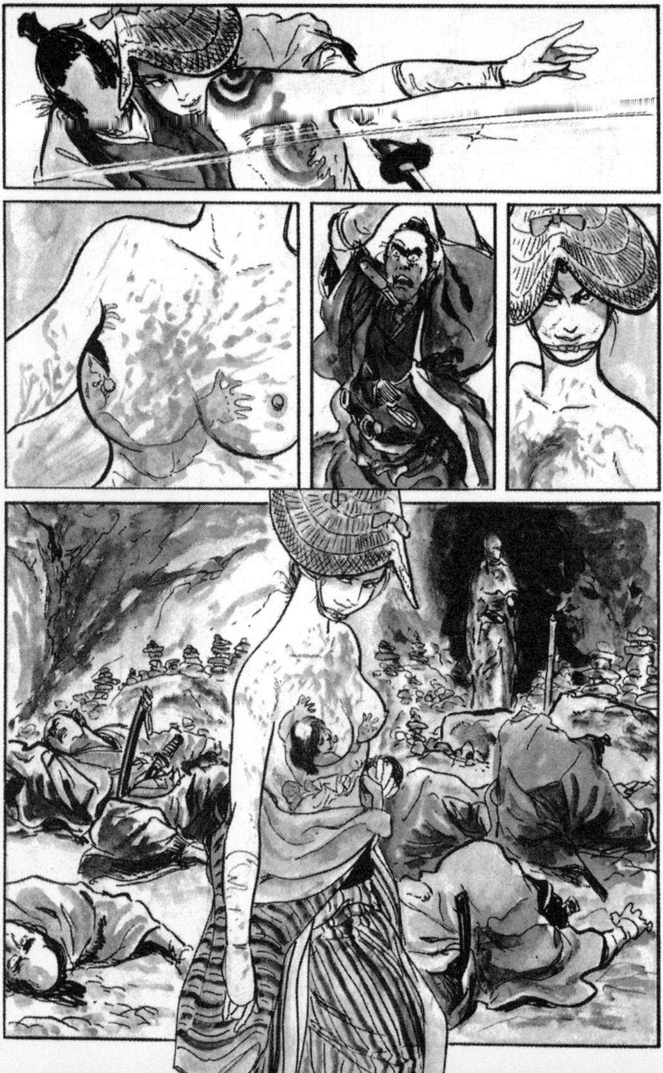

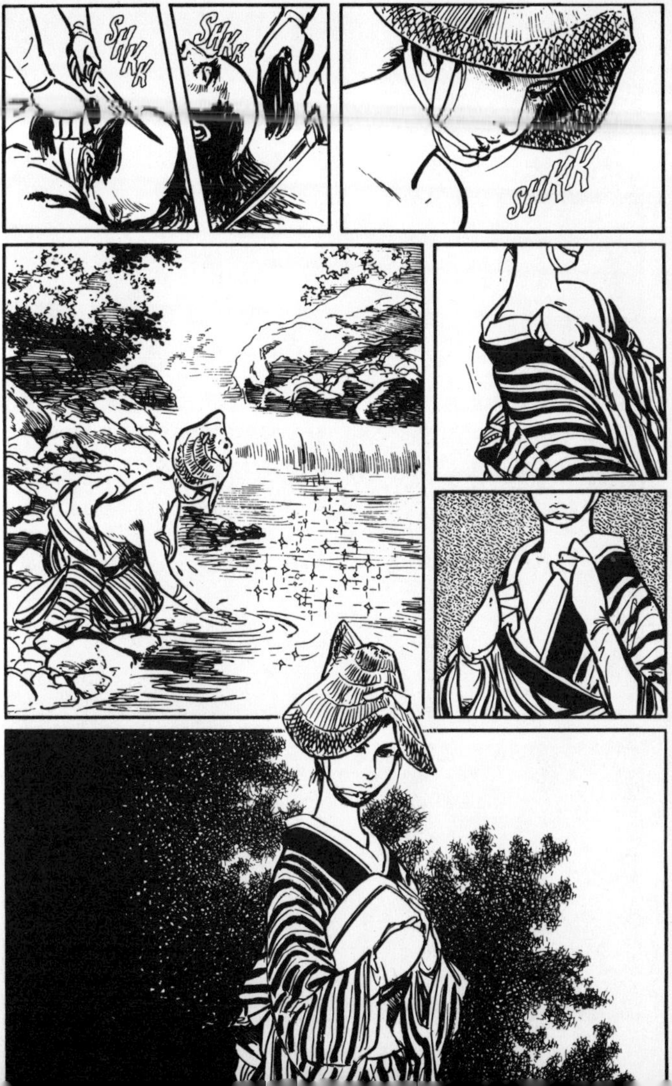
SHKK
SHKKK
SHKKK

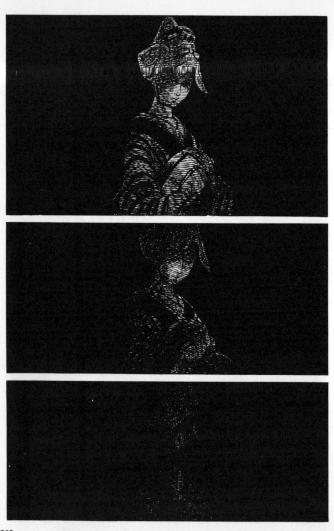

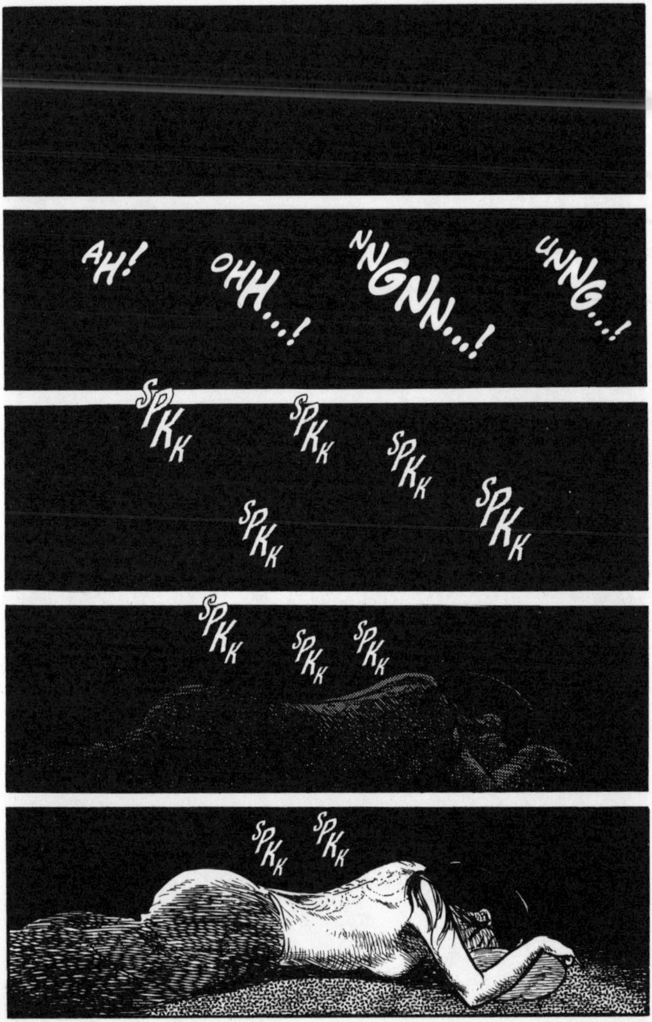
AH!
OHH...!
NNGNN...!
UNNG...!
SPKK
SPKK
SPKK
SPKK
SPKK
SPKK
SPKK
SPKK
SPKK
SPKK

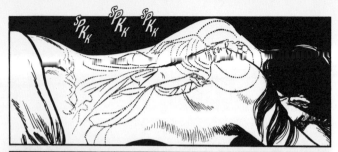

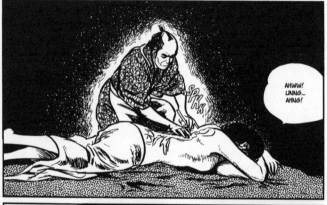

AHWW! UNNG... AHNG!

WINTER'S THE TIME FOR TATTOOS, IT IS... THE CLIENT DOESN'T SWEAT, SEE? THE INK DRIES QUICK.

UHH! OWW!

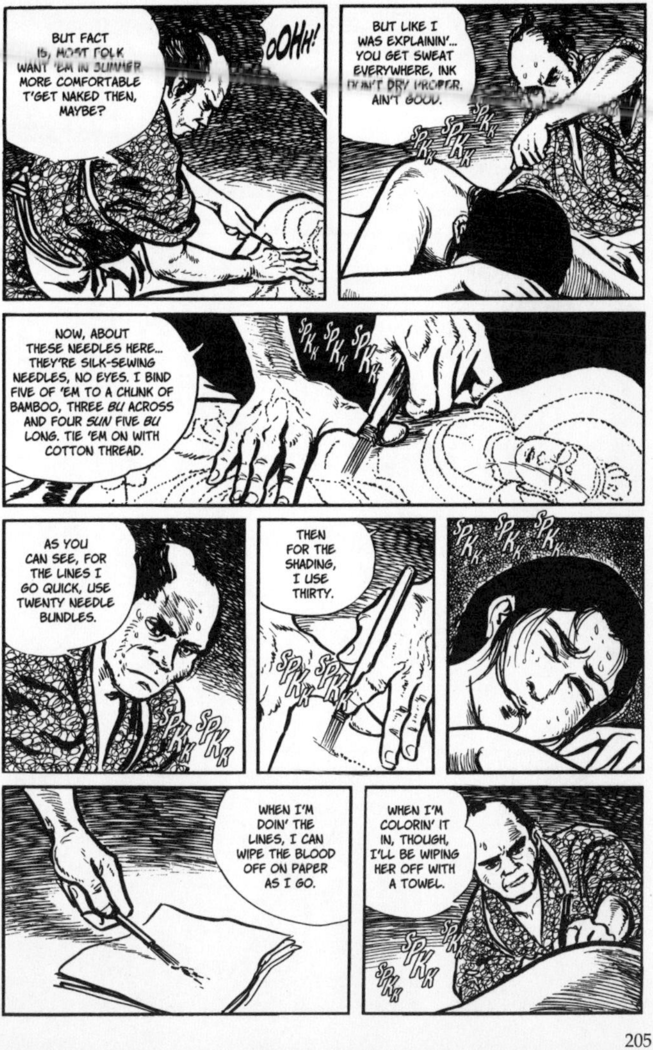
BUT FACT IS, MOST FOLK WANT 'EM IN SUMMER. MORE COMFORTABLE T'GET NAKED THEN, MAYBE?
OOHH!
BUT LIKE I WAS EXPLAININ'... YOU GET SWEAT EVERYWHERE, INK DON'T DRY PROPER. AIN'T GOOD.
SPKK SPKK SPKK
NOW, ABOUT THESE NEEDLES HERE... THEY'RE SILK-SEWING NEEDLES, NO EYES. I BIND FIVE OF 'EM TO A CHUNK OF BAMBOO, THREE *BU* ACROSS AND FOUR *SUN* FIVE *BU* LONG. TIE 'EM ON WITH COTTON THREAD.
SPKK SPKK SPKK
AS YOU CAN SEE, FOR THE LINES I GO QUICK, USE TWENTY NEEDLE BUNDLES.
SPKK SPKK
THEN FOR THE SHADING, I USE THIRTY.
SPKK SPKK
SPKK SPKK SPKK
WHEN I'M DOIN' THE LINES, I CAN WIPE THE BLOOD OFF ON PAPER AS I GO.
WHEN I'M COLORIN' IT IN, THOUGH, I'LL BE WIPING HER OFF WITH A TOWEL.
SPKK SPKK SPKK

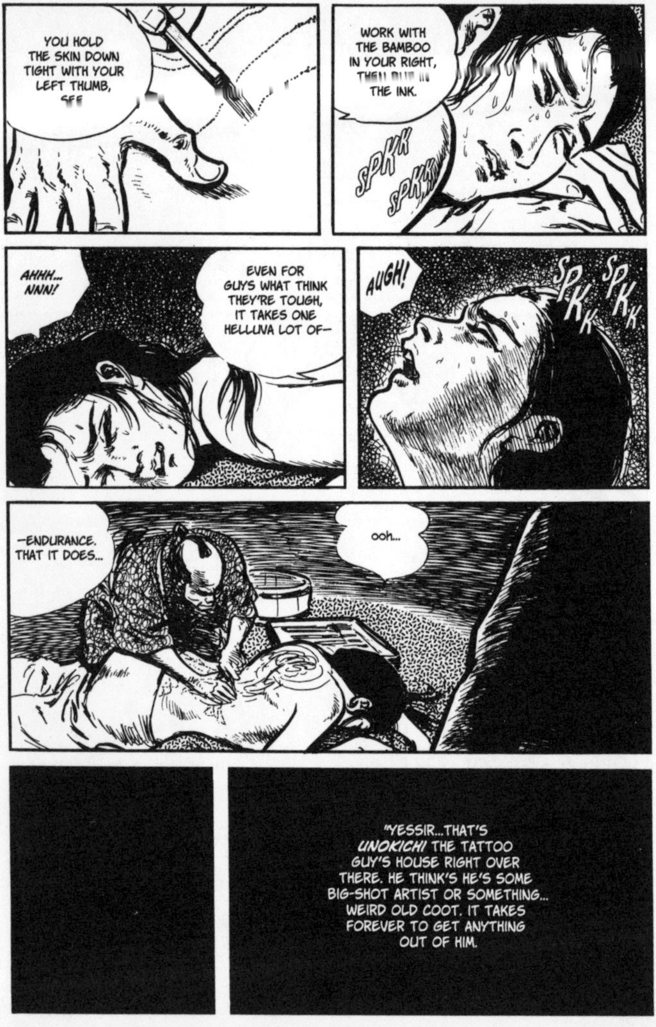
YOU HOLD THE SKIN DOWN TIGHT WITH YOUR LEFT THUMB,
WORK WITH THE BAMBOO IN YOUR RIGHT,
THE INK.
SPKK SPKK
AHHH... NNN!
EVEN FOR GUYS WHAT THINK THEY'RE TOUGH, IT TAKES ONE HELLUVA LOT OF—
AUGH!
SPKK SPKK
—ENDURANCE. THAT IT DOES...
ooh...
"YESSIR...THAT'S UNOKICHI THE TATTOO GUY'S HOUSE RIGHT OVER THERE. HE THINK'S HE'S SOME BIG-SHOT ARTIST OR SOMETHING... WEIRD OLD COOT. IT TAKES FOREVER TO GET ANYTHING OUT OF HIM.

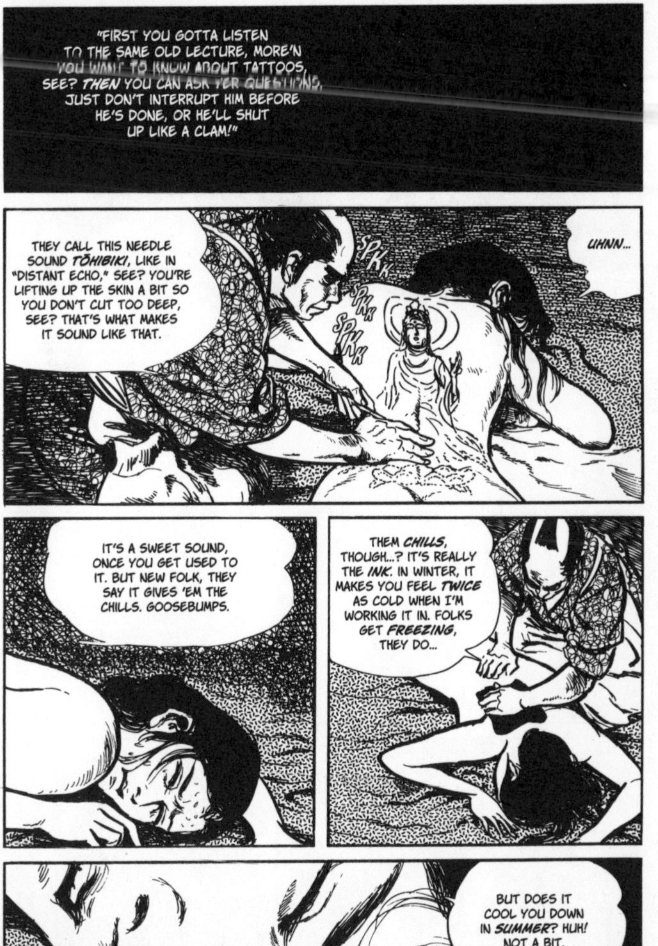
"FIRST YOU GOTTA LISTEN TO THE SAME OLD LECTURE, MORE'N YOU WANT TO KNOW ABOUT TATTOOS, SEE? THEN YOU CAN ASK YER QUESTIONS. JUST DON'T INTERRUPT HIM BEFORE HE'S DONE, OR HE'LL SHUT UP LIKE A CLAM!"
THEY CALL THIS NEEDLE SOUND TŌHIBIKI, LIKE IN "DISTANT ECHO," SEE? YOU'RE LIFTING UP THE SKIN A BIT SO YOU DON'T CUT TOO DEEP, SEE? THAT'S WHAT MAKES IT SOUND LIKE THAT.
SPKK
SPKK
SPKK
UHNN...
IT'S A SWEET SOUND, ONCE YOU GET USED TO IT. BUT NEW FOLK, THEY SAY IT GIVES 'EM THE CHILLS. GOOSEBUMPS.
THEM CHILLS, THOUGH...? IT'S REALLY THE INK. IN WINTER, IT MAKES YOU FEEL TWICE AS COLD WHEN I'M WORKING IT IN. FOLKS GET FREEZING, THEY DO...
BUT DOES IT COOL YOU DOWN IN SUMMER? HUH! NOT A BIT.

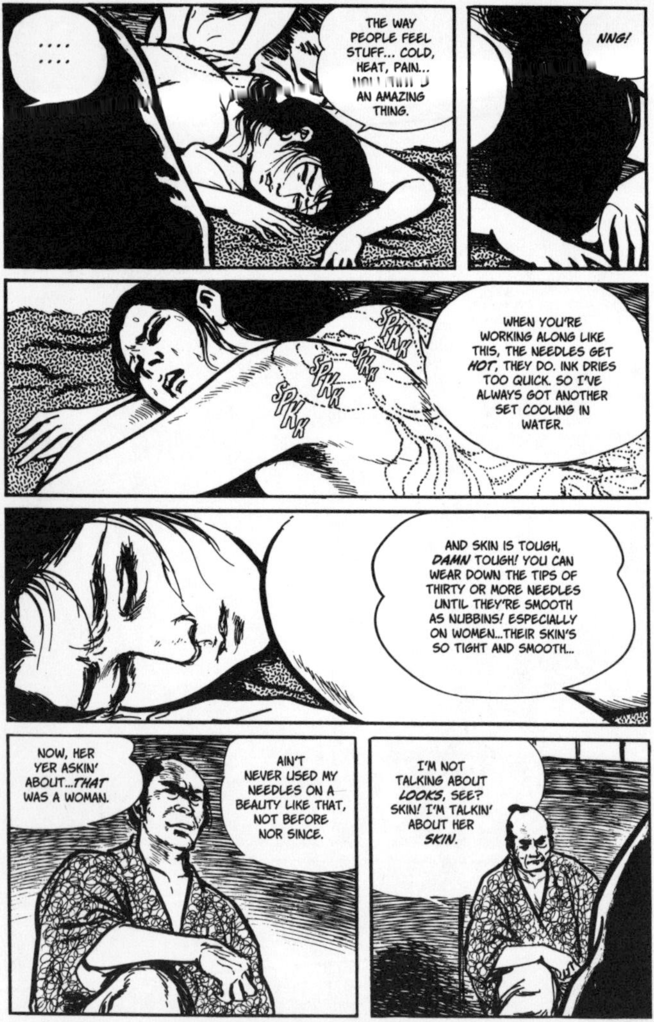
....
....
THE WAY PEOPLE FEEL STUFF... COLD, HEAT, PAIN... AN AMAZING THING.
NNG!
WHEN YOU'RE WORKING ALONG LIKE THIS, THE NEEDLES GET *HOT*, THEY DO. INK DRIES TOO QUICK. SO I'VE ALWAYS GOT ANOTHER SET COOLING IN WATER.
SPKK SPKK SPKK SPKK
AND SKIN IS TOUGH, *DAMN* TOUGH! YOU CAN WEAR DOWN THE TIPS OF THIRTY OR MORE NEEDLES UNTIL THEY'RE SMOOTH AS NUBBINS! ESPECIALLY ON WOMEN...THEIR SKIN'S SO TIGHT AND SMOOTH...
NOW, HER YER ASKIN' ABOUT...*THAT* WAS A WOMAN.
AIN'T NEVER USED MY NEEDLES ON A BEAUTY LIKE THAT, NOT BEFORE NOR SINCE.
I'M NOT TALKING ABOUT *LOOKS*, SEE? SKIN! I'M TALKIN' ABOUT HER *SKIN*.

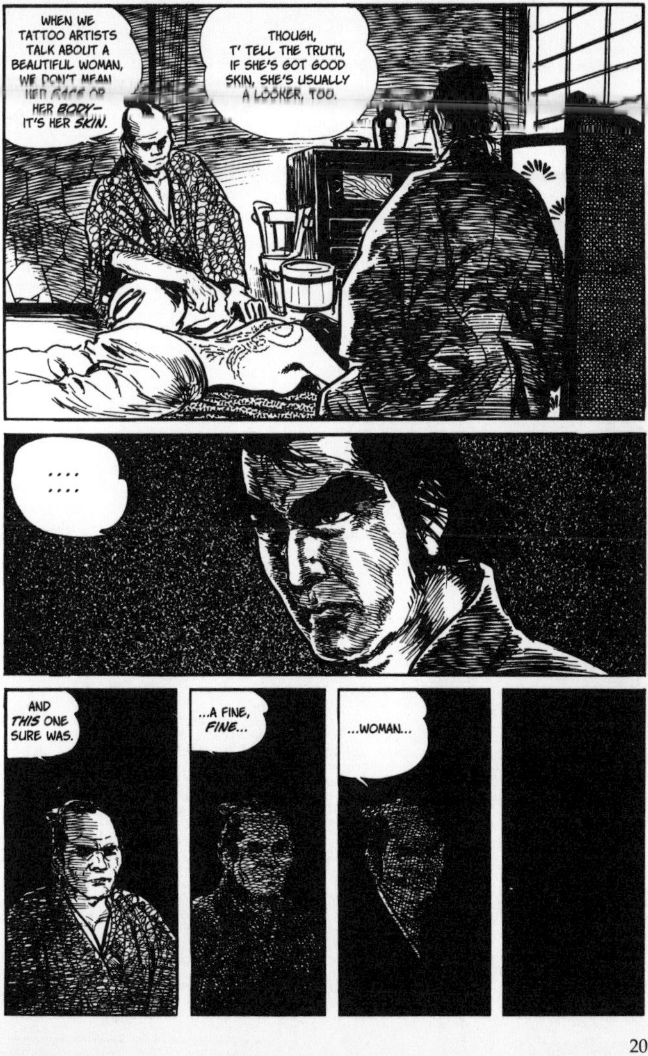
WHEN WE TATTOO ARTISTS TALK ABOUT A BEAUTIFUL WOMAN, WE DON'T MEAN HER FACE OR HER *BODY*— IT'S HER *SKIN*.
THOUGH, T' TELL THE TRUTH, IF SHE'S GOT GOOD SKIN, SHE'S USUALLY A LOOKER, TOO.
....
....
AND *THIS* ONE SURE WAS.
...A FINE, *FINE*...
...WOMAN...

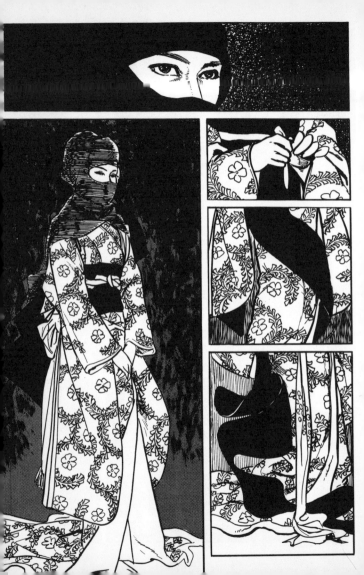

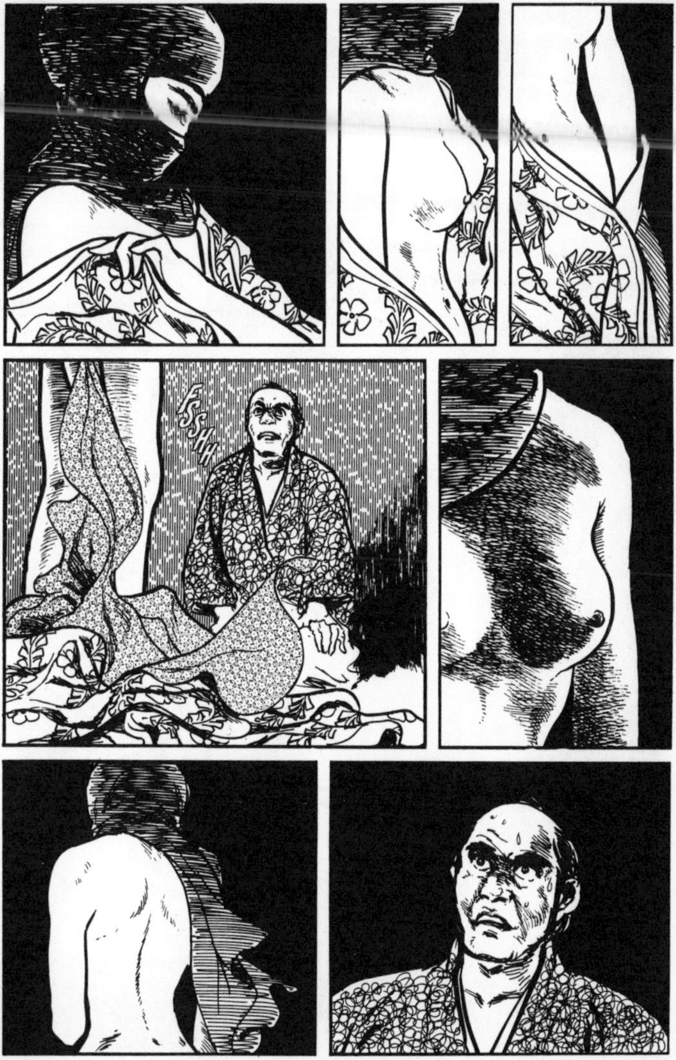
FSSHH

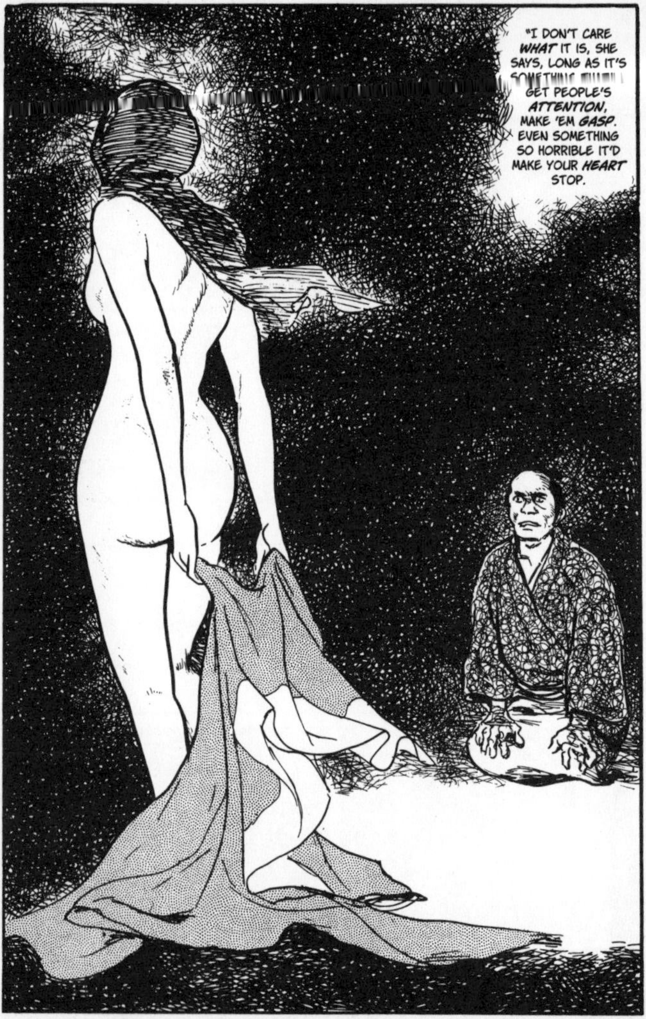
"I DON'T CARE *WHAT* IT IS, SHE SAYS, LONG AS IT'S SOMETHING GET PEOPLE'S *ATTENTION*, MAKE 'EM *GASP*. EVEN SOMETHING SO HORRIBLE IT'D MAKE YOUR *HEART* STOP.

"OR MAYBE SOMETHING TO DRIVE MEN MAD WITH *LUST*.

...ANYTHING.

GIVE ME THE MOST *SHOCKING* TATTOO YOU CAN!

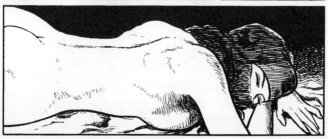

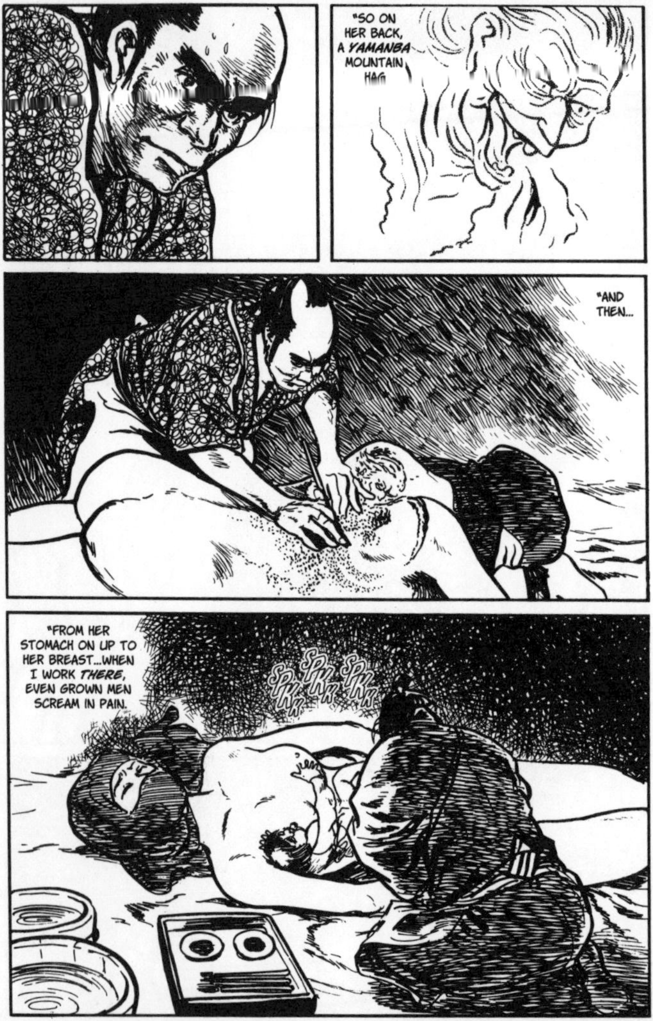
"SO ON HER BACK, A *YAMANBA* MOUNTAIN HAG
"AND THEN...
"FROM HER STOMACH ON UP TO HER BREAST...WHEN I WORK *THERE*, EVEN GROWN MEN SCREAM IN PAIN.
SPKKK SPKKK SPKKK

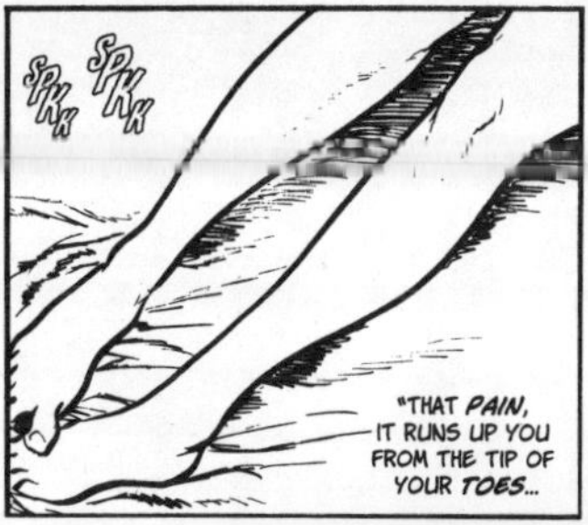
SPKK SPKK
"THAT *PAIN*, IT RUNS UP YOU FROM THE TIP OF YOUR *TOES*...
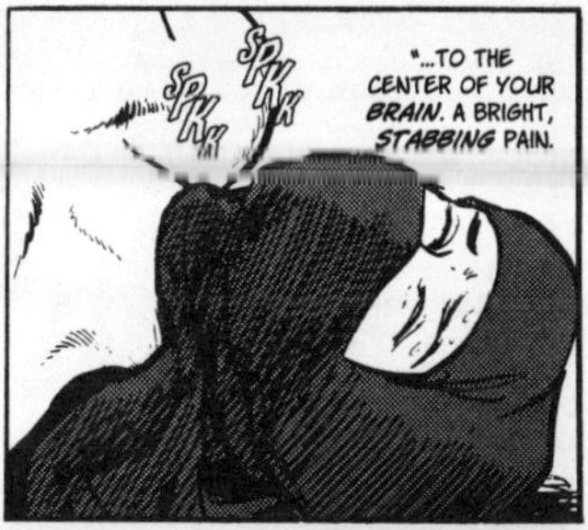
SPKK SPKK
"...TO THE CENTER OF YOUR *BRAIN*. A BRIGHT, *STABBING* PAIN.
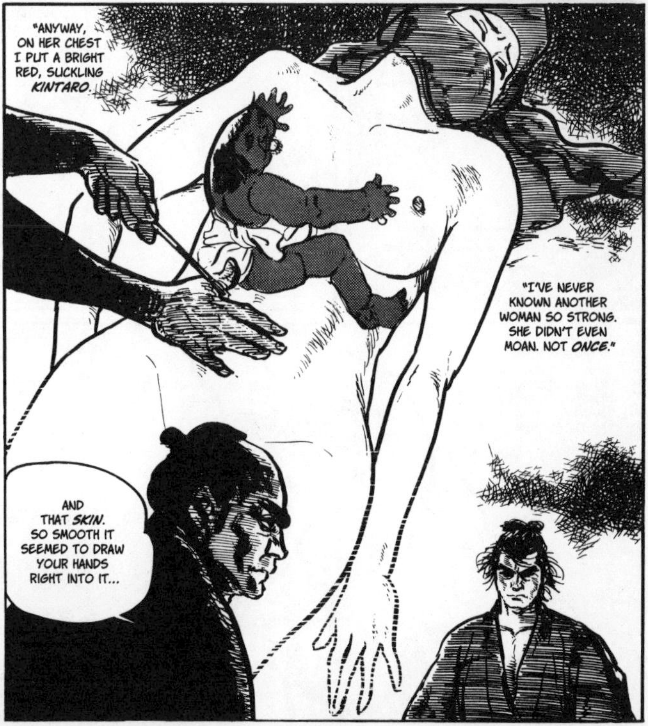
"ANYWAY, ON HER CHEST I PUT A BRIGHT RED, SUCKLING *KINTARO*.
"I'VE NEVER KNOWN ANOTHER WOMAN SO STRONG. SHE DIDN'T EVEN MOAN. NOT *ONCE*."
AND THAT *SKIN*. SO SMOOTH IT SEEMED TO DRAW YOUR HANDS RIGHT INTO IT...

BUT AS I ~~WAS WORKING~~ *I WORKED* SOMETHING!

"FIRST I'D THOUGHT MAYBE SHE WAS A DANCER, BUT I WAS *WRONG*.

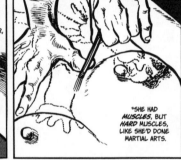

"SHE HAD *MUSCLES*, BUT *HARD* MUSCLES, LIKE SHE'D DONE MARTIAL ARTS.

"UNDER THOSE RICH *CURVES* WAS A *HARD BODY*...I'LL *SWEAR* THAT WOMAN HAD TRAINED WITH THE *SWORD*.

"I'VE HEARD *DAIMYŌ* TAKE ON WOMEN FIGHTERS SOMETIMES. *BESSHIKI-ONNA*, THEY CALL 'EM. SO IT COMES TO ME, MAYBE THIS WOMAN'S ONE OF *THEM*.

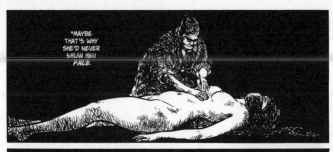

"MAYBE THAT'S WHY SHE'D NEVER SHOW HER FACE.

"STILL, FOR A WOMAN FROM A *BUKE* FAMILY TO GO THE REST OF HER LIFE WITH A *MOUNTAIN HAG* ON HER BACK AND A *KINTARO* FEEDING ON HER BREAST... WHAT THE *HELL* WAS SHE THINKIN'...?

"THAT TATTOO WAS A *MASTERPIECE*, MEBBE THE BEST OF MY LIFE! BUT I'VE WORRIED EVER SINCE THAT I DID HER WRONG..."

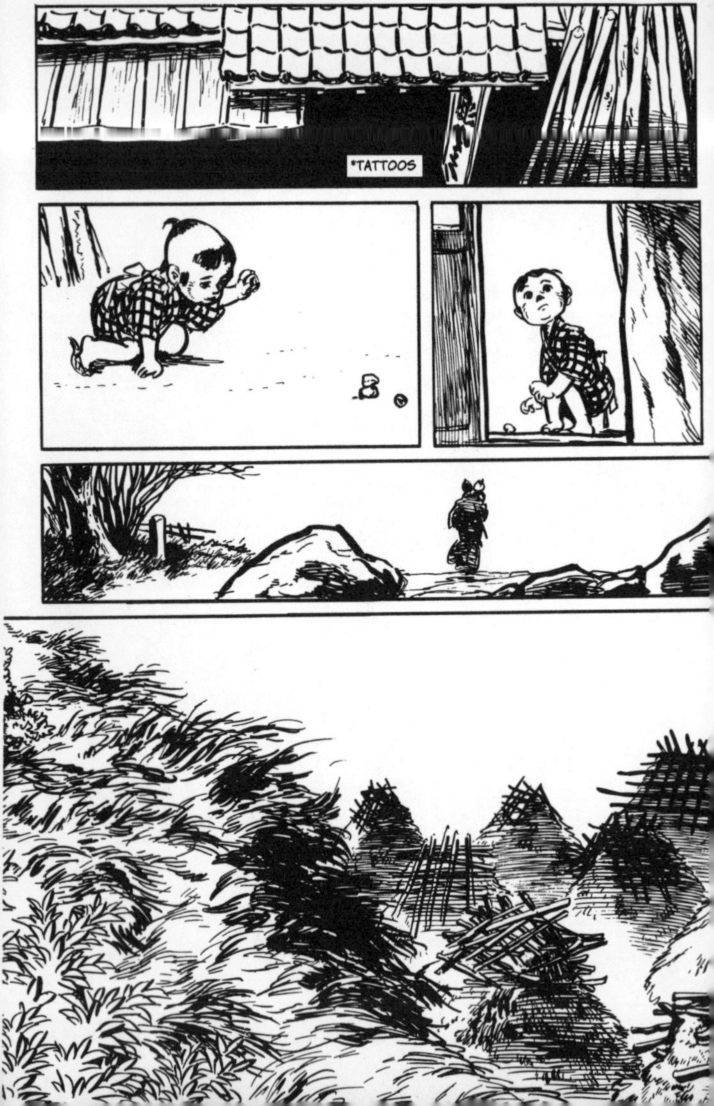
*TATTOOS

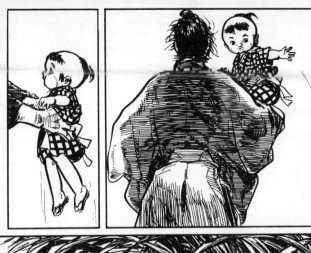

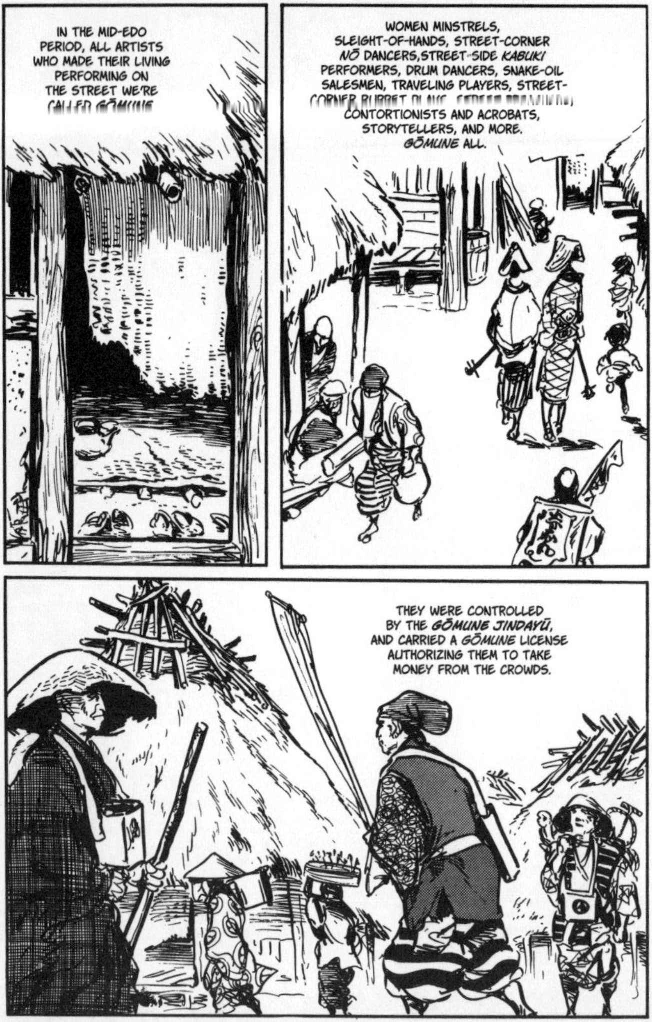
IN THE MID-EDO PERIOD, ALL ARTISTS WHO MADE THEIR LIVING PERFORMING ON THE STREET WE'RE CALLED GŌMUNE
WOMEN MINSTRELS, SLEIGHT-OF-HANDS, STREET-CORNER NŌ DANCERS, STREET-SIDE KABUKI PERFORMERS, DRUM DANCERS, SNAKE-OIL SALESMEN, TRAVELING PLAYERS, STREET-CORNER PUPPET PLAYS, STREET
CONTORTIONISTS AND ACROBATS, STORYTELLERS, AND MORE. GŌMUNE ALL.
THEY WERE CONTROLLED BY THE GŌMUNE JINDAYŪ, AND CARRIED A GŌMUNE LICENSE AUTHORIZING THEM TO TAKE MONEY FROM THE CROWDS.

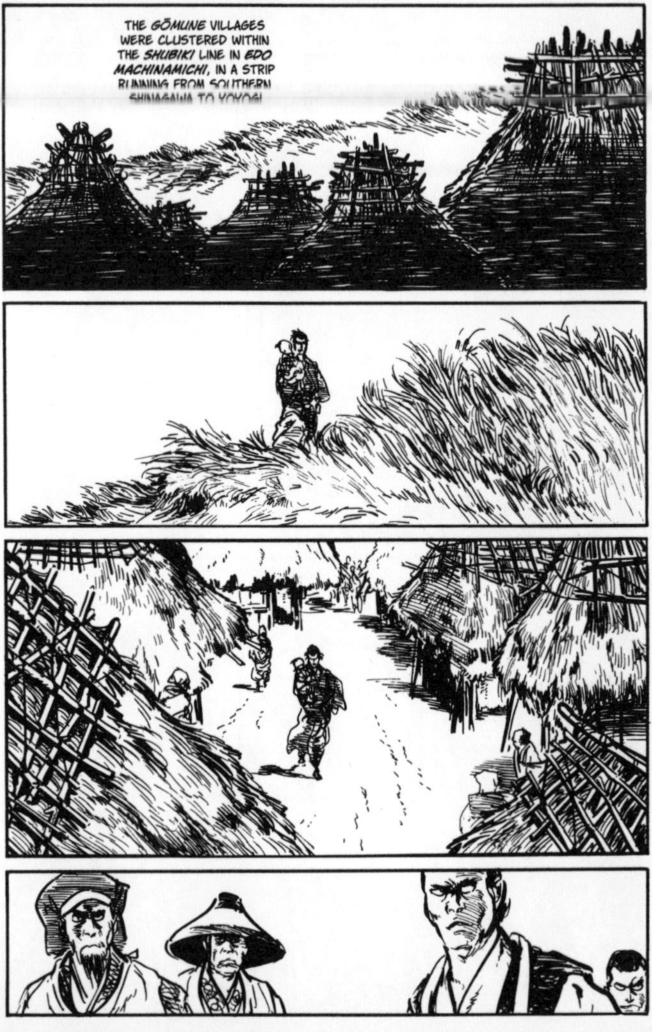
THE GŌMUNE VILLAGES WERE CLUSTERED WITHIN THE SHUBIKI LINE IN EDO MACHINAMICHI, IN A STRIP RUNNING FROM SOUTHERN SHINAGAWA TO YOYOGI.

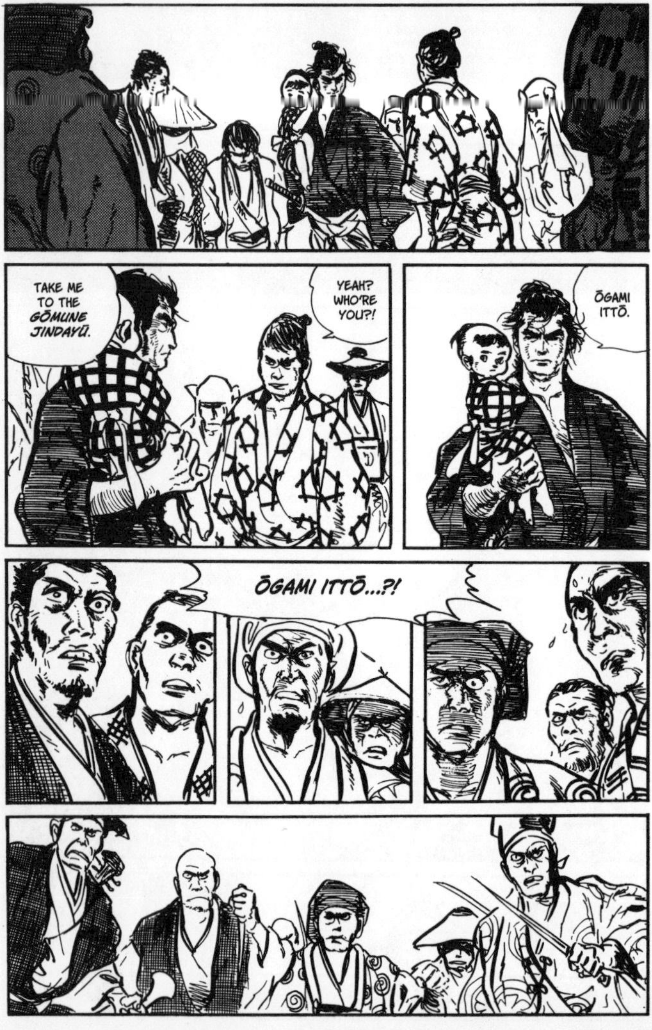

TAKE ME TO THE GŌMUNE JINDAYŪ.
YEAH? WHO'RE YOU?!
ŌGAMI ITTŌ.
ŌGAMI ITTŌ...?!

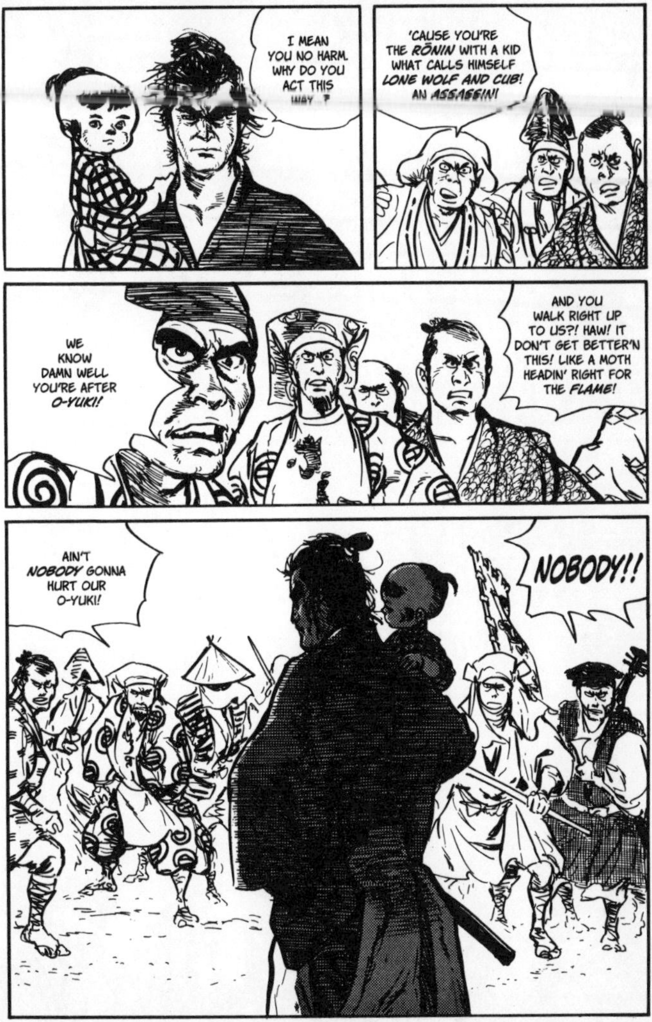
I MEAN YOU NO HARM. WHY DO YOU ACT THIS WAY..?
'CAUSE YOU'RE THE *RŌNIN* WITH A KID WHAT CALLS HIMSELF *LONE WOLF AND CUB!* AN *ASSASSIN!*
WE KNOW DAMN WELL YOU'RE AFTER *O-YUKI!*
AND YOU WALK RIGHT UP TO US?! HAW! IT DON'T GET BETTER'N THIS! LIKE A MOTH HEADIN' RIGHT FOR THE *FLAME!*
AIN'T *NOBODY* GONNA HURT OUR O-YUKI!
NOBODY!!

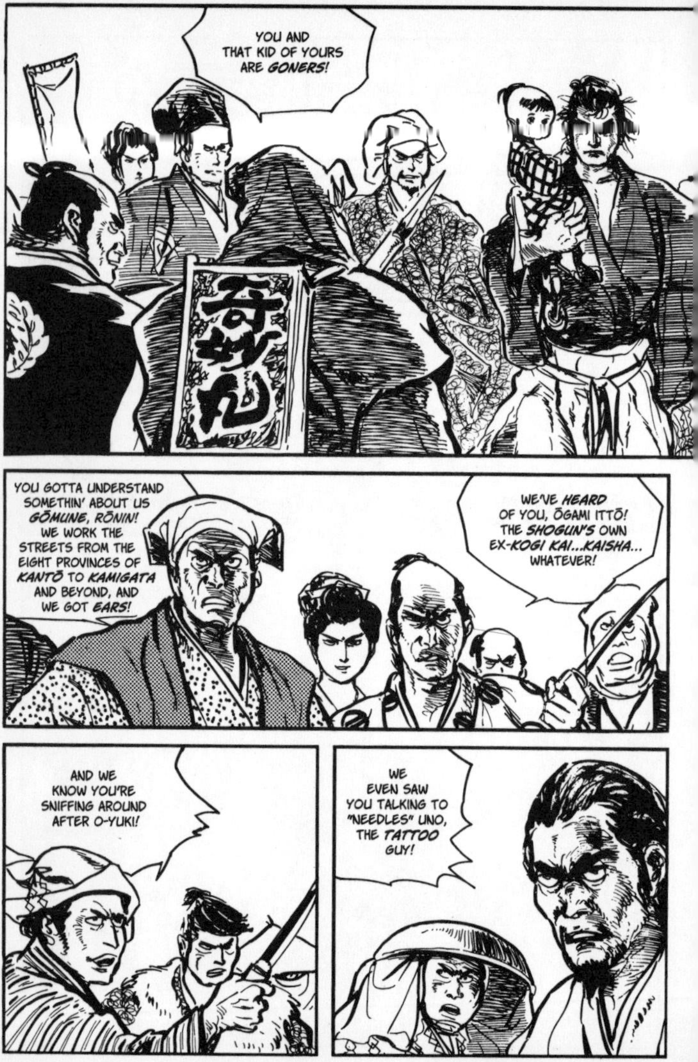
YOU AND THAT KID OF YOURS ARE GONERS!
YOU GOTTA UNDERSTAND SOMETHIN' ABOUT US GŌMUNE, RŌNIN! WE WORK THE STREETS FROM THE EIGHT PROVINCES OF KANTŌ TO KAMIGATA AND BEYOND, AND WE GOT EARS!
WE'VE HEARD OF YOU, ŌGAMI ITTŌ! THE SHOGUN'S OWN EX-KOGI KAI...KAISHA... WHATEVER!
AND WE KNOW YOU'RE SNIFFING AROUND AFTER O-YUKI!
WE EVEN SAW YOU TALKING TO "NEEDLES" UNO, THE TATTOO GUY!

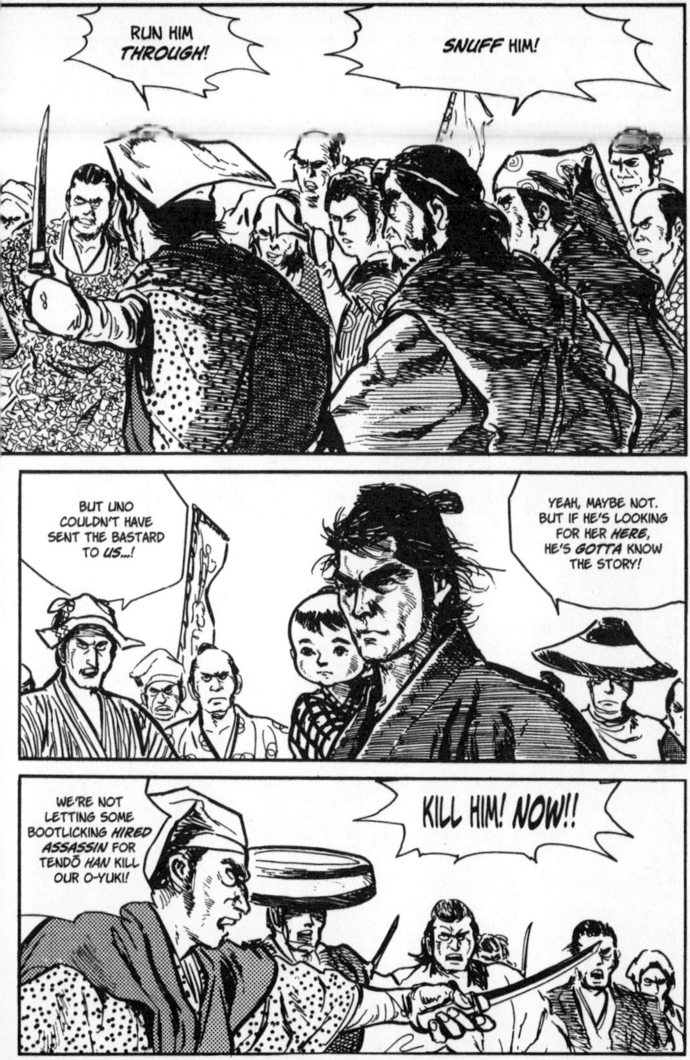
RUN HIM THROUGH!
SNUFF HIM!
BUT UNO COULDN'T HAVE SENT THE BASTARD TO US...!
YEAH, MAYBE NOT. BUT IF HE'S LOOKING FOR HER HERE, HE'S GOTTA KNOW THE STORY!
WE'RE NOT LETTING SOME BOOTLICKING HIRED ASSASSIN FOR TENDŌ HAN KILL OUR O-YUKI!
KILL HIM! NOW!!

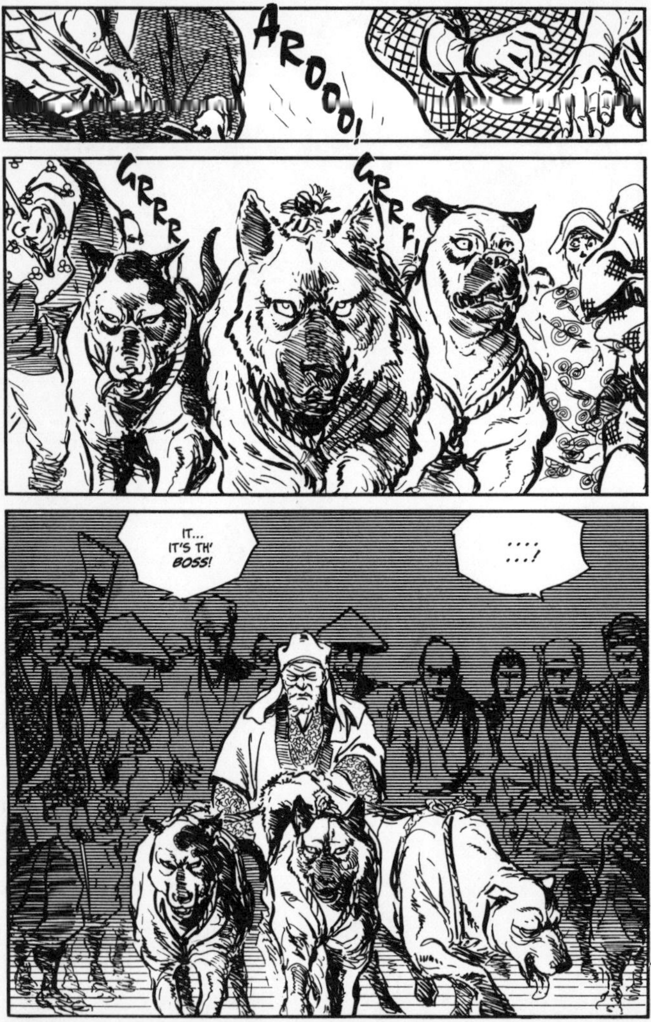
AROOOO!
GRRRF!
GRRRR
....
...!
IT...
IT'S TH' BOSS!

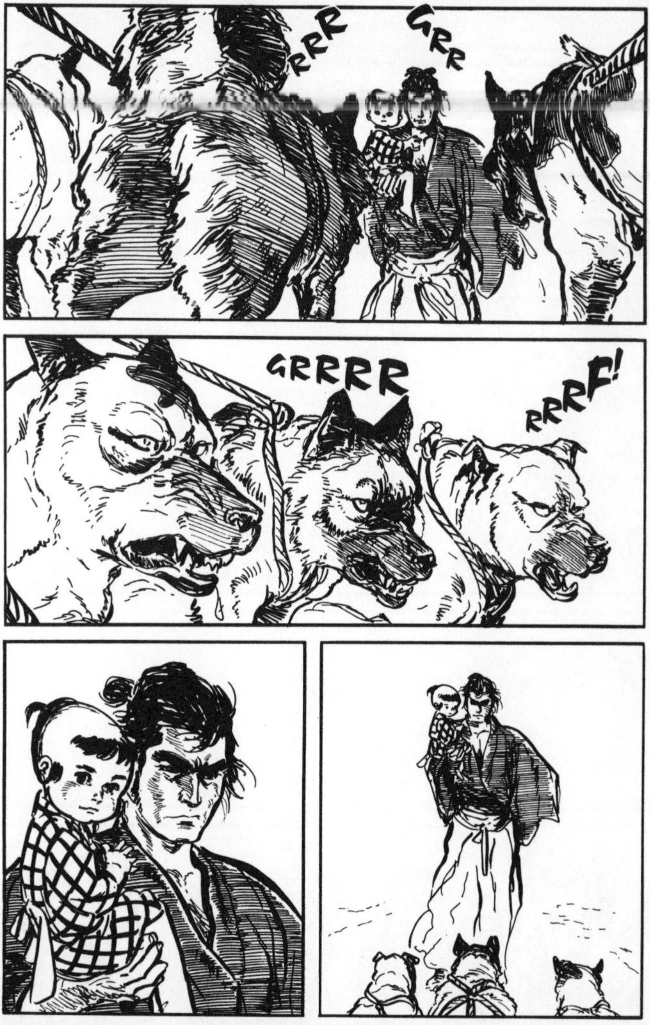
GRR
RRR
RRRF!
GRRRR

BEASTS BE A BETTER JUDGE OF HATE AND MURDER THAN ANY HUMAN BE.

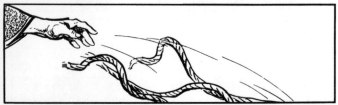

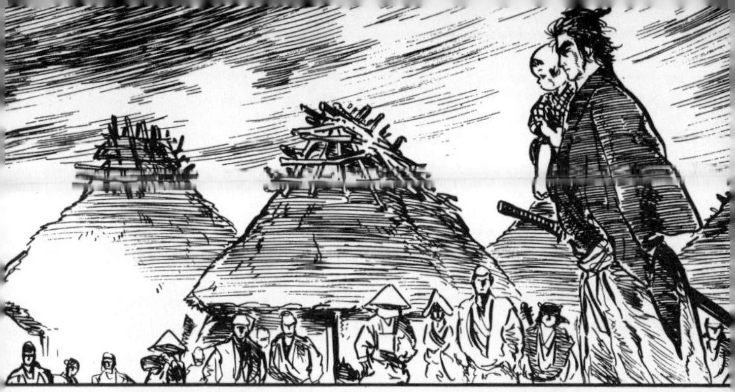

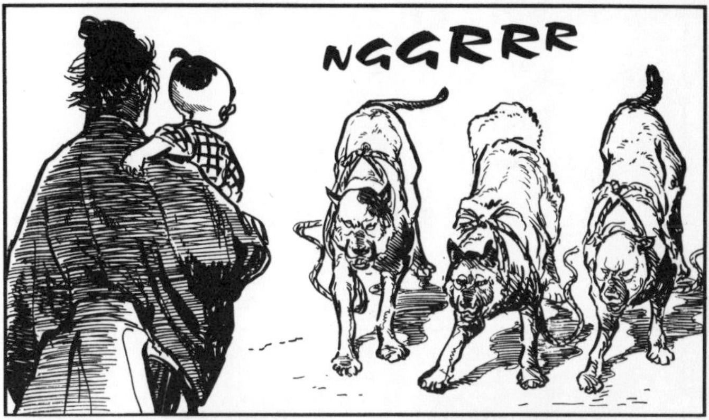
NGGRRR

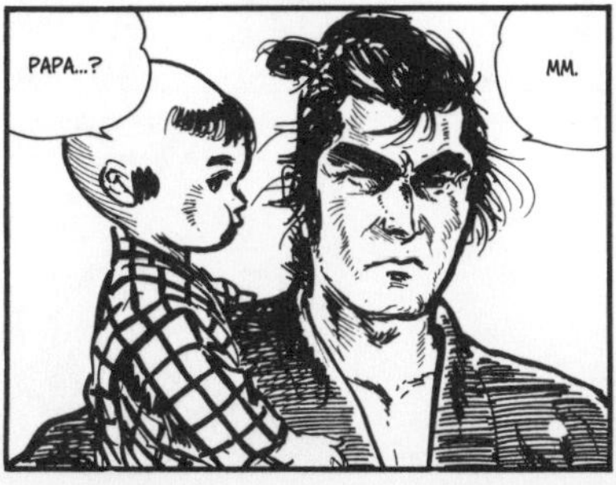
PAPA...?
MM.

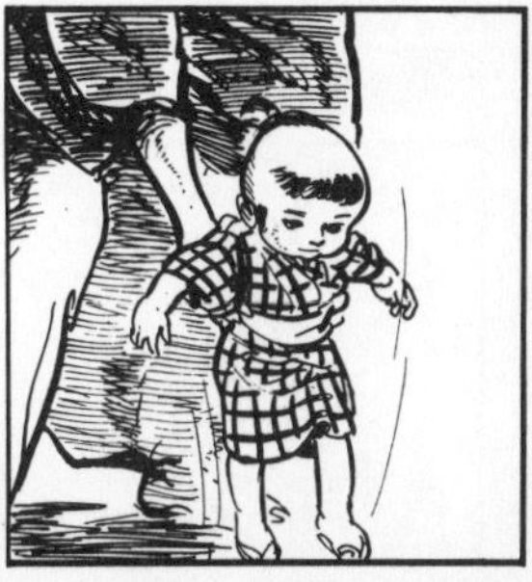

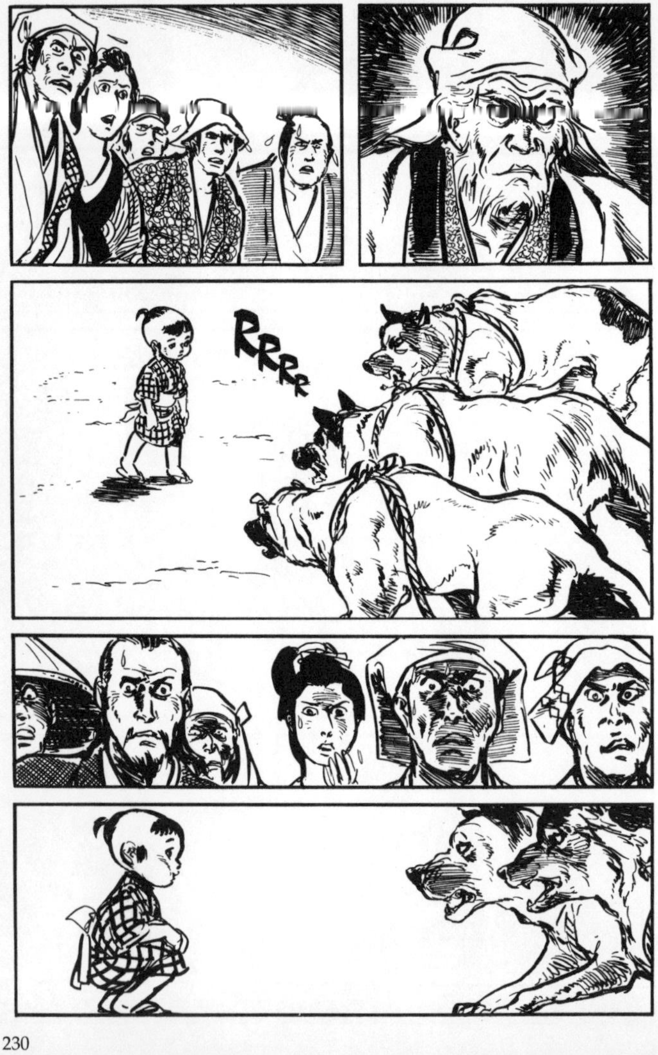
RRRR

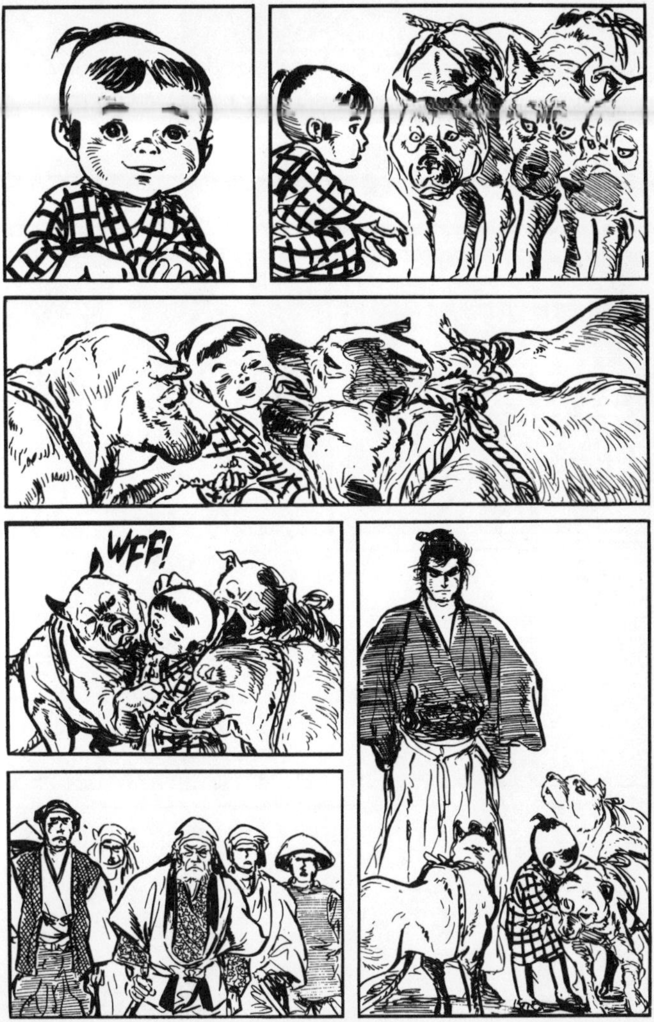
WFF!

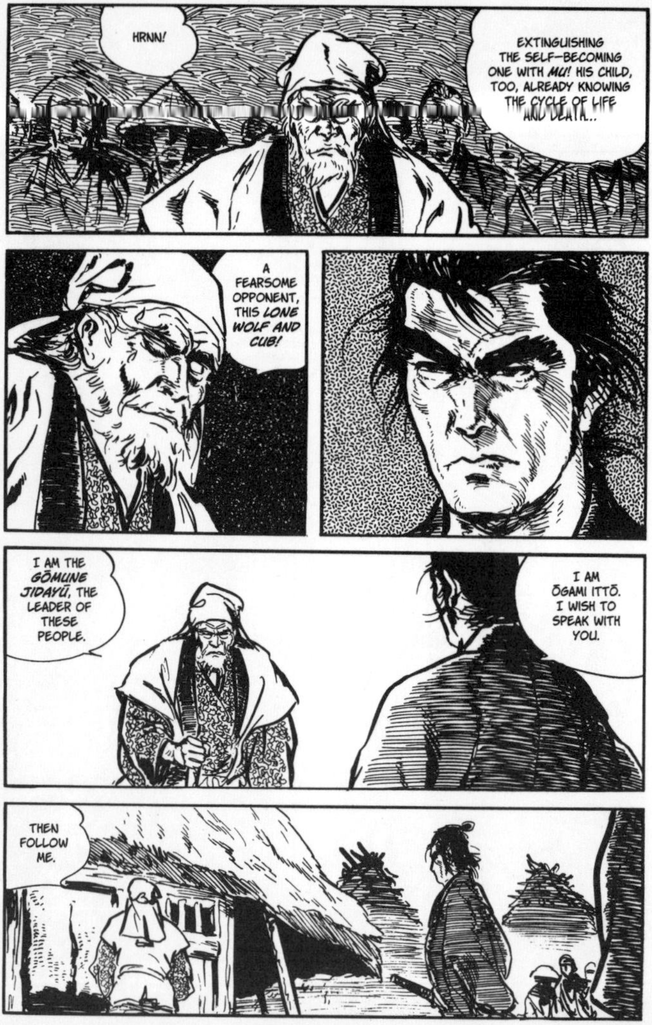
EXTINGUISHING THE SELF—BECOMING ONE WITH *MU!* HIS CHILD, TOO, ALREADY KNOWING THE CYCLE OF LIFE AND DEATH...
HRNN!
A FEARSOME OPPONENT, THIS *LONE WOLF AND CUB!*
I AM ŌGAMI ITTŌ. I WISH TO SPEAK WITH YOU.
I AM THE *GŌMUNE JIDAYŪ*, THE LEADER OF THESE PEOPLE.
THEN FOLLOW ME.

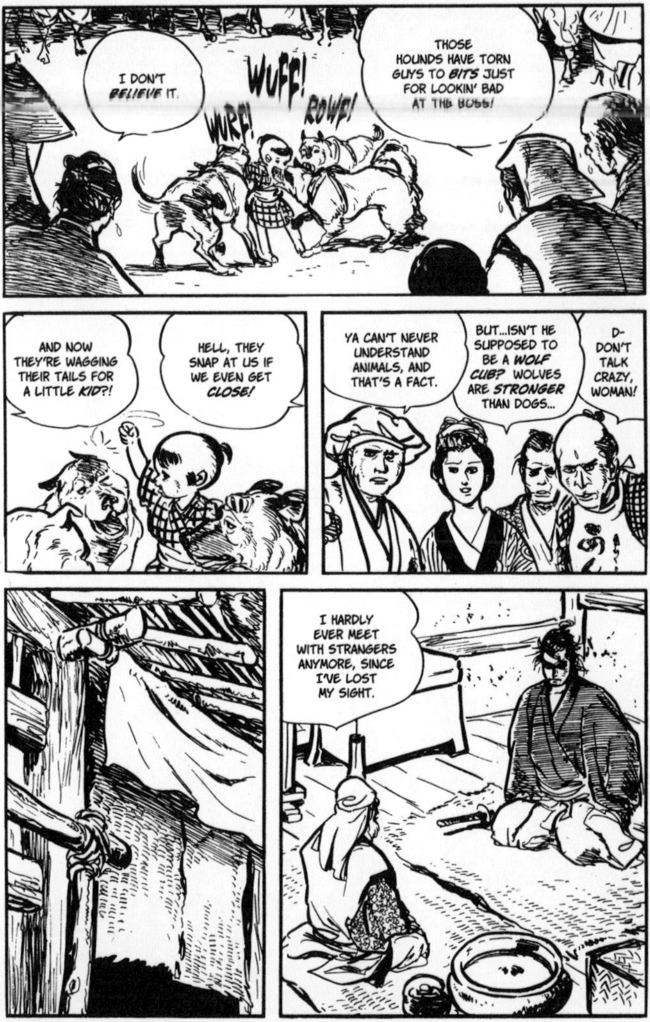
I DON'T BELIEVE IT.
WUFF!
WUFF!
ROWF!
THOSE HOUNDS HAVE TORN GUYS TO BITS JUST FOR LOOKIN' BAD AT THE BOSS!
AND NOW THEY'RE WAGGING THEIR TAILS FOR A LITTLE KID?!
HELL, THEY SNAP AT US IF WE EVEN GET CLOSE!
YA CAN'T NEVER UNDERSTAND ANIMALS, AND THAT'S A FACT.
BUT...ISN'T HE SUPPOSED TO BE A WOLF CUB? WOLVES ARE STRONGER THAN DOGS...
D-DON'T TALK CRAZY, WOMAN!
I HARDLY EVER MEET WITH STRANGERS ANYMORE, SINCE I'VE LOST MY SIGHT.

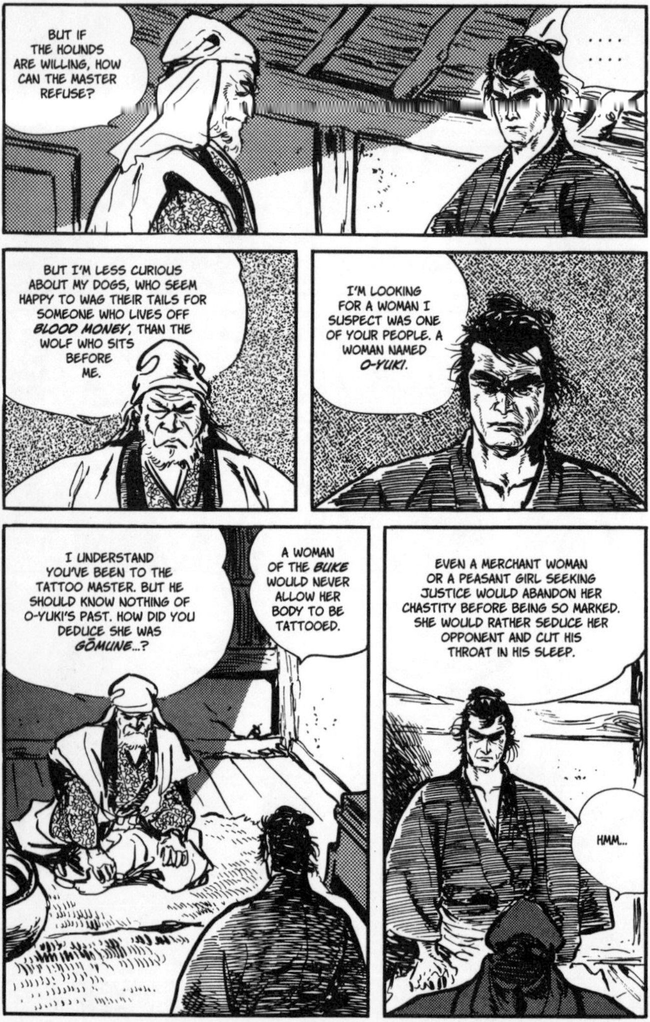
BUT IF THE HOUNDS ARE WILLING, HOW CAN THE MASTER REFUSE?
....
....
BUT I'M LESS CURIOUS ABOUT MY DOGS, WHO SEEM HAPPY TO WAG THEIR TAILS FOR SOMEONE WHO LIVES OFF *BLOOD MONEY*, THAN THE WOLF WHO SITS BEFORE ME.
I'M LOOKING FOR A WOMAN I SUSPECT WAS ONE OF YOUR PEOPLE. A WOMAN NAMED *O-YUKI*.
I UNDERSTAND YOU'VE BEEN TO THE TATTOO MASTER. BUT HE SHOULD KNOW NOTHING OF O-YUKI'S PAST. HOW DID YOU DEDUCE SHE WAS *GŌMUNE*...?
A WOMAN OF THE *BUKE* WOULD NEVER ALLOW HER BODY TO BE TATTOOED.
EVEN A MERCHANT WOMAN OR A PEASANT GIRL SEEKING JUSTICE WOULD ABANDON HER CHASTITY BEFORE BEING SO MARKED. SHE WOULD RATHER SEDUCE HER OPPONENT AND CUT HIS THROAT IN HIS SLEEP.
HMM...

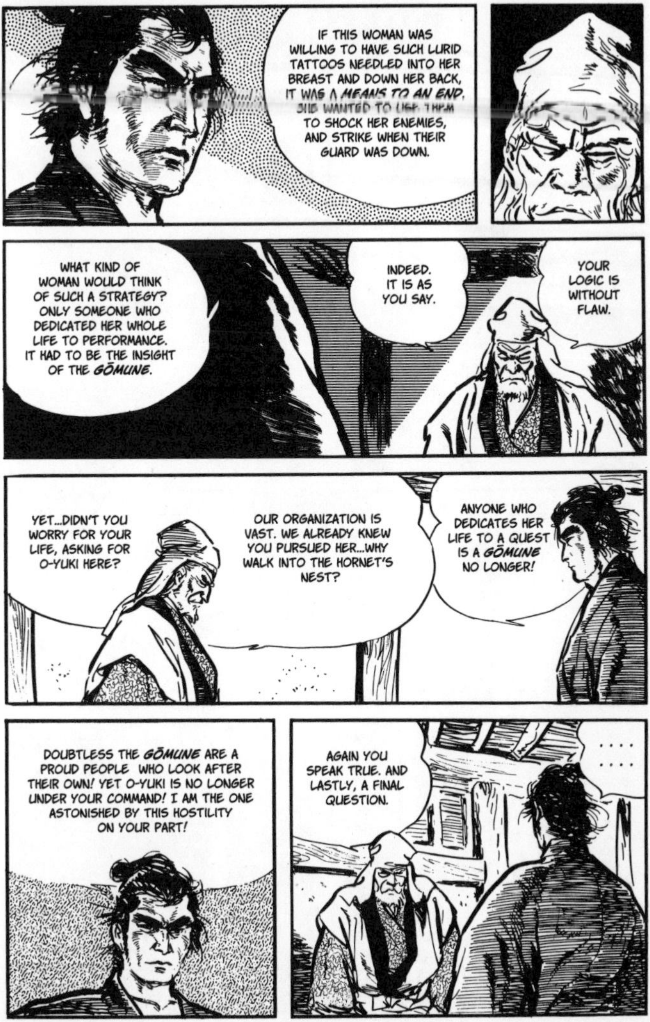
IF THIS WOMAN WAS WILLING TO HAVE SUCH LURID TATTOOS NEEDLED INTO HER BREAST AND DOWN HER BACK, IT WAS A *MEANS TO AN END.* SHE WANTED TO USE THEM TO SHOCK HER ENEMIES, AND STRIKE WHEN THEIR GUARD WAS DOWN.
WHAT KIND OF WOMAN WOULD THINK OF SUCH A STRATEGY? ONLY SOMEONE WHO DEDICATED HER WHOLE LIFE TO PERFORMANCE. IT HAD TO BE THE INSIGHT OF THE *GŌMUNE*.
INDEED. IT IS AS YOU SAY.
YOUR LOGIC IS WITHOUT FLAW.
YET...DIDN'T YOU WORRY FOR YOUR LIFE, ASKING FOR O-YUKI HERE?
OUR ORGANIZATION IS VAST. WE ALREADY KNEW YOU PURSUED HER...WHY WALK INTO THE HORNET'S NEST?
ANYONE WHO DEDICATES HER LIFE TO A QUEST IS A *GŌMUNE* NO LONGER!
DOUBTLESS THE *GŌMUNE* ARE A PROUD PEOPLE WHO LOOK AFTER THEIR OWN! YET O-YUKI IS NO LONGER UNDER YOUR COMMAND! I AM THE ONE ASTONISHED BY THIS HOSTILITY ON YOUR PART!
AGAIN YOU SPEAK TRUE. AND LASTLY, A FINAL QUESTION.
....
....

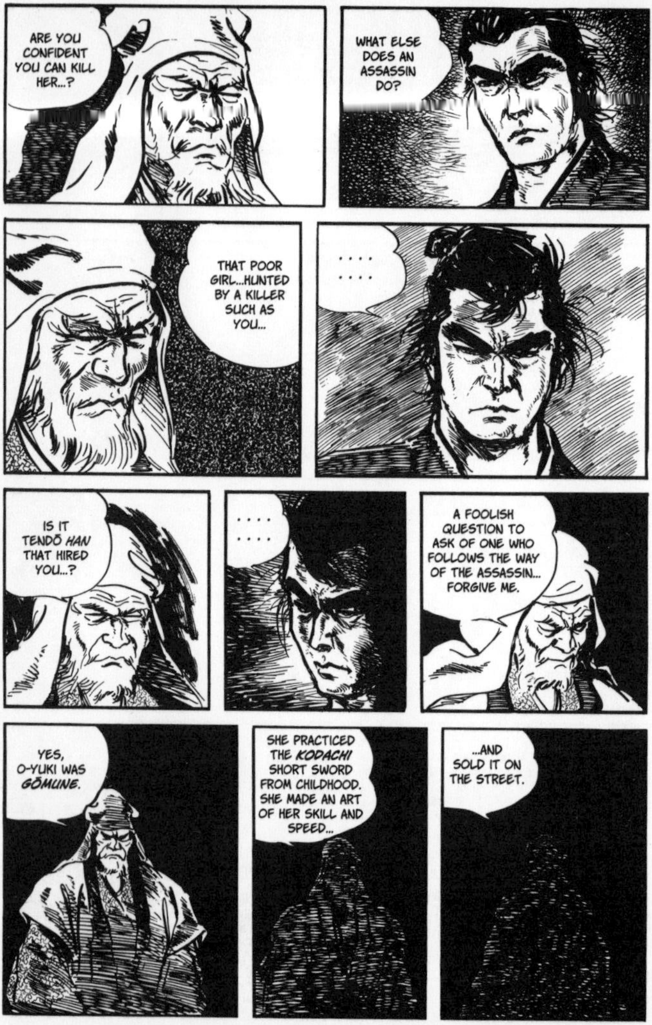
ARE YOU CONFIDENT YOU CAN KILL HER...?
WHAT ELSE DOES AN ASSASSIN DO?
THAT POOR GIRL...HUNTED BY A KILLER SUCH AS YOU...
. . . .
. . . .
IS IT TENDŌ *HAN* THAT HIRED YOU...?
. . . .
. . . .
A FOOLISH QUESTION TO ASK OF ONE WHO FOLLOWS THE WAY OF THE ASSASSIN... FORGIVE ME.
YES, O-YUKI WAS *GŌMUNE*.
SHE PRACTICED THE *KODACHI* SHORT SWORD FROM CHILDHOOD. SHE MADE AN ART OF HER SKILL AND SPEED...
...AND SOLD IT ON THE STREET.

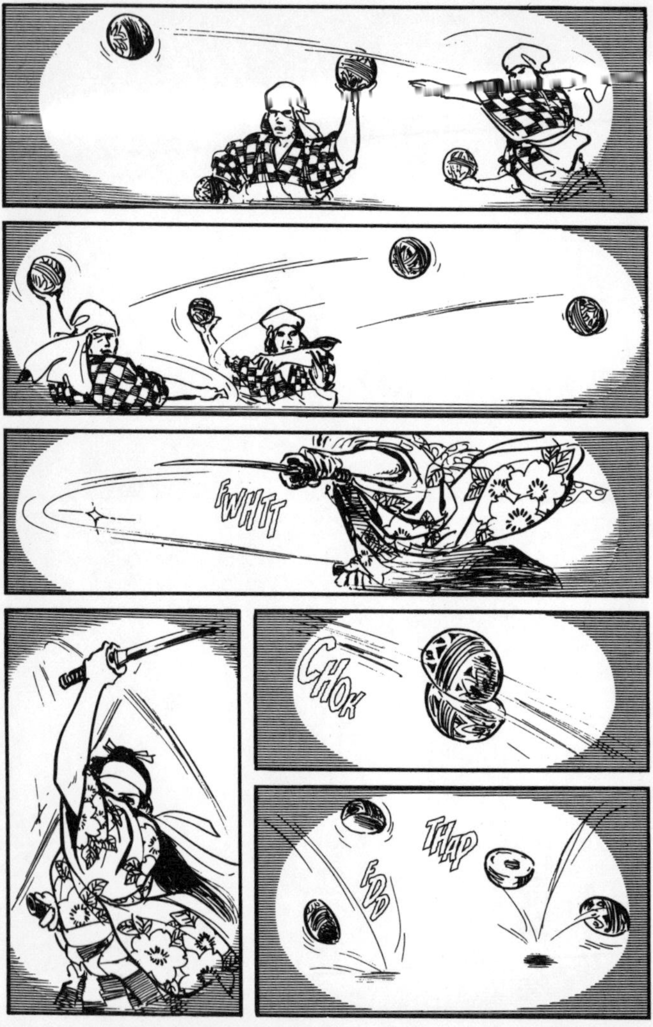
FWHTT
CHOK
THAP
FDD

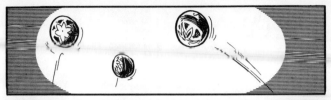

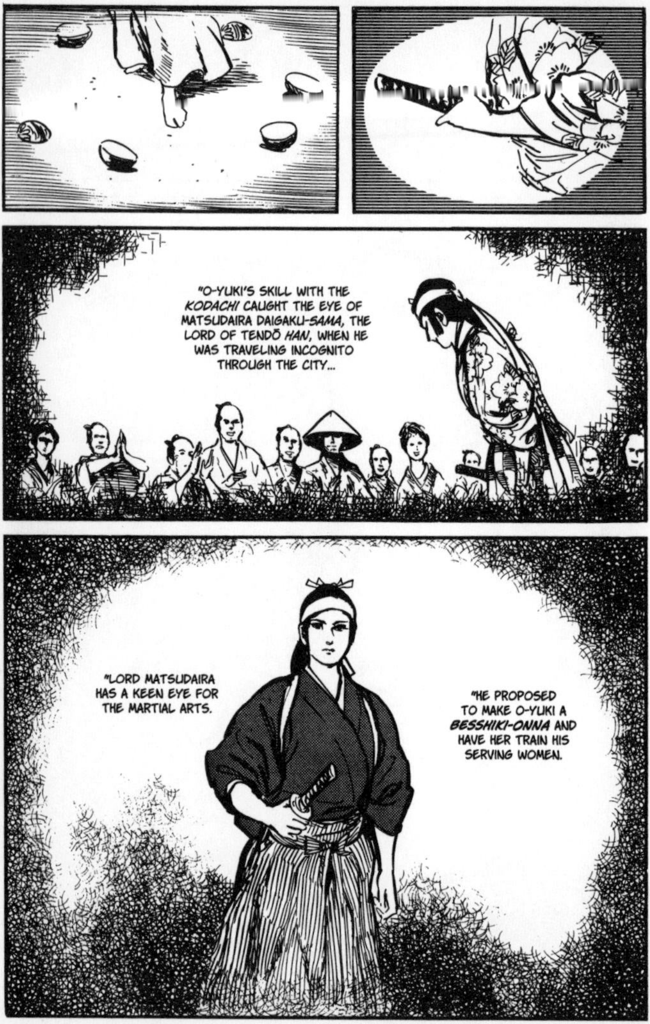
"O-YUKI'S SKILL WITH THE *KODACHI* CAUGHT THE EYE OF MATSUDAIRA DAIGAKU-*SAMA*, THE LORD OF TENDŌ *HAN*, WHEN HE WAS TRAVELING INCOGNITO THROUGH THE CITY...
"LORD MATSUDAIRA HAS A KEEN EYE FOR THE MARTIAL ARTS.
"HE PROPOSED TO MAKE O-YUKI A *BESSHIKI-ONNA* AND HAVE HER TRAIN HIS SERVING WOMEN.

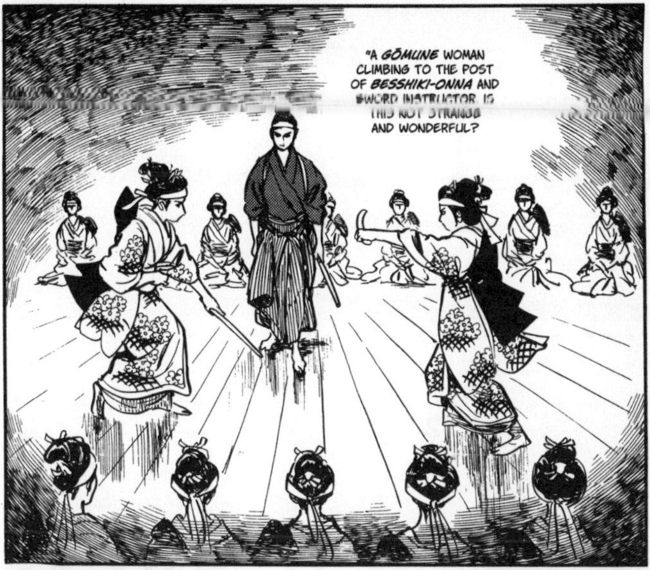
"A GŌMUNE WOMAN CLIMBING TO THE POST OF BESSHIKI-ONNA AND SWORD INSTRUCTOR, IS THIS NOT STRANGE AND WONDERFUL?

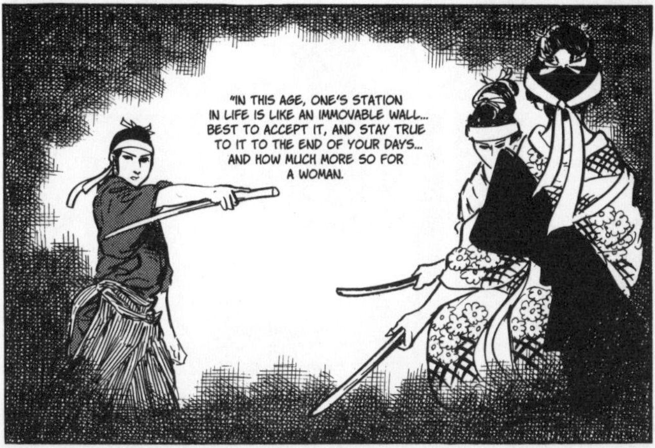
"IN THIS AGE, ONE'S STATION IN LIFE IS LIKE AN IMMOVABLE WALL... BEST TO ACCEPT IT, AND STAY TRUE TO IT TO THE END OF YOUR DAYS... AND HOW MUCH MORE SO FOR A WOMAN.

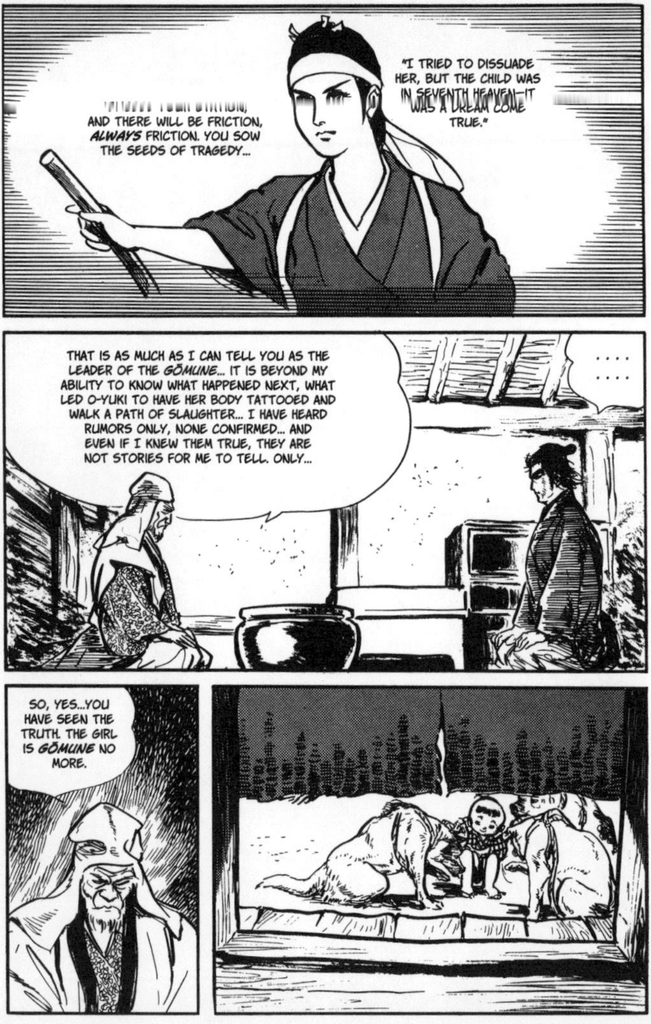
"I TRIED TO DISSUADE HER, BUT THE CHILD WAS IN SEVENTH HEAVEN—IT WAS A DREAM COME TRUE."
AND THERE WILL BE FRICTION, *ALWAYS* FRICTION. YOU SOW THE SEEDS OF TRAGEDY...
....
....
THAT IS AS MUCH AS I CAN TELL YOU AS THE LEADER OF THE *GŌMUNE*... IT IS BEYOND MY ABILITY TO KNOW WHAT HAPPENED NEXT, WHAT LED O-YUKI TO HAVE HER BODY TATTOOED AND WALK A PATH OF SLAUGHTER... I HAVE HEARD RUMORS ONLY, NONE CONFIRMED... AND EVEN IF I KNEW THEM TRUE, THEY ARE NOT STORIES FOR ME TO TELL. ONLY...
SO, YES...YOU HAVE SEEN THE TRUTH. THE GIRL IS *GŌMUNE* NO MORE.

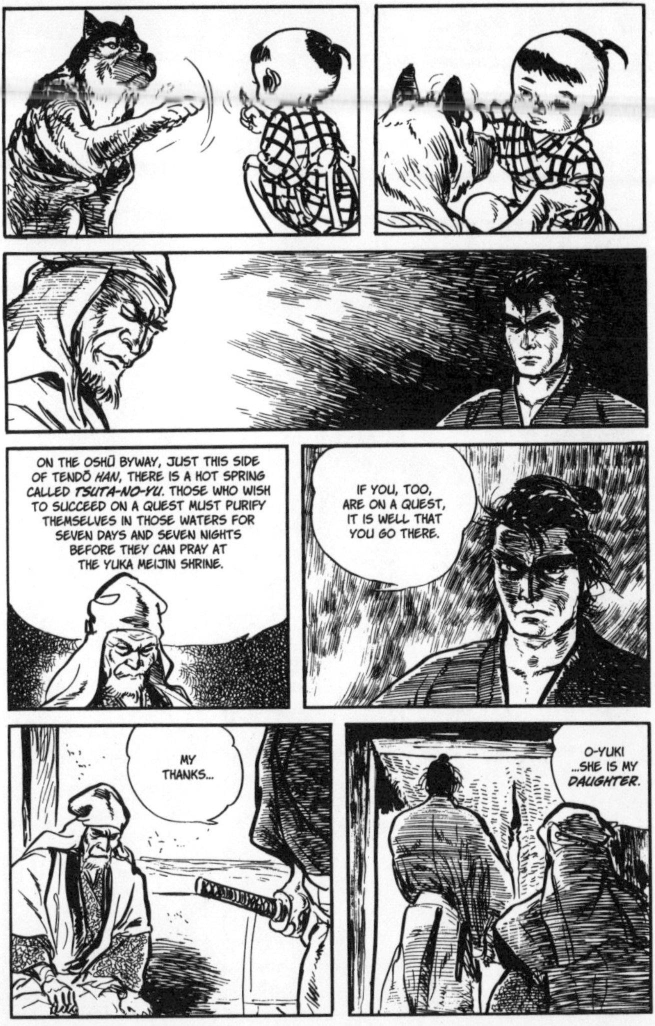
ON THE OSHŪ BYWAY, JUST THIS SIDE OF TENDŌ *HAN*, THERE IS A HOT SPRING CALLED *TSUTA-NO-YU*. THOSE WHO WISH TO SUCCEED ON A QUEST MUST PURIFY THEMSELVES IN THOSE WATERS FOR SEVEN DAYS AND SEVEN NIGHTS BEFORE THEY CAN PRAY AT THE YUKA MEIJIN SHRINE.
IF YOU, TOO, ARE ON A QUEST, IT IS WELL THAT YOU GO THERE.
MY THANKS...
O-YUKI ...SHE IS MY *DAUGHTER*.

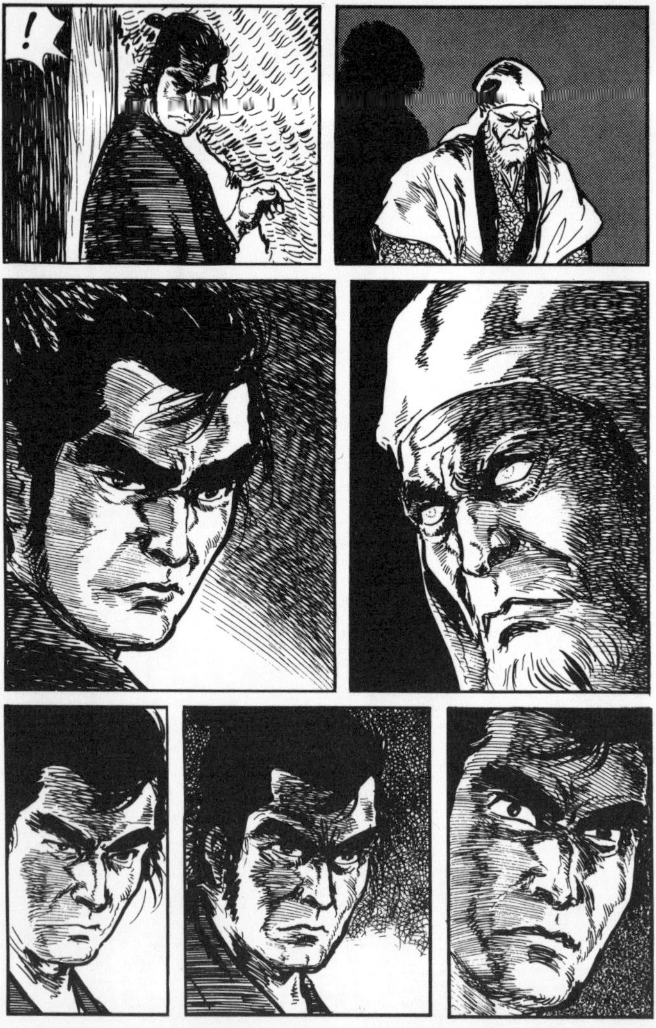
!

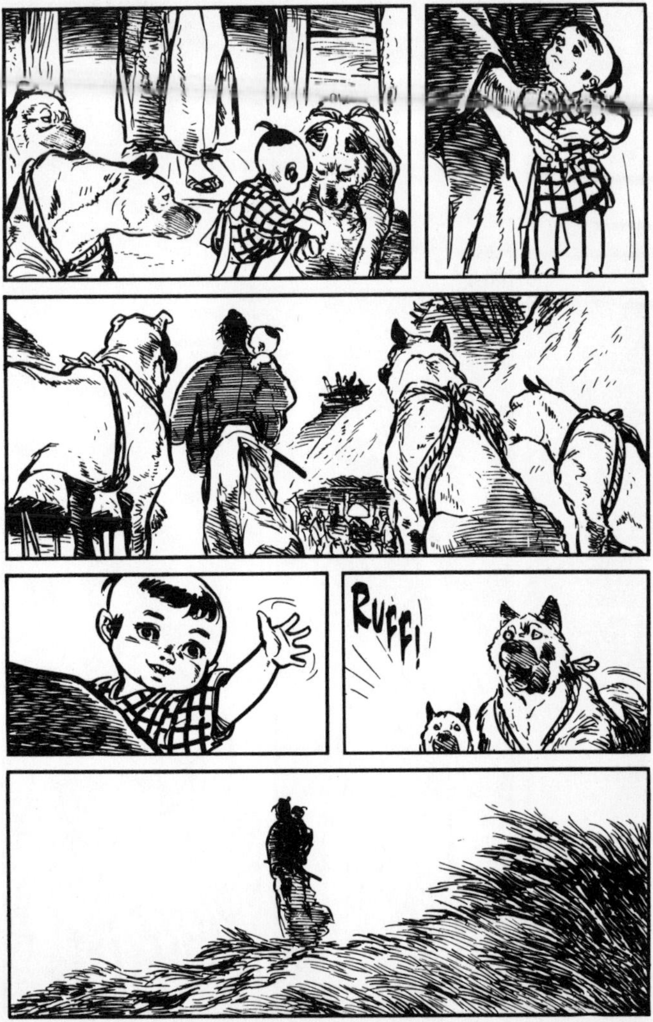
RUFF!

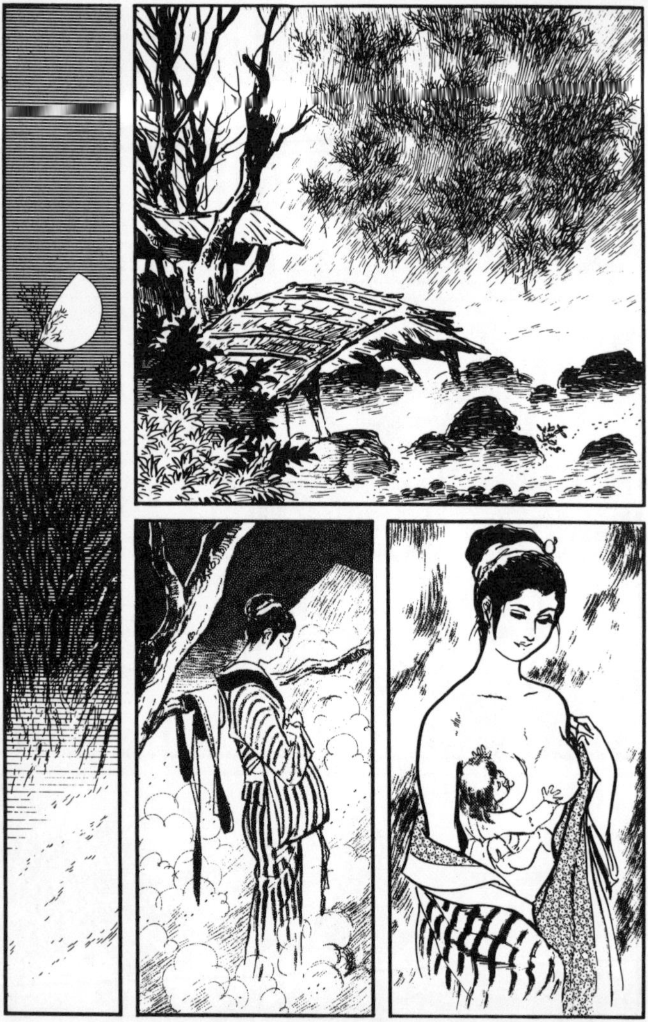

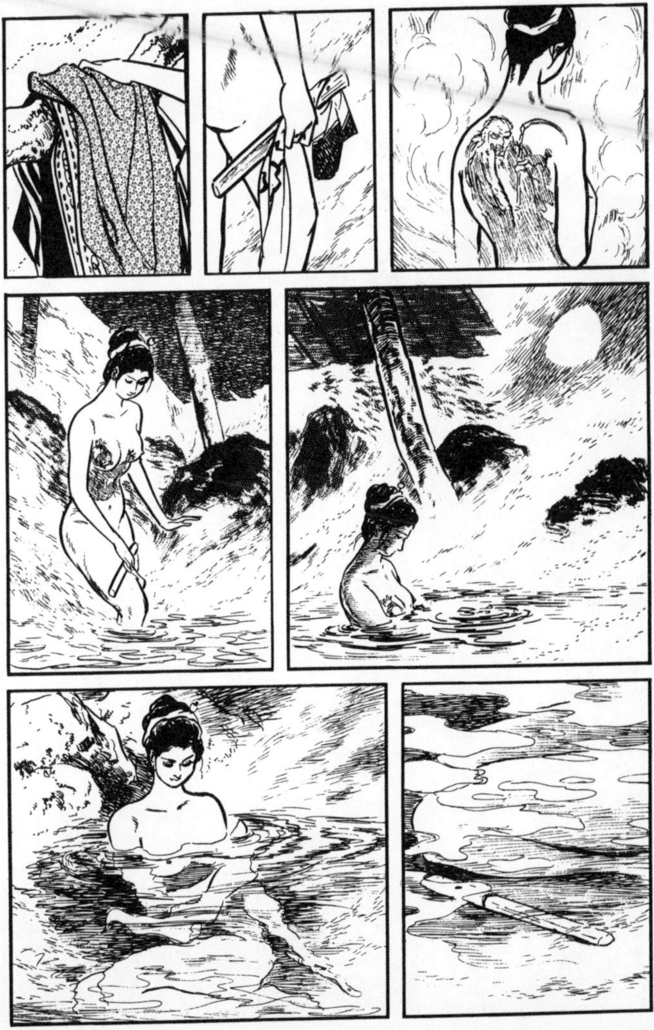

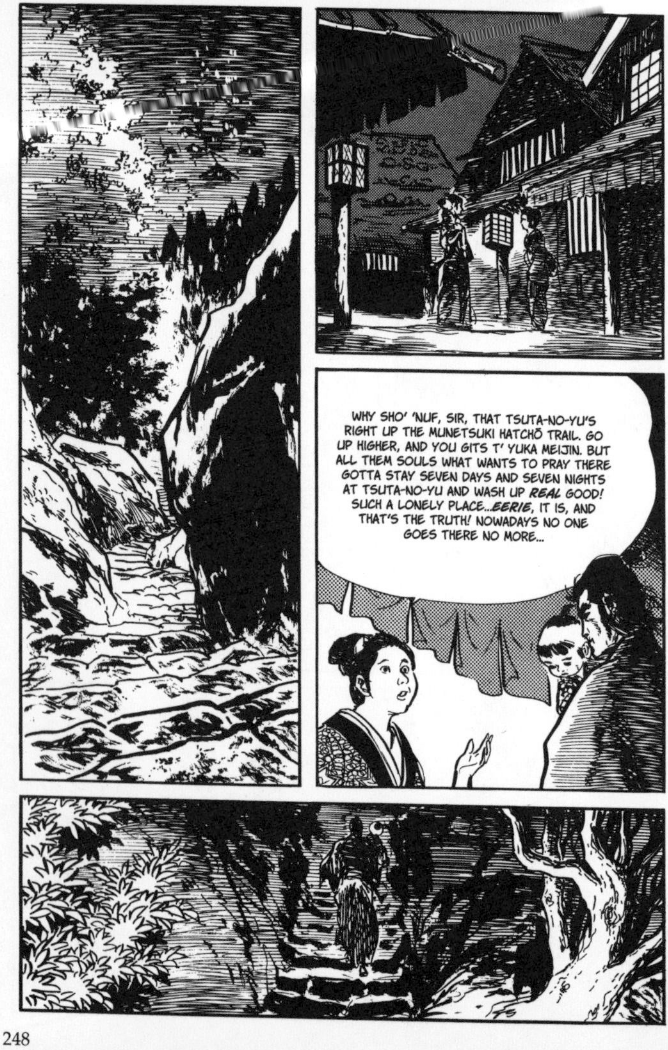
WHY SHO' 'NUF, SIR, THAT TSUTA-NO-YU'S RIGHT UP THE MUNETSUKI HATCHŌ TRAIL. GO UP HIGHER, AND YOU GITS T' YUKA MEIJIN. BUT ALL THEM SOULS WHAT WANTS TO PRAY THERE GOTTA STAY SEVEN DAYS AND SEVEN NIGHTS AT TSUTA-NO-YU AND WASH UP *REAL* GOOD! SUCH A LONELY PLACE...*EERIE*, IT IS, AND THAT'S THE TRUTH! NOWADAYS NO ONE GOES THERE NO MORE...

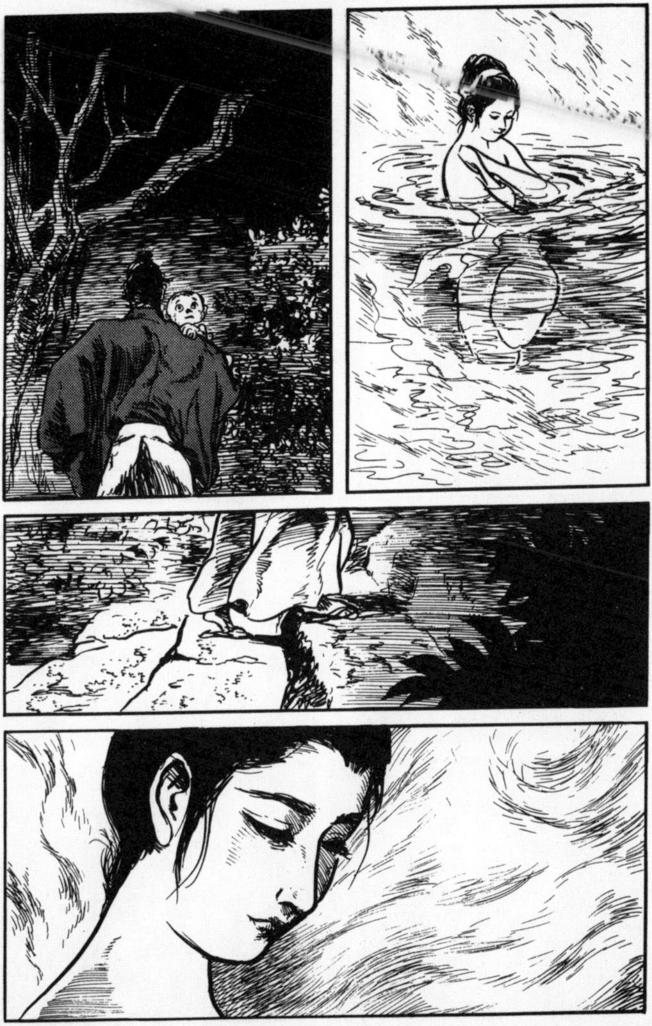

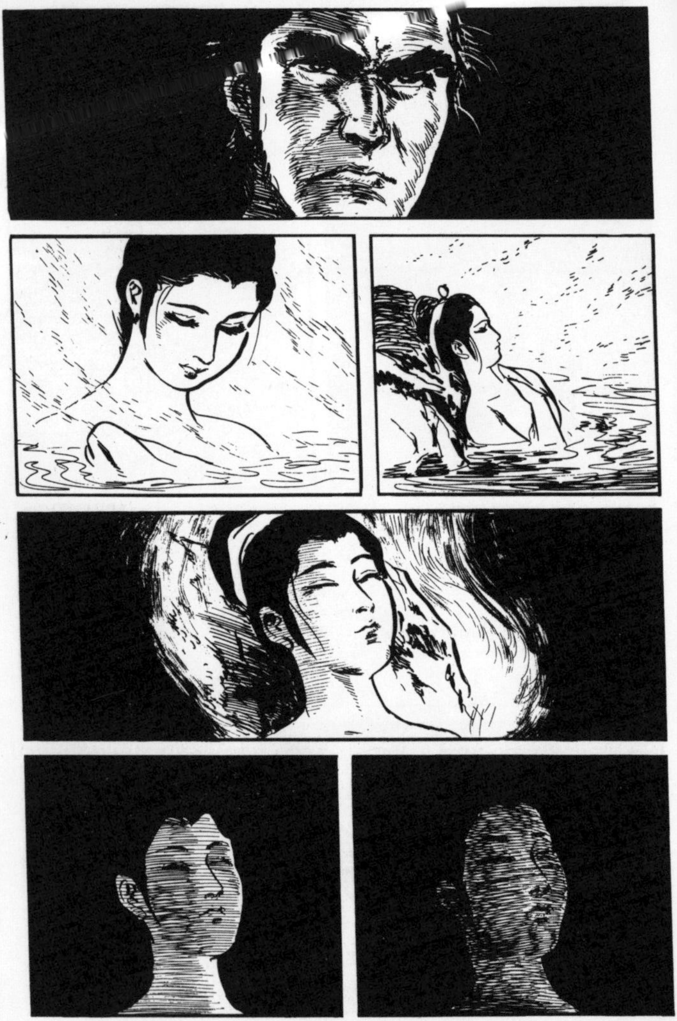

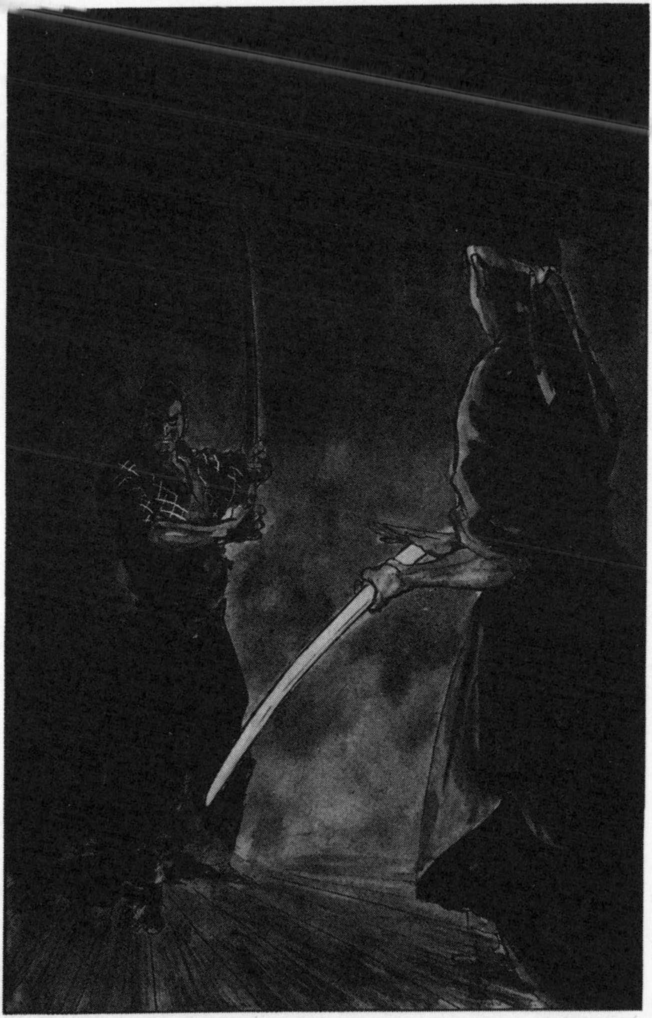

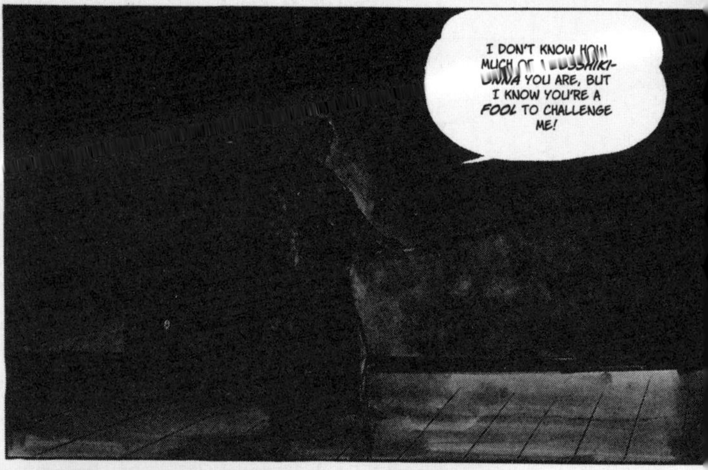
I DON'T KNOW HOW MUCH OF SHIKI-UNNA YOU ARE, BUT I KNOW YOU'RE A FOOL TO CHALLENGE ME!
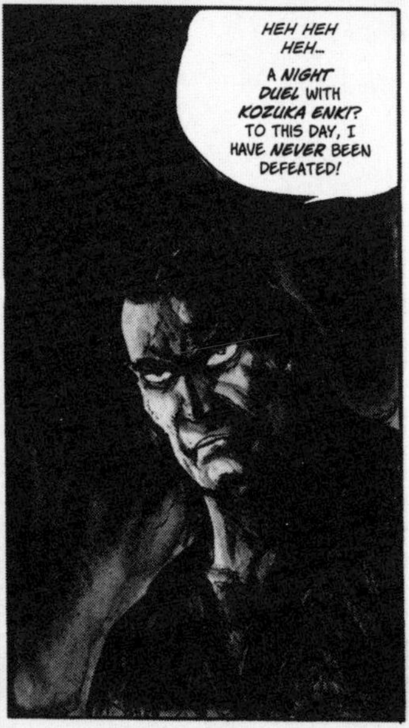
HEH HEH HEH... A NIGHT DUEL WITH KOZUKA ENKI? TO THIS DAY, I HAVE NEVER BEEN DEFEATED!
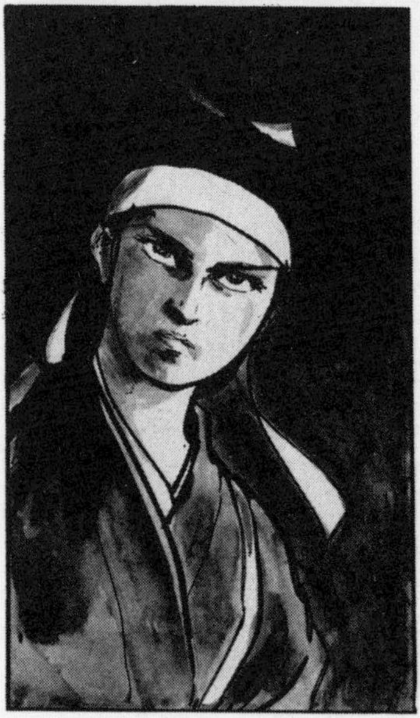

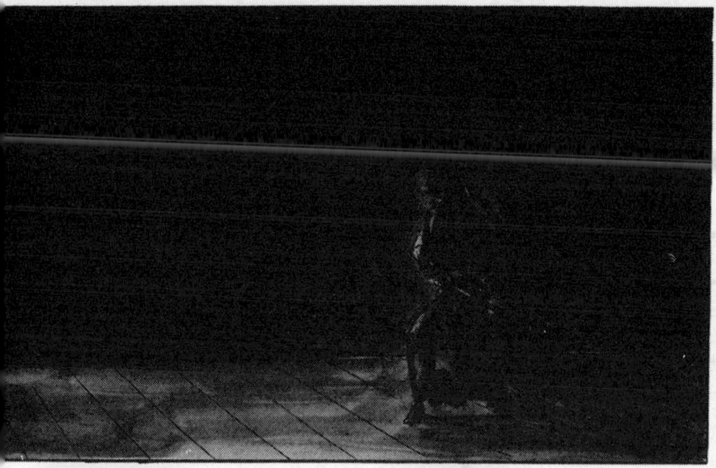

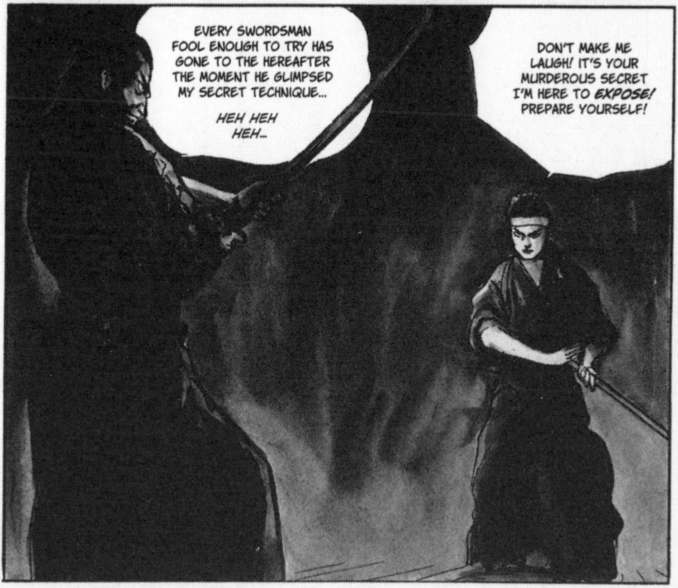
EVERY SWORDSMAN FOOL ENOUGH TO TRY HAS GONE TO THE HEREAFTER THE MOMENT HE GLIMPSED MY SECRET TECHNIQUE...
HEH HEH HEH...
DON'T MAKE ME LAUGH! IT'S YOUR MURDEROUS SECRET I'M HERE TO EXPOSE! PREPARE YOURSELF!

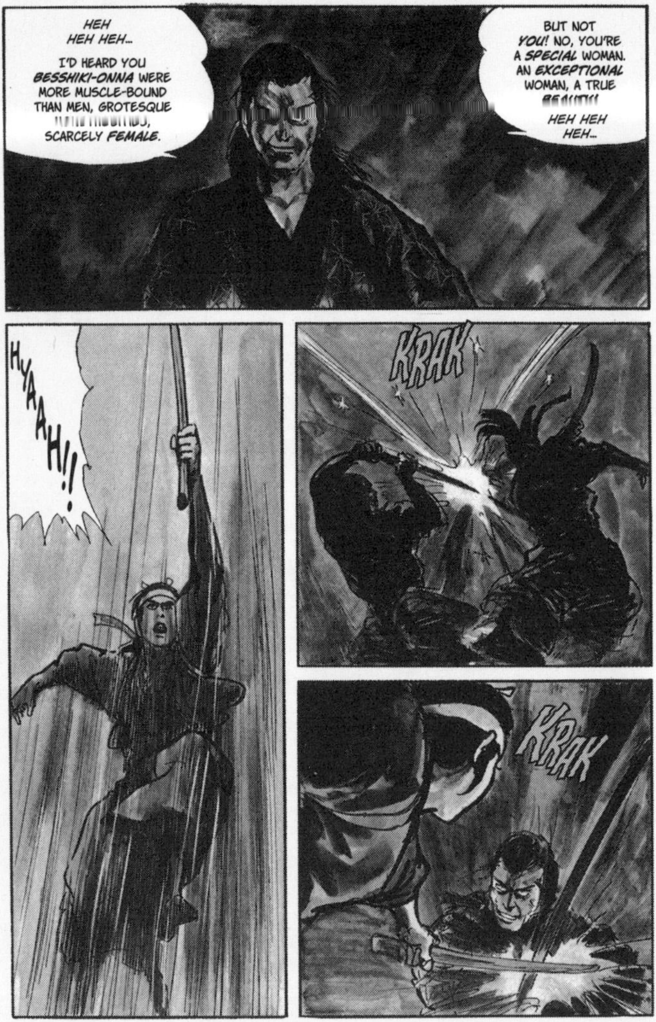
HEH HEH HEH...
I'D HEARD YOU *BESSHIKI-ONNA* WERE MORE MUSCLE-BOUND THAN MEN, GROTESQUE
SCARCELY *FEMALE*.
BUT NOT *YOU!* NO, YOU'RE A *SPECIAL* WOMAN. AN *EXCEPTIONAL* WOMAN, A TRUE
HEH HEH HEH...
HYAAAH!!
KRAK
KRAK

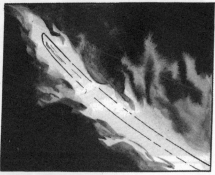

HEH HEH HEH...

WHAT ARE YOU *STARING* AT? LOOK AT THE *SWORD* AND YOU *LOSE*!

255

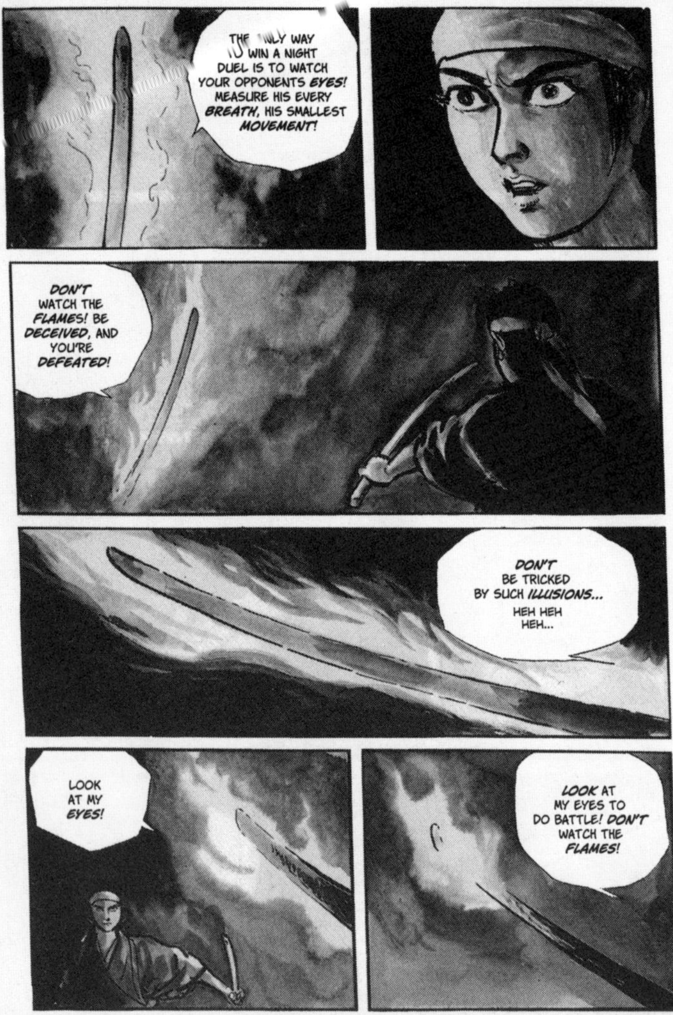
THE ONLY WAY TO WIN A NIGHT DUEL IS TO WATCH YOUR OPPONENTS EYES! MEASURE HIS EVERY BREATH, HIS SMALLEST MOVEMENT!
DON'T WATCH THE FLAMES! BE DECEIVED, AND YOU'RE DEFEATED!
DON'T BE TRICKED BY SUCH ILLUSIONS... HEH HEH HEH...
LOOK AT MY EYES!
LOOK AT MY EYES TO DO BATTLE! DON'T WATCH THE FLAMES!

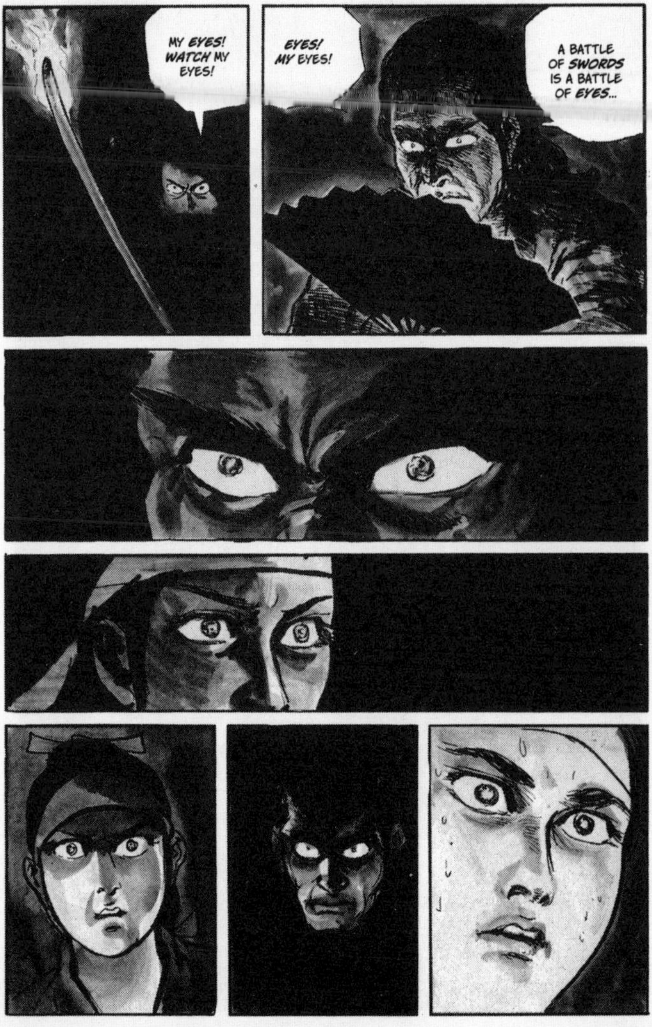
A BATTLE OF SWORDS IS A BATTLE OF EYES...
EYES! MY EYES!
MY EYES! WATCH MY EYES!

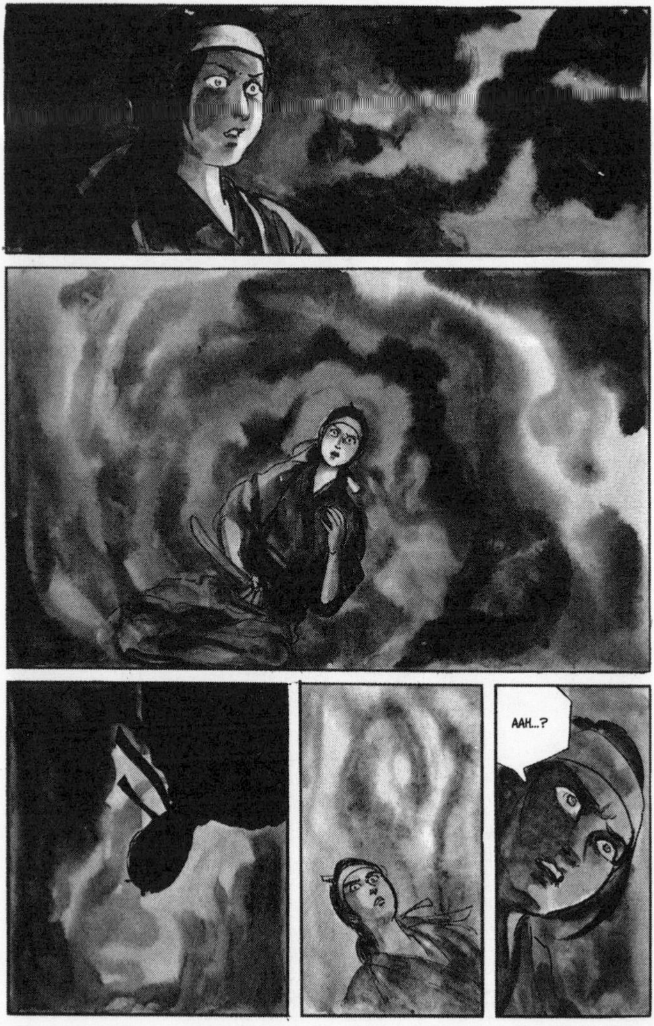
AAH...?

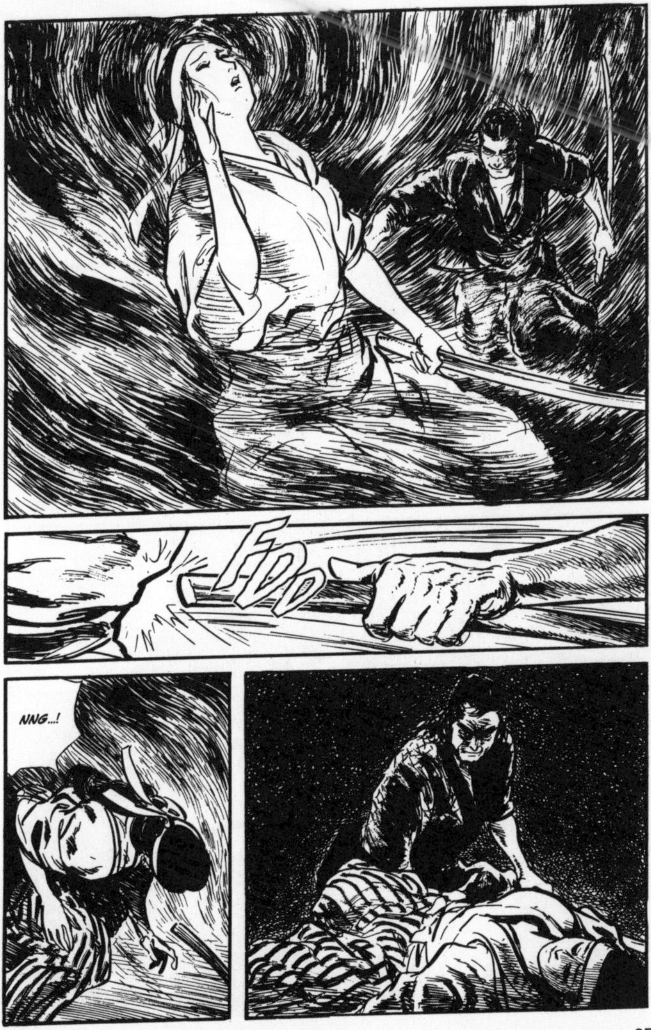
NNG...!

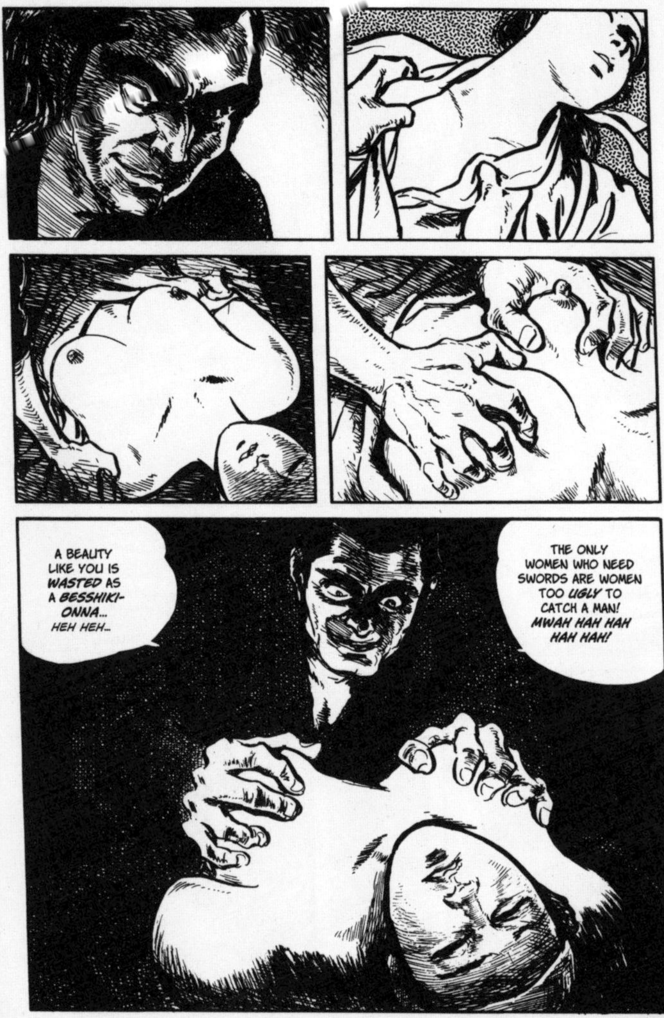
A BEAUTY LIKE YOU IS *WASTED* AS A *BESSHIKI-ONNA*... HEH HEH...
THE ONLY WOMEN WHO NEED SWORDS ARE WOMEN TOO *UGLY* TO CATCH A MAN! *MWAH HAH HAH HAH HAH!*

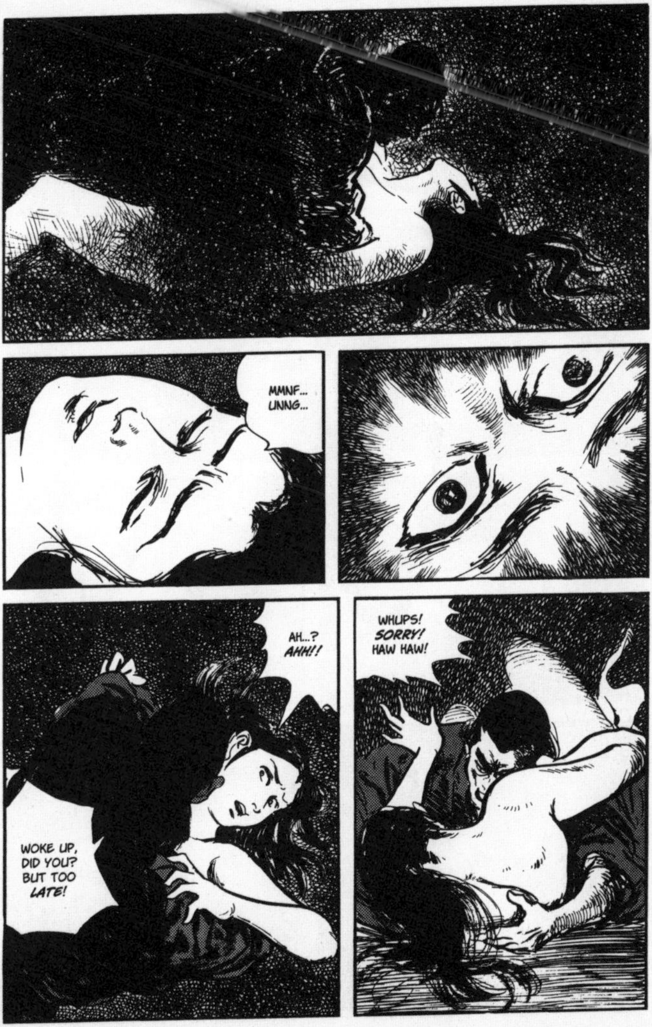
MMNF... UNNG...
WHUPS! *SORRY!* HAW HAW!
AH...? *AHH!!*
WOKE UP, DID YOU? BUT TOO *LATE!*

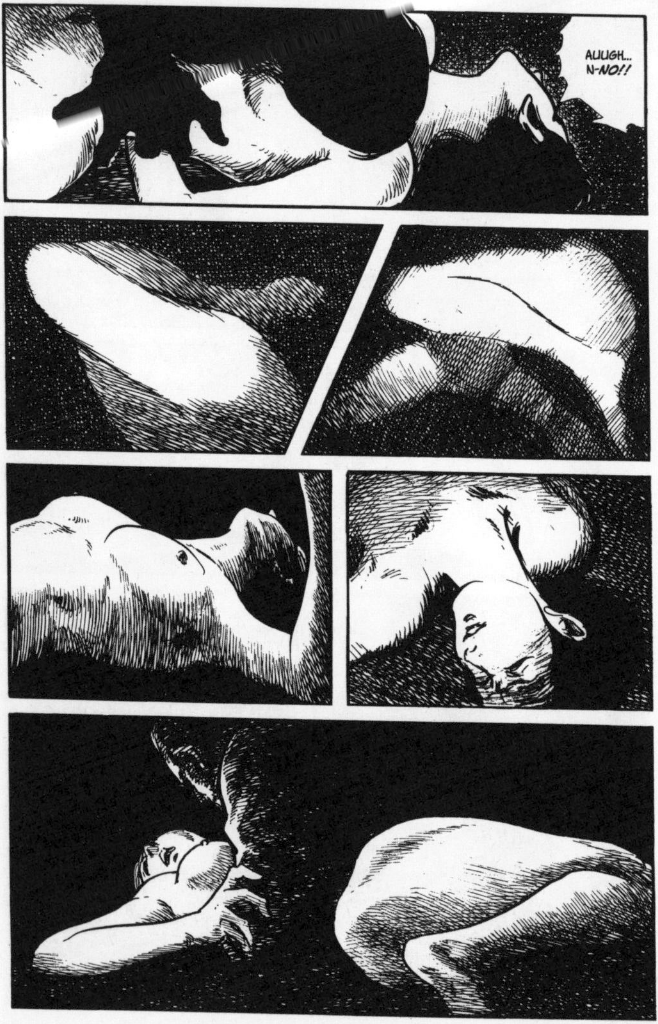
AUUGH... N-NO!!

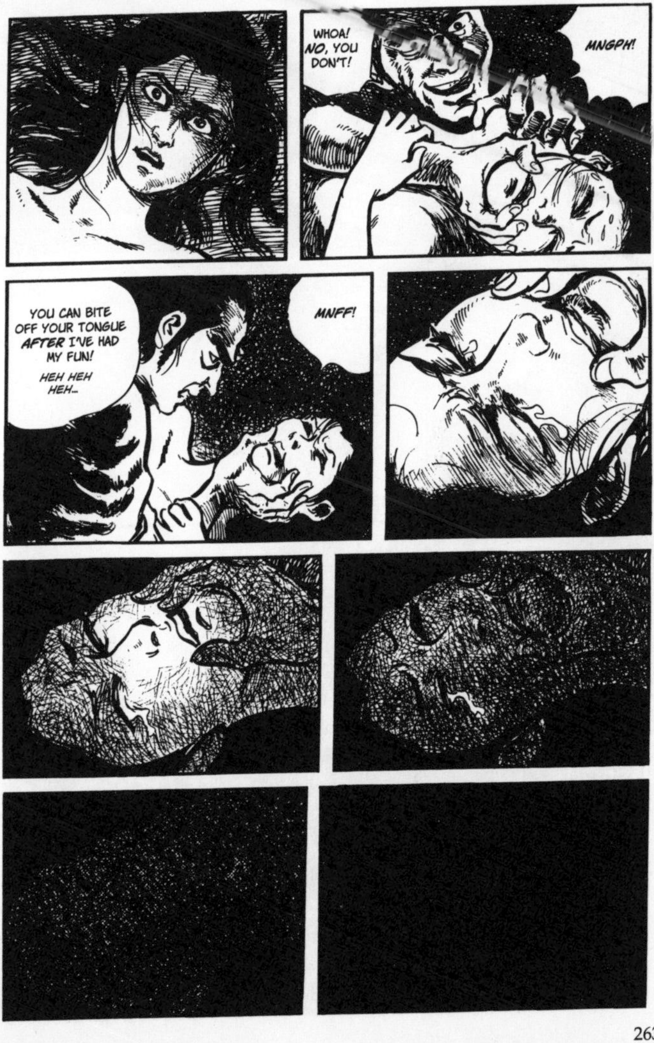
MNGPH!
WHOA! NO, YOU DON'T!
MNFF!
YOU CAN BITE OFF YOUR TONGUE AFTER I'VE HAD MY FUN!
HEH HEH HEH...

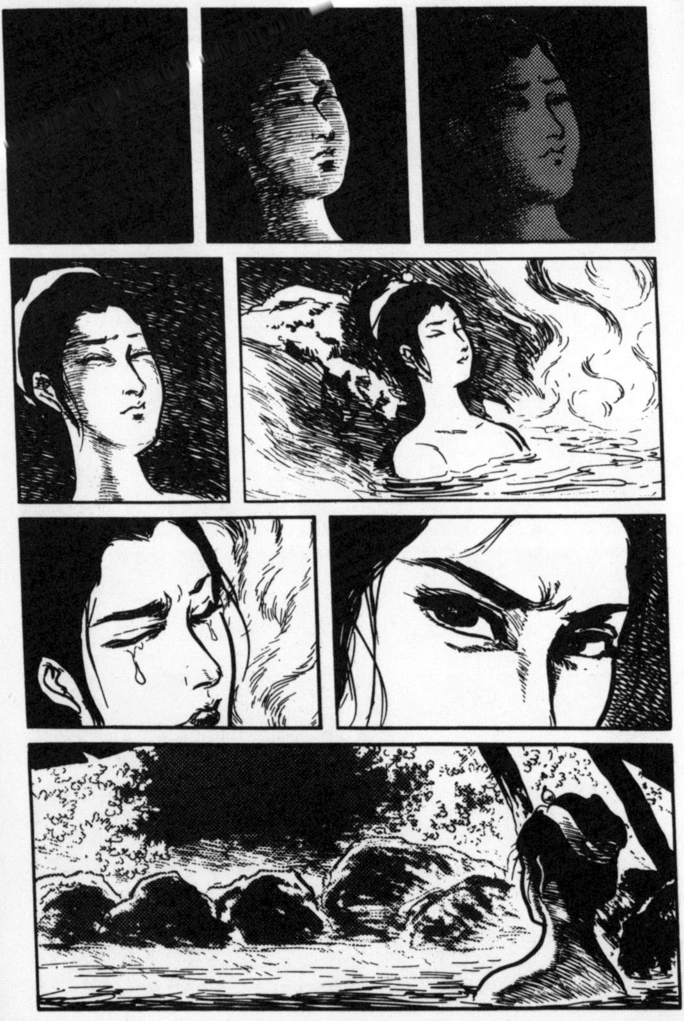

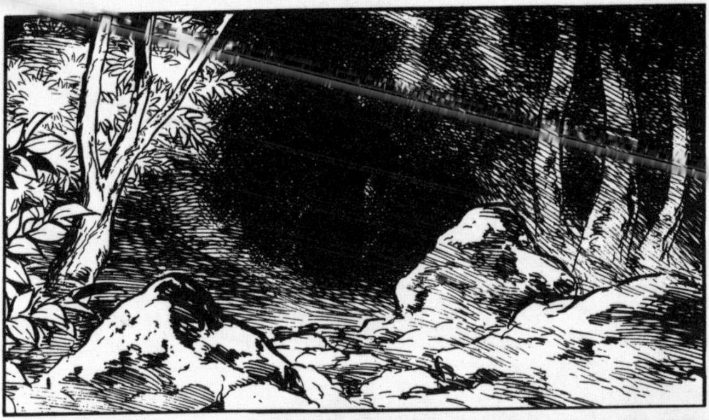
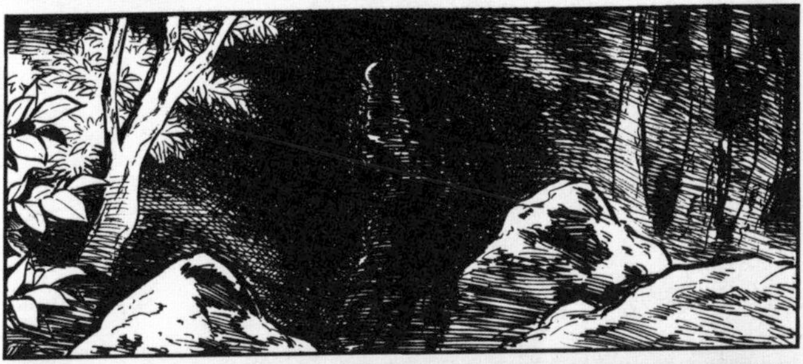
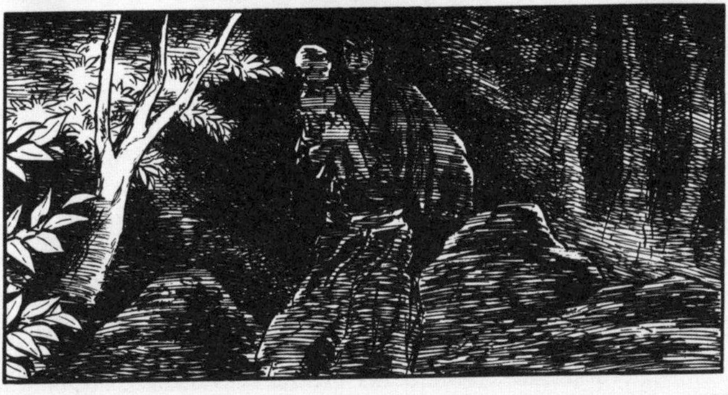

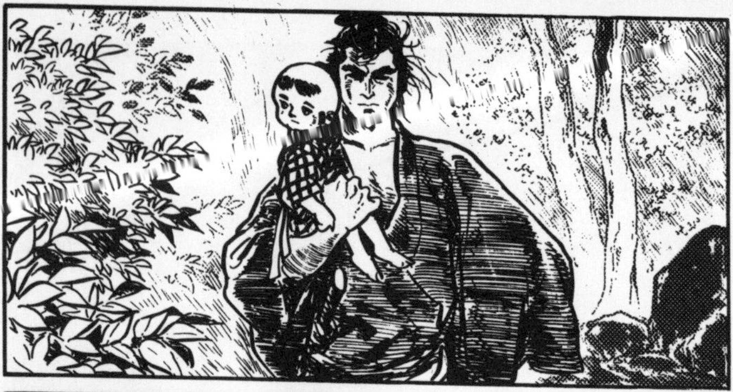

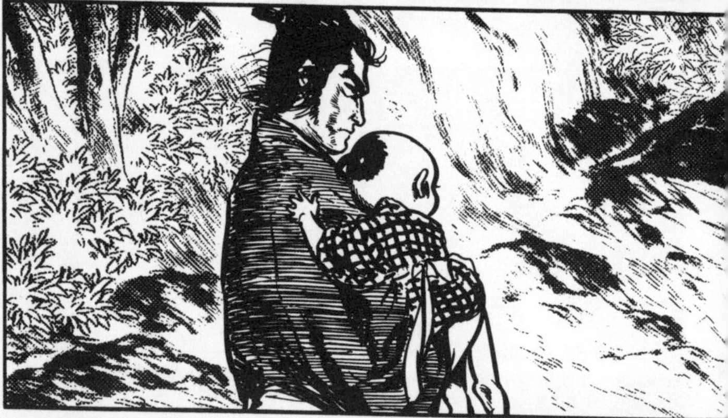

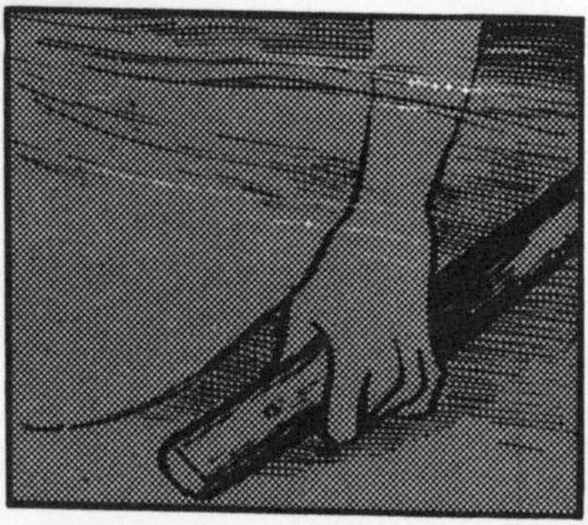

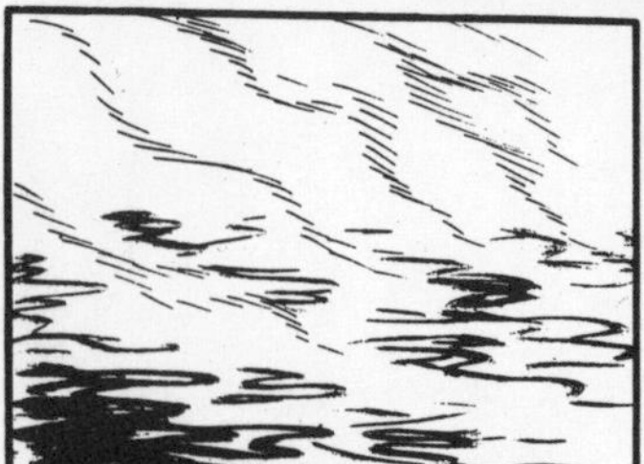

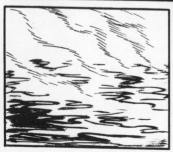

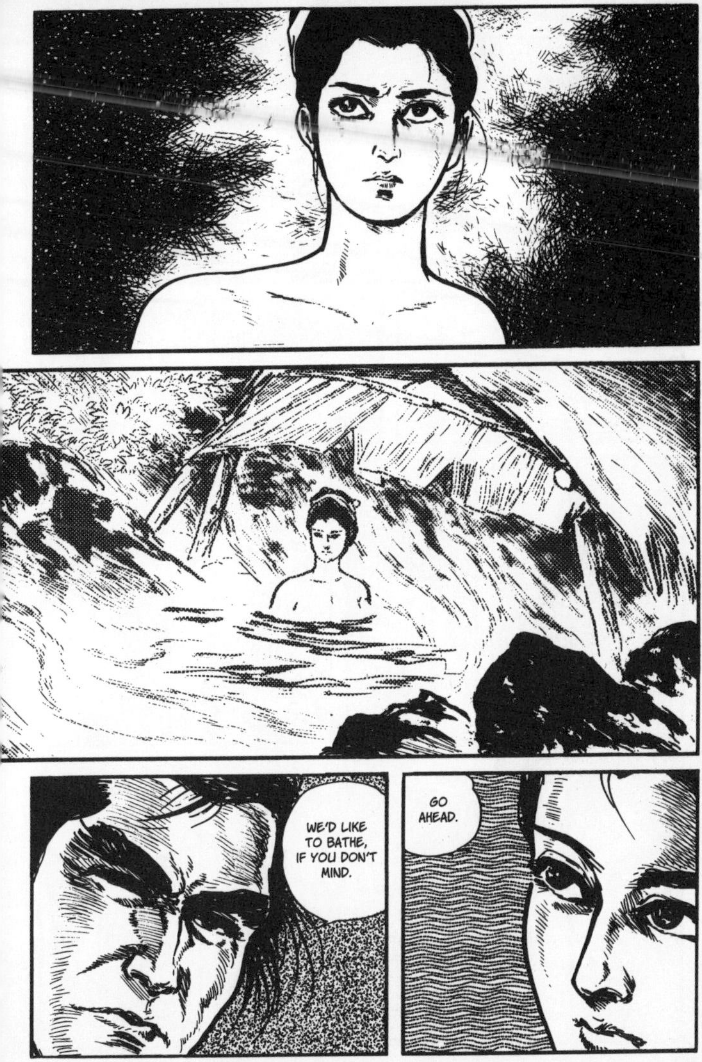
WE'D LIKE TO BATHE, IF YOU DON'T MIND.
GO AHEAD.

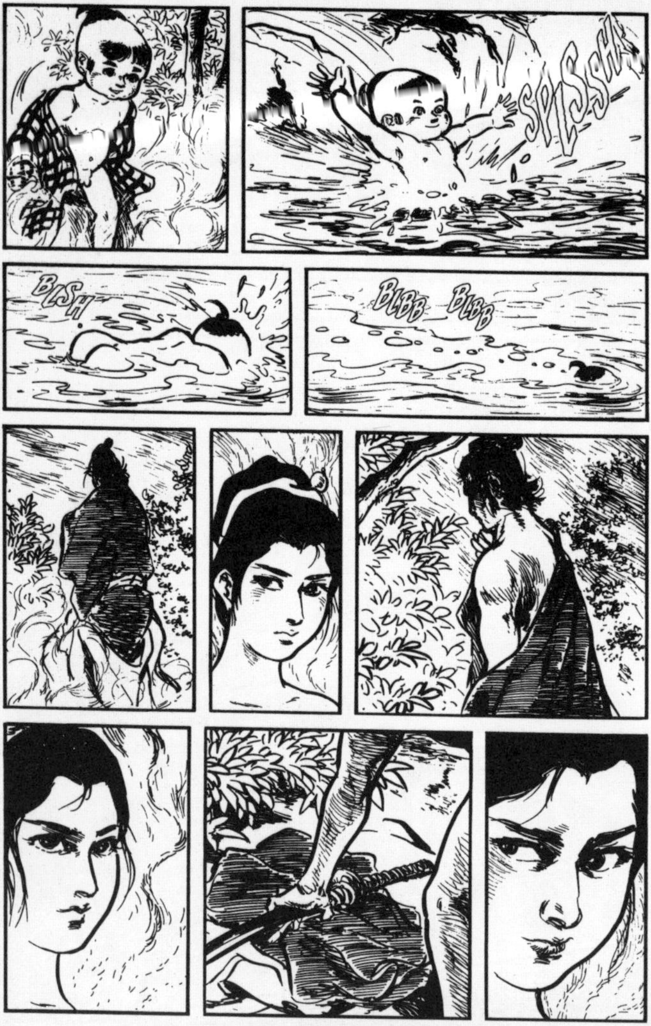
SPLSSHA
BLBB BLBB
BLSH

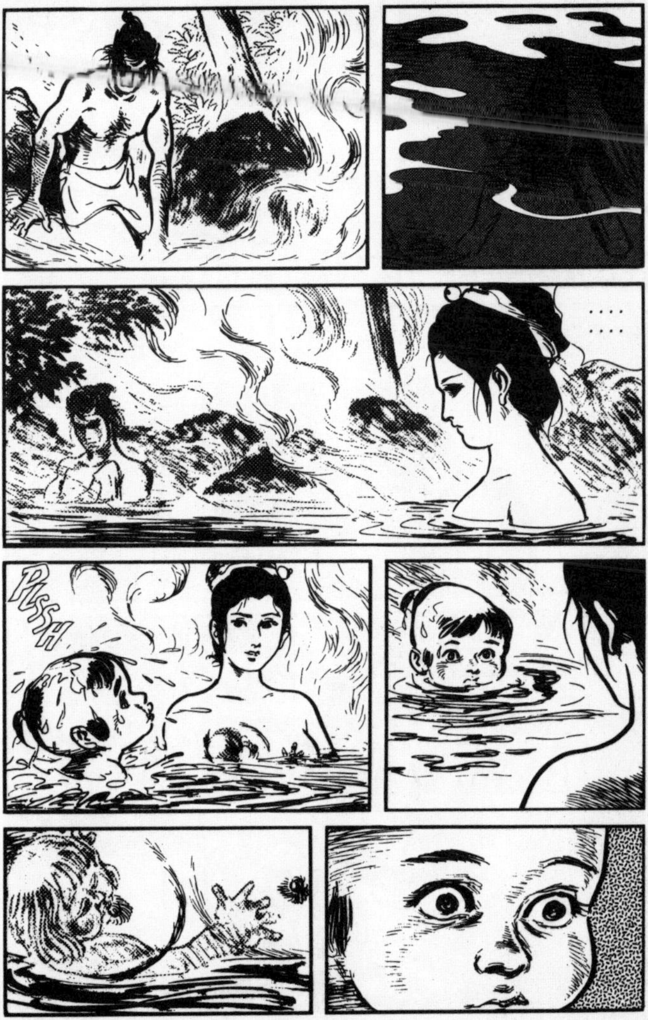
. . . .
. . . .
PUSSH

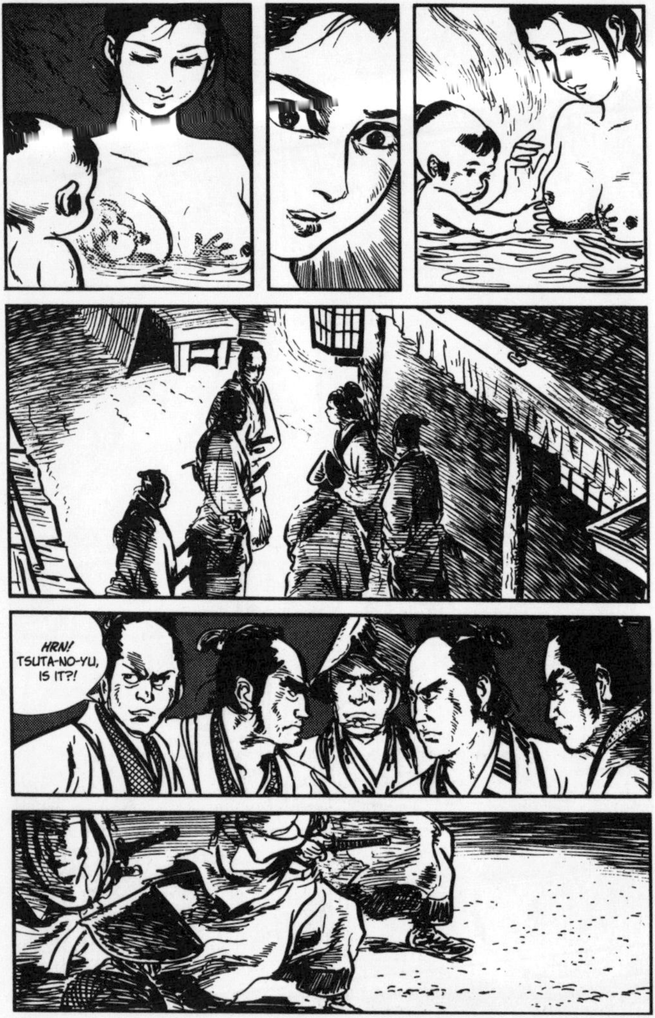
HRN!
TSUTA-NO-YU,
IS IT?!

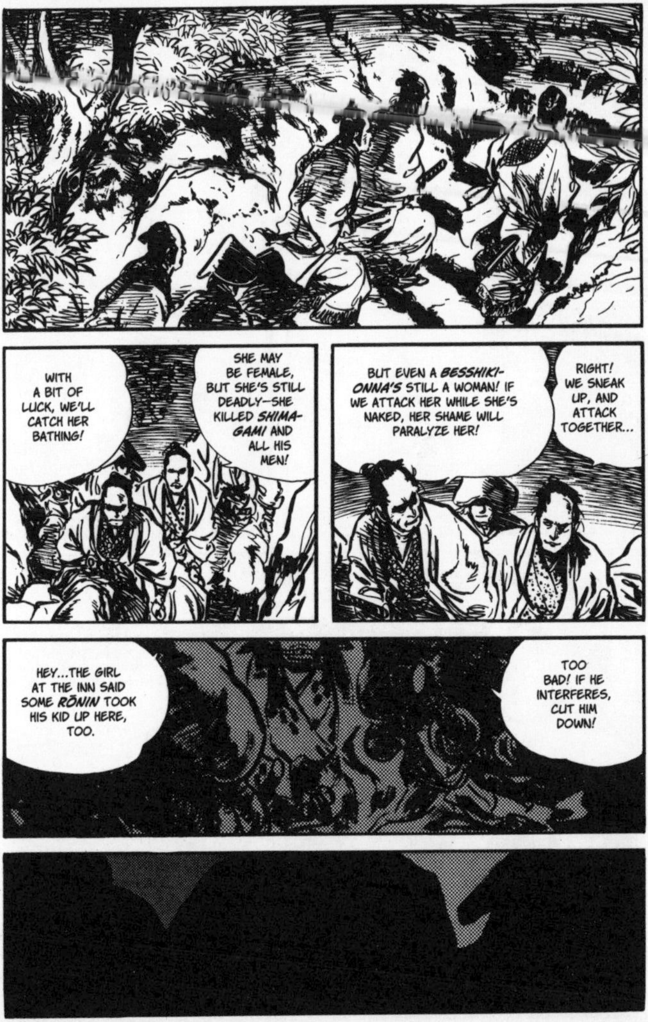
WITH A BIT OF LUCK, WE'LL CATCH HER BATHING!
SHE MAY BE FEMALE, BUT SHE'S STILL DEADLY—SHE KILLED *SHIMAGAMI* AND ALL HIS MEN!
BUT EVEN A *BESSHIKI-ONNA'S* STILL A WOMAN! IF WE ATTACK HER WHILE SHE'S NAKED, HER SHAME WILL PARALYZE HER!
RIGHT! WE SNEAK UP, AND ATTACK TOGETHER...
HEY...THE GIRL AT THE INN SAID SOME *RŌNIN* TOOK HIS KID UP HERE, TOO.
TOO BAD! IF HE INTERFERES, CUT HIM DOWN!

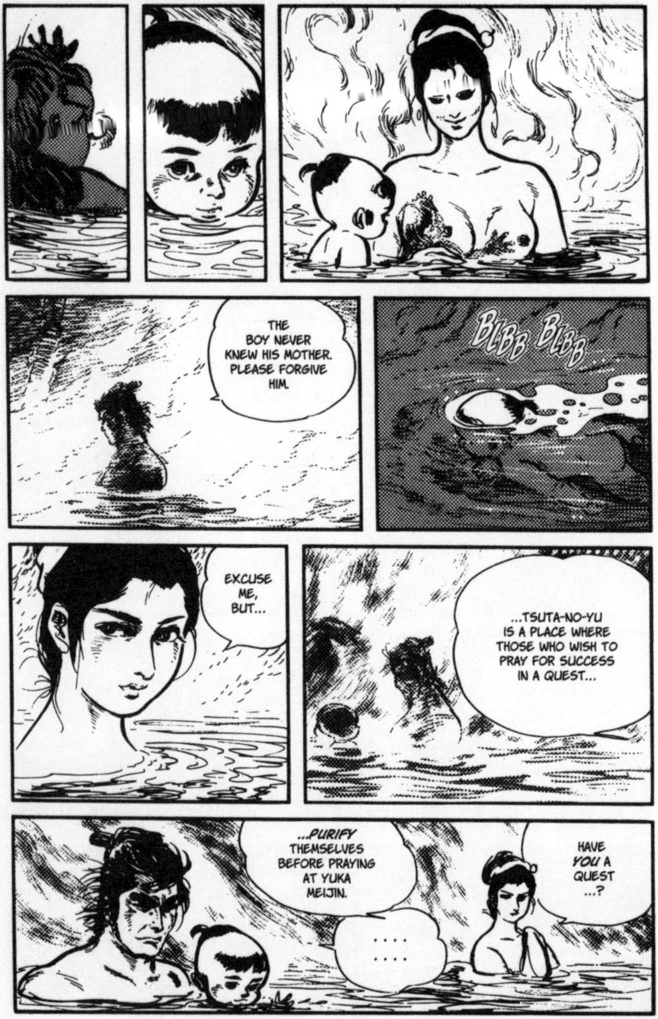
THE BOY NEVER KNEW HIS MOTHER. PLEASE FORGIVE HIM.
BLBB BLBB
EXCUSE ME, BUT...
...TSUTA-NO-YU IS A PLACE WHERE THOSE WHO WISH TO PRAY FOR SUCCESS IN A QUEST...
...PURIFY THEMSELVES BEFORE PRAYING AT YUKA MEIJIN.
....
....
HAVE YOU A QUEST ...?

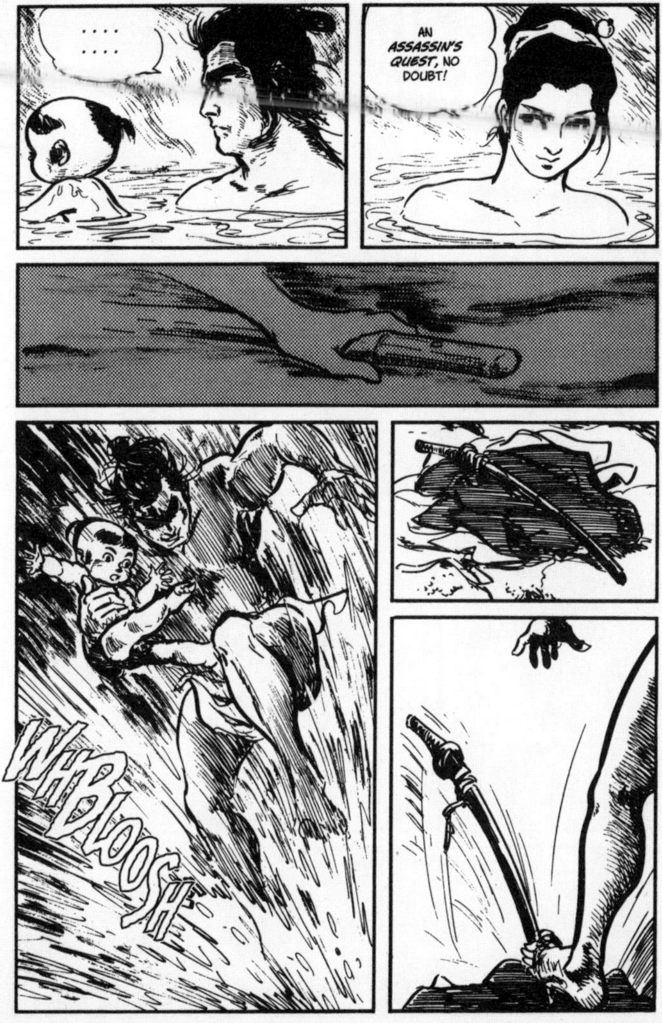
AN ASSASSIN'S QUEST, NO DOUBT!
.... ....
WHBLOOSH

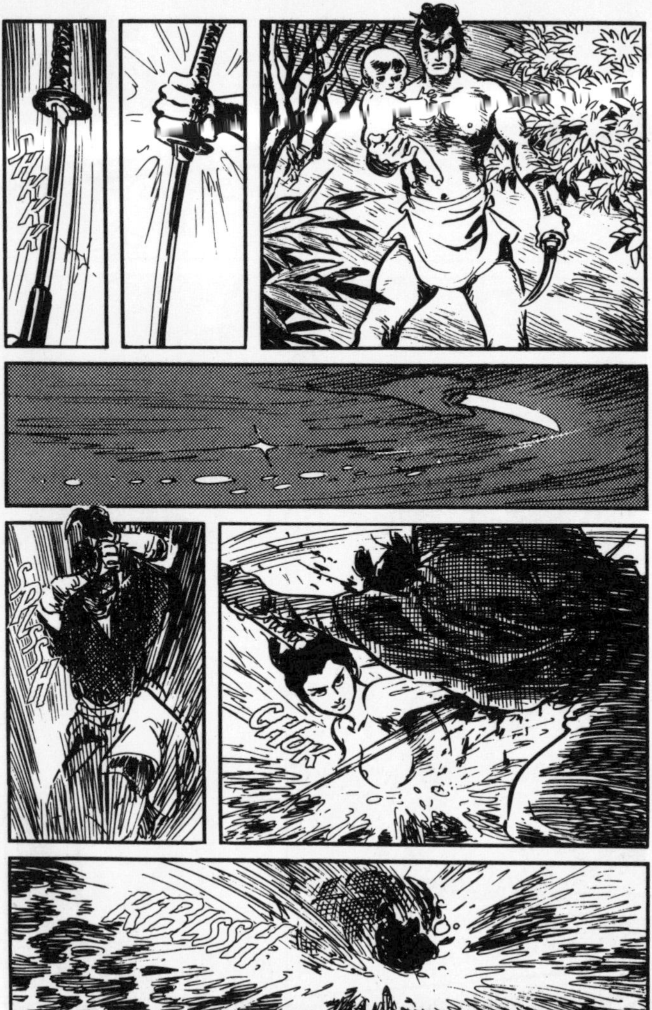
SHKKKK
SPLSSH
CHUK
KBLSSH!

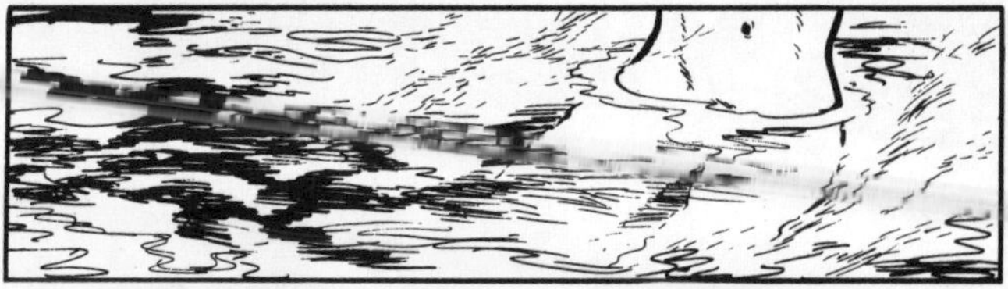
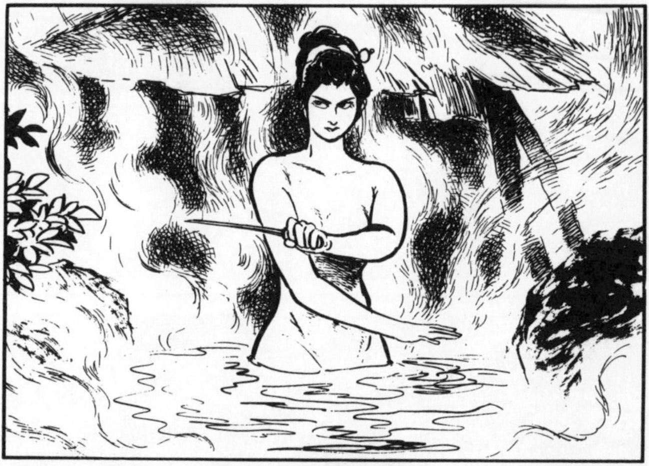
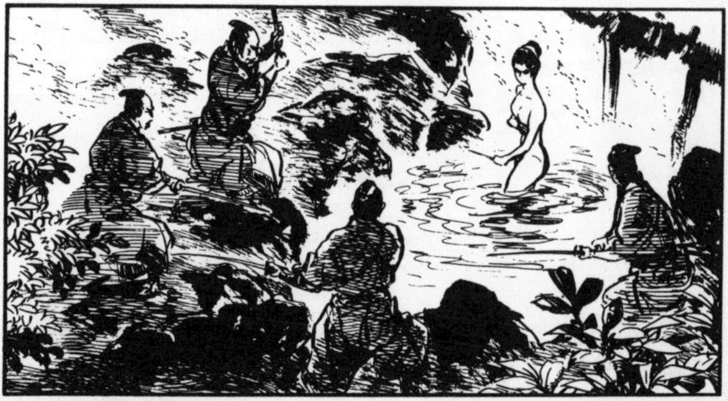

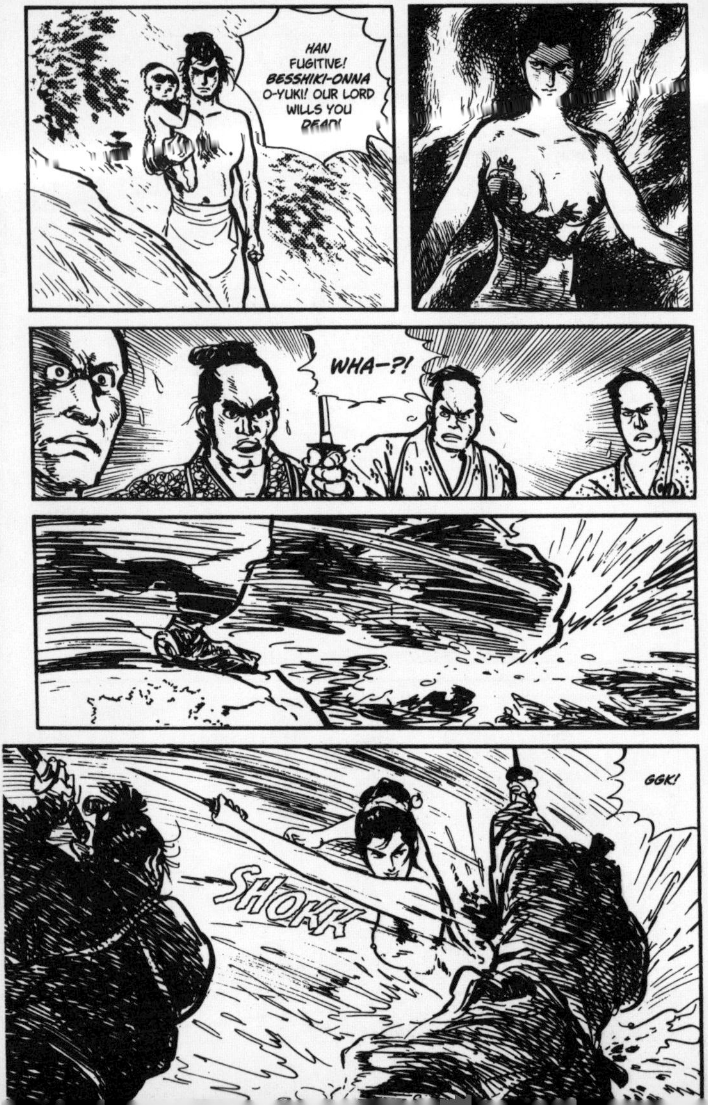
HAN FUGITIVE! BESSHIKI-ONNA O-YUKI! OUR LORD WILLS YOU DEAD!
WHA-?!
SHOKK
GGK!

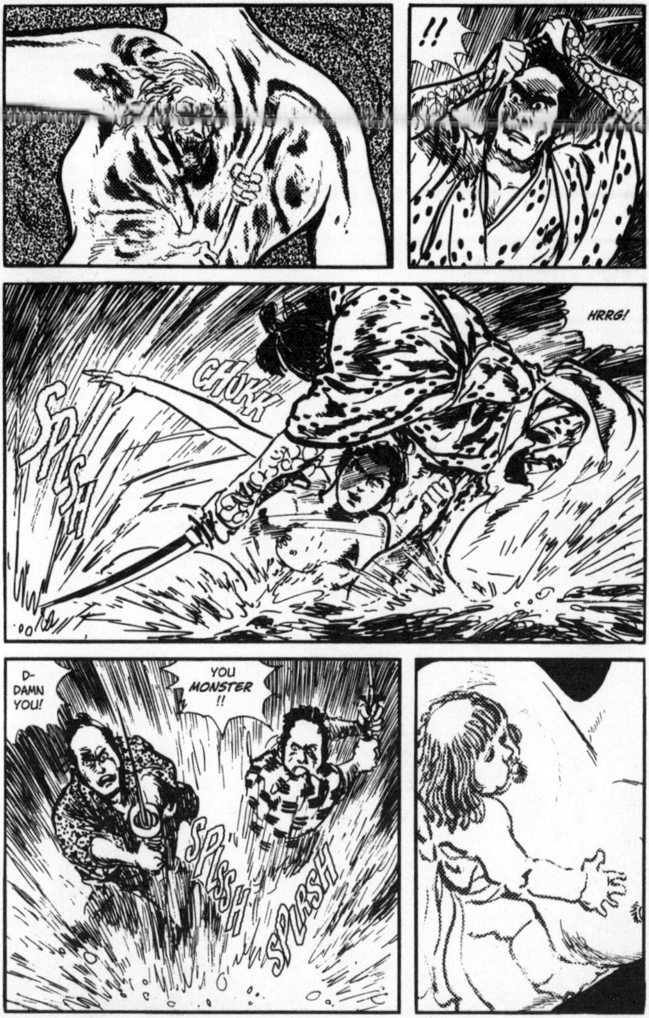
!!
HRRG!
CHOKK
SPLSH
YOU MONSTER !!
D-DAMN YOU!
SPLSSH
SPLASH

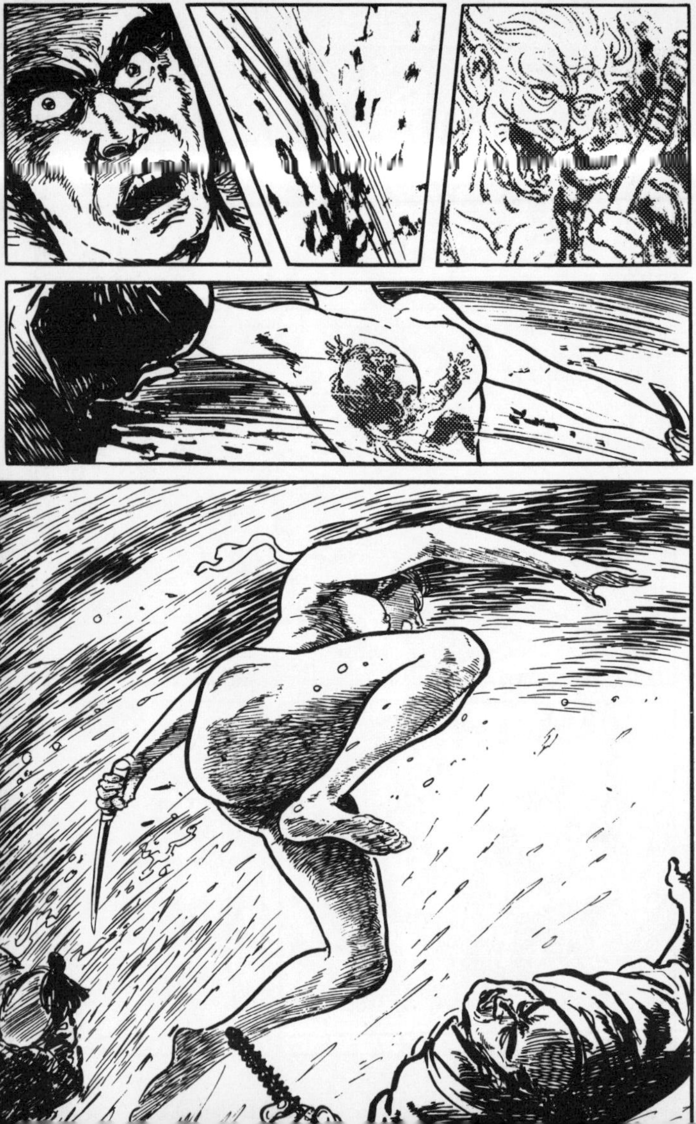

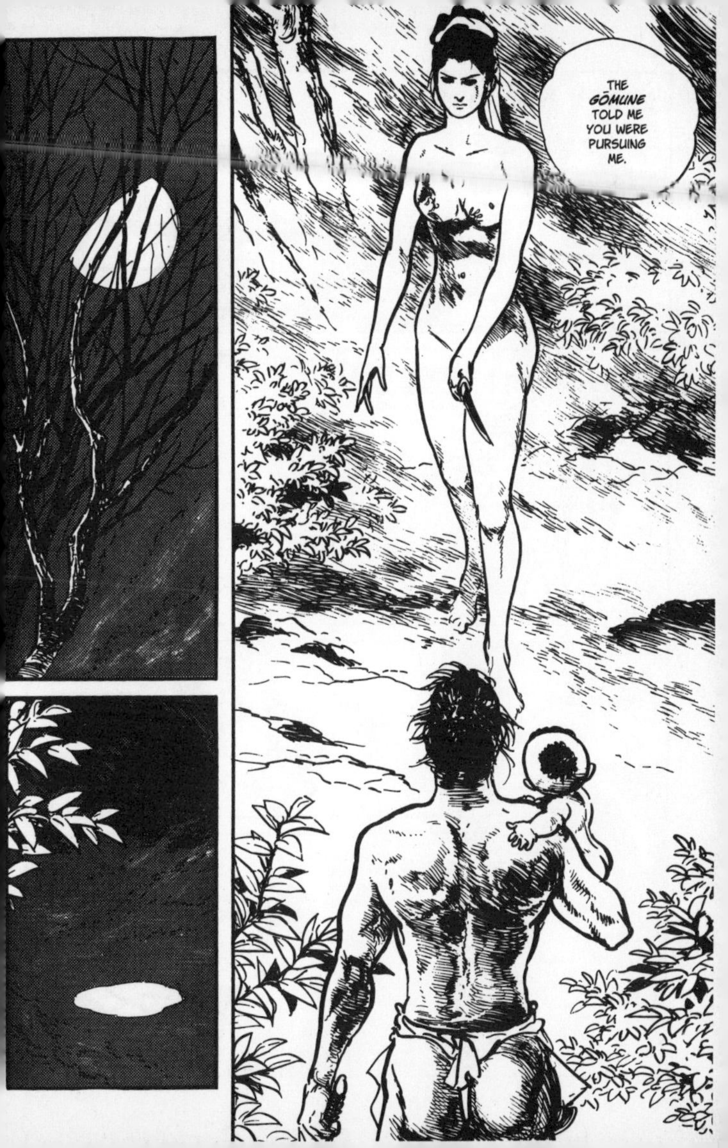
THE GŌMUNE TOLD ME YOU WERE PURSUING ME.

AND YOUR NAME...*LONE WOLF AND CUB!*

BUT YOU HAVE NO *SAKKI!* I'VE BEEN WATCHING YOU! AND I'VE...

. . . .

A KILLER WITH NO *BLOOD LUST.* SO *STRANGE!*

I KNOW IT'S *POINTLESS* TO ASK THE ASSASSIN...

. . . .

...YET THERE IS ONE THING THE *HUNTED* WOULD ASK HER *HUNTER.*

WHO HIRED YOU TO *KILL* ME...?!

BEFORE I ANSWER...

...TELL *ME* WHY YOU CUT OFF THE *MAGE* OF THE MEN YOU HAVE KILLED.

I AM A FUGITIVE FROM *TENDŌ HAN!!* OF COURSE OUR LORD IN HIS ANGER IS SENDING MEN TO *EXECUTE* ME!

IF I CUT OFF THE *MAGE* OF MY PURSUERS AND SEND THEM BACK...

AH. I SEE.

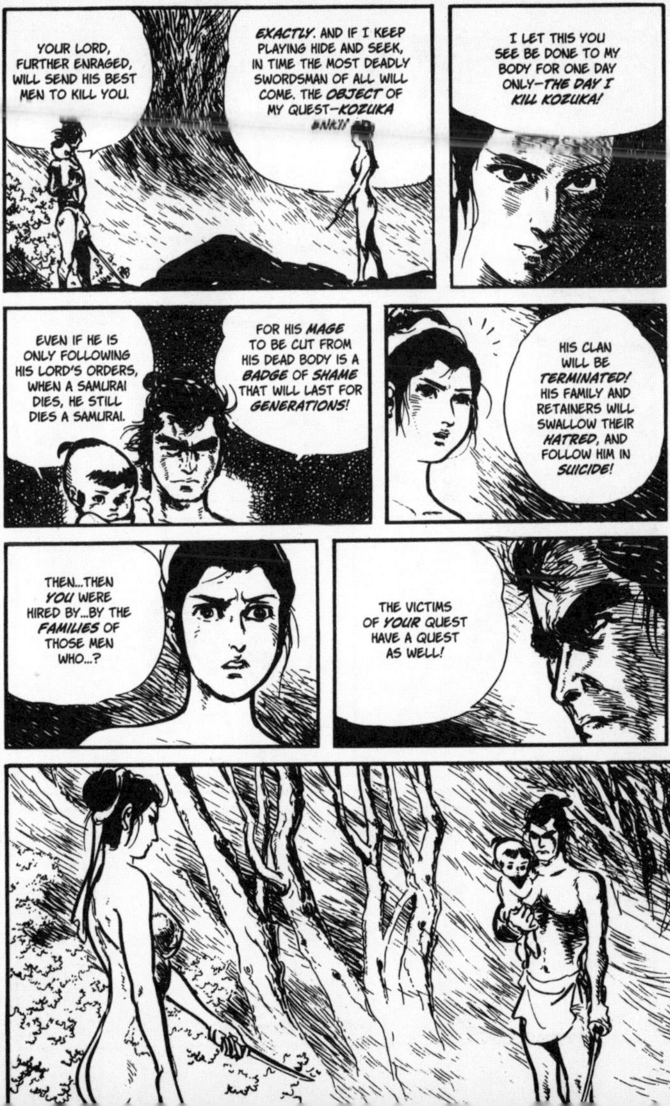
YOUR LORD, FURTHER ENRAGED, WILL SEND HIS BEST MEN TO KILL YOU.
EXACTLY. AND IF I KEEP PLAYING HIDE AND SEEK, IN TIME THE MOST DEADLY SWORDSMAN OF ALL WILL COME. THE OBJECT OF MY QUEST—KOZUKA ENKI!
I LET THIS YOU SEE BE DONE TO MY BODY FOR ONE DAY ONLY—THE DAY I KILL KOZUKA!
EVEN IF HE IS ONLY FOLLOWING HIS LORD'S ORDERS, WHEN A SAMURAI DIES, HE STILL DIES A SAMURAI.
FOR HIS MAGE TO BE CUT FROM HIS DEAD BODY IS A BADGE OF SHAME THAT WILL LAST FOR GENERATIONS!
HIS CLAN WILL BE TERMINATED! HIS FAMILY AND RETAINERS WILL SWALLOW THEIR HATRED, AND FOLLOW HIM IN SUICIDE!
THEN...THEN YOU WERE HIRED BY...BY THE FAMILIES OF THOSE MEN WHO...?
THE VICTIMS OF YOUR QUEST HAVE A QUEST AS WELL!

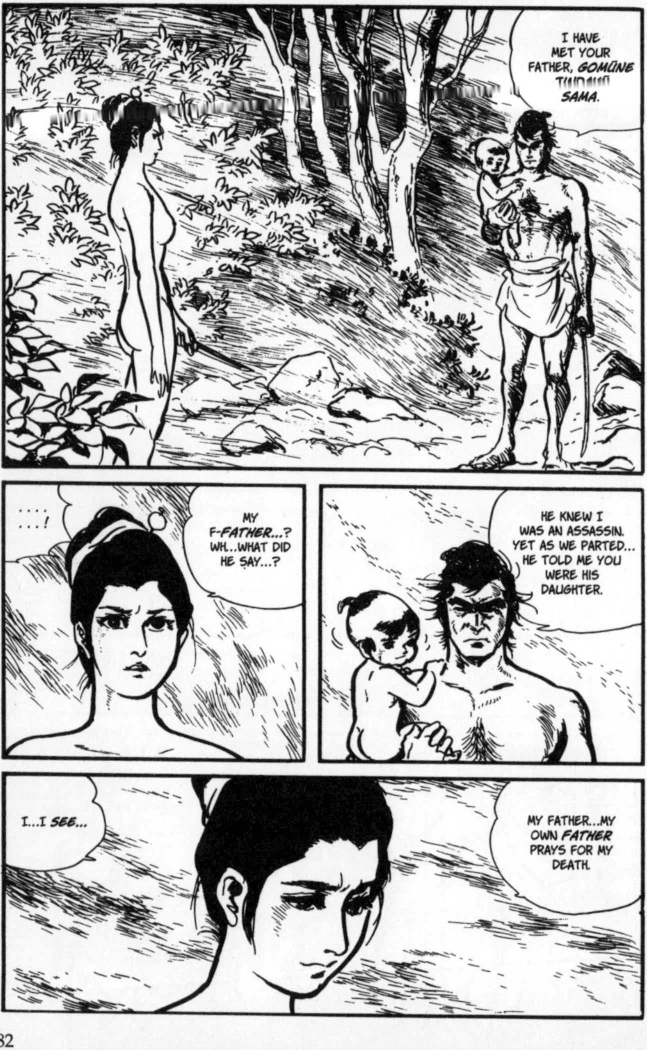
I HAVE MET YOUR FATHER, GOMŪNE SAMA.
....
...!
MY F-FATHER...? WH...WHAT DID HE SAY...?
HE KNEW I WAS AN ASSASSIN. YET AS WE PARTED... HE TOLD ME YOU WERE HIS DAUGHTER.
I...I SEE...
MY FATHER...MY OWN FATHER PRAYS FOR MY DEATH.

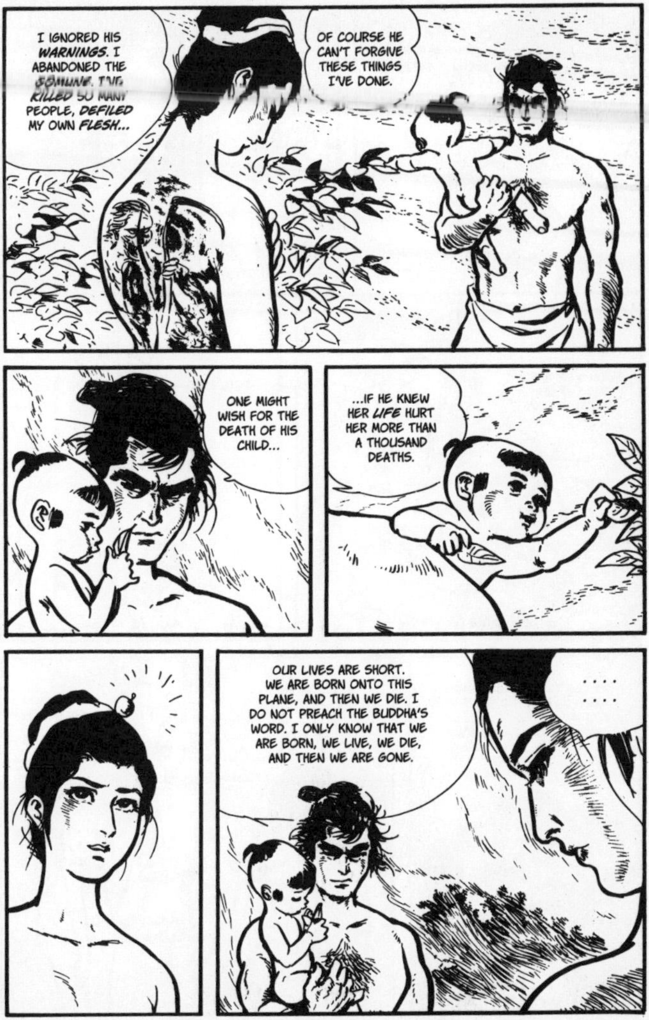
I IGNORED HIS *WARNINGS*. I ABANDONED THE *SOMUNE*. I'VE *KILLED* SO MANY PEOPLE, *DEFILED* MY OWN *FLESH*...
OF COURSE HE CAN'T FORGIVE THESE THINGS I'VE DONE.
ONE MIGHT WISH FOR THE DEATH OF HIS CHILD...
...IF HE KNEW HER *LIFE* HURT HER MORE THAN A THOUSAND DEATHS.
OUR LIVES ARE SHORT. WE ARE BORN ONTO THIS PLANE, AND THEN WE DIE. I DO NOT PREACH THE BUDDHA'S WORD. I ONLY KNOW THAT WE ARE BORN, WE LIVE, WE DIE, AND THEN WE ARE GONE.
....
....

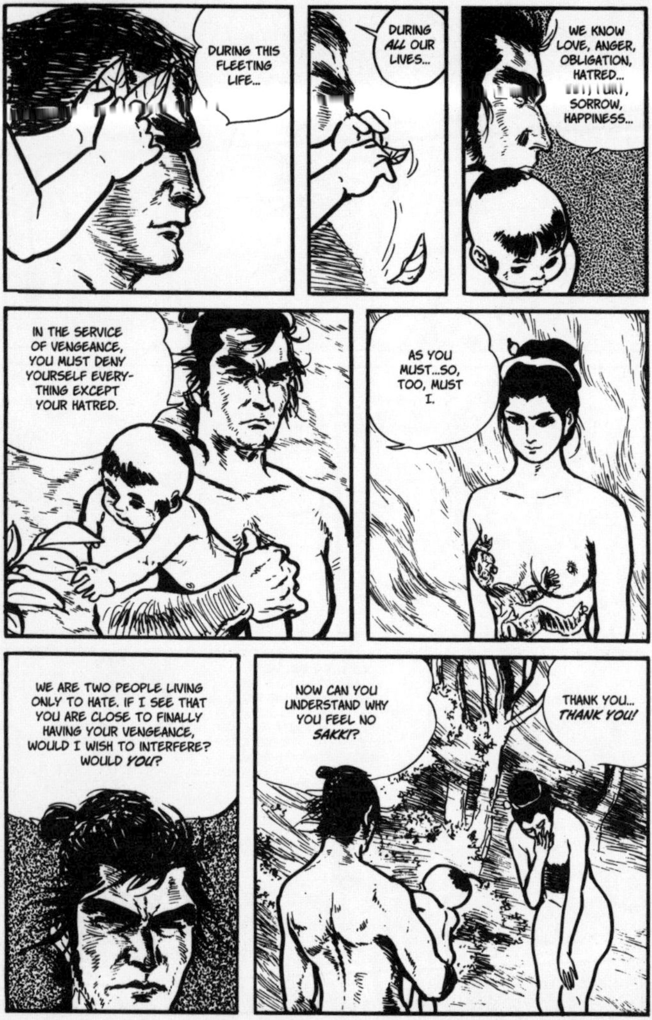

DURING THIS FLEETING LIFE...
DURING *ALL* OUR LIVES...
WE KNOW LOVE, ANGER, OBLIGATION, HATRED... [redacted], SORROW, HAPPINESS...
IN THE SERVICE OF VENGEANCE, YOU MUST DENY YOURSELF EVERY-THING EXCEPT YOUR HATRED.
AS YOU MUST...SO, TOO, MUST I.
WE ARE TWO PEOPLE LIVING ONLY TO HATE. IF I SEE THAT YOU ARE CLOSE TO FINALLY HAVING YOUR VENGEANCE, WOULD I WISH TO INTERFERE? WOULD *YOU*?
NOW CAN YOU UNDERSTAND WHY YOU FEEL NO *SAKKI*?
THANK YOU... *THANK YOU!*

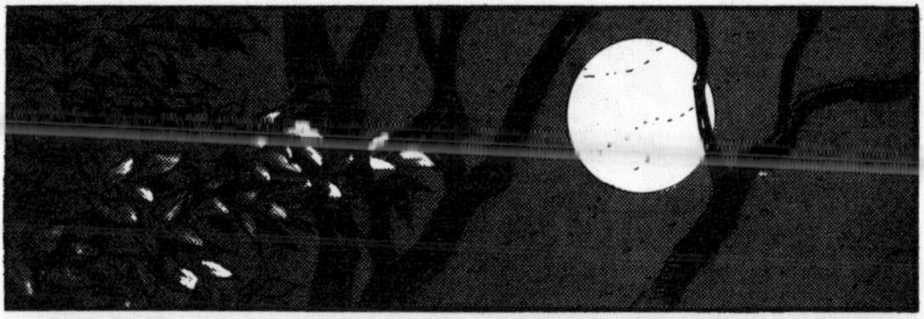
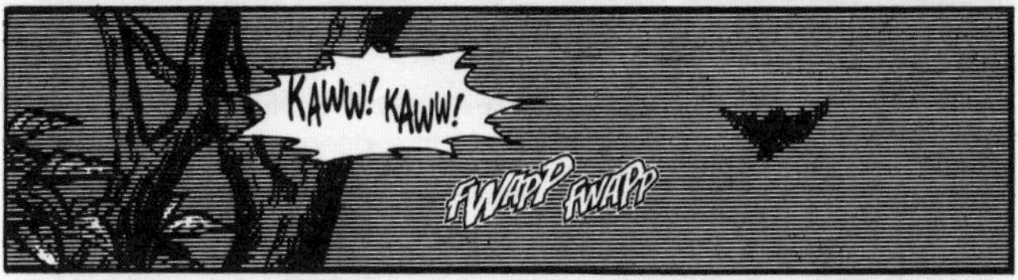
KAWW! KAWW!
FWAPP FWAPP
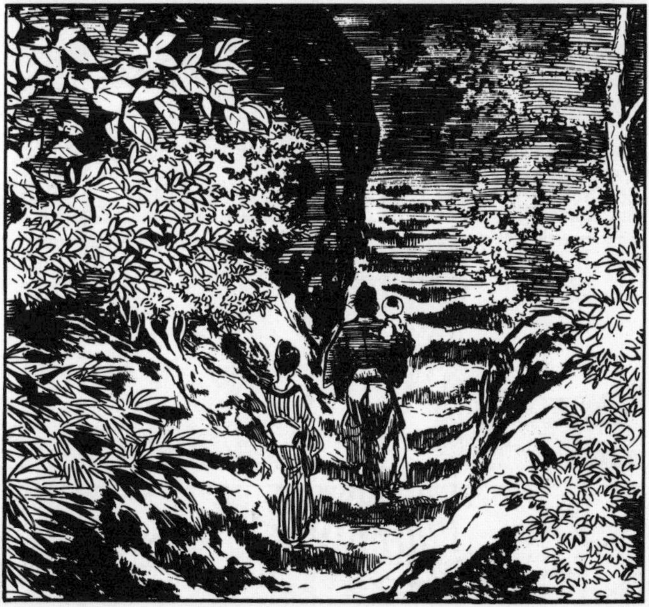

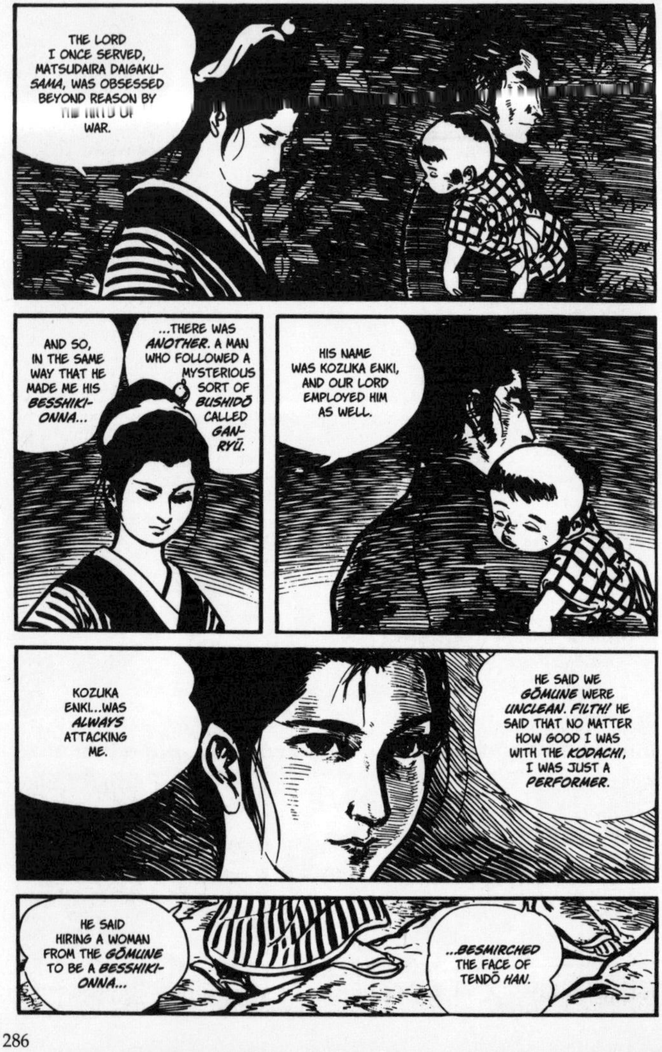
THE LORD I ONCE SERVED, MATSUDAIRA DAIGAKU-SAMA, WAS OBSESSED BEYOND REASON BY WAR.
AND SO, IN THE SAME WAY THAT HE MADE ME HIS BESSHIKI-ONNA...
...THERE WAS ANOTHER. A MAN WHO FOLLOWED A MYSTERIOUS SORT OF BUSHIDŌ CALLED GAN-RYŪ.
HIS NAME WAS KOZUKA ENKI, AND OUR LORD EMPLOYED HIM AS WELL.
KOZUKA ENKI...WAS ALWAYS ATTACKING ME.
HE SAID WE GŌMUNE WERE UNCLEAN. FILTH! HE SAID THAT NO MATTER HOW GOOD I WAS WITH THE KODACHI, I WAS JUST A PERFORMER.
HE SAID HIRING A WOMAN FROM THE GŌMUNE TO BE A BESSHIKI-ONNA...
...BESMIRCHED THE FACE OF TENDŌ HAN.

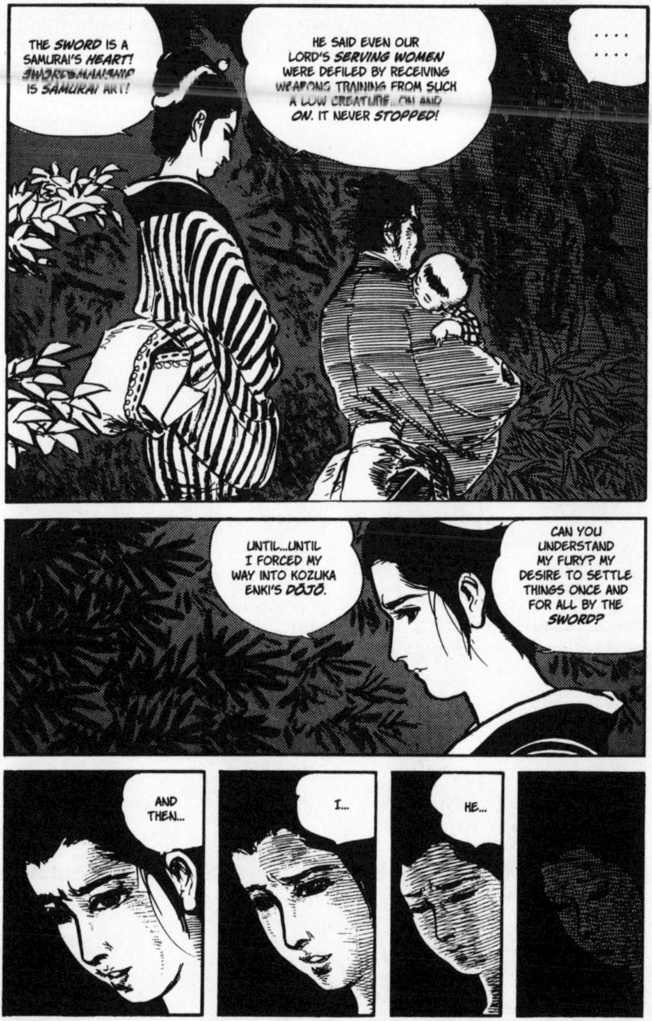
THE SWORD IS A SAMURAI'S HEART! SWORDSMANSHIP IS SAMURAI ART!
HE SAID EVEN OUR LORD'S SERVING WOMEN WERE DEFILED BY RECEIVING WEAPONS TRAINING FROM SUCH A LOW CREATURE...ON AND ON. IT NEVER STOPPED!
. . . .
. . . .
UNTIL...UNTIL I FORCED MY WAY INTO KOZUKA ENKI'S DŌJŌ.
CAN YOU UNDERSTAND MY FURY? MY DESIRE TO SETTLE THINGS ONCE AND FOR ALL BY THE SWORD?
AND THEN...
I...
HE...

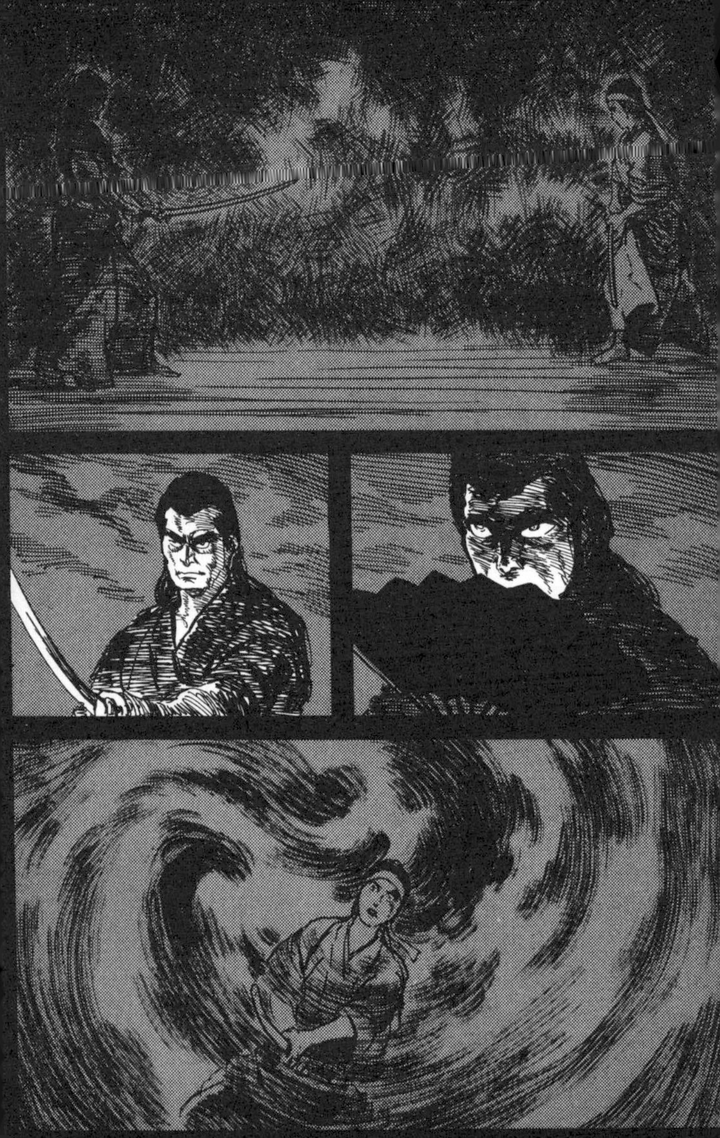

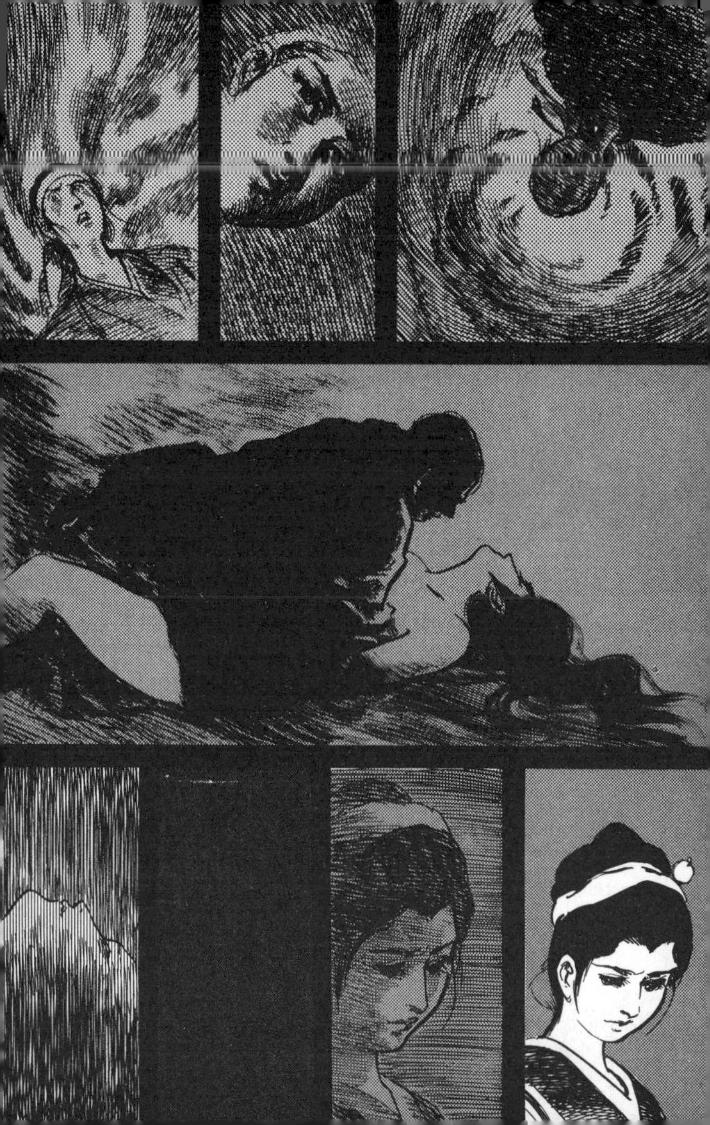

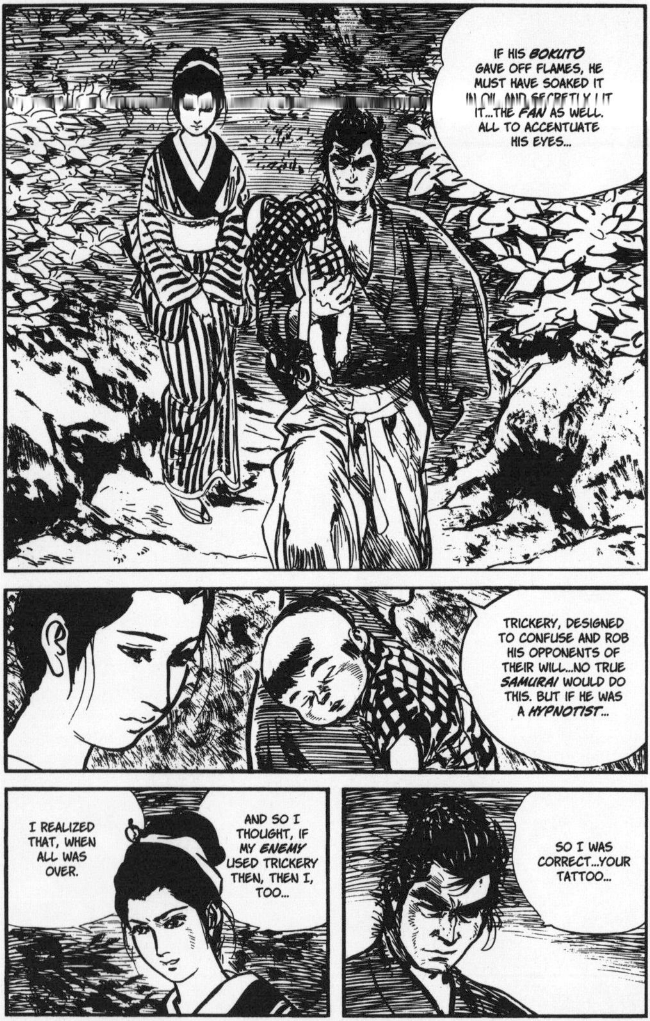
IF HIS *BOKUTŌ* GAVE OFF FLAMES, HE MUST HAVE SOAKED IT IN OIL AND SECRETLY LIT IT...THE *FAN* AS WELL. ALL TO ACCENTUATE HIS EYES...
TRICKERY, DESIGNED TO CONFUSE AND ROB HIS OPPONENTS OF THEIR WILL...NO TRUE *SAMURAI* WOULD DO THIS. BUT IF HE WAS A *HYPNOTIST*...
I REALIZED THAT, WHEN ALL WAS OVER.
AND SO I THOUGHT, IF MY *ENEMY* USED TRICKERY THEN, THEN I, TOO...
SO I WAS CORRECT...YOUR TATTOO...

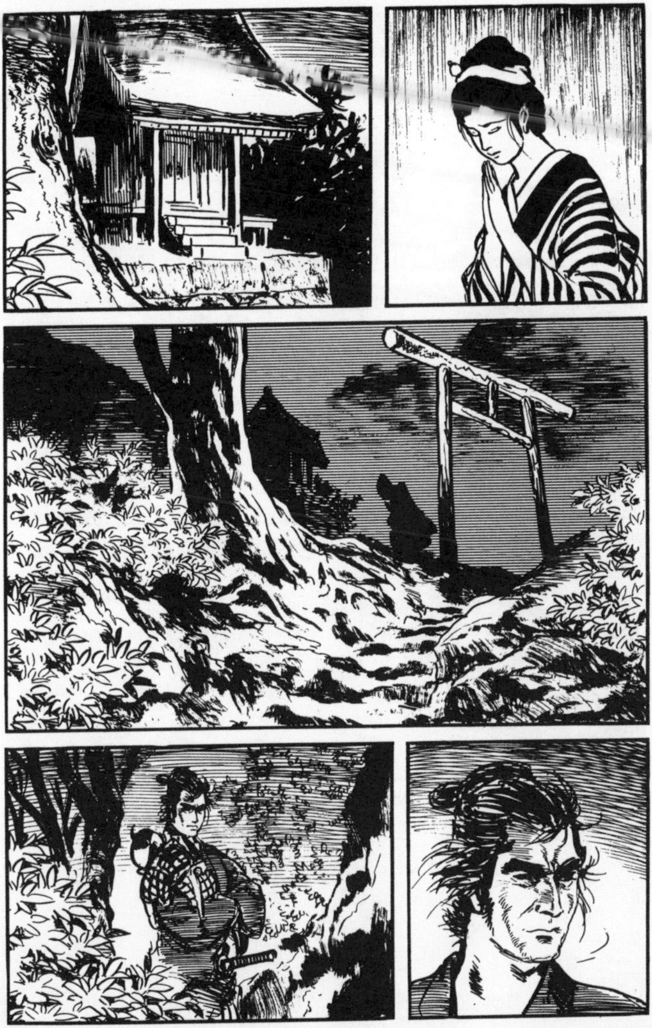

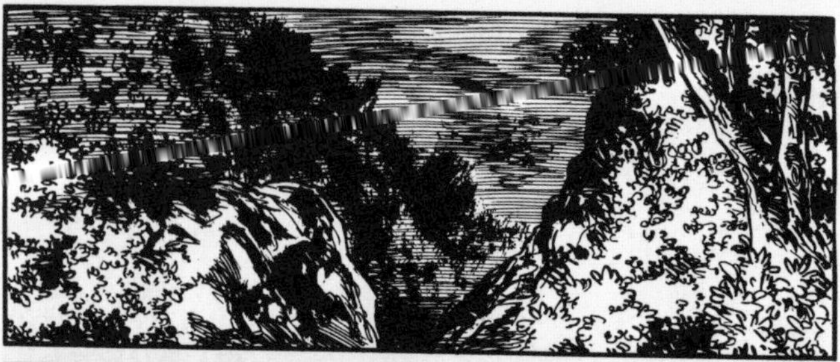
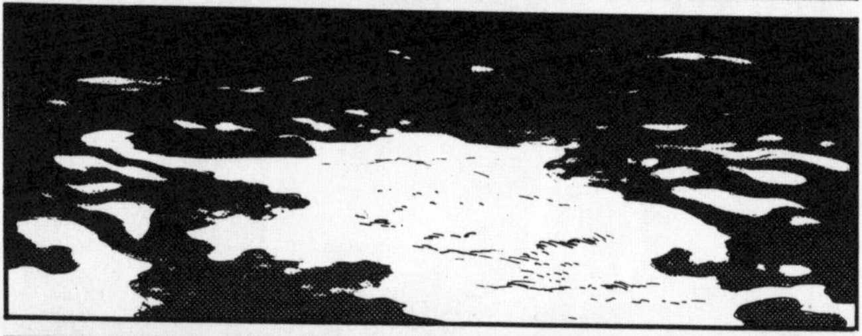
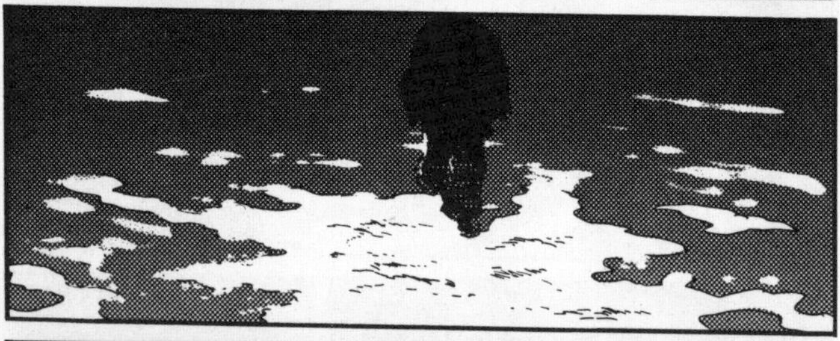
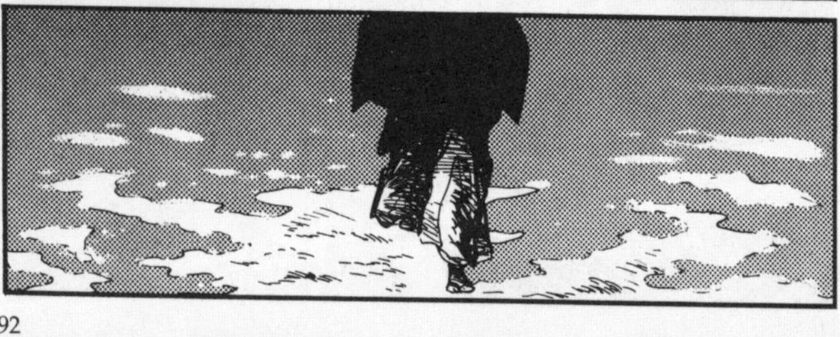

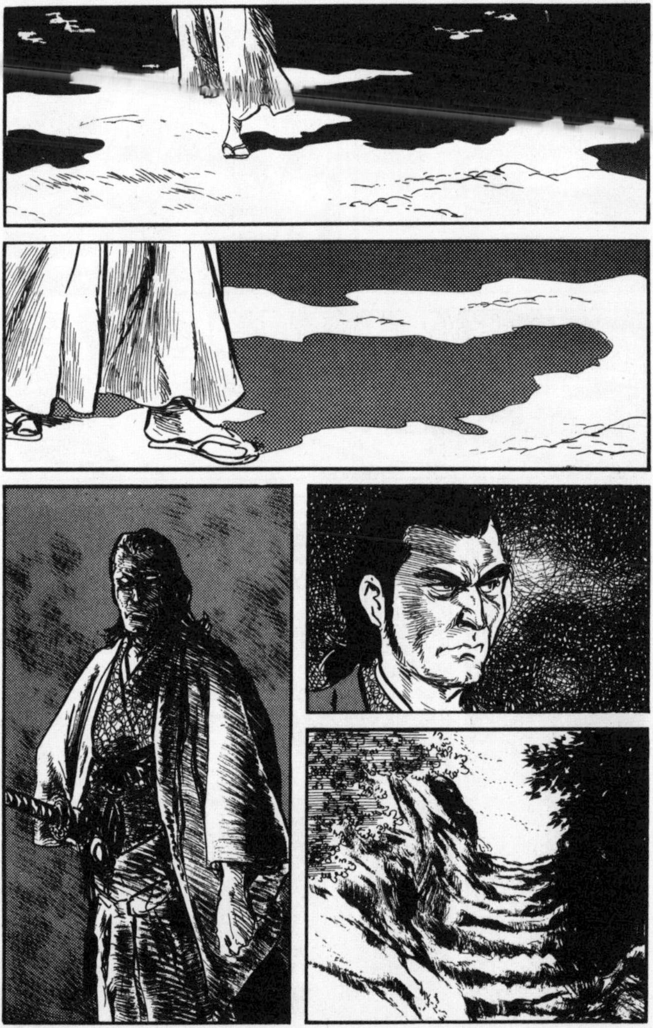

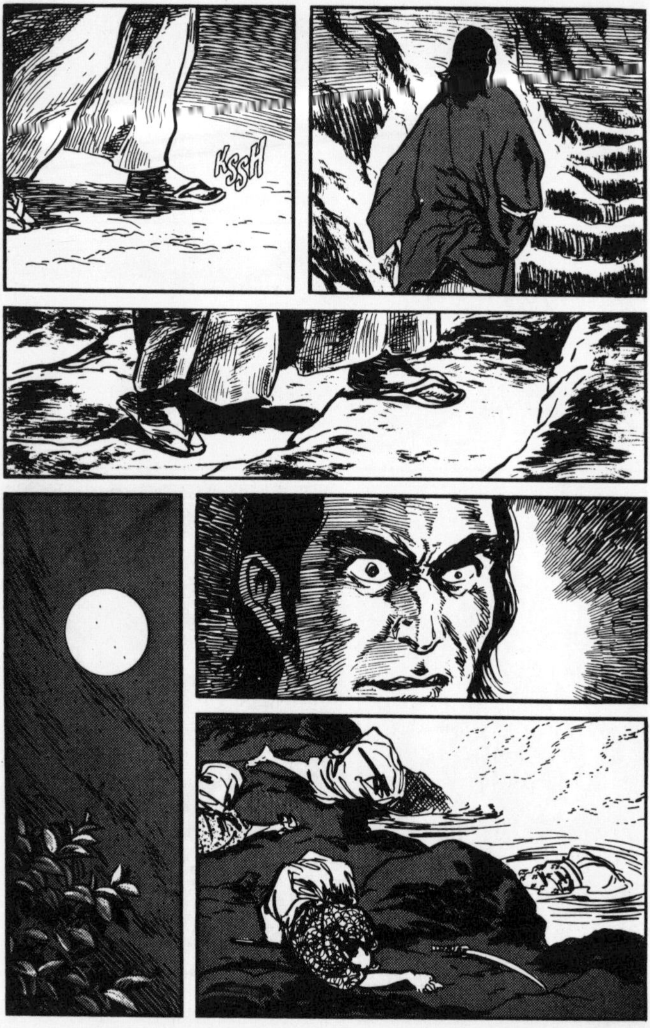
KSSH

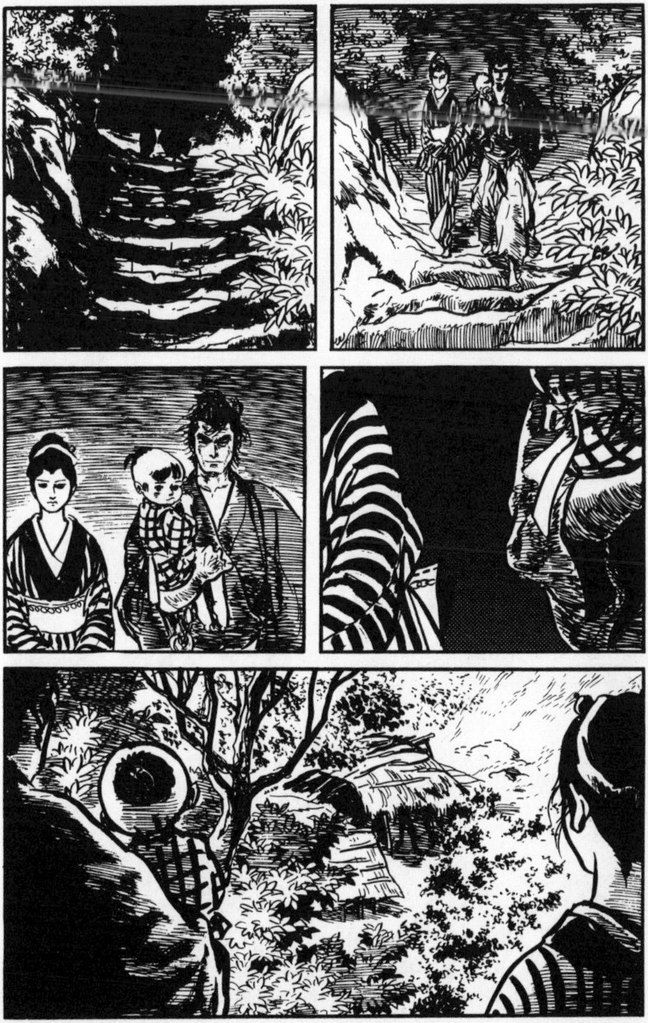

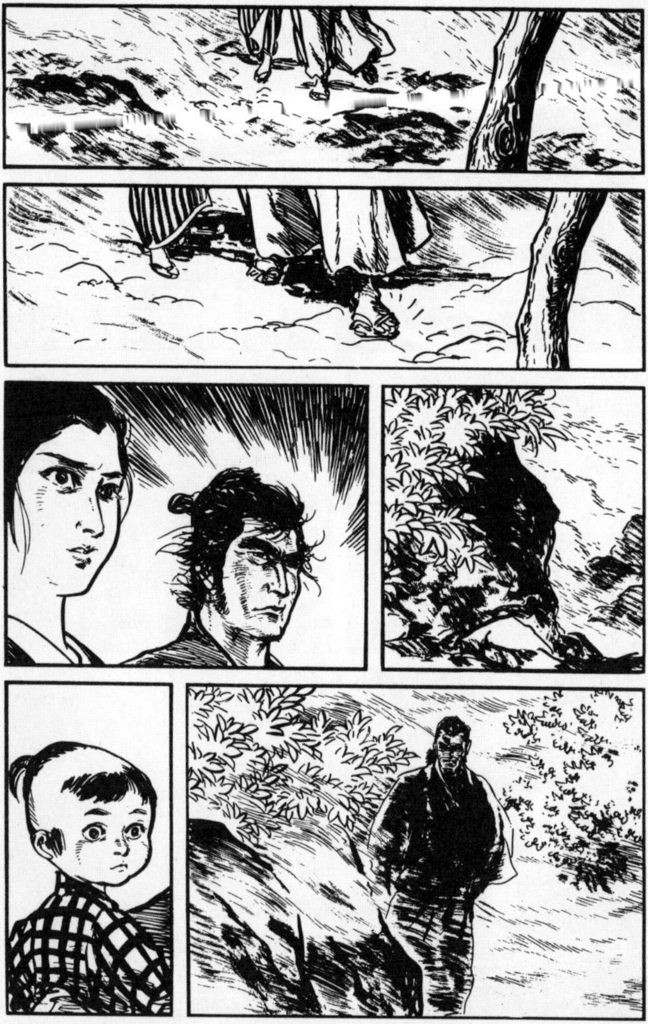

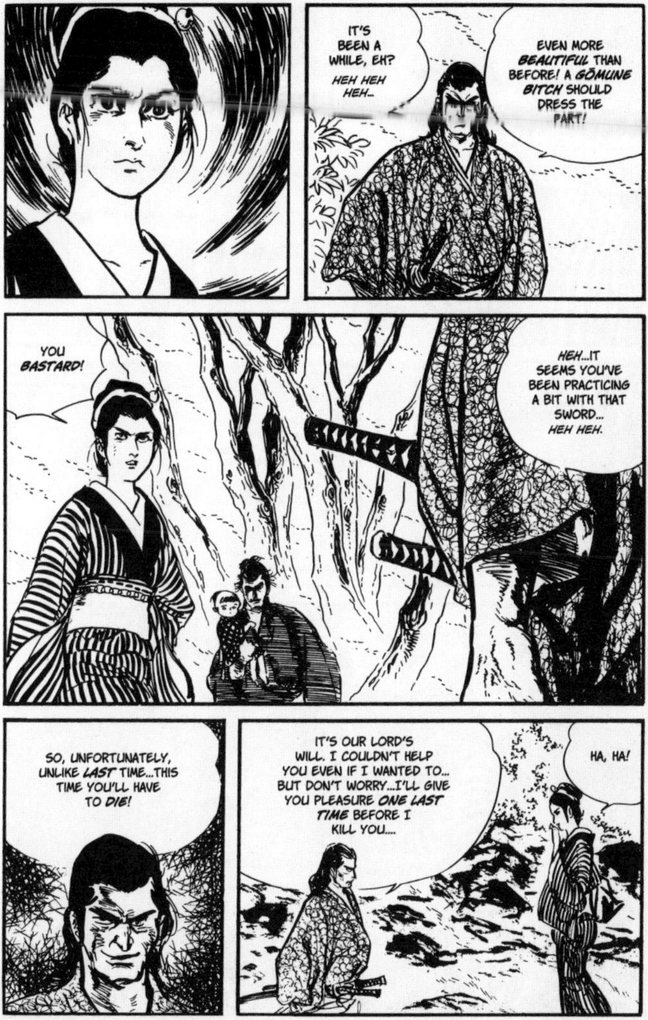
IT'S BEEN A WHILE, EH? *HEH HEH HEH*...
EVEN MORE *BEAUTIFUL* THAN BEFORE! A *GŌMUNE BITCH* SHOULD DRESS THE PART!
YOU *BASTARD!*
*HEH*...IT SEEMS YOU'VE BEEN PRACTICING A BIT WITH THAT SWORD... *HEH HEH.*
SO, UNFORTUNATELY, UNLIKE *LAST* TIME...THIS TIME YOU'LL HAVE TO *DIE!*
IT'S OUR LORD'S WILL. I COULDN'T HELP YOU EVEN IF I WANTED TO... BUT DON'T WORRY...I'LL GIVE YOU PLEASURE *ONE LAST TIME* BEFORE I KILL YOU....
HA, HA!

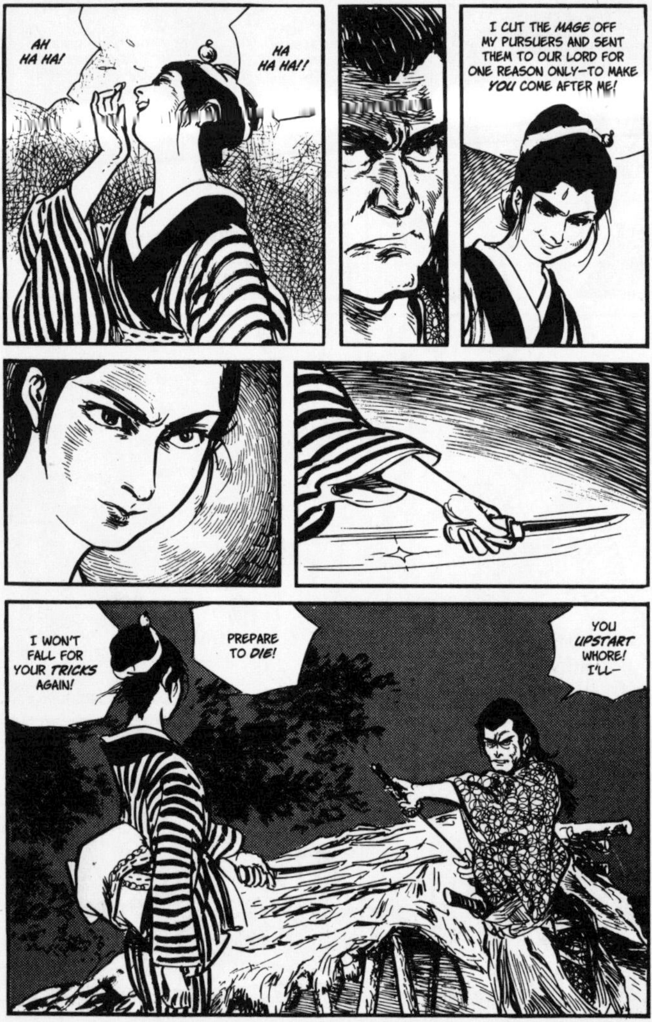
AH HA HA!
HA HA HA!!
I CUT THE MAGE OFF MY PURSUERS AND SENT THEM TO OUR LORD FOR ONE REASON ONLY—TO MAKE YOU COME AFTER ME!
I WON'T FALL FOR YOUR TRICKS AGAIN!
PREPARE TO DIE!
YOU UPSTART WHORE! I'LL—

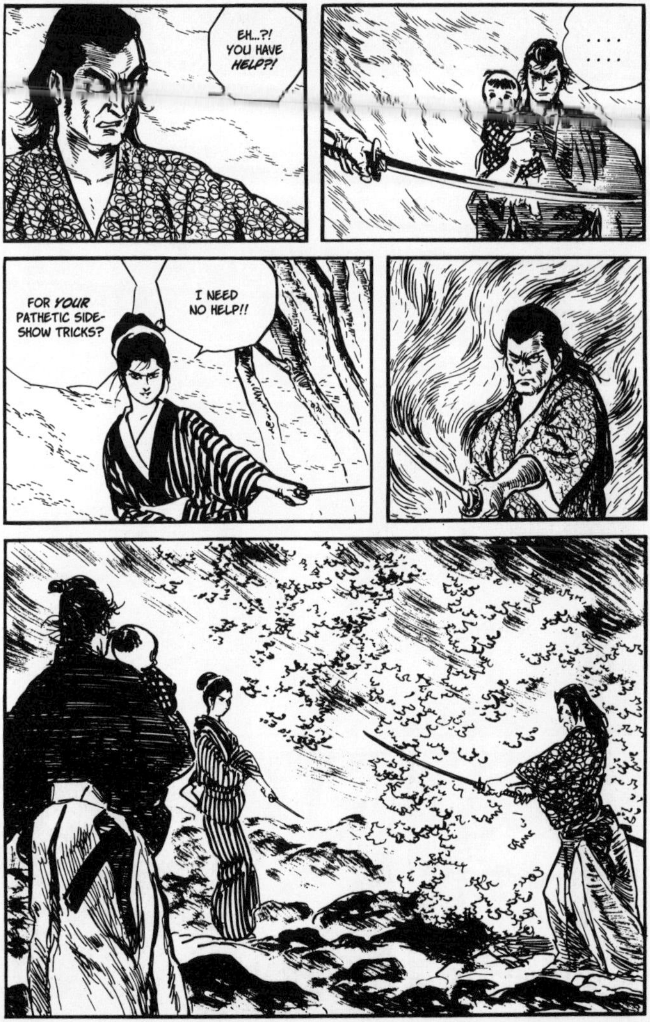
....
....
EH...?! YOU HAVE *HELP?!*
I NEED NO HELP!!
FOR *YOUR* PATHETIC SIDE-SHOW TRICKS?

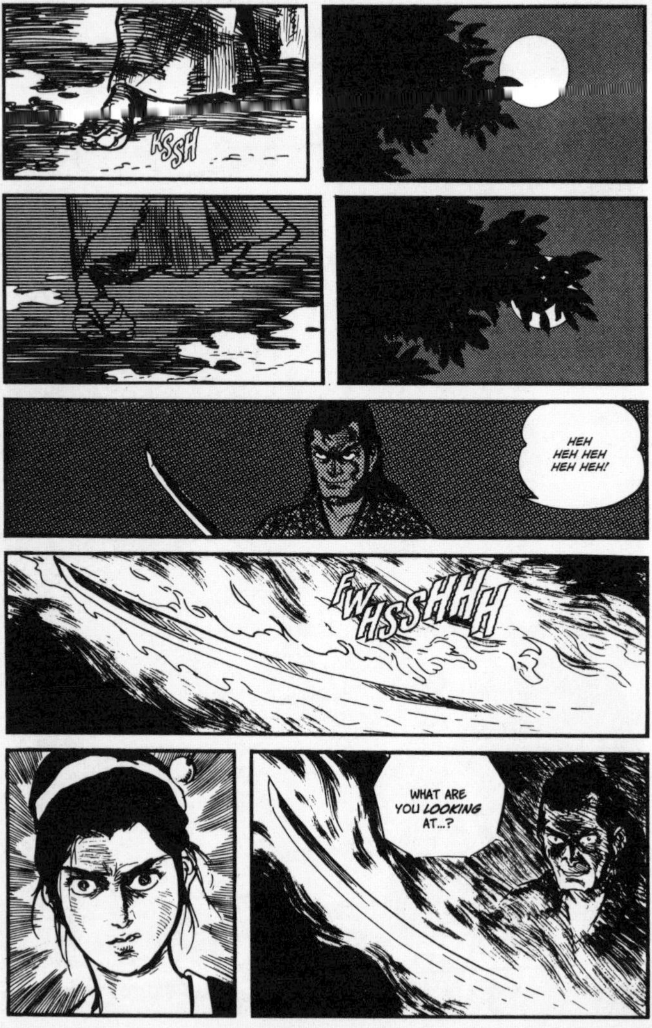
KSSH
HEH HEH HEH HEH HEH!
FWHSSHHH
WHAT ARE YOU LOOKING AT...?

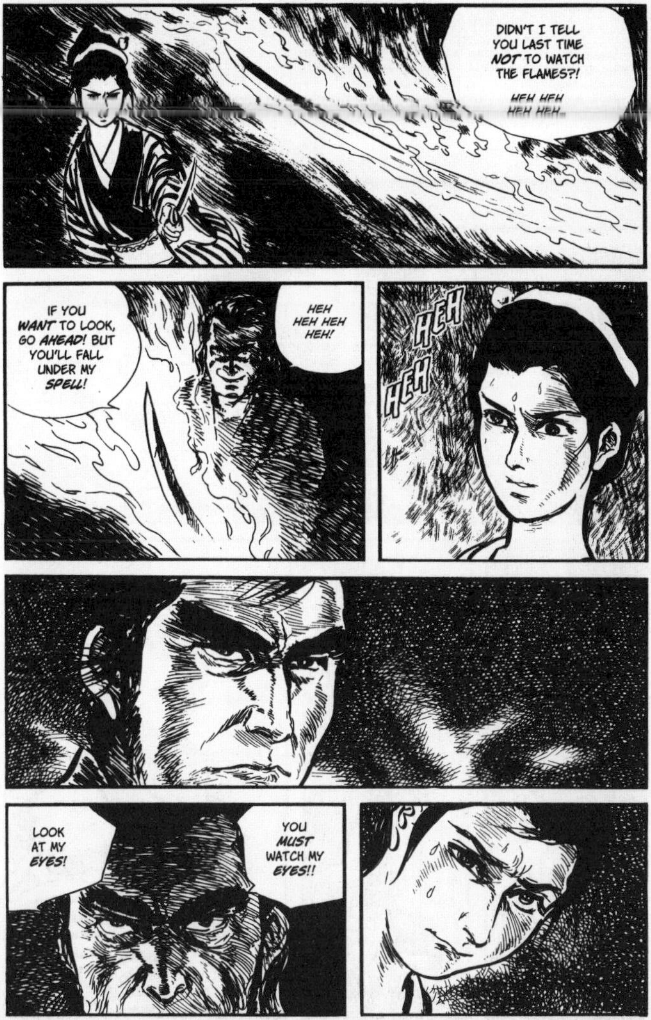
DIDN'T I TELL YOU LAST TIME NOT TO WATCH THE FLAMES?!
HEH HEH HEH HEH...
IF YOU WANT TO LOOK, GO AHEAD! BUT YOU'LL FALL UNDER MY SPELL!
HEH HEH HEH HEH!
HEH HEH
LOOK AT MY EYES!
YOU MUST WATCH MY EYES!!

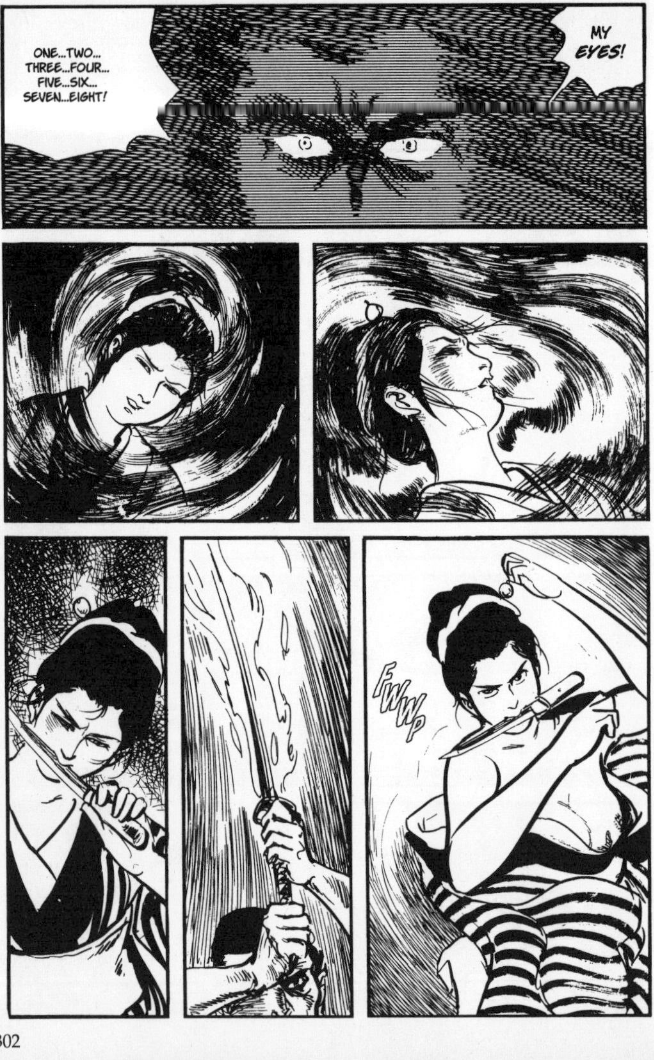
MY EYES!
ONE...TWO... THREE...FOUR... FIVE...SIX... SEVEN...EIGHT!
FWWP

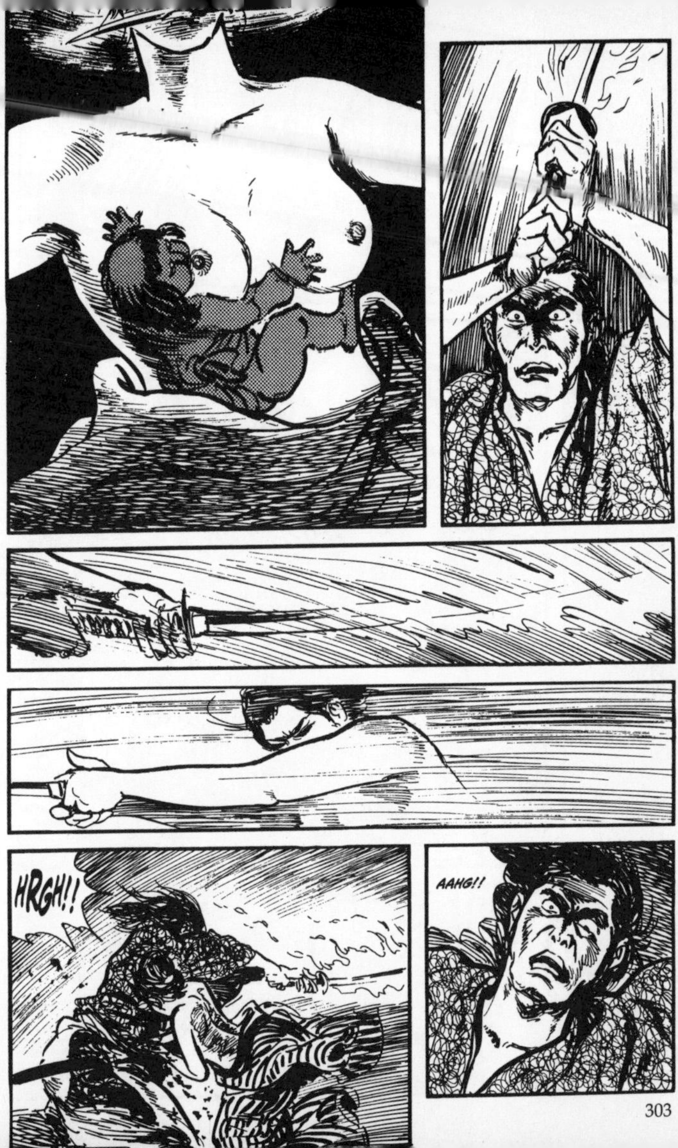
AAHG!!
HRGH!!

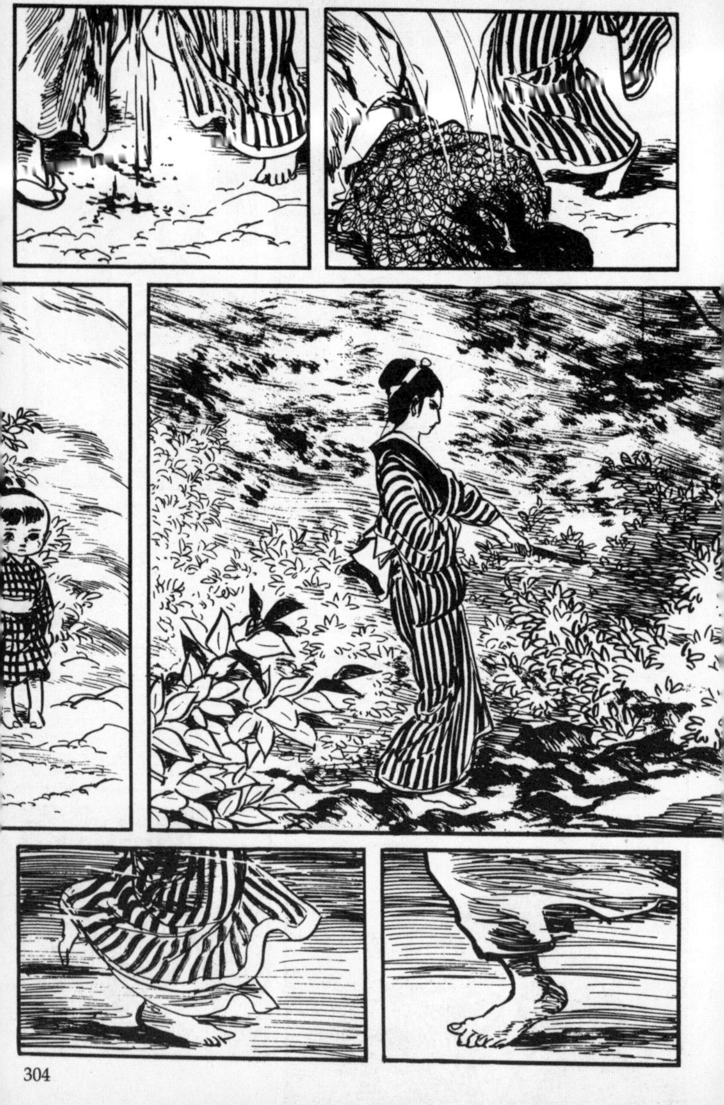

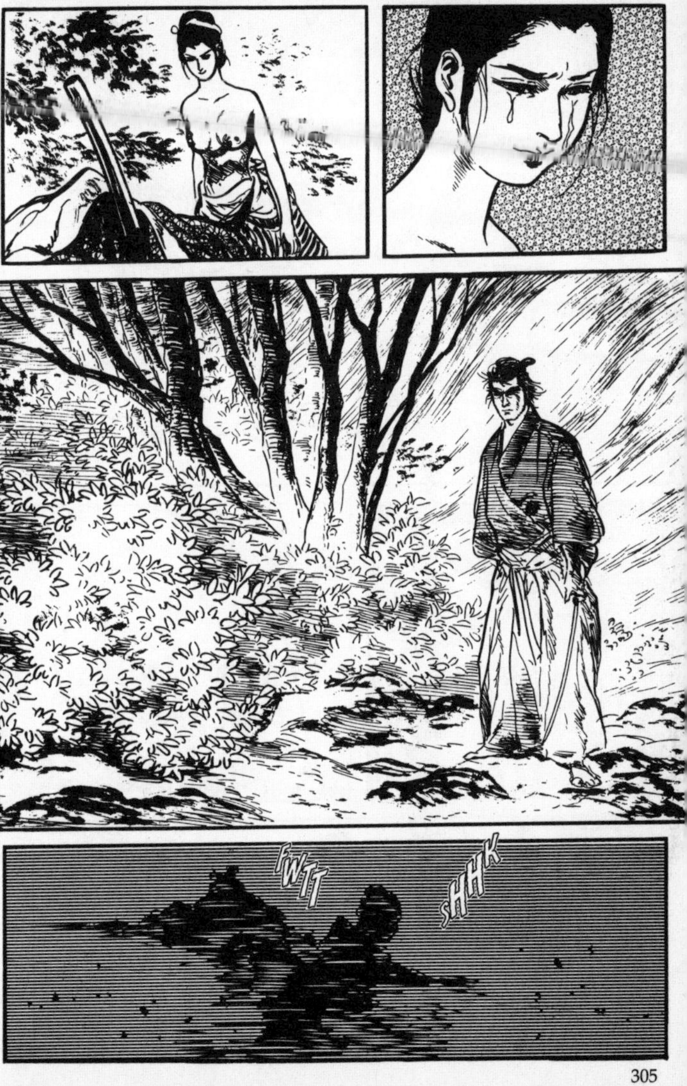
sHHK
FWTT

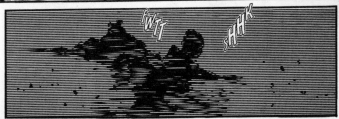

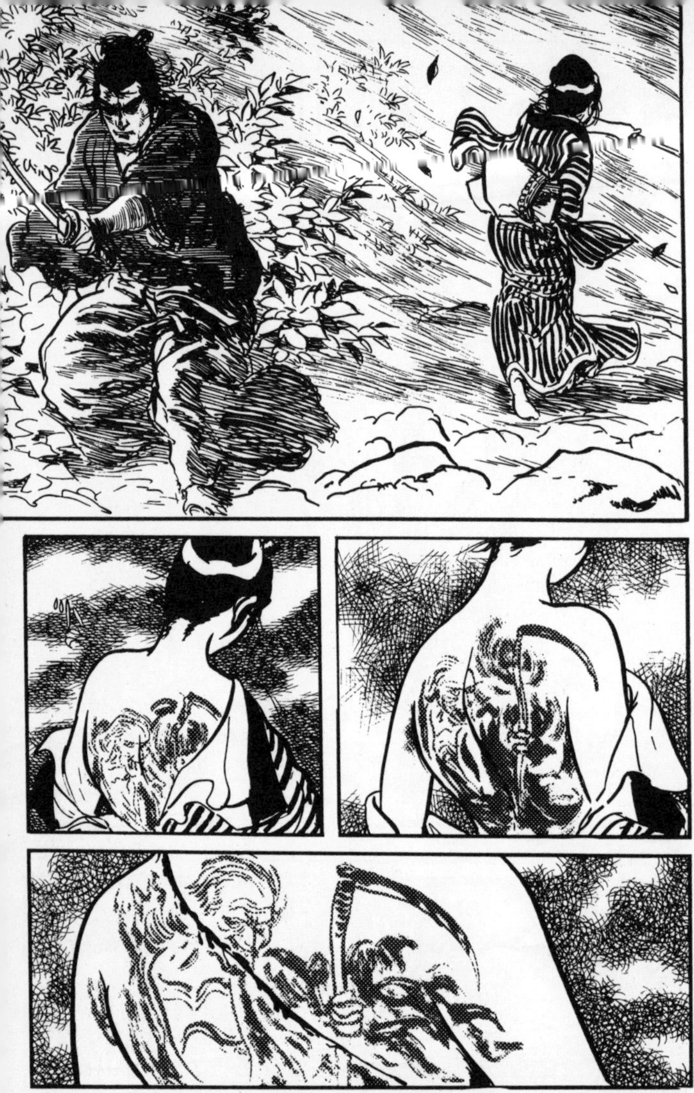

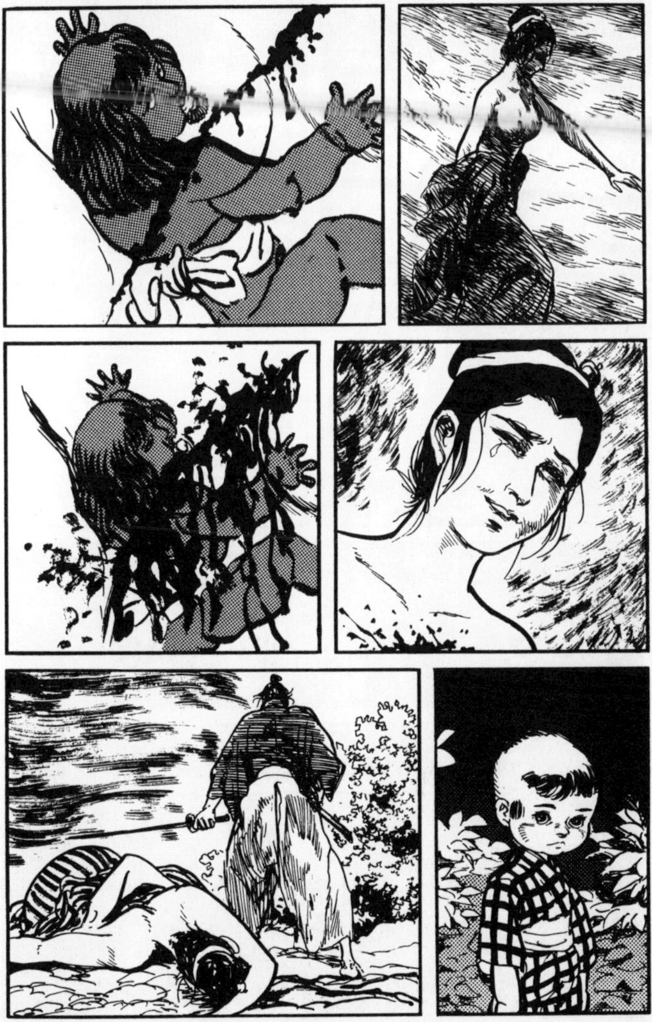

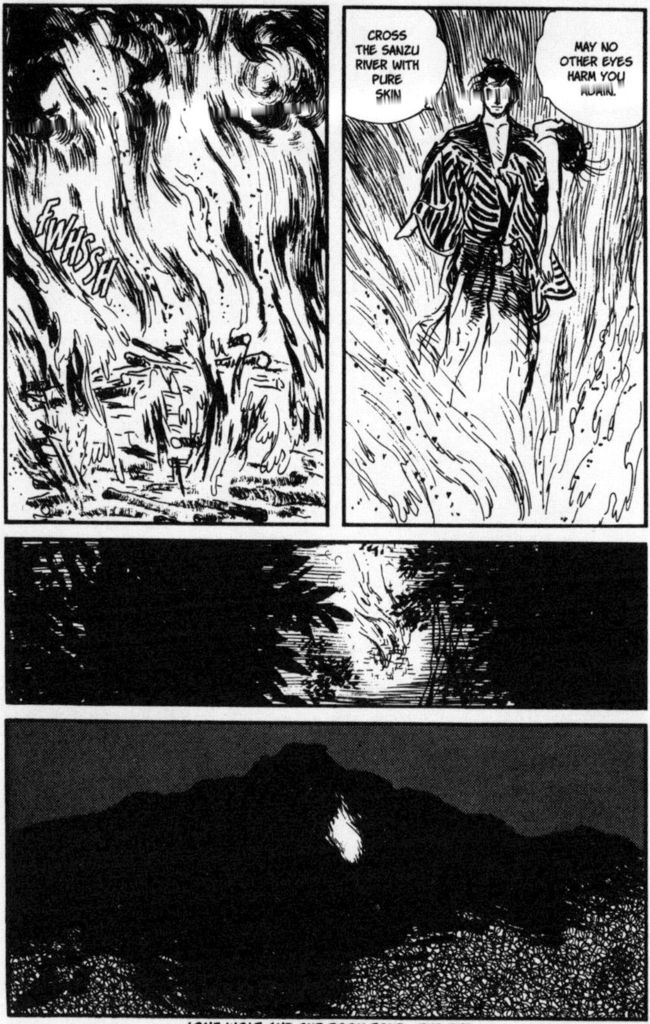
FWHSSH
CROSS THE SANZU RIVER WITH PURE SKIN
MAY NO OTHER EYES HARM YOU AGAIN.

*LONE WOLF AND CUB BOOK FOUR: THE END*
*TO BE CONTINUED*

# GLOSSARY

**adauchi**

Revenge killing. It was accepted practice in the Edo period to kill the person who had killed one's lord or relatives. If the case was strong, the authorities would turn a blind eye to the killing.

**bokutō**

A wooden practice sword.

**bu**

Approximately 3 millimeters.

**buke**

A samurai household.

**bushidō**

The way of the warrior.

**currency**

*mon* – A copper coin.
*kan* – A bundle of 1,000 *mon*.
*monme* – A silver piece.
*ryō* – A gold piece, worth 60 *monme* or 4 *kan*.

**daimyō**

A feudal lord.

**dōtanuki**

A battle sword. Literally, "sword that cuts through torsos."

**Edo**

The capital of medieval Japan and the seat of the shogunate. The site of modern-day Tokyo.

**han**

A feudal domain.

**hatamoto**

*Daimyō* considered utterly loyal to the Tokugawa clan, with the right to meet the shōgun face to face. Their title, "standard bearers," came from history, when the warriors who would be promoted in peacetime to *hatamoto* had been the most trusted allies of Tokugawa Ieyasu, the first of the Tokugawa shōguns.

**hollyhock crest**

Each samurai family had a family crest considered synonymous with the clan itself. The Tokugawa clan crest was a three-leafed hollyhock. To point one's sword toward the shogun's crest was to point your sword toward the shogun himself, an unforgivable act of treason.

**honorifics**

Japan is a class and status society, and proper forms of address are critical. Common markers of respect are the prefixes *o* and *go*, and a wide range of suffixes. Some of the suffixes you will encounter in *Lone Wolf and Cub*:

*chan* – for children, young women, and close friends

*dono* – archaic; used for higher-ranked or highly respected figures

*sama* – used for superiors

*san* – the most common, used among equals or near-equals

*sensei* – used for teachers, masters, respected entertainers, and politicians

## jizō

Local deities, represented by simple stone statues by the roadside. Often decorated with red cloth bibs.

## kabuki

The best-known traditional Japanese theater, with elaborate staging and costumes. Tremendously popular with the townspeople of Edo.

## Kamigata

The area around the imperial capital of Kyoto and the merchant city of Osaka. Now referred to as Kinki.

## kan

6 *shaku*, approximately 1.8 meters.

## Kantō

Literally, "east of the gate." Eastern Japan, north of the mountain chain around Mount Fuji, especially the region around Edo, present-day Tokyo.

## kasezue

Literally, "deer staff." Distinguished by its antler-like cutting prongs.

## kintaro

A legendary feral child, with red skin and superhuman strength.

## kōgi kaishakunin

The shogun's own second, who performed executions ordered by the shogun.

## kurobiki, shubiki

Edo was a castle town that rose up around the moats and ramparts of Edo castle, the stronghold of the Tokugawa clan. The central core of the city, administered by the *machi-bugyō* (Edo city commissioner) and home to the households and estates of *daimyō* and samurai, was demarcated on official maps by a black line, the *kurobiki*. An outer red line, or *shubiki*, marked the limits of Greater Edo, the *go-funai*. In the middle Edo period, the samurai class occupied some sixty percent of the city's land, and temples and shrines another twenty percent. That left only twenty percent of the land for a burgeoning civilian population exceeding one million.

## machi-bugyō

The Edo city commissioner, combining the post of mayor and chief of police. A post held in monthly rotation by two senior Tokugawa vassals, in charge of administration, maintaining the peace, and enforcing the law in Edo. Their rule extended only to commoners; samurai in Edo were controlled by their own *daimyō* and his officers. The *machi-bugyō* had an administrative staff and a small force of armed policemen at his disposal.

## mage

Pronounced *mah-gay*. The samurai's topknot.

## mu

Nothingness. A crucial concept in Zen Buddhism, and a goal of all the martial arts. Clearing the mind of all extraneous thoughts and connections, to exist wholly in the moment, freed of all attachment to life and the world around you.

## namu

From the Sanskrit *namas*: "take refuge in the Buddha." A common prayer for the dead.

## nō

Traditional theater, performed in masks on a bare stage. Favored by the samurai class.

## rōnin

A masterless samurai. Literally, "one adrift on the waves." Members of the samurai caste who have lost their masters through the dissolution of *han*, expulsion for misbehavior, or other reasons. Prohibited from working as farmers or merchants under the strict Confucian caste system imposed by the Tokugawa shogunate, many impoverished *rōnin* became "hired guns" for whom the code of the samurai was nothing but empty words.

## ryū

Often translated as "school." The many variations of swordsmanship and other martial arts were passed down from generation to generation to the offspring of the originator of the technique or set of techniques, and to any *deishi* students that sought to learn from the master. The largest schools had their own *dōjō* training centers and scores of students. An effective swordsman had to study the different techniques of the various schools to know how to block them in combat. Many *ryū* also had a set of special, secret techniques that were only taught to school initiates.

## sakki

The palpable desire to kill, directed at another person. Sometimes called blood lust. Based on the concept of *ki*, or energy, found in spiritual practices and Japanese martial arts like Aikido. These body energies can be felt beyond the physical self by the trained and self-aware.

## sanpin

A derogatory term for low-rank samurai. From the losing three-and-one combination in dice games.

## seisatsu yodatsu

Under the four-caste social system imposed by the Tokugawa shogunate, the samurai class had the unquestioned right to kill those in lower castes, often for the smallest of insults and infractions.

## shaku

10 *sun*, approximately 30 centimeters.

## sun

Approximately 3 centimeters.

# KAZUO KOIKE

Though widely respected as a powerful writer of graphic fiction, Kazuo Koike has spent a lifetime reaching beyond the bounds of the comics medium. Aside from co-creating and writing the successful *Lone Wolf and Cub* and *Crying Freeman* manga, Koike has hosted television programs; founded a golf magazine; produced movies; written popular fiction, poetry, and screenplays; and mentored some of Japan's best manga talent.

*Lone Wolf and Cub* was first serialized in Japan in 1970 (under the title *Kozure Okami*) in *Manga Action* magazine and continued its hugely popular run for many years, being collected as the stories were published, and reprinted worldwide. Koike collected numerous awards for his work on the series throughout the next decade. Starting in 1972, Koike adapted the popular manga into a series of six films, the *Baby Cart Assassin* saga, garnering widespread commercial success and critical acclaim for his screenwriting.

This wasn't Koike's only foray into film and video. In 1996, *Crying Freeman*, the manga Koike created with artist Ryoichi Ikegami, was produced in Hollywood and released to commercial success in Europe and is currently awaiting release in America.

And to give something back to the medium that gave him so much, Koike started the *Gekiga Sonjuku*, a college course aimed at helping talented writers and artists — such as *Ranma 1/2* creator Rumiko Takahashi — break into the comics field.

The driving focus of Koike's narrative is character development, and his commitment to character is clear: "Comics are carried by characters. If a character is well created, the comic becomes a hit." Kazuo Koike's continued success in comics and literature has proven this philosophy true.

# GOSEKI KOJIMA

Goseki Kojima was born on November 3, 1928, the very same day as the godfather of Japanese comics, Osamu Tezuka. While just out of junior high school, the self-taught Kojima began painting advertising posters for movie theaters to pay his bills.

In 1950, Kojima moved to Tokyo, where the postwar devastation had given rise to special manga forms for audiences too poor to buy the new manga magazines. Kojima created art for *kami-shibai*, or "paper-play" narrators, who would use manga story sheets to present narrated street plays. Kojima moved on to creating works for the *kashi-bon* market, bookstores that rented out books, magazines, and manga to mostly low-income readers. He soon became highly popular among *kashi-bon* readers.

In 1967, Kojima broke into the magazine market with his series *Dojinki*. As the manga magazine market grew and diversified, he turned out a steady stream of popular series.

In 1970, in collaboration with Kazuo Koike, Kojima began the work that would seal his reputation, *Kozure* *Okami* (*Lone Wolf and Cub*). Before long the story had become a gigantic hit, eventually spinning off a television series, six motion pictures, and even theme song records. Koike and Kojima were soon dubbed the "golden duo" and produced success after success on their way to the pinnacle of the manga world.

When *Manga Japan* magazine was launched in 1994, Kojima was asked to serve as consultant, and he helped train the next generation of manga artists.

In his final years, Kojima turned to creating original graphic novels based on the movies of his favorite director, Akira Kurosawa. Kojima passed away on January 5, 2000 at the age of 71.

# RONIN REPORT

By Tim Ervin Gore

## Weapons Glossary: Part One

Swords are by far the most romantic instruments of death in Japanese feudal history; from the graceful long sword, also called a *daito* or *katana*; and the shorter but powerful *wakizashi*; to the *tanto* used in the infamous *seppuku* act. Magnificent enough to supplant the noble horse and bow as the weapon of choice for samurai, the blade took on an almost religious significance, its art refined and secretive, both in the making and the wielding.

And the practice of making a good sword was kept secretive. Creating such a weapon is painstaking, scientific, and exact, and the art is practically lost. In the *Samurai Sword* handbook by John Yumato, much can be learned about the construction and identification of swords. But in writing *Lone Wolf and Cub*, Koike and Kojima showed a marked fascination with the plethora of dangerous and exotic weapons which evolved in feudal Japan. Many of these weapons can be found in common reference books, but quite a few are too obscure for a quick study. The following is a brief index of some of the weapons found in the first four volumes of *Lone Wolf and Cub*.

Fig. 1. *tanto*

In traditional Japanese sword smithery, three traditional sizes of swords evolved over a long period of time. The *tanto* (fig. 1) was the most commonly available. Often, under decree of stiff shogun rule, commoners were prohibited from carrying blades at all, aside from those used in agriculture and industry. When the peasants decided to rise up against the ruling warrior factions, fewer dangerous weapons made it easier to quell the unruly citizens. However, when it was authorized (or out of sight), the simple and concealable *tanto* was the secret pillow partner, often wielded by women, and easily hidden in the folds of one's robes. Dogged by its reputation as a belly-slicing suicide instrument, the *tanto* was a useful second sword to the thrifty samurai. These knives were generally less than 12 inches in blade length, and, due to a largely utilitarian role, not always of the highest quality.

Fig. 2. *wakizashi*

The *wakizashi* (or *kodachi*) (fig. 2), a medium sized sword 1-2 feet in length, was a stout and useful weapon. In *Lone Wolf and Cub*, Ogami's *dotanuki* is identified as a *wakizashi*, and a mean one at that. Miyamoto Musashi, a renowned samurai from the early 1600s, established a style of carrying and wielding swords that would change the face of the samurai forever, that of carrying two swords (or *dai-sho*), and fighting with both at the same time. This new method popularized the making of swords in pairs. Though occasionally a samurai would choose to pair his long sword with a *tanto*, the samurai elite most likely carried a *wakizashi* as the match of his *daito*.

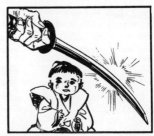

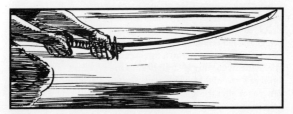

Fig. 3. *daito*

The *daito* (*odachi, katana*) (fig. 3), long and graceful, was the polished trophy of the samurai elite. Such swords of high quality and reputable manufacture were highly treasured and handed down through generations. This is the sword most romanticized in literature, film, and manga. A *daito* sword was usually over 2 feet in length, occasionally built longer to match the will and height of the samurai who wielded it. Being the main battle blade of the samurai, the *daito* was created with extreme precision, accounting for generations upon generations of secretive smithery. The methods of the archaic master swordsmiths were lost in waves of less violent times, as the masters themselves turned their skills and shops over to more modern uses, such as the manufacture of scissors and other tools. Their swords, however, still grace the walls of museums and collectors, many in fine condition, a testimony to their makers.

Fig. 4. *kozuka*

A samurai may have kept a few small knives for utility and tactical purposes, occasionally mounted in the hilt of a *daito*. These knives may have been used for throwing at an enemy or a last-ditch cut to the throat. The larger of these knives was the *kozuka* (fig. 4), which makes numerous appearances in the *Lone Wolf and Cub* series. An example of Koike and Kojima's use of such a weapon occurs in "The Flute of the Fallen Tiger" (*LW&C* Vol. 3), in which one of the Bentenrai brothers throws a small knife past the face of a mouthy commoner in a threatening gesture. Ogami returns the blade by tossing it straight into the scabbard of one of the brother's swords. As a side note, it should be mentioned that a few pages after the appearance of this *kozuka*, Ogami refers to it as a *kogara* — a small bird. But as Ogami's blade is referred to as a *dotanuki*, so would other blades be named after their performance. So, a small blade made to fly swiftly through the air might have been called a *kogara*. Even more interesting were *wari-bashi* (split chopsticks). These small knives were likely to be quite handy for any number of uses. According to Yumoto's handbook, *wari-bashi* were used to secure one's hair, and their bases could handily be used as ear cleaners.

But the sword was not the first weapon, and its exclusive availability made it scarce amongst the fighting foot soldiers. Instead, many soldiers employed spears and spear-like instruments to occasionally administer slow death upon their enemies. One particularly effective method of fighting was the use of a spear from horseback (fig. 5), as shown in "Suio School Zanbato" (*LW&C* Vol. 1). Skill

Fig. 5. spear from horseback

with a spear was a highly regarded art, and coupled with the furious gallop of a powerful horse, the weapon was difficult to avoid and painfully effective. A pierced torso from a charge with a spear left many unfortunate soldiers groaning in pools of blood, awaiting merciful death.

Fig. 6. *naginata*

Such an offensive created the need for a properly defensive weapon. Taking up this duty was the incredibly effective *naginata* (fig. 6). With a long, wooden handle and a curved, one-sided blade, the *naginata* was a vicious instrument akin to the halberd, historically used to chop the legs of cavalry horses and fight swordsmen at a safe distance. In *Lone Wolf and Cub*, Ogami's spring-loaded cart handles are a form of *naginata*, which he employs with deadly effect. Although the long blades of Ogami's spring-loaded pole-arms look a bit like the similar *nagamaki*, the handle of the weapon is longer than the blade, which was apparently the measure of difference between the two weapons. The *naginata* is a graceful weapon and is a popular modern martial art form.

In *Lone Wolf and Cub*, many pages are devoted to exploring the effectiveness of these standard war weapons, but Koike and Kojima seemed to enjoy the less conventional weapons and their tactical uses. One such weapon, or rather, an extension of numerous weapons, was the weighted chain. In *Classical Bujutsu*, an excellent study of Japanese martial tradition, Don Draeger describes the sickle and chain, or *kusarigama* (fig. 7), a multi-resourceful weapon. Casual observance of many Japanese martial traditions exposes likely evolutions of weapons, and some of the

Fig. 7. *kusarigama*

more impressive weapons derived from agricultural tools. Though pedestrian on its own, the addition of a light chain with an iron weight on the end changed the sickle into a death trap. Thrown by an expert, the weight could break bones (or trees, according to Koike and Kojima), and the chain could wrap around an opponent and his arms, leaving him vulnerable to the sickle's blade. An excellent example of the *kusarigama* and its use is shown at the end of "Close Quarters" (*LW&C* Vol. 3), in which Ogami finds himself face-to-face with a master of the *kusarigama* and is challenged to get beyond the reach of the iron weight at the end of the chain. The sickle aside, the weighted chain makes numerous appearances in *Lone Wolf and Cub*. In "A Father Knows

His Child Heart, as Only a Child Can Know His Father's" (*LW&C Vol. 1*), a weighted chain is planted in the staff of one of Ogami's opponents. In "Eight Gates of Deceit" (also in Vol. 1), a woman attacks Ogami with a short sword and weighted chain, suggesting that there were many schools of study integrating such weapons.

Koike and Kojima's fascination with exotic weapons extends beyond what can be found in most reference books. In "The Flute of the Fallen Tiger," the three Bentenrai brothers carry individual, specialized weapons of destruction. One brother carries a simple sword, but wields it in a special way, while another swings a short iron club, and the third brandishes a bladed bear claw. The iron club (fig. 8) was a useful weapon to many samurai. This pictured iron club is shorter than most surviving examples, and it seems to have a wooden haft, but the iron end works in the same way: brutal, bloody bludgeoning. In "The Bell Warden" (*LW&C* Vol. 4), three brothers specialize in weapons that present Ogami with new challenges. The *manrikisa*, the *sanjinrai*, and the *injiuchi tsubute* are each dangerous hand-to-hand combat weapons (see p. 45).

Fig. 7. iron club

With the motivation to outmaneuver the other schools and combatants, the samurai took it upon himself to learn the ways of all weapons in existence. Given the assortment of these dangerous objects, and the way each person creates his or her own variation, one could imagine what a challenge it would be to be Ogami Itto. It takes time to learn so much about the art of death, but such study was necessary to earn the position of *kogi kaishakunin* — which helps explain why it angered the Lone Wolf to spend such an effort only to be bested by corruption. Like the lost art of swordsmithing, the ever-changing art of war, and the ever-present involvement of politics, would eventually drain the warrior from us all.

*Special thanks to Stan Sakai.*

**LONE WOLF AND CUB**
Kazuo Koike and
Goseki Kojima
*Collect the complete
?8 volume series!*

**VOLUME 1:**
**THE ASSASSIN'S ROAD**
ISBN: 1-56971-502-5 $9.95
**VOLUME 2:**
**THE GATELESS BARRIER**
ISBN: 1-56971-503-3 $9.95
**VOLUME 3:**
**THE FLUTE OF
THE FALLEN TIGER**
ISBN: 1-56971-504-1 $9.95
**VOLUME 4:**
**THE BELL WARDEN**
ISBN: 1-56971-505-X $9.95
**VOLUME 5:**
**BLACK WIND**
ISBN: 1-56971-506-8 $9.95
**VOLUME 6:**
**LANTERNS FOR THE DEAD**
ISBN: 1-56971-507-6 $9.95
**VOLUME 7:**
**CLOUD DRAGON, WIND TIGER**
ISBN: 1-56971-508-4 $9.95
**VOLUME 8:**
**CHAINS OF DEATH**
ISBN: 1-56971-509-2 $9.95
**VOLUME 9:**
**ECHO OF THE ASSASSIN**
ISBN: 1-56971-510-6 $9.95
**VOLUME 10:**
**DRIFTING SHADOWS**
ISBN: 1-56971-511-4 $9.95

**VOLUME 11:**
**TALISMAN OF HADES**
ISBN: 1-56971-512-2 $9.95
**VOLUME 12:**
**SHATTERED STONES**
ISBN: 1-56971-513-0 $9.95
**VOLUME 13:**
**THE MOON IN THE EAST,
THE SUN IN THE WEST**
ISBN: 1-56971-585-8 $9.95
**VOLUME 14:**
**DAY OF THE DEMONS**
ISBN: 1-56971-586-6 $9.95
**VOLUME 15:**
**BROTHERS OF THE GRASS**
ISBN: 1-56971-587-4 $9.95
**VOLUME 16:**
**GATEWAY INTO WINTER**
ISBN: 1-5671-588-2 $9.95
**VOLUME 17:**
**THE WILL OF THE FANG**
ISBN: 1-56971-589-0 $9.95
**VOLUME 18:**
**TWILIGHT OF THE KUROKUWA**
ISBN: 1-56971-590-4 $9.95
**VOLUME 19:**
**THE MOON IN OUR HEARTS**
ISBN: 1-56971-591-2 $9.95
**VOLUME 20:**
**A TASTE OF POISON**
ISBN: 1-56971-592-0 $9.95
**VOLUME 21:**
**FRAGRANCE OF DEATH**
ISBN: 1-56971-593-9 $9.95
**VOLUME 22:**
**HEAVEN AND EARTH**
ISBN: 1-56971-594-7 $9.95

**VOLUME 23:**
**TEARS OF ICE**
ISBN: 1-56971-595-5 $9.95
**VOLUME 24:**
**IN THESE SMALL HANDS**
ISBN: 1-56971-596-3 $9.95
**VOLUME 25:**
**PERHAPS IN DEATH**
ISBN: 1-56971-597-1 $9.95
**VOLUME 26:**
**STRUGGLE IN THE DARK**
ISBN: 1-56971-598-X $9.95
**VOLUME 27:**
**BATTLE'S EVE**
ISBN: 1-56971-599-8 $9.95
**VOLUME 28:**
**THE LOTUS THRONE**
ISBN: 1-56971-600-5 $9.95

**LONE WOLF 2100**
Mike Kennedy and
Francisco Ruiz Velasco
*The stylish, futuristic
re-imagining of the classic
Lone Wolf and Cub*

**VOLUME 1:**
**SHADOWS ON SAPLINGS**
ISBN: 1-56971-893-8 $12.95
**VOLUME 2:**
**THE LANGUAGE OF CHAOS**
ISBN: 1-56971-997-7 $12.95
**VOLUME 3:**
**PATTERN STORM**
ISBN: 1-59307-079-9 $12.95

---

## Available from your local comics shop or bookstore!

To find a comics shop in your area, call 1-888-266-4226 • For more information or to order direct:
• On the web: www.darkhorse.com • E-mail: mailorder@darkhorse.com
• Phone: 1-800-862-0052 or (503) 652-9701 Mon.-Sat. 9 A.M. to 5 P.M. Pacific Time
*Prices and availability subject to change without notice

*Dark Horse Comics:* Mike Richardson *publisher* • Neil Hankerson *executive vice president*
Tom Weddle *vice president of finance* • Randy Stradley *vice president of publishing* • Chris Warner *senior books editor*
Anita Nelson *vice president of sales & licensing & marketing* • David Scroggy *vice president of product development*
Lia Ribacchi *art director* • Dale LaFountain *vice president of information technology*
Darlene Vogel *director of purchasing* • Ken Lizzi *general counsel*